THE LIFE OF WILLIAM AUGUSTUS, DUKE OF CUMBERLAND

THE LIFE OF WILLIAM AUGUSTUS, DUKE OF CUMBERLAND

BY
Andrew Henderson

EDITED BY
Roderick Macpherson

Routledge
Taylor & Francis Group
LONDON AND NEW YORK

First published 2010 by Pickering & Chatto (Publishers) Limited

2 Park Square, Milton Park, Abingdon, Oxon OX14 4RN
711 Third Avenue, New York, NY 10017, USA

Routledge is an imprint of the Taylor & Francis Group, an informa business

First issued in paperback 2017

BRITISH LIBRARY CATALOGUING IN PUBLICATION DATA

Henderson, Andrew, 1717–1776.
The life of William Augustus, Duke of Cumberland. – (Roxburghe Club)
1. Cumberland, William Augustus, Duke of, 1721–1765. 2. Jacobite Rebellion, 1745–1746. 3. Great Britain – History – George II, 1727–1760 – Biography. 4. Henderson, Andrew, 1717–1779 – Correspondence. I. Title II. Series III. Macpherson, Roderick. IV. Roxburghe Club. 941'.072'092–dc22

ISBN-13: 978-1-8519-6063-7 (hbk)
ISBN-13: 978-1-138-11306-0 (pbk)

Typeset by Pickering & Chatto (Publishers) Limited

DEDICATED AND PRESENTED TO
THE PRESIDENT AND MEMBERS OF
THE ROXBURGHE CLUB
BY
LORD REES-MOGG
2010

ROXBURGHE CLUB

MMX

CONTENTS

ROXBURGHE CLUB

FOREWORD

Andrew Henderson (1717–76) was my great grandfather's great grandfather. He was an eyewitness of the history of the mid-eighteenth century, particularly the '45 revolt. He was a journalist, historian, biographer, mathematics tutor, publisher and bookseller, most of which are professions I also have followed. He had for many years a bookseller's shop in Westminster Hall, and lived in Great College Street, behind Westminster Abbey, a part of London in which I lived for thirty years. I feel a natural affinity to him, as our lives and interests have overlapped to such a degree. I am very grateful to Mr Roderick Macpherson who in this Roxburghe Club Edition of Henderson's most significant work, *The Life of William Augustus, Duke of Cumberland*, has discovered new and interesting material about Henderson's earlier life.

Henderson was a brave controversialist who made the case for the pro-Hanoverian Whig cause in Scotland. The Hanoverians defeated Bonnie Prince Charlie, but lost the romantic battle of reputation. Only a minority of Scots, now as then, would actually be Jacobites, but many Scots mistakenly assume that the Jacobite side was the side of patriotism. In fact, the Hanoverians gave Scotland, as well as England, a constitutional monarchy which allowed liberal democracy to develop. The alternative would probably have been the French style of absolute monarchy.

In his controversies, Henderson fought the Jacobites, including the Jacobistical Samuel Johnson. He fought the novelist and literary power broker Dr John Tobias Smollett, and he defended the reputation of the Duke of Cumberland, the victor of Culloden. He taught geometry to George III. He had courage as well as a journalist's eye for detail and for a colourful phrase. I feel proud of him.

WILLIAM REES-MOGG

INTRODUCTION

The monuments in the Valhalla of British men of letters, surnamed by letter 'H' – the *Dictionary of National Biography* (1891) and the *Oxford Dictionary of National Biography* (2004) – bear witness to the long period of obscurity in which has been mouldering the reputation of the Whig historian Andrew Henderson. Neither his year of birth nor of death can be traced on those epitaphs. Moreover, the newer work claims there is no evidence of his ever marrying. Fortunately, Ralph Henderson's *Records of My Family*, published privately in 1926, preserves the essential biographical details. They are quoted here, on his authority: Andrew Henderson was born at Lilliesleaf, Roxburgh, on 26 February 1717 and died at South Minns, Hertfordshire, in February 1776, at the age of fifty-nine. He married Sarah, daughter of Thomas Radford, of Stourbridge, and they had five sons, John (b. 1759), Francis (b. 1762), Thomas (b. 1765), William (b. 1768) and Andrew (b. 1771).[1]

Howsoever respectable may have been his home life, the family historian records that Henderson, who had trained for the ministry of the Church of Scotland, received an anonymous letter in 1767, warning him that the Jacobites were spreading the report that he had been 'excluded from the pulpit on account of gracelessly throwing off the cloak of outward sanctity'.[2] Research now shows that in 1741 a church court, considering charges against Henderson, heard tell of his alleged 'licentious and odious opinion, that fornication was no crime'. Henderson would have his revenge on his accusers, the Reverend Mr Rose of Nairn and the Reverend Mr Munro of Auldearn, thereafter of Tain. This was taken in the pages of *The Life of William Augustus, Duke of Cumberland,* published in 1766 and now reissued in this volume. It is, as Henderson's biographer of 1891 suggests, his best work.[3]

Henderson's papers survived a fire at his home in 1761. 'A terrible fire on the 8th July but I escaped' is an entry in his diary for the year of this disaster. A grandson of Andrew Henderson recorded in 1813 that the author 'was burnt out of his house and lost the greater part if not the whole of his papers and property'.[4] A pitiful account of poor Henderson's despair comes from the same note:

> being in bed when the fire broke out, his wife awoke him, he put on his stockings, but finding that the fire had got such a hold that there was no prospect of saving anything, he threw himself back on the bed with an apparent desire to be consumed by the flames, as nothing but future misery and want presented itself to his view, and it was with the greatest difficulty he could be moved from his perilous situation.

Certainly mishaps befell several of his writings, their troubles being occasioned not only because of that fire. His manuscript 'History of the Hendersons', which tribe he is said to have traced to the Swedes,[5] also survived into the nineteenth century; but Ralph Henderson lamented that the work had since disappeared, and all efforts to trace it had proved unsuccessful.[6] Henderson worked on a 'History of Scotland from 1748' and had a completed manuscript by 1771.[7] The attempts to publish this evidently provided yet another of those eighteenth-century literary altercations with which his name is associated.

> We have four anonymous letters addressed to Andrew about this same time, warning him that there was a Jacobite plot to carry him off and lodge him in a madhouse; telling of the abuse spoken against him by Wm. Guthrie and a clergyman at Slaughter's Coffee House, Andrew having attacked Guthrie in the preface of his History [of Scotland],

writes Ralph Henderson.[8] Here are some further comments in the family volume of 1926:

> When, in 1767, Andrew began to publish his History of Scotland in weekly parts, the whole trouble culminated in a law suit, brought against him by Hamilton (who was then printing William Guthrie's History of Scotland) in order to prevent Andrew from publishing his History. This suit Andrew lost, and he says 'was consequently, through the scheming villainly [*sic*] of a miscreant, drowned in poverty and want.' ... Of Andrew's History of Scotland only four numbers were printed, and they are all in existence. The MS. of the History is also preserved, lacking the first 183 pages, presumably the part that was printed.[9]

The full list of Henderson's publications, however, shows how prodigious was his output and how large a body of work is still available for study. His publications commenced in 1746 with his first offering in praise of the Duke of Cumberland: *Expeditio militaris, sive Britannia liberate, Carmen in honorem Cumbriae ducis illustrissimi*. (Henderson refers in print to his 'two Sapphic Odes on his Royal Highness the Duke of Cumberland.')[10] *The History of the Rebellion, 1745 and 1746* – 'By an Impartial Hand, who was an Eye-witness to most of the Facts' – appeared first in Edinburgh, then in London, both in 1748. Henderson mentions some of the circumstances that delayed its publication. Explaining how he had been 'sent up in June 1747' to be an assistant at Watts's Academy, which, he found, was quite a London sanctuary for Jacobites, he writes this of his book: 'Though I had brought up the impression, yet I was not allowed to publish it, for fear of giving offence.'[11] That the London edition was published in January of 1748[12] indicates that the Edinburgh book must have been set by the previous year. Although the London version, or 'Second Edition Revised and Corrected' bore to have been 'Reprinted from the Edinburgh Edition', being sold by the very same bookseller and publisher, R. Griffiths, at the Dunciad in Ludgate Street, in fact they were different works. The Edinburgh edition had 232 pages, while the London one had 126. The new preface for the London audience advertised, 'The Young Chevalier, &c., Sold by Griffiths, London', as quite 'a Second Part to this Work.' Whereas the London edition ends with another calling of attention to that 'Pamphlet lately published', the Edinburgh book, in more dignified fashion, advertised the author's admiration of the Duke of Cumberland:

> And now that he is at the Head of our Armies, it is the Duty of every British subject to pray to the God of Battles, that his Success may be as great Abroad as at Home; that so Laurel after Laurel may surround the Head of him, whom Europe yet admires.
>
> FINIS.

Indeed, the further editions of *History of the Rebellion*, all published at London, add more variations to Henderson's text. Charles Sandford Terry, in his bibliography of Jacobite history, noted that the title had two editions in 1753: one of 360 pages, the other of 370, with illustrations.[13] 'Twice pirated and three times reprinted' are the author's proud remarks about the work.[14] Although Ralph Henderson notes that 'Andrew's History of 1745 is frequently quoted by Sir Walter Scott in the Tales of a Grandfather',[15] in fact it was the manuscript narrative by Lord Elcho that better forms the basis of Scott's telling in the Tales.[16] However popular it once was – and it is still useful, as the contemporary account of events that was most widely known – in 1944 the Roxburghe Club published Henrietta Tayler's devastating critique on the reliability of Henderson's history:

> ... among other ludicrous errors [Henderson] states that Prince Charles Edward fought with the French at Dettingen and commanded them at Tournai! His account of the Prince's wanderings is also fantastic in the extreme. He causes him to assume woman's clothes on two separate occasions, to visit the Isle of Mull and a number of other places to which he never went, and finally lands him at Boulogne instead of Roscoff.[17]

His anonymous *Life of John, late Earl of Stair ... with characters of the Young Chevalier and other persons*, was published, also at London, in 1748. (Possibly this is the pamphlet to which his advertisement referred.) *Arsinoe, or The Incestuous Marriage, a Tragedy* came from the press, under his name, in 1752. The *DNB* judges it 'a worthless play' – 'never acted, nor, indeed, ever deserved such an honour'.[18] His biographical works continued with an anonymous History of Charles XII King of Sweden (1750). Lives of Frederick, King of Sweden (1752), Dr Archibald Cameron (1753), Field-Marshal Daun (1757), Field-Marshal Keith

(1758) and William the Conqueror (1764), preceded Henderson's best known biography, that of the Duke of Cumberland (1766).

These are the titles of pamphlets, as confirmed to be by him, from the *DNB* article: *Consideration on the question whether the Act of Parliament establishing a militia through England ought to extend to Scotland in time of War* (1760); *Dissertation on the Royal Line and first Settlers in Scotland* (1771); *A Letter to the Right Reverend Father in God William Lord Bishop of Chester, on occasion of his sermon preached before the House of Lords on Jan. 31st, 1774* (1774); *A Letter to Dr Samuel Johnson on his Journey to the Western Isles* (1775); and *A Second Letter to Dr Samuel Johnson* (1775). Ralph Henderson gives a much more extensive list.[19]

The present volume, collecting the 1766 *Life of William Augustus, Duke of Cumberland* and the two pamphlets of 1775 addressed to Samuel Johnson, contains much autobiographical information about Henderson. The preface to *Cumberland* states the author 'was born five miles South east of the Tweed, in the Shire of Roxburgh, where my predecessors by both parents lived for five hundred years before'. He mentions his father, as master of the grammar school of Nairn, in the footnote at p. 173. The first 'Letter to Dr Samuel Johnson', in the very first paragraph, mentions Henderson's considerable knowledge of Scotland. He says he is familiar with Sir Robert Henderson's gardens, at Fordell and Otterstoun.[20] He writes of his knowledge of the isles of Coll and Tiree, and happily places himself, on 13 December 1737 and again in September 1766, on 'a considerable high mountain' at the southern part of Tiree, commanding a wonderful view. He writes of 'my abode for 15 months in the Isles'. Henderson tells of having travelled in Badenoch, and in April 1741 being at Invernahaven. He writes of Mull and claims intimate acquaintance with the Reverend Mr McQueen in Skye and Mr McLean in Mull. He had the honour of being personally known to the late Duke of Argyll. He writes of having been tutor to Colonel Dugald Campbell, whose father was the sheriff of Argyllshire.

From Ralph Henderson's volume we can add that Francis Henderson (b. 1655, in Teviotdale) and his wife, Margaret Douglas, who lived in the village of Denholme, in the parish of Cavers, in Teviotdale, were the parents of John, the father of Andrew.[21] John, probably the younger of two brothers, was born in 1685. The other brother, Francis, was a clockmaker in Denholme, whose death, aged fifty-four, occasioned a poem in Latin by his brother.[22] In 1715 John Henderson married Margaret, daughter of Andrew Angus, bailie of Selkirk. They had one son, the author, and a daughter who died young. 'Mr John Henderson' had in 1702, at the early age of seventeen, been appointed master of the school at Lilliesleaf. He ceased to be master there in 1716, according to Ralph Henderson; yet he records that John Henderson was styled 'merchant burgess of Selkirk' at the time of his marriage. The family history further states that 'in 1720 he became what would now be called a bankrupt'.[23]

'Being scarce turned five years old I went north with the best of Fathers', writes Henderson in the preface to *Cumberland* of the year 1722, when his father was appointed master of the school at Nairn.[24] The designation 'John Henderson: Edinburgensis mercator' in a manuscript of verses and letters, dated 1732,[25] indicates that the father was later to return to his mercantile life in the south. Letters dated 1727 and 1729 place Andrew at school at Dornoch, Sutherland. According to his own account, the school at Nairn and the Universities of Aberdeen and Edinburgh were the places of his formal education.[26] The records of Marischal College, Aberdeen, confirm that an 'And. Henderson' was there from 1731 to 1735, where he received the degree of Master of Arts.[27] Having done some teaching in Edinburgh, he became tutor to the Countess of Stair's nephew, to the son of Colonel Young, the Earl of Stair's aide-de-camp, and to Colonel Dugald Campbell.[28]

Ralph Henderson states that Andrew Henderson was 'in Argyleshire and the Isles, 1736–1741.' He adds, 'From 1741 onwards he appears to have been in Edinburgh ... In January, 1745, he became a "probationer" under the Presbytery of Edinburgh, and there is a testimonial in his favour from that body, dated May 4th, 1747.' This passage includes the following statement, further research into which now gives a fuller picture of the author's whereabouts and public displays of character in the very period leading up to the Jacobite rising in 1745: 'there is no proof that he was ever admitted to the Ministry, though it is a family tradition that through his journeying to see his mother, who was dying, on the "Lord's Day," he was dismissed from the Ministry'.[29]

Henderson describes his father as 'a truly divine man, and who understood classical learning as well as any man in Europe'.[30] The future author's own education had qualified him for entry to training for the supreme professional elite of eighteenth-century Scotland, the ministry of the Church of Scotland. Letters from later years, available to Ralph Henderson in 1926, styled Andrew 'Reverend' and 'Preacher of the Gospel'.[31] Why did such a one, with these advantages, not become ordained in the Established Church, but rather impelled, in June 1747, to go to London, first as mathematical master at Watts's Academy and thereafter to set up as a bookseller at Dean Swift's Head, Longacre, soon thereafter at Westminster Hall?[32] The reasons why Andrew Henderson turned from being a preacher of the Gospel to an author and seller of books are indicated in the papers of the General Assembly of the Church of Scotland, Main Series, entitled on the spine, 'Assembly Papers 1743', but containing interesting material about Henderson from the years 1740 to 1745. The papers preserve a lengthy account of the complaint against Henderson, as considered by the Presbytery of Forres and Synod of Moray. Not only had he to confess himself guilty of the enormity of having travelled on the Sabbath without going to church, but the circumstances also clearly indicate that he had lied to his local minister about his non-attendance at divine worship that day:[33]

> Forres, April 17th 1740.
>
> The Presbytery having heard that Mr Andrew Henderson Preacher of the Gospel lately come to this Bounds had given offence by travelling upon the thirtieth day of March last being the Lords Day from Elgin to Nairn without attending publick Worship recommended it to Masters Rose & Munro to Enquire into that affair and report Meantime to cause Cite him to next Dyet of Presbytery in Case they see cause.[34]
>
> Forres, May 29th 1740.
>
> Mr Rose reported that he and Mr Munro had called for and Enquired Mr Andrew Henderson anent his travelling from Elgin to Nairn in terms of former appointment but that he had refused to give any Accountt of said affair to them and that they therefore had caused Cite him to this Dyet of Presbytery for the Scandals of Sabbath Profanation, Lying & Prevarication and he being called and not compearing Mr Rose further reported that he had since last Dyet of Presbytery caus'd Cite him also to appear before the Presbytery of Edinburgh for Immoralities alleadged to be Committed by him there having received a letter from the Moderator of that Presbytery for that Effect ...[35]

The August meeting of the Forres presbytery agreed to put the following questions to Henderson:

> *1mo.* Whether he had upon March 30th being the Lords Day travelled from Nairn without attending upon publick Worship. *2do.* Whether he said to Mr Rose at Nairn or any other that he heard Sermon that Day at Forres & that Mr Squire[36] lectured in the Corinthians. *3tio.* Whether he had not oftner than once said that he heard Sermon that Day at Forres and Endeavoured to Confirm any in the belief of it.[37]

Henderson, having required that the charges be put to him in writing and considered his response, gave the following answers:

> *1mo.* That he had travelled upon the last Lords Day of March ... and is heartily sorry that he should have been fatally Constrained to neglect attendance upon publick Worship, a thing which his Soul abhors. *2do.* That upon Mr Rose's asking whether he was at Sermon answered overly at Forres ... as also that after twice or thrice being asked where the Text was answered unawares, I believe in the Corinthians ... *3tio.* That upon Mr Rose's taking the advantage of him to ask Questions before 2 witnesses & upon saying, You say the Lecture was in Corinthians, he reply'd ... but declares that he never Endeavoured to Confirm any Person in the Belief of it ...[38]

At Elgin, on 23 October 1740, Henderson, 'being heard at full length', was suspended. He, again being 'heard at great length' in April of the following year, then caused much more about himself to be recorded over the affair. Although he would produce a favourable account of his conduct from the Edinburgh presbytery, his own accusations against others quite undid his credit with that of Forres, as these extracts show:

> Compeared Mr Andrew Henderson and Jas. Fraser his procurator ... Votes marked, it carryed by great majority ... Therefore the Synod did & hereby do suspend & discharge the said Mr Henderson from preaching the Gospel until the next meeting of Synod at Forres the 3rd Tuesday Aprile next, Mr Henderson being call'd in this was intimated to him and the Moderator tendered him a very serious and grave rebuke, exhorting him to greater Circumspection in his behaviour.[39]
>
> Forres, Aprile 22d. 1741.
>
> Resumed ... Thereafter the Members of Synod taking a complex view of this whole affair, reconsider'd Mr Henderson's former Confession & finding that he had left the Bounds of Synod soon after last meeting and was but lately returned that Members of Presbytery of Forres nor others of the Synod were capable of advancing any thing in his favours but to the contrary, observing that for the short time he had resided at Nairn the place of his usual abode in this Countrey he had given up 1st Attendance on Ordinances as dispens'd by Mr Rose his parish Minister on pretence as he said that he was not edifyed, That in his defences before the Synod he had instead of discovering an humble Sense of his Sins and Sorrow for the Offence he had given to the Synod so as to oblige them to suspend him from the Exercise of his License as a Probationer, That to the contrary he seem'd too much to defend the Crimes he had formerly confessd and pretended Sorrow for, and moreover to the great Offence of the Synod had heated some of the Members at the Bar in most rude, slanderous & unchristian Manner, upon all we the following State of a Question was agreed to, If the Synod shall longer continue Mr Henderson under the sentence of Suspension or deprive him altogether of his License as a probationer. Rolls being called & Votes marked it carryed by a very great Majority ... [to] continue Mr Henderson under Sentence of Suspension from the Exercise of preaching the Gospel & recommend it to the Presbytery of Forres to enquire into his Conduct while in their Bounds in regard that several Scandals were allegd against him that were not formerly in process. Mr Henderson then called and the Sentence intimated to him, whereupon he protested against it, appeald from it to the next General Assembly for Reasons to be given in in due time and thereupon askd and took Instruments in the Clerk's Hands and cravd Extracts and further protested that as Mr Rose Minister of Nairn in a very prejudging & injurious Manner laid before the Synod several gross Scandals against him, viz. frequent Drunkenness, dancing, and maintaining the licentious and odious Opinion, as also inculcating upon Women, That Fornication was no Crime, he craves that Mr Rose according to form of process give some account of their probability & undertake to make out the libel under pain of being censured as a Slanderer.[40]
>
> Elgin, October 21 1741.
>
> Compeared [Henderson]. He had resided at Edinburgh since last Meeting of Synod [and] he had brought along with him Certificate from that Presbytery which was presented & read in presence of Synod the Tenor whereof follows: 'These are to certify that Mr Andrew Henderson came to the Bounds of this Presbytery of Edinburgh cloathed with a License from the Presbytery of Mull to preach the Gospel & that he did preach in several of our Churches till it was rumoured that he had misbehaved in

> a house then said to be of bad fame & till this Presbytery had an Account that he was suspended from the foresaid license by the Presbytery of Forres & Synod of Murray from which he appealed to the General Assembly, where a protest was against him for not proscuting the said Appeal & that upon Enquiry into the said Misbehaviour and about the foresaid House ... nothing was made out either against him or it and ... he has been employd as a probationer yet during his abode here, ... without offence & with Approbation in teaching the Youth in about this City & therefore there is nothing known here why he may not be as hereby he is recommended as a person fit for teaching the lang[illeg.] and other parts of useful learning wherever he shall be regularly employd within the Bounds of any other Presbytery where Providence hereafter may order his Lot. In Testimony whereof these presents are by Order of ye Presbytery subscribd at Edinburgh the 30th Septr. 1741 by Sic Subscribitur Robt. McIntosh.'[41]

Henderson renewed his former protest against Rose and appealed to the next General Assembly. Then – as in a scene of Scottish drama – he wondered aloud of seeing a dagger before him:

> Mr Henderson while standing at the Synod's Barr and while the Clerk was writing out the above protest openly expressd himself in these Words, 'I believe Mr Daniel Munro woud cut my throat if he coud'. Mr Henderson being asked if he owned these Words to be his, answered he did because he was [of] opinion that Mr Munro was just then insinuating something to his disadvantage and because that contrary to Form of Process he had dilated him without previously informing him & for other reasons to be insisted on in due time. The Synod was justly offended at this, appointed their Moderator immediately to rebuke Mr Henderson but reserve the further Consideration of this offence till next Synod, to which Mr Henderson is appointed to be summoned apud acta accordingly the Moderator sharply reprimanded him for his Indiscretion and summoned him apud acta to next Synod.[42]

This present volume republishes the revengeful lines that Henderson later directed against the reputation of Mr Daniel Munro,[43] 'Daniel Monro, minister of Tain ... was an uncouth man, a monster of impiety, wickedness, and ill-nature'(see p. 173). The related footnote adds further to the insult: 'He was afterward turned out of his church for fighting and other immoralities.' Mr Alexander Rose, minister of Nairn, was also humiliated in *Cumberland* (see p. 197), where he is called 'one Rose Macinucater,[44] minister of Nairn, a wretch of such uncommon wickedness of heart, that such a one ought never to have been born ... ; and to complete his ruin he died farmer, grazier, adulterer, smuggler, and bankrupt'. The *Fasti* just says that Rose was ordained on 7 July 1730 and died on 16 December 1757.[45] Rose has suffered the indignity of having his detractor's opinion kept permanently in print since 1961, for John Prebble's *Culloden*[46] quotes the *Cumberland* page, nicely contrasting Henderson's rant with the reporting of another incident:

> A boy of seventeen was accused of spying for the Rebels, and was tried for it standing before a court-martial on the heather. Drummers of the Inlying Picquet beat him bravely to the gallows, and he hung there for ten minutes before Macinucater Rose of Nairn won him a reprieve from the Duke [of Cumberland]. This was His Royal Highness's clemency, it [15 April] being his birthday.[47]

To this Prebble adds, 'But if this were the same Macinucater Rose of Nairn ... there must have been some good in him. Though that, too, Andrew Henderson would no doubt have considered disgraceful.'[48]

Returning to the Church of Scotland's papers, we next find the 'Reasons of Appeal Mr Andrew Henderson against the Synod of Murrays Sentence.' This section contains an interesting item: the following certificate of Henderson's moral character, given at Edinburgh, 12 November 1744, under the hands of David White, James McGibbon and Colin Campbell, all deacons:

> These are to certify that Mr Andrew Henderson Preacher of the Gospel did reside in the House of Archibald Heron late Deacon of the Shoemakers in Edinburgh who has and still does retain a good & pious Character, since the Beginning of June 1743 till the 18th October last, during which time his Behaviour was every way agreeable to the Character of a Probationer so far as we could observe or hear having particular Acquaintance of him.[49]

Henderson gave in the following petition, backed 'Edinr. 13 May 1745':

> Unto the Very Reverend the Moderator and remnant, Members of the General Assembly of the Church of Scotland. The Petition of Mr Andrew Henderson humbly sheweth, That your Petitioner having been suspended by the Very Reverend the Synod of Moray for travelling upon a Sabbath to see his Mother who was sick upon his Father's Death and for saying, upon Mr Rose the Minister of Nairn's asking where was you at Sermon, overly at Forres, These and none other are the Crimes laid to his Charge ...[50]

He achieved his purpose for, by act of the provincial synod of Moray, dated 16 October 1745, reponing him to the exercise of his licence as a preacher of the Gospel, he was reinstated.[51] By 26 November 1746 he had resolved to leave Edinburgh and, evidently thinking himself quite the hero of an incident in the capital, sought an extract 'of what is minuted with regard to that generous action of relieving a modest Woman from a Rape'.[52]

The intemperate language of the disgraced probationer, however – he who publicly, scandalously supposed a minister of the Kirk to be in character a cut-throat – became a feature no less of the writings of the historian. As a pamphleteer in the eighteenth-century tradition, we may allow him his sneering disdain of Dr Johnson and his 'execrable treatise'. But from his *History of the Rebellion* let this be taken, almost at random, as an example of the sometimes wildly opinionated author. Here he writes about the Sutherlands, a clan loyal to the Hanoverian cause, to which Henderson was himself so ardently attached. His having accepted the myths of Clanchattan – to which, in his day, it was supposed that the Sutherlands and Macphersons were sprung – is really the only excess here that could be excused:

> Much degenerated from the Bravery of their Ancestors, and far from equalling that of the MacPhersons, who are of the same Stock ... In short, those People [the Sutherlands] are as poor, their Tempers as barbarous and inhuman as cruel and revengeful, as those of the worst of the Rebels, but less active, more stupid, and not at all given to that outward Civility, which the latter, by a natural Air peculiar to themselves, affect to shew to Strangers who come among them.[53]

There can be no escaping the field of Culloden in any treatment of Henderson's work. Material from his *History of the Rebellion* reappears in *Cumberland*, as one would expect: any assessment of Cumberland's reputation most closely concerns his actions in 1746. The battle is referred to in the *Second Letter to Dr Samuel Johnson*, in the part advertised as 'An impartial Character of Doctor [Tobias] Smollet':

> His account of the Duke of Cumberland's conduct in Scotland is shocking; 'for fifty miles round all was silence, horror and desolation'? whereas there was scarce a hut pulled down, a stone displaced, or a person killed who was not actually in arms, even on the day of the battle of Culloden, much less afterwards, nor have I the least reason to alter the account contained in my history of the rebellion, a book which underwent five editions, and was first published by Mr Griffiths Anno 1748, when he invited me to write the history of Scotland.'[54]

Henderson's bitter resentment of criticism of Cumberland, 'one of the most illustrious princes that ever lived',[55] is evident in this passage:

> Such was the Battle of Culloden, which the enemies of the Government have so cruelly represented, to the shame and reproach of the illustrious Leader, who, under God, was the chief instrument of the victory. The whole account given of it by Tobias Smollet is one continued misrepresentation.'[56]

The juxtaposition in this present volume of the Duke of Cumberland and Dr Johnson makes too delicious a combination of characters to allow for complete restraint. The Duke's enduring role in the Jacobite historical narrative begins on 28 November 1745,[57] when he took command of General Sir John Ligonier's army: and this was done at Lichfield, Johnson's birthplace. Did Samuel Johnson carry arms in the Jacobite army? On such a notion, let us simply read the argument – at one extreme of an old debate – made accessible in this newspaper cutting from 1925,[58] entitled 'Johnson the Jacobite',[59] reviewing a publication by the Hon. Sir Charles Russell (1863–1928), who assumed the presidency of The Johnson Society (Lichfield) in that year (according to the society's website):

> Under this title Sir Charles Russell has put forth a pamphlet, which will be a startling surprise to those who think of that essential Englishman, Samuel Johnson, as a large and cumbrous person, plagued by constant ill health and by the accumulated *sitzfleisch* that comes of a sedentary life. In fact, he revives Croker's suggestion that the famous man of letters ... was actually 'out' in the Jacobite rising of 1745. Croker's authority has been generally discredited, it is true, owing to the brilliant way in which Macaulay carried out his threat of 'dusting the varlet's jacket.' But the dust has settled since then, and, when the canons of modern criticism are applied in this case of a personal attack, we find that the dull and painstaking Croker was a more reliable writer than the greatest of Whig historians. ... There is no rest for the Whiggish in these critical days, so we refrain from pressing home the attack against Macaulay and all his works. After all, Sir Charles Russell, working out Croker's hint in detail, makes out a very good case for his belief that Johnson actually fought in the Forty-Five. In the first place, we know nothing at all about Johnson's life in the years 1745–46, and this spell of obscurity can be explained on the assumption that he found it expedient to disappear from the public gaze, while the hand of authority was hard on the rebels and all who sympathized with them. Secondly, there can be no doubt that Johnson was possessed not only of personal courage but also of the fighting man's temperament ... Thirdly, he came from a country that was strongly pro-Stuart, where they actually hunted a fox in a red uniform with plaid-clad hounds as a symbolical act of political faith, and his own Jacobite sympathies were often very strongly expressed. Indeed, it seems unlikely that this born fighter would have sat with arms folded while his rightful Prince was marching in triumph through the Midlands, his own homeland. Fourthly, when he passed through the Highlands in Boswell's company, the fact that he looked upon many scenes of the agelong struggle 'with lack lustre eye,' may be a proof, as Hazlitt thought, that they were already familiar to him or associated in his mind with interests that he durst not explain. Fifthly, and finally, how came he to have the musket, sword, and belt, which Boswell saw hanging in his closet? It is all a fascinating speculation, and it is possible to believe it without losing any of our affectionate admiration for one of the greatest of Englishmen.

A. N. Campbell-Maclachlan, whose work on Cumberland's career in 1745–7 was published in 1876, notes that William Augustus – by comparision with Charles Edward – had found 'but scant chroniclers'. However, the author says nothing of his predecessors; Henderson is but briefly quoted, and without citation.[60] Jonathan Oates gives the most recent review of the biographical literature on the Duke of Cumberland.[61] Of the very first biography, Henderson's, published in 1766, a year after Cumberland's death, this is the assessment: 'It shows Cumberland in an impossibly good light during every phase of his life.'[62] Observing that only a few historians have cared to defend Cumberland, the Hon. Evan Charteris[63] is described as the 'first important one'.[64] Charteris comments on the early biographer's 'never-failing enthusiasm ... Henderson wrote in the Georgian era, and was not unmindful of those having authority'.[65] However, as Oates writes, it is John Prebble's *Culloden* – first published in 1961, and never out of print since then – that could claim to be the most influential single work on the subject.[66] Prebble does not praise Henderson: he calls him Cumberland's 'servile biographer'.[67] In an age when television's power holds sway, however, Henderson's informing of Prebble, and Prebble's advising of Peter Watkins, the director of the famous BBC film, *Culloden* (1964), probably marks the highpoint of Henderson's historical influence in recent times. Positioned behind a wall, looking on through a telescope, Henderson the eyewitness is a character in the film. He shouts his commentary to camera as cannonballs fly; the film audience meets Henderson in the very act of capturing his picture of a battle which, as much as any in British history, retains a fascination in the public mind. The film and the eyewitness's role in it have since been the subject of scholarly comment:

> The docudrama shows a 'Whig historian' interpreting the fighting from afar, hidden behind a wall of stones and dependent on the lens of a telescope to discern the course of events. Hinting that such a poorly placed eyewitness can hardly be trusted for an informed account, the film forces viewers to question evidence. As one reviewer noted, it offers a considerable contrast from the old CBS television docudrama that confidently announced, 'You Are There.' *The Battle of Culloden* makes us wonder: 'Are We There?' It asks, in effect, which version of events is to be believed.[68]

Prebble's talents in choosing his historical writing themes do much to illustrate why Henderson, panegyrist for the Duke of Cumberland, should so soon have been ignored as a historian in his own right. Cumberland's claim to glory was in conquering British loyalties to the Chevalier de Saint Georges, the Jacobites' King James VIII and III, and the foe of Culloden, the Young Chevalier. Prebble's *The King's Jaunt: George IV in Scotland, August 1822 'One and twenty daft days'* (1988), gives its whole third part to the theme of Hanoverian George IV as 'Heir to the Chevalier'. As Prebble quotes from the *Edinburgh Observer*, 'We are now all Jacobites, thorough-bred Jacobites, in acknowledging George IV.' This is all part of the wizardry of Sir Walter Scott. 1822 marks the key point of a process which sought to catch the glamour and legitimacy of the Jacobites for the Georgites. It might even be said to culminate in such influential fictions as this:

> On the death of Prince Charles Edward and his brother, Prince Henry Benedict, the Cardinal Duke of York, the male line of the Royal Stuarts ended, and the Cardinal left his personal heirlooms to George III., thus (in absence of any *duthus* which he could settle) tacitly nominating him tanist of the old Royal line.[69]

As Prebble writes, quoting Scott, '"We are THE CLAN, and our King is THE CHIEF." By one persuasive paragraph the great-grandson of German Geordie and the great-nephew of Bloody Cumberland had become a Highland chief.'[70] Borrowing Henderson's own words, 'that union, on which the strength, the power, nay, and the glory of Great Britain do so entirely depend',[71] had simply no use for exhortations that 'the name of the hero be fixed upon every heart, and be remembered with a becoming gratitude'.[72] Truly he had been a king's beloved son: 'Never was a son more endearing to a father than the Duke of Cumberland'.[73] But, whatever the 'transcendent virtues which adorned the Duke of Cumberland',[74] affection for him died – either in 1760, with the death of George II; or in 1776, with the passing of Henderson, who had supposed the Duke's life 'so truly glorious a theme'.[75]

'The 16th April was the Beginning of a Jubilee only interrupted by the Misery of those who had forefeited their Lives to publick Justice.'[76] Certainly medals were struck: the motto on the medal of the Cumberland Society, 'instituted at Inverness the 17th day of April, 1746, in grateful Remembrance of the Service done our King and Country by his Royal Highness the Duke of Cumberland in extinguishing the Rebellion at the Battle of Culloden', translated as, 'The deed is done, it is finished, he is perished'.[77] Writing again of the events of 1746, but twenty years later, Henderson alludes to the efforts of some of the Jacobite chiefs to regroup and continue the rising until the end of May.[78] Cluny Macpherson's regiment – fully intact, having missed Culloden, and left undisturbed in Badenoch by British government troops for a whole month after the battle of 16 April[79] – was a focus for efforts to regroup and rally the Jacobite army. Only when a large party of Macphersons surrendered their arms late in May, did the Jacobites' formal resistance to the British army come to an end.[80] It is absurd to claim, as Henderson does, that the victorious Duke of Cumberland thereafter 'took nothing from his enemies, except the power of hurting'.[81] The comment that prisoners, transported to the colonies, 'procured a more comfortable sustenance than if they had remained at home'[82] – however hackneyed the excuses for Highland depopulation have since become – puts the writer beyond the line of possibility for a historian. But could Henderson (and the Church of Scotland) have been right to judge Cumberland 'the Deliverer of his country'?[83] Instead of stressing Cumberland's 'moderation and lenity',[84] the heroic aspect, if to be glimpsed at all, is in seeing whether the Duke was right to judge it unsafe to grant the wished-for mercy advocated by others in the Hanoverian establishment. One thinks especially of the Duke's contrasting opinions on this with those of Lord President Forbes of Culloden.[85] 'He wishes for lenity, if it can be with safety,' wrote Cumberland, 'which he thinks, but I don't.'[86]

'The Forty-five had not seriously threatened to remove George from the throne', claims W. A. Speck.[87] But, as the Jacobite army was advancing, why should we not believe that there was some truth in George II's legendary outburst after a nightmare: '*de Great Glenbogged was coming*'?[88] Cumberland feared future troubles; he had 'only weakened the madness but not at all cured, and I tremble for fear that this vile spot may still be the ruin of this Island and of our Familly'. So he wrote in July 1746, on being recalled from Scotland to London – in which city the brave 'Marcellus' would transform into 'Butcher'.[89] He too would have been right to fear the influence of 'Old Glenbucket'. Major General

John Gordon of Glenbucket's journey to Rome in 1737 to visit King James has caused some historians to make Glenbucket chiefly responsible for there having been a rising in 1745.[90] He travelled to Rome in company with 'Mr Peter Grant the Churchman':[91] this is the Abbé Grant, who saw to it that Charles Edward Stuart was received in state at the English, Scots and Irish Colleges in Rome in April 1766 as King Charles III.[92] Cumberland had died the previous year; 1766 was the very year of the publication of Henderson's biography.

If that clerical kissing of hands in homage in Rome could just be dismissed as a futile gesture, let it be remembered that Abbé Grant's nephew, the French colonel and spy, Baron Grant de Blairfindy,[93] would, in 1767, be sending the first of his reconnaissance reports to the Duc de Choiseul about the state of British defences against a projected invasion.[94] Had a *lettre de cachet* not put the great minister into exile in 1770, there is evidence to show it probable that a French invasion of Britain would soon have been launched. As Grant de Blairfindy's reports explicitly show, the future of 'le Roi Charles Edouard' was an integral part of the whole mission[95] – at least so far as Grant was concerned. There are hints that the spy's father, John Grant, had been a deserter from a government regiment, who joined his brothers (officers in Glenbucket's regiment)[96] in the Jacobite army; moreover, that he was listing men in Banffshire for service in the French army in 1750.[97] It appears that, other than the burning by troops of the house of Blairfindy in Glenlivet,[98] no punishment is recorded as having been inflicted upon any members of this dangerous family by the British state.[99] Perhaps, after all, history may marvel at the Duke of Cumberland's 'moderation and lenity not to be found in ancient times, and scarce to be believed in times to come'?[100] It seems that some instances of it did not obviously favour his family's interest, for Jacobite schemes would last long beyond his victory at Culloden.

Roderick Macpherson,
Glasgow, 15 April 2009.

Notes:

1. Ralph Henderson, *Records of My Family* (Carlisle: Chas. Thurnam, 1926), pp. 16 and 23. His sources were four of Henderson's diaries, covering the years 1759 to 1771. The date of marriage is not referred to in print. However, this is the entry relating to the birth of John, at Westminster: '1759 Sat. August 25th ½ pm tertian, born a male child, every way beautiful and comely, whom may the eternal Jehovah bless for ever and ever as also the Mother.' (Ibid., p. 22.)
2. Ibid., p. 18.
3. [H. R. Tedder], *Dictionary of National Biography*, vol. 9, p. 395.
4. R. Henderson, *Records of My Family*, p. 23.
5. Ibid., p. 21.
6. Ibid., p. 7.
7. Alexander Du Toit, *Oxford Dictionary of National Biography*, vol. 26, p. 297.

8. R. Henderson, *Records of My Family*, p. 20
9. Ibid.
10. Henderson's *Cumberland,* p. 293.
11. Ibid.
12. *Cumberland,* preface.
13. Charles Sandford Terry, *The Rising of 1745: With a Bibliography of Jacobite History 1689–1788* (London: D. Nutt, 1900). 'The Lond. 1753 edit. is virtually a new work.'
14. R. Henderson, *Records of My Family*, p. 19.
15. Ibid., p. 20.
16. Alice Wemyss, *Elcho of the '45*, ed. John Sibbald Gibson (Edinburgh: Saltire Society, 2003), p. 226.
17. Henrietta Tayler (ed.), *The History of the Rebellion in the Years 1745 and 1746* (Oxford: Roxburghe Club, 1944), p. xx. She states here that Henderson's Edinburgh edition appeared in 1747 and that the 1748 London edition is a reprint of that. She also points to Elcho's manuscript as the source from which Sir Walter Scott drew so much.
18. [Tedder], *DNB*, quoting *Biographia Dramatica* (1812), vol. 2, p. 38.
19. R. Henderson, *Records of My Family*, pp. 25–6.
20. Of this prominent family of the name, Ralph Henderson writes: 'All efforts to trace the exact connection have failed, but it would seem probable that Francis [the grandfather of Andrew] was descended from either a younger brother or an uncle of the first Baronet, Sir John Henderson of Fordell'. (*Records of My Family*, p. 8.)
21. R. Henderson, *Records of My Family*, p. 8
22. Ibid., pp. 10 and 13.
23. Ibid., p. 13.
24. Ibid.
25. Ibid.
26. Ibid., p. 16.
27. Du Toit, *ODNB*, p. 296.
28. R. Henderson, *Records of My Family*, p. 17.
29. Ibid., pp.17 and 18.
30. *Cumberland*, p. 173 fn.
31. R. Henderson, *Records of My Family*, p.18.
32. [Tedder], *DNB*.
33. National Archives of Scotland (NAS), CH1/2/82 ff. 164–213. (Abbreviations expanded.)
34. Ibid., f. 169.
35. Ibid.
36. John Squyre, minster of Forres, 1718–58. (Hew Scott, *Fasti Ecclesiæ Scoticannæ*, vol. 6 (Edinburgh: n. p., 1926), p. 422.)
37. NAS, CH1/2/82, f. 169.
38. Ibid.
39. Ibid., f. 171.
40. Ibid.
41. Ibid., f. 173.
42. Ibid., f. 174.
43. Munro was transferred to the parish of Tain on 13 June 1745, having previously been minister at Auldearn, since 1736. He died in 1748. (Scott, *Fasti Ecclesiæ Scoticannæ*, vol. 7 (Edinburgh, 1928), p.71.)

44. Henderson refers to the name *MacInnucater* as one of the 'Northern Clans'. (*History of the Rebellion*, Edinburgh edn, p. 63). Macnucater, 'son of the fuller', is Englished as Walker (George F. Black, *The Surnames of Scotland*, New York Public Library, 1946, p. 553).
45. Scott, *Fasti Ecclesiæ Scoticannæ*, vol. 6, p. 443.
46. John Prebble, *Culloden* (London: Secker & Warburg, 1961), p. 194.
47. Ibid., p. 17.
48. Ibid., p. 194.
49. NAS, CH1/2/82, ff.186 and 188.
50. Ibid., f. 184.
51. Ibid., f. 185.
52. Ibid., f. 206.
53. Henderson's *History of the Rebellion*, Edinburgh edn, pp. 59–60; cf. London edn, p. 45. The London edition gives a further insult by Henderson, perhaps with Mr Daniel Munro in mind: 'Of the Monroes I shall only observe, that the same Character will fit them, as that I have here given of the People of Sutherland.'
54. Henderson's *Second Letter to Dr Johnson*, pp. 313–14.
55. *Cumberland*, p. 280.
56. Ibid., p. 260.
57. Tayler (ed.), *The History of the Rebellion*, p. 101.
58. *The Morning Post*, 17 February 1925, p. 8, col. 3. 'Here is', at any rate, an addition to the historical Apocrypha which need not be accepted as absolute truth, but may be studied for edification.
59. For a recent treatment of Johnson's Jacobitism, see Jonathan Clark and Howard Erskine-Hill (eds), *Samuel Johnson in Historical Context* (Houndsmills and New York: Palgrave, 2002); especially the first essay by Paul Monod, 'A Voyage out of Staffordshire; or, Samuel Johnson's Jacobite Journey', pp. 11–43.
60. A. N. Campbell-Maclachlan, *William Augustus, duke of Cumberland; being a sketch of his military life and character, chiefly as exhibited in the general orders of H. R. H., 1745–1747* (London: Henry S. King & Co., 1876), pp. 3, 4, 12 and 13.
61. Jonathan Oates, *Sweet William or the Butcher? The Duke of Cumberland and the '45* (Barnsley: Pen & Sword Military, 2008).
62. Ibid., p. 3.
63. Author of *William Augustus, Duke of Cumberland. His Early Life and Times (1721–1748)* (London: E. Arnold, 1913); *William Augustus, Duke of Cumberland and the Seven Years War* (London: Hutchinson, 1925); *A Short Account of the Affairs of Scotland in the Years 1744, 1745, 1746 by David, Lord Elcho* (memoir and annotations by Charteris) (Edinburgh, 1907). (This last mentioned work refers (p. 29) to Abbé Grant as a spy for the British government, which is open to question.)
64. Oates, *Sweet William or the Butcher?*, p. 13.
65. Hon. Evan Charteris, *William Augustus, Duke of Cumberland His Early Life and Times (1721–1748)* (London, 1913), p. 12.
66. Oates, *Sweet William or the Butcher?*, p. 8.
67. Prebble, *Culloden*, p. 127.
68. Robert Brent Toplin, 'The Filmmaker as Historian', *American Historical Review*, 93:5 (December 1988), pp. 1210–27, p. 1219, making reference to Ina Rae Hark, 'On Eyewitnessing History: The Compromised Spectator in Peter Watkins' *Culloden*', *South Atlantic Quarterly*, 84 (Summer 1985), pp. 294–301, p. 301.

69. Thomas Innes of Learney, *The Tartans of the Clans and Families of Scotland* (Edinburgh and London, W. & A. K. Johnson Limited, 1938), p. 280.
70. John Prebble, *The King's Jaunt: George IV in Scotland, August 1822* (London: Collins, 1988), p. 100.
71. *Cumberland,* preface.
72. Ibid., p. 272.
73. Ibid., p. 336.
74. Ibid., p. 371.
75. Ibid., preface.
76. *History of the Rebellion*, Edinburgh edn, p. 202; London edn (1748), p. 121.
77. Noel Woolf, *The Medallic Record of the Jacobite Movement* (London: Spink, 1988), p. 103; Michael Sharp, *Jacobite and anti-Jacobite Medals,* The Royal Stuart Society, Paper lxxiv (2008), p. 13.
78. *Cumberland,* p. 198.
79. Alan G. Macpherson, *A Day's March to Ruin – a documentary narrative of the Badenoch Men in the 'Forty-Five and biography of Col. Ewan Macpherson of Cluny, 1706–1764* (Newtonmore: Clan Macpherson Association, 1996), pp. 163 *et seq.*
80. Oates, *Sweet William or the Butcher?*, p. 121.
81. *Cumberland*, p. 191.
82. Ibid., p. 271.
83. Ibid., p. 272.
84. Ibid., p. 269.
85. George Menary, *The Life and Letters of Duncan Forbes of Culloden, Lord President of the Court of Session 1685–1747* (London: A. Maclehose & Co., 1936), p. 287. Forbes was 'that old woman who talked to me of humanity,' according to a saying of Cumberland. (Tayler, *The History of the Rebellion*, p. xv.)
86. Philip W. Sergeant, *Rogues and Scoundrels* (London, 1924), p. 241.
87. W. A. Speck, *The Butcher: The Duke of Cumberland and the Suppression of the 45* (Oxford: Blackwell, 1981), p. 203.
88. Alistair and Henrietta Tayler, *Jacobites of Aberdeenshire and Banffshire in the Forty-Five* (Aberdeen: Milne & Hutchison, 1928), p. 252.
89. Sergeant, *Rogues and Scoundrels*, p. 242.
90. Tayler and Tayler, *Jacobites of Aberdeenshire,* p. 250. Glenbucket's 'Memoriall to The King', personally delivered in January 1738, was a document 'of extraordinary interest' (as the editor, Henrietta Tayler, describes it), published in the Roxburghe Club volume of 1944, pp. xxvii–viii.
91. Tayler and Tayler, *Jacobites of Aberdeenshire*, p. 255.
92. Lesley Lewis, *Connoisseurs and Secret Agents in Eighteenth Century Rome* (London: Chatto & Windus, 1961), p. 217.
93. Charles Grant, Vicomte de Vaux, *Mémoires Historiques, Généalogiques, Politiques, Militaires, &c. de la Maison de Grant* (London: n.p., 1796), pt 2, p. 363.
94. See Margaret Cotter Morison, 'The Duc de Choiseul and the Invasion of England, 1768–1770, *Transactions of the Royal Historical Society*, 3rd series, vol. 4 (1910), pp. 83-115; J. W. Thompson and S. K. Padover, *Secret Diplomacy – A Record of Espionage and Double-dealing: 1500–1815* (London: Jarrolds, 1937), pp. 171–3.
95. Lord Mahon, *History of England from the Peace of Utrecht*, vol. 5, 1763–74 (London: John Murray, 1851), appendix xix, 'Intended Invasion of England', pp. xix–xxi (the quotation at the last page).

96. Alastair Livingstone of Bachuil, C. W. H. Aikman and Betty Stuart Hart (eds), *Muster Roll of Prince Charles Edward Stuart's Army 1745–46* (Aberdeen: Aberdeen University Press, 1984), pp. 121–2. John Grant's brothers were William, of Blairfindy; Alexander, Logan [Laggan] of Blairfindy; and James, in the same place. Two of William's sons were also officers in Glenbucket's regiment.
97. James Allardyce (ed.), *Historical Papers relating to the Jacobite Period 1699–1750*, vol. 2 (Aberdeen: New Spalding Club, 1896), pp. 563–4.
98. Tayler and Tayler, *Jacobites of Aberdeenshire*, p. 101.
99. There is no evidence known to confirm the story of Abbé Grant having been brought up to London as a rebel in the year 1745–6, in the same ship with Lords Balmerino, Kilmarnock, etc., as appears in Henry Swinburne's *The Courts of Europe at the Close of the Last Century*, ed. C. White, (London: Henry Colburn, 1841), vol. 1, p. 210.
100. *Cumberland*, p. 191.

His Royal Highness,

William Duke of Cumberland

Engravd for the Life of the Duke. /

THE LIFE OF WILLIAM AUGUSTUS DUKE OF CUMBERLAND.

CONTAINING
A Circumstantial and Historical Account of the Times for the last Forty-four Years.

By ANDREW HENDERSON, M.A.

Author of the History of the REBELLION.

Quique sui memores alios fecere merendo. VIRG.

LONDON:

Printed for J. RIDLEY, in St. James's-Street; Z. STUART, in Pater-noster-Row; W. RICHARDSON and L. URQHUART, at the Royal Exchange; and the Booksellers in Westminster-Hall.

M DCC LXVI. / / /

TO

HER ROYAL HIGHNESS

The Princess AMELIA,

This LIFE of

Her ROYAL BROTHER the

DUKE OF CUMBERLAND

IS DEDICATED,

With the profoundest Respect and Regard,

By Her Royal Highness's most obedient,

Most devoted and humble Servant,

And. Henderson, /

PREFACE.

If the actions of good men, who have defended religion and the liberties of their country, ought to be recorded, then there need be no apology for publishing a Life of his Royal Highness William Augustus *Duke of* Cumberland: *I must only apologize for myself, in undertaking so arduous a task, and so truly glorious a theme.*

Two Gentlemen of great worth and probity, being pleased with my History of the Rebellion, *fixed upon me as a person who had, with some care, enquired into the transactions of that period, when the conduct of his Royal Highness was every way conspicuous; that performance was published at* London *in* January 1748, *after I had left* Watts's *academy, to which I had been sent up, as mathematical master, by a Gentleman of great learning, who is now steward upon one of the largest estates in* North Britain. *My book was twice pirated, and three times reprinted, an honour done to no other account of these troubles; and Mr.* Griffiths *the publisher (if alive) will do me the justice to acknowledge how desirous I was to rectify every mistake that might have crept into it, and still am, being always ready to embrace truth whereever it is to be found.*

Unfortunately for this performance, it differs widely from Dr. Tobias Smollett's *History almost in every particular: and however willing I may be to yield to that Gentleman in every point of literature, yet I must confess that my opportunities of knowing* Scotland *were no less than his, or what any of his votaries can pretend to.*

I was born five miles south east of the Tweed, *in the shire of* Roxburgh, *where my predecessors by both my parents lived for five hundred years before: connected / in blood with those of the surnames of* Scott *and* Douglass, *I can say with great truth,*

> No parricide nor rebel yet was known
> In all my line; let each excuse his own.

Being scarce turned of five years, I went to the North with the best of fathers. While at the universities of Aberdeen *and* Edinburgh, *I had opportunities of being acquainted with Gentlemen from different parts of the kingdom, especially as I was tutor to the Countess of* Stair's *nephew, and to Mr.* Thomas Young, *son to Colonel* Young, *Lord* Stair's *aid de camp. I likewise taught in the high school of* Edinburgh, *by which, with my being tutor to Colonel* Dugald Campbell *in* Argyleshire, *I had occasion to know every county in* Scotland *but three, and also to be in several of the isles.*

As to inserting the manifestoes of the Pretender, it was by the advice of some eminent Clergymen and Officers of State, in order to lay open the pernicious tendency of the Adventurer's attempt, whose object was the dissolution of that union, on which the strength, the power, nay, and the glory of Great Britain *do so entirely depend; and consequently to set forth what gratitude is due from every* Protestant *and* Englishman *to him, whose valour and conduct defeated the daring and impious project.*

As to the events which fell not within my own view, I have taken them from the best evidence, as I have those upon the continent; and am fully satisfied of the truth of most of the matters herein contained. /

CONTENTS.

THE LIFE OF WILLIAM DUKE OF CUMBERLAND.

BOOK I.

CONTENTS.

A short Account of the Family of Hanover, – *the Birth of the Duke of* Cumberland, – *his Education and Advancement,* – *the Death of Sir* Isaac Newton, – *and of King* George I. – *the War in* 1739–1743, – *and a Description of the Battle of* Dettingen.

AMONG the several princes of Germany, who are distinguished for riches, or eminent in power, there is not one at this time beyond the Electoral House of Hanover; the country is among the most fertile in the circle of Lower Saxony; it is well watered with rivers, remarkable for fine horses, yields a revenue / of 600,000 *l. per annum,* and furnishes an army of 30,000 men; their descent might be traced up to the Pagan gods of ancient Rome, and ever since the year 490 they have been possessed of principalities in the Lower Saxony, which, united together, formed a very great and considerable dukedom about the middle of the 14th century, known by the name of Brunswick-Lunenburgh, to distinguish it from Brunswick-Wolfenbuttle, of which they were descended: two of these dukes of Lunenburgh wore the Imperial diadem, an evident token of their importance in the empire, and a plain indication that they were not unworthy the choice which a nation, far more powerful than the Germanic body, made of them to wear a crown more brilliant and illustrious than that of any emperor, or other potentate.

On the head of George I. Elector of Hanover, was the English diadem conferred, in consequence of his being the nearest Protestant heir to the British throne: there was indeed an heir nearer, but then he was a Roman Catholic, and the person, viz. King Charles I. by whom the descent came, had been put to death by the hands of a common executioner. The Duke of Savoy, grandfather to the present King of Sardinia, is the person meant: he was the grandson of Philip, Duke of Orleans, and of Henrietta of England, daughter to that unfortunate prince, whose reign was so unhappy, and whose exit was so fatal and unprecedented: it has long been a dispute among politicians, whether or not the descendant from a man, who had died upon a scaffold, was to have the preference to one, whose ancestors had not been so publicly stigmatized; for my part, I am always for remedying injuries, and think that any person ought to be regarded the more, on account of / the hardships suffered by his immediate ancestors, provided the same have been the effect of injustice and cruelty, or, in other words, have been wholly undeserved: a circumstance extremely doubtful in the case of King Charles I. whose connections with France were the source and spring not only of his calamity, but perhaps one of the prevailing motives with the British parliament to pass over his offspring in the act of settlement, and to fix the crown upon the head of a prince eminent for his virtues, distinguished by his bravery, and admired for his economy and conduct; the circumstance of being descended from a prince, who had stood in a field of blood for the Protestant religion at the famous battle of Prague, anno 1620, was not a small incident in his favour, and to give it a further sanction the Duke of Lunenburgh himself fought in that engagement on the side of the Protestant army: however, these qualifications, fortunate as they were, would not have entirely weighed with them, had not the superior qualities of George I. commanded respect and dignity; he had served in the armies of the empire against France and the Turks, and had come with a body of 10,000 men to the relief of Vienna, 1683, then besieged by the Turkish army, consisting of 200,000 men, commanded by the Grand Seignor in person, hitherto flushed with slaughter, crowned with conquest, and become courageous through an obstinate inveteracy against the Christian name: in a word, his Majesty King George I. was thoroughly acquainted with the art of war, and in the year 1708 commanded the army of the Empire upon the Rhine. Monsieur Voltaire, notwithstanding his attachment to his native country, and to the

Stuart family, is yet forced, as it were against his will, to bestow upon him the finest and the most exalted / encomiums; for at the very time when he is charging him with an oppressive ambition, in attacking the King of Sweden, while ready to be devoured by a number of enemies too powerful for him, he is obliged to own that he was adored by his German subjects, that he hated the pride of Majesty, and delighted to converse in great familiarity with a few old courtiers. He was, continued he, one of the wisest Kings in Europe, and perhaps the only one who could taste upon a throne the pleasures of friendship and a private life*.

The family of Hanover are naturally soldiers, born with all the ardour of a military genius; an instance of which we shall give in our late sovereign. He came to the army of the Allies in the month of June 1708, then commanded by Prince Eugene of Savoy, and by the Duke of Marlborough, under the direction of which last he was entirely put by the Elector his father. As the crown of England, upon the decease of William Duke of Gloucester, son to Queen Anne, did by the act of settlement devolve upon the heirs of the Princess Sophia, Dutchess Dowager of Hanover, so the young Prince wanted to signalize himself, by engaging among those over whom he was one day to govern; and soon an opportunity offered: for on the 11th of July that year was fought the terrible battle of Oudenarde between the army of the Allies, and that of France commanded by the Duke de Vendosme, and animated by the presence of the Dukes of Burgundy and Berry, attended by the old Chevalier de St. George, in favour of whom the House of Bourbon seemed to interest herself seriously. As the Pretender to / the throne of England was in the opposite army, so the young Electoral Prince of Hanover, judging of the spirit of his rival by his own, thought he would undoubtedly charge at the head of the Gens d'Armes, in order to give a proof of his being worthy to wear that crown, which he had so lately sought after, and therefore wanted not to be outdone in point of courage and magnanimity. He intreated the Duke of Marlborough to suffer him to charge in the first line of the British cavalry, and at the head of the regiment of Greys. The Duke however, ready to comply with any proposal from his Highness on any other occasion, yet was inflexible to the most earnest solicitations as to this particular; for he looked upon the young man as Prince of Wales, the property of the people of Great Britain, and consequently not to be exposed to the doubtful

* History of Charles XII, Book VII.

fates and calamities of an engagement. This being the case, he watched an opportunity of joining the Hanoverian cavalry, and rode into the foremost rank just as they were advancing to the charge: opposite to these was a party of the Gens d'Armes, a circumstance which only fired the young hero; he charged with all the intrepidity and valour that could be expected from the most enterprizing and resolute soldier, and when his horse was shot under him, he fought on foot until another was brought to remount him. In a word, he was in the hottest place of the firing; every action was done as with forethought, and from the best laid plans of operation; he was only mistaken in one thing; the Dukes of Burgundy and Berry, with the Chevalier, were not in the field; for by the advice of Vendosme, the two first went up to the spire of an high steeple, from thence to behold the progress of the battle; and the Chevalier was so complaisant as to attend them. / However, their stay was but short; for on seeing the clouds of smoke, and hearing the firing, which was both loud and terrible, they hastened down, and each of them mounted a courser, which stood ready for them, and so galloped off to a further distance.

But though the conduct of the Dukes of Burgundy, Berry, and the Chevalier, was no less shameful for them, than the behaviour of the Electoral Prince of Hanover was glorious for him; yet a Prince* of the Duke of Marlborough's experience and judgment was not to dispense with a strictness of discipline, which is the vital principle, whence, as from a fountain, is derived the health, the safety, and welfare of every army. He ordered him to be tried by a court-martial. The Prince appeared, and, like Epaminondas of old, he generously, and openly confessed his having charged at the head of his father's cavalry. The defence was not sustained; he was degraded from the rank of a major-general to that of a corporal, and the report being made to the Elector his father, the same was approved by him. However, the suspension was soon taken off, the Prince was honourably restored to his dignity, and the army in general, from this sudden eclipse of his station, began to look upon his aspect as more brilliant after the clouds were blown over that had darkened it for a time; and with his employment he regained the favour and affection of his father, of which he seemed in some measure to have been deprived.

* He was Prince of Mildelhielm, an honour conferred on him, anno 1704, by the Emperor Leopold, on account of the battle of Hockstet.

Every action of King George I. seemed to be dictated, as it were, by wisdom itself; he knew how to reconcile jarring interests, and was well acquainted with men and with things; his tenderness / toward his children was not the least conspicuous among his virtues; he came to the peaceable possession of the British throne on the decease of Queen Anne without bloodshed. He landed at Greenwich on the 18th of September 1714, attended with his eldest son, and was there received by the lords of the regency, the officers of state, and a prodigious concourse of nobility, and other persons of distinction, and on the 20th made his public entry into the city of London, attended by the Prince riding on his right hand, and by two hundred coaches and six of others, who waited upon him. There was a thorough change in the ministry; all who had stickled for a separate peace with France were discharged; the Duke of Marlborough, whose fame had filled every court in Europe, was made generalissimo; the Duke of Argyle was made commander of the forces in Scotland; the Earl of Stair was sent Embassador into France; and such as were connected with these great men shared the Royal favour. It was no wonder that a Prince of such uncommon penetration and goodness as King George I. should deal tenderly with his children; he had only two, a daughter and a son; the former of whom was at that time Queen of Prussia, and has favoured the world with a race of Princes, who, at the time of writing this, are looked upon to be among the best accomplished commanders in Europe; the latter was our late Sovereign, known by the name of George II. who swayed the British sceptre almost thirty-three years. He had by his Royal consort Queen Caroline two sons and five daughters; the first of whom, Frederic Prince of Wales, was a mirror of good-nature, generosity, and virtue; and the second, the subject of these memoirs, was possessed of all the accomplishments that can either / render a man amiable in private life, or make him shine with lustre in an exalted station. The great and shining qualities of his ancestors united in him; nor did he, like other heroes, carry them to such excess, as to render them hurtful or pernicious: by his care, vigilance, and circumspection, he held them in their due poise, and knew, like the skillful marksman, how to use them, and when it was most proper to exert them to advantage. It is of him we intend to write what has come to our knowledge concerning his person and actions.

He was born at Leicester-house on the 26th of April 1721, N.S. an event which not a little contributed to appease the minds of the people then exasperated to the highest degree, by the great and singular losses which many gentlemen of large and opulent estates had lately sustained.

The project of the South Sea Company, in the year 1720, was one of those schemes that may discover the blindness of those that are set upon acquiring riches, and the hidden arts that men, intent upon villainy, and who had abandoned conscience, were able to effectuate. Under pretence of reducing the public funds into one capital, and of paying off the national debt, did the contrivers of the South Sea stock procure the sanction of the legislature; their scheme was first approved by the parliament on the 1st of February 1720, and in April following received the Royal assent. It was strange that a trading nation could not see into the impropriety of trading to advantage to such distant regions: for whether the navigation to those seas be by the Cape of Good Hope, or by sailing to the southward of the Straits of Magellan, as Lord Anson did in the year 1742, yet the voyage is dangerous through the variety of climates, the profits are uncertain, and at that time the coasts of / these remote places were only known to the Spaniards, who concealed them, as in a repository: however a prospect of gaining, cent. upon cent. engaged many to put in large sums in the South Sea stock: the rich citizens of this great metropolis laid in very large sums, gentlemen of fortune borrowed money upon their paternal estates, to trade with: it was no new thing, to see a thousand pounds paid down for one hundred employed in the South Sea capital, which soon amounted to two millions: and for the further encouragement, the contrivers paid some poor people very large and considerable sums, while the opulent and wealthy received little more than fair promises. In a word, rich men became poor and the poor became rich by this scene of iniquity: which, about the latter end of August, began to open, and continued so to do till Michaelmas, when the stock fell from 1000 l. to 150 l. and before the Christmas following all was detected: many great and antient families were reduced to the lowest ebb of misery: many ladies of fortune were from this reduced to the alternative of starving or going into a workhouse, where far from meeting with such usage as the intention of the charity proposed, or as humanity and goodness suggested, they were insulted by the matrons, of whom better things might have been expected, and frequently dragged by the hair of the head from one apartment to another, and thrown down stairs with violence at last. Nor did the evil stop here, for while the contrivers of the South Sea scheme were impoverishing men of property with chimerical projects, others, whose views were more generous, whose intentions were more candid and fair, projected schemes of a more salutary nature, and under the name of companies, wanted to form societies for the manufactory of / linen, and the advancement of the fisheries, which last is an inexhaustible source of wealth to the inhabitants of Great Britain and Ireland: but these, with other schemes of the like kind, were not only refused by the privy council, but suppressed by public proclamation: for as the South Sea project had ruined many, and that above one million and an half sterling had been lost by individuals, the clamour was so loud against some contrivers, thought to be in the secret of the whole, that the nation in general was put in a ferment, and our trade both foreign and domestic was well high ruined.

But tho' the fraud was detected by Sir Robert Walpole, who thereupon was made Chancellor of the Exchequer and first Commissioner of the Treasury, tho' the money (1,450,000 l.) found in the repositories at the South Sea house was appropriated to the sufferers, yet the complaints continued to be both loud and piercing, till the time of the birth of prince William, when these began to subside: he was baptized by the name of William, a name very propitious for England, for Holland, and in short for the Protestant cause: the birth of a son born to the Royal family, and among ourselves, was singularly pleasing to the public, and the more so on account of the name given him; and what not a little tended to enhance the satisfaction, they had been deprived of a former prince of that name: a coolness, whether political or real is but a circumstance, that had subsisted between the King and his Son, was intirely removed: the ordinary guards that attended the Prince of Wales were restored, and did duty at Leicester-house as before the misunderstanding; and, to shew that the harmony was perfect and intire, the Prince of Wales the year following accompanied his Royal Father in a tour to Hampshire, when he visited Winchester, the / docks, yards, arsenals, magazines and shipping in the port and harbour of Portsmouth, and returning by the way of Guilford in Surrey to his palace at Kensington, he procured an universal affection and applause: nor must we pass over in silence that the year of this Prince's birth was remarkable for the first trial of inoculation in England: the experiment was made with success upon some convicts in Newgate, and now seems universally to be received in this country as salutary and useful: the greatest physicians in this island seem to have approved of it; even in Kent, where the small-pox is looked on as the pestilence, it has been received; at Maidstone, which is certainly a fine situation, and a place of great commerce and trade, it is almost tried upon every individual, and I have been credibly informed, that out of a very great number who have gone through the operation, only one young lady died. However to treat in this place upon inoculation, a subject which I don't pretend to understand, would be preposterous, and yet one cannot pass over that the question, whether it be more advantageous to the public? is at this time under the consideration of the learned: the different physicians in Europe have the matter before them, and time will produce the decision, which I hope will be for the preservation of mankind, and which no morbid views or self-interest of any individual ought ever to preponderate against.

Whether the intire and cordial reconciliation between the King and his Son, proceeded from the great tenderness or regard which he always shewed toward the Princess of Wales and her offspring, or to the complacency which he discovered at the birth of a prince, in the midst of a people over whom Providence had set him, certain it is that no man ever discovered a greater satisfaction and delight / than did King George the First in this young Prince, whose charms even in a state of infancy were significant of his approaching greatness: the Princess of Wales was so fond of him that she carried him in her lap whether in a coach or chair upon a visit, or even when taking a tour or airing into the country. Numbers of people have crowded from all corners of the city to look at the Mother and her Son: the innate comeliness and native grace stamped upon every feature, and legible in every attitude of the one, with the Royal tenderness and care so visible in the several manœuvres of the other, procured an universal love, veneration, and esteem. The city was full of the prints of the Princess of Wales sitting with her Son upon her knee; the generous and tender-hearted frequently shed tears at the sight, and poured out their blessings upon both; the disaffected themselves were forced to yield their tribute of praise, envy itself was dumb and lost in wonder, factions were silent, and both friends and enemies vied in their encomiums. The King himself at the first installation of Knights after the birth of the Prince created him a Knight of the Bath, and put the red ribband, the ensign of it, about him with his own hand: his Majesty rightly judged it most proper to begin with this Order, as its principal design was to relieve the orphan, the widow, and those who had none to help them; for he had observed such shining instances of goodness and generosity in the heart of the Prince even during his childhood, that he thought him worthy of this honour even upon the footing of his own merit. Scarce had he begun to walk when he was observed to feel for the poor; and such engaging sallies of goodness and the sagacity dropped from him on every occasion, as could not fail of raising both affection and esteem. / One day the Princess was going to Kensington, to pay her compliments to the King: and as the coach passed through Hyde-park a multitude of poor people crowded about it, as usual: her Highness being exceeding popular, held up the child in her arms, that they might see him: without hesitating a moment he threw among them what silver he had in his hand; and being checked for his rashness, as the people began to struggle about the spoil, he calmly answered with an endearing smile, which was ever most familiar to him; 'O, madam, ought not I to love my loyal subjects?' The Princess seemed to storm at the expression, and said, 'You little rogue, how come you to say my subjects, they are only the King's.' 'O, madam, (answered he) I meant the loyal subjects; for I know that they are only the subjects of my royal Grand-father.'

Such shining and transcendent goodness could not fail of being highly pleasing to the King, who at the grand installation of thirty-seven knights of the different orders, on the 25th of May 1725, made him a Knight of the Bath. The ceremony was in the Abbey of Westminster; to which the companions marched in their robes, and from thence to a very grand and most magnificent entertainment: and to shew further the high respect and regard which the King bore him, he was created Baron of the isle of Alderney, Viscount of Trematon in Cornwall, Earl of Kennington, in Surrey, Marquis of Berkhamstead in Hertfordshire; and, on the 15th of July 1726, was created Duke of Cumberland.

In this disposition and with such encouragements he was taken from the women, or rather from the Princess of Wales herself, and placed under the tuition of Mr. Philips, a man naturally of a good / disposition, and endowed with a considerable stock of the Latin language. The tutor had no less authority over his pupil than if he had been the son of an ordinary mechanic: for no lady upon earth kept her children under a stricter discipline and in more subjection than did the then Princess of Wales. Mr. Phillips soon found a genius of the first order to form, a disposition intirely tractable, and a readiness to obey, that would have endeared one of a low rank to any who had the care of his education. He soon became acquainted with the Latin tongue: he was particularly attentive to such lines as contained precepts of virtue and morality. Among others he became enamoured with this expression:

> *Omnia si perdas, famam servare memento.*
>
> Strive to deserve a good and glorious name;
> Though all be lost, preserve an honest fame.

Nor did he only acquire a knowledge in the Latin language beyond what princes generally do, he was committed to the care of Mr. Palairet, for learning the French language, and to write. Under him he soon became acquainted with that tongue, so as to speak it fluently at the age of twelve years, as he did both the German and the Italian. He greatly delighted in the company of the illustrious Sir Isaac Newton; a man whom the Princess honoured much with her conversation, and on whom she bestowed the elogium uttered by the queen of Sheba with regard to Solomon; *I have* (said she) *at last found a man capable of resolving all my hard questions*. His Highness read Justin and Quintus Curtius with great assiduity, and was so taken with Ovid's Metamorphoses, that he could repeat the two incomparable orations of Ajax and Ulysses before the chieftains of Greece for the arms of Achilles; / a production which Cicero declares to be, in his opinion, infinitely preferable to any thing that ever came from the pen of a Grecian orator, Demosthenes himself not excepted. But this application to the languages did not hinder his pursuing such exercises as nature seemed principally to have designed him for. When but five years old he raised a company of young boys, much about his own age, whom he marshalled and trained up according to the method which at that time appeared to him most convenient and satisfactory; and being a daily spectator of the maneouvres and evolutions of the different corps in the regiments of guards, he, to the astonishment of all who saw him, drew up his little battalion in so regular and orderly a manner, that the King his grandfather was delighted therewith, and even discovered an unusual complacency before the foreign ambassadors when he saw his grandson appear at the head of his corps within the area of the court at St. James's. His authority among them was every way full and directory: their private quarrels were decided with moderation and temper; virtues intirely significant of true magnanimity. There was no repining at his decisions; plaintiff and defendant were equally pleased. Before he was full eight years old he could manage a horse; which, with other violent exercises that seemed to engross the most of his attention and discovered his inclination to war, laid the early foundation of a sound and vigorous constitution, which enabled him to support fatigue to the admiration of thousands, and which none but himself was thought capable to undergo.

Hitherto every thing tended to encourage him, nor was there any interruption to that serene tranquillity which had attended him since the first moment of his coming into the world, till the 20th / of March 1727, when the great Sir Isaac Newton died, to the universal regret of those who admired him, loved him, and lost him. His Highness appeared troubled, and honoured the funeral of that great man with his presence.

The loss of his Grandfather soon followed: for his Majesty had, on the 26th of May 1727, put an end to the session of parliament by a most gracious speech from the throne; in which, after thanking them for their zeal and readiness in expediting the public business, he informed them of the siege of Gibraltar by the Spaniards; that the Crown of Sweden had acceded to the treaty of Hanover, notwithstanding the opposition of the Court of Vienna, and that an actual convention had been signed between Great Britain, France, and Denmark: and in a particular and lively manner represented the absolute necessity of augmenting our marine, and of equipping several fleets for immediate service. This being over, he, on the 3d of June, after naming the Regency in his absence, embarked on board the Caroline yacht at Greenwich; and in two days landed at Gravendael, in the province of Holland. Going on board a yacht belonging to the States General, he arrived at Vaert on the 7th, where he rested that night, and next morning set out for Hanover, escorted by a party of the Dutch guards, that were ordered to wait upon him during his stay in their territory. About eleven o'clock at night of the 9th he came to Delde, and eat pretty heartily at supper; but particularly of a melon, which seemed not to have been properly prepared. Setting off by three next morning, for Linden, he was attacked by a fit of the cholic soon after; but here finding his appetite had failed him, he was blooded: for his great desire was to arrive in his own dominions; and so, contrary to / the remonstrance of his friends, he again went into his coach; but, being seized with a lethargic disorder, he dropped his head on the gentleman's breast that sat near him, and said, *It is all over with me*. However the coach proceeded, and he arrived that night at the palace of his brother the Duke of York in

Osnaburgh; where, being again blooded, he was put to bed, and, about one o'clock in the morning of the 11th expired, with little or no struggle, in the sixty-ninth year of his age, and in the fourteenth of his reign; and was succeeded by his only son George the IId; who, with his spouse Queen Caroline, was crowned in Westminster Abbey on the 11th of October thereafter.

When the news of the King's death first reached Leicester-house, there was more than an ordinary consternation, and none appeared more affected than the Duke of Cumberland: the consideration that this chasm in the Royal Family paved a way to his own greater dignity, could not make the least impression upon him, or diminish that grief which naturally rose for the unexpected death of the King. He was sent out of town for some time, in order to divert his concern, and did not return till about a week before the coronation of his Royal Parents; when, according to the custom of other Kings, they dined in Westminster-hall, and on the subsequent lord mayor's day honoured the city banquet with their presence.

From this time he became more and more beloved, not only by the King and Queen, but by all the Royal Family, admired by the foreign ambassadors, and the delight of the people of Great Britain, whose satisfaction was enhanced by his being born among them. In short, he increased in stature and wisdom, his character daily shone with the brighter lustre, he grew in the esteem of his parents, / and in favour with the public. On the 18th of May 1730, he was elected a knight companion of the most noble order of the garter, and was installed at Windsor on the 13th of June 1731.

His Highness, by being a companion of these orders, had an opportunity of being better acquainted with those of the several dignities; and as many of these threw up their places in the year 1733, in consequence of their disagreement with Sir Robert Walpole about the excise scheme, so he discovered a visible concern at losing the company of some great and illustrious personages, such as the Earl of Chesterfield, the Earl of Stair, and some others, for whom he had always entertained the highest personal honour and regard. However, the uneasiness arising from these sudden changes, which generally prevail at courts, and take their rise sometimes from the most trivial causes, did not hinder his application to the sciences, and in a particular manner to the study of geometry; for which science he had discovered an uncommon inclination, having heard the Queen converse with the immortal Sir Isaac Newton upon the theory of the tides, the nature and cause of the winds, monsoons, the path of comets, the nature of light, and the power of refracting telescopes, the eclipses of the sun and moon, the occultation of the stars, the laws and theory of motion and gravity, the figure of the earth, the laws by which the planets were retained and guided in their orbits, the intrinsic value of money: in a word, what nature had before denied to human eyes was discovered by the eyes of this great man's understanding.

> *Nature and nature's laws were hid in night.*
> *God said, Let* Newton *be, and there was light.* /

His modesty and goodness of heart added lustre to that treasure of divine knowledge which he had acquired by the strength of his genius and the diligence of his application. He established the truth of revealed religion upon evidence that was irresistible: he formed to the belief of it by conversation and argument, and excited to the practice of its different rules by a shining and amiable example. The several branches of human knowledge were equally familiar to him; and if at any time a gentleman communicated to him a treatise upon some particular part, to which he had devoted his attention, Sir Isaac would, upon the perusal of it, discover things that had escaped the author, or give hints to a further improvement: this Mr. Mills, the author of the Conic Sections, which goes by his name, experienced, to his great satisfaction. Mr. Gregory and Dr. Keil happily experienced the same thing.

Fortunate in the company of so great a man, his Highness applied to the study of Euclid's Elements, that basis and foundation of all mathematical learning; and having digested the doctrine of plain and spherical trigonometry, both of which he understood extremely well, he gave his attention to the theory of navigation, and taking the plans of towns; and, having studied the conic sections, he proceeded to learn fortification and gunnery, all which he understood at the age of fifteen years; at which time the present Princess Dowager of Wales arrived in England, when Prince William, being looked upon as the most accomplished young gentleman of his age, the admiration of the Royal Family, the ornament of the Court, and to be possessed of so transcendent and princely an address, that at the marriage of the Prince of Wales, he / gave the hand of the bride into that of her future consort.

About this time the Royal Family seemed to be divided in their opinion about the bent of the Duke's genius, whether he would be fitter for the sea or land service. The King intended him for the former, since in time he might arrive at the station of lord high admiral of England, as Prince George of Denmark was before. For this purpose he visited Portsmouth and Spithead, went on board the ships in the harbour in all the habit of a sailor, never appearing as one of the Royal Family, in the insolence of power, but in the mildness and moderation of a generous and condescending temper: but then he was prevented from following this business by the death of the Queen, on the 20th of November 1737. Every one was affected with the loss; the court, the city, the army, the counties and people equally felt it, and equally lamented her death, she being a pattern of virtue both in domestic and public life, a mother of her people, brilliant in her character, and glorious in the goodness of her heart. She was four times guardian of the realm in the absence of her Royal Husband.

The death of the Queen and the peaceable tranquillity of the nation hindered his acting upon the watry element: however, there soon happened an occasion in which he was to display those talents which hitherto were but guessed at, and now appeared in all their lustre and brightness. And here it will not be improper to give an account of the rise of the war 1739: a war which was no less serious and terrible than the most sanguine that had happened in Europe for many years. /

The Court of London had by the peace of Utrecht* obtained liberty to send an Assiento ship annually to the West Indies, and the private men on board often carried over such goods as were contraband; complaints were frequently made upon the subject; but the enemies of Great Britain, no less envious of her welfare than of the tranquillity of Spain, did by every art possible blow up the coal of dissension, which at length kindled into an open war between the two powers: it began in America, and soon reached to Europe; while peace and tranquillity reigned in the latter, the guarda costas in the islands of Cuba, Hispaniola, and other places of the West Indies, committed depredations of the worst kind upon the vessels trading to the British settlements. The first ship was the Pearl of Kingston, taken off the Havannah in the month of May 1739; three guarda costas attacked her at once, twice boarded her, and were twice repulsed with loss, and with bloodshed. A net was spread upon the main deck of the Pearl, which twice

* 1713.

threw the assailants into the sea; some were drowned, and others being taken up, discovered the cause of their disaster. To make sure of the Pearl they contrived a method of cutting the net, at the very time when they were boarding the vessel. The crew of the Pearl endeavoured again to throw the assailants overboard; but the netting being broken, they were seized all at once, as they were bowing down to take hold of the ends thereof. Being overpowered and taken prisoners, they were not treated as by a generous enemy; for after detaining them eight days at sea, they carried them into the Havannah, which they entered naked as they were born, and there / continued upon a short allowance for seven months, when a cartel ship arrived, and gave an account of the actual declaration of war.

In every commercial state some people deal in illicit goods to the prejudice of the fair trader. The kingdoms of Great Britain and Spain, with their respective settlements, have ever been overrun with that false set of men; for they are to be found not only in Europe, but through the whole extent of the West Indies and the Leeward Islands, particularly in those of Cuba and Hispaniola.

The English merchants had liberty from the Court of Madrid to supply the Spanish colonies with negroes purchased in Guinea, and other parts of Africa. This negro traffic, which forces the husband from the arms of his wife, the wife from the embraces of her husband, and both from their parents and friends, cannot be expected to proceed with a proper regard to justice and humanity. Under different pretexts this branch of trade was miserably perverted and abused; by agreement thirty-three piasters were to be paid to the Spanish governor of every place where the slaves were sold, for every one of those that were disposed of. This trade was of singular advantage to the South Sea Company, who by the treaty were to furnish the colonies with four thousand eight hundred negroes, for whom they pay the thirty-three piasters *per* head, and for their farther encouragement they obtained a privilege of selling eight hundred without any duty; but the greatest advantage reaped by England above other nations, was the permission granted in the year 1716 of sending a ship annually to Porto Bello on the isthmus of Panama.

This vessel, which was to be of no more than five hundred tons, was in 1717, by agreement, raised to eight hundred and fifty, though in reality / and by abuse to a thousand, which could carry two million weight of goods; and these were but the least part of that commerce. A pinnace attended the vessel to carry provisions to it; and according to some was continually going backward and forward, took in loads of goods in the British colonies, conveyed them to the vessel, which by this constant supply answered the end of a whole fleet; besides other vessels frequently carried goods to the company's ship, from whence they returned to the several settlements in America with such commodities as the inhabitants wanted.

The Spanish governors, like those of other nations, not always actuated by principles of moderation and lenity, treated the British traders with rigour and severity, not duly considering that there were smugglers among themselves, and that a connivance with these was the occasion of what was complained of. The smugglers were so faithful to each other, as to agree upon signals, which they perfectly well knew; sometimes the innocent were confounded with the guilty; sums lawfully due to the former were detained on account of illicit gain made by the latter: and thus the Spanish colonies were abused by the English traders, ruined by their own smugglers, and cheated out of their substance by the governors among themselves.

M. de Voltaire, treating of this subject, seems to deviate from his usual politeness; a great many English, says he, became pirates with impunity. On the coast of Florida they met with some Spaniards that were sounding for some galleons that had been shipwrecked, and out of whom they had recovered to the amount of 400,000 piasters; part of the crew were murdered, and the money was seized. The Spaniards demanded satisfaction for / these outrages from the English governors in those quarters; but the English freebooters, when they took a Spanish vessel, used to sink it, with all the crew, after they had gutted it, that there might remain no proof of their villainy: at other times they sold those Spaniards in their own colonies; and when these wretches demanded justice of the English governors, those who had sold them got off, by pretending that from their swarthy complexion they had taken them for negroes. The pirates understood each other, and divided the spoils with the judges, and then gave out that they had been tried by their peers.

The Spanish guarda costas frequently revenged themselves of these cruel hostilities; for taking a great many vessels they used the crews extremely ill: they were put under the hatches, and laid in irons; carried into the Havannah and other parts naked as they were born, and there confined to a dungeon; out of which hardships they were, by the humanity of the natives, partly relieved.

In the mean time negotiations were set on foot, both at London and Madrid, for terminating the differences in America. By the convention of Pardo, of the 14th of January 1739, the Court of Spain, upon ballancing accounts with the South Sea Company, engaged to pay them ninety thousand pounds in four months, reserving to herself a power of making a deduction of what the Company might be indebted to the Spaniards. This became the subject of a fresh quarrel, which, with the accounts of private merchants, produced a war, wherein each nation expended a thousand times more than the demand of either.

During these transactions one Jenkins, the captain of a vessel that had been taken, presented himself before the House of Commons in the beginning / of April 1739, with his nose slit, and wanting his ears, that had been cut off. He appeared to be a plain open man, and his condition gaining credit to his words, he asserted, that he had carried on no contraband trade, but was taken on the American coast by a Spanish guarda costa, whose commander seized his ship, laid the crew in irons, and had left him these infamous tokens; 'Gentlemen,' said he, 'after mangling me in this manner, they threatened to put me to death: I expected it, and recommended my soul to God, but the revenge of my cause to my country.' These words, uttered with an emphasis significant of the man's situation and hardships, raised pity in the whole assembly; the citizens of London crowded to see Jenkins, and loudly demanded a war.

The House of Commons was greatly divided in their opinions; Sir Robert Walpole and his party were desirous to reconcile matters; while the opposite party, by their harangues, inflamed the minds of the people to such a degree, that a war with Spain was openly and loudly called for, as the most advantageous step that could possibly then be taken: every wise remonstrance against involving two mother countries for the iniquitous practice of some smugglers at a distance, was laughed at and ridiculed. In a word, it was the general opinion that a war with Spain would be advantageous to Great Britain, though now it is found that any rupture between the two crowns is hurtful to the trade and commerce of both in general, and to many rich and opulent cities in particular; for the merchants of both monarchies keep up so close a correspondence even in the time of war, that the British traders have constantly been interested in the Spanish commerce, while / they were arming for the destruction of that monarchy; so that when a British privateer took a prize, they really plundered their own countrymen.

Never was more eloquence displayed than in the speeches made at that time in both Houses of Parliament, nay, I question if the studied harangues pronounced at Athens and at Rome, upon almost similar occasions, are superior to the extemporaneous discourses of Sir William Wyndham, Lord Carteret, Sir Robert Walpole, the Earl of Chesterfield, the Duke of Argyle, Mr. Pitt, Mr. Pultney, and Sir William Yonge. These discourses were but the natural effect of that liberty, which the British nation has been hitherto careful to maintain. It is true, the spirit of party runs through them all, and the real state of affairs is generally disguised under the shades of eloquence and rhetoric, or by the subtlety of argument; for while the ministerial party represented the government in a flourishing condition, the patriots affirmed, that the nation was ruined and undone. 'Where are those days,' cried a member in the House, 'when a minister declared, that no power in Europe should fire a single cannon, without leave first obtained from England.' At last the voice of the nation stifled the arguments of the ministers of state, and a run of addresses from every quarter determined the King; letters of reprisal were delivered out to merchants and privateers, and war was was declared against Spain Oct. 23, 1739.

At first the sea was the theatre of action, in which the privateers of each nation began to seize the merchant ships both in Europe and in America, as it were jointly destroying that very commerce for which they were fighting; and in a short time proceeded to greater hostilities, both sides being / intent to wreck upon the fair trader the vengeance that was due only to a nest of smugglers. Admiral Vernon was sent to the West Indies with a formidable squadron of nine ships of the line. He set sail with these on the 3d of August, and by the way of Cape Ortugal, E. of the Groyne, of Madeira and Antigua, he arrived on the 12th of October at Port Royal in Jamaica without any advantage, on account of the position of the enemy, whom at that time he could not annoy; however, to keep up the spirits of his countrymen, he attempted the conquest of Porto Bello, which on the 21st of November he effected; but being unable to leave a garrison in it, he was obliged to return to Jamaica, both to curb the insolence of the privateers, and for preserving the health of the land forces, who were daily mouldering away by sickness and fatigue, owing to the change of air, and their own want of experience.

The account of Vernon's success at Porto Bello arriving in England created a general joy, as if the harbour there had been the only place of refuge for the Spanish privateers, which swarmed in those seas. The Duke of Cumberland, then in the 18th year of his age, discovered an unusual satisfaction, and did not fail, on every occasion, to express the deep sense he had both of the personal valour of Admiral Vernon, and of the mighty action which he atchieved. Indeed men of more experience than his Highness were imposed upon by that paltry conquest. The Two Houses of Parliament congratulated the King upon the success, and wrote a letter of thanks to the Admiral; the towns, the cities, the army and the navy, ecchoed his encomium, and the clergy themselves from their pulpits sounded the Admiral's applause; nay, to such a degree did his fame grow, that they / judged him capable of the greatest atchievements, nay, of working impossibilities!

No sooner came the news of Vernon's having sailed to lay siege to Carthagena in the gulph of Mexico, than perceptions were made to celebrate the taking of it; and at the very time when he was raising the siege, viz. April 1741, after a fruitless and ill-conducted attack upon Fort Lazae, entirely owning to a difference subsisting between the Admiral and General Wentworth, a medal was struck in honour of the conquest; on one side of this imaginary medal were to be seen the haven and outworks of the place, with this motto: *He has taken Carthagena.* And on the reverse was Admiral Vernon, with these words: *To the avenger of his country.*

Such imaginary trophies did not fail to excite the disgust and obstinacy of the enemy. Admiral Vernon had in fact done little or nothing, the conquest of Porto Bello with six ships only! might have been effected with the sixth part of the force, the Spanish guarda costas multiplied in the West Indies, the Court of Madrid kept rejoicings for no less than three successive days for the repulse at Carthagena; their privateers now more than ever infested the ports of the Mediterranean and the ocean; and daily captures were carried into Ferrol and St. Sebastians. The expedition under Vernon was of infinite loss to the nation, and our disaster before Carthagena, in which 700 men fell unrevenged, not only eclipsed our glory among foreigners, but raised the demand of our enemies, and influenced France to join more openly against us; for she sent a strong squadron under the command of the Marquis d'Antin to Martinico, with secret orders not only to act in an hostile manner / against the subjects of Great Britain, either jointly with the Spaniards, or separately by themselves, but even to concert measures with them for attacking Jamaica; and at the same time declared, that she could not longer remain an idle spectator of the losses which Spain sustained in America, where indeed her ruin had been inevitable, provided a good understanding had subsisted between the commanders of the different appointments.

The King of Great Britain remonstrated against this armament by his ambassador at the Court of Versailles, to whom Cardinal Fleury used this expression: 'My Lord, there is a difference between arming and declaring war; it is true, the King, my master, has promised a neutrality; but as unforeseen accidents may happen, it is prudent to be prepared against all events.'

The nation, under these circumstances, was now apprehensive of a war with France, and began to utter great discontent, throwing the blame on the ministry for not having more effectually reinforced Vernon, to whom they imputed nothing of the fatal disaster, though indeed from his obstinacy he was the origin and spring of *all*, he being a man of weak understanding, strong prejudices, boundless arrogance, a stern look and overbearing passions.' A powerful fleet of twenty-one sail of the line and three fireships were ordered on a secret expedition; from whence great things were expected: Sir John Norris, Admiral of the Red, hoisted his flag on board the unfortunate Victory of 110 guns*. Many of the first quality went on board her, and the Duke of Cumberland embarked as a volunteer; and here he continued from the 1st of July till 18th of / September, when he disembarked at Spithead, but little pleased with the paradings of a fleet fitted out at a vast expense, and which engrossed the attention almost of all Europe. His Highness from this time judged that the sea would not furnish such scenes of action as the land; and therefore preferring the latter, he followed a military life ever after. Indeed there soon opened a scene both by land and by water; the armies of France were traversing from one end of Germany to the other; they had already fixed the Imperial diadem upon the head of the Elector of Bavaria, to the exclusion of the present Empress Dowager, and in contempt of the Pragmatic Sanction, which confined it to the heirs whatsoever of the House of Austria. Several battles had been fought in Bohemia between the Austrians and Prussians with various success, which only tended to bring on further

* This ship was lost soon after.

rapine and cruelty. As the sea-engagement off Toulon was but a sequel of what happened at Dettingen, it will not be improper to take a view of that war, in which his Highness had so great and so considerable a share.

The scheme of France was to overturn the House of Austria, and to make a partition of her dominions; and the interest of Great Britain was to save her, and keep them entire. To support the Pragmatic Sanction, the British and Hanoverian troops were put in motion, the command of which last was committed to the Earl of Stair, a nobleman of the greatest abilities, being no less remarkable as a soldier than a statesman, and skilled in all the arts of command. He had been a Lieutenant General under the Duke of Marlborough, who was his patron and friend; for at the time of the union of the crowns of England and Scotland, the temporal interest of North Britain was in the / family of Stair. His Lordship's uncle was president of the Court of Session, the chief places in the Exchequer and Customs were vested in the branches of the Dalrymple family, and one of these held the office of Lord Advocate, an office of the same kind with that of Attorney General.

Under the patronage of Marlborough he was sent ambassador to King Augustus on his reascending the throne of Poland; he was afterwards dispatched as ambassador extraordinary and plenipotentiary to the Court of France upon the peace of Utrecht; by his care, vigilance, and activity, he traversed all the projects in favour of the Chevalier de St. George; the fame of his negotiations sounded through Europe, and the magnificent entry which he made into Paris on the accession of the present French Monarch to the crown, filled every mouth with admiration and astonishment; his disgrace since the year 1733, when he resigned all his places, now tended to make him more conspicuous; his very actions in private life were like so many gems to set off the brilliancy of his character; he had improved his estate in a very singular manner, and had laid out his gardens at Castle Kennedy with such elegance and taste, that they might be said to vye with those of Marli and Versailles. On his return to court after an absence of nine years, he became the favourite and admiration of all; the Duke of Cumberland was constantly with him, and brought several of the nobility of the same age with himself to his Lordship's levees.

As this nobleman was a consummate statesman, an excellent commander, and knew the temper and genius of the principal officers both civil and military in France, so he was judged to be the fittest person not only to persuade the States General to take part in the war, which seemed to be inevitable, / but to command the British troops, in case things should come to an extremity. Accordingly he was sent over to the Hague, in order to traverse the negotiations of the Marquis de Fenelon, who was endeavouring to persuade the States into a neutrality: however, both the French and British ambassadors were unsuccessful; for the States General would neither openly declare against France, nor yet would they embrace a neutrality, though often solicited thereto by Mynheer Van Hoey, their ambassador at Paris.

During the summer of the year 1742, he continued with the troops upon the frontiers of Brabant, and in that time gained so much upon the affections of the soldiers, that they were ready to march wherever he should be pleased to direct them. It was this nobleman's talent to shine among the great, but to familiarize himself with those of an inferior station; an enemy to whatever was ungenerous and oppressive, he rectified an abuse which procured him universal respect and satisfaction: the horses dung, which before him had been the perquisite of the commanding officers, was now appropriated for the use of the private men; and though he had an offer of any regiment, yet he preferred the Iniskilling dragoons as a corps of worth and high reputation, and who had stood by him both at the battles of Ramillies and Malplaquet. Indeed his Lordship's choice was commendable, as by it he shewed steadiness of temper, and a disposition not subject to change; he had built barracks for them near his residence in the shire of Galloway; he furnished the horses of the private men with hay and stabling at the moderate rate of two shillings *per* week through the year; the officers dined daily with him, a dozen at a time by rotation; and no drago nor private / man ever came to his house without being hospitably and chearfully entertained; and what was still more encouraging, he gave eight pence *per diem* to above 300 of the private men, whom he employed in fencing his parks, cutting ditches, and laying out his inclosures. Happy for the Duke of Cumberland to learn the first rudiments of the art of war under the eye of so distinguished and so great a commander, who soon had an opportunity given him of shewing these great abilities with which the world had hitherto confessed him to be endowed.

The Marshal Duke de Noailles, a nobleman of the first rank in France, and one of her most experienced commanders, was in the neighbourhood of Aschaffenberg, upon the Maine, with an army of 80,000 men, the flower of three armies*, already destroyed by the sword, by famine, and fatigue. The march of the troops was a point of delicacy: Marshal Noailles wanted to hinder the junction of the Hessians with the English, and Lord Stair was desirous to effect it. For doing this he caused them to march in the night-time; to set out about the dusk of the evening, and not to halt till next morning about sun-rise. The generals and private men were equally anxious to know the place where they were to halt, and where they were intended; and yet such was their confidence in the superior understanding of their leader, that none of them ever complained. However at last Sir Philip Honeywood, general of foot, ventured to ask the Earl, where was the intended place of halting? 'Can you,' said his Lordship, / 'keep a secret, Sir Philip?' 'As well,' replied Sir Philip, 'as any man living.' Upon my word,' said his Lordship, 'and so can I.' And thus Sir Philip retired, without any other satisfaction but that of mutual compliments.

By this march, which marked a superiority of skill and genius, he reached Aschasenberg time enough to join the King, who was just come from Hanover, attended by several general officers, among whom was the Duke of Cumberland, who then ranked as a major general. The Duke of Noailles was willing to prevent their junction with the Hessians, and to cut off their provisions; which last was effected: for he drew so near the town, that nothing could go out or into it, on account of his patroling parties, and to cross over the stone bridge at Aschaffenburgh was preposterous, and giving the enemy a visible advantage. Indeed the concern for the troops prompted Lord Stair to cross the river with a party, in order to view the position of the enemy: however, he had almost fallen into their hands: for a party of men came out of an avenue, where they were lying in ambush, and fired upon the party attending his lordship, whose hat was shot through, and fell from him: his party retired, and the enemy did not think fit to pursue.

During the stay of the troops here, an exact discipline was observed among them, and the troops both of Great Britain and Hanover were brought, from the example of their officers, to treat each other with con-

* One commanded by M. Maillebois, which marched into Hanover; one by M. Broglio, which took the rout of Hesse; and the third by the Duke de Belleisle, which had desolated Bohemia, and almost laid waste the city of Prague.

fidence and humanity. The intention of the French general was to cut off the provisions of the allies, and to waste and consume them in a country where they could not get supplies. The Earl of Stair saw into the extent of his views, and took his measures accordingly: and / indeed the more circumspection was necessary on his part, as the British army was in general composed of men, the fortieth part of whom had never seen an engagement; nor indeed was he much better off with respect to his generals, many of whom had rather rose by a parliamentary interest, than by merit, and on account of their experience: however he had some very able and distinguished commanders. Such as the generals Clayton and Campbell, Sir Philip Honeywood and the Earl of Crawford. The Hanoverians were not more experienced: the only corps of veterans consisted of 300 Austrians, lately arrived.

But it was not so with the troops of the enemy; for during the years 1741 and 1743 many of them had served in Italy and upon the Rhine, many of them had served in the Ottoman army against the Germans and Russians, and lately carried arms among the troops of Prussia: some had fought at the battle of Czaslow, when the Prussian monarch defeated the Austrians under Prince Charles of Lorrain, after an obstinate resistance: many of the regiments of the Duke de Noailles' army had served at the battle of Frauenberg, between Prince Lobkowitz and the Marshals Belleisle and Broglio, in which battle the Austrians indeed quitted the field, but left the enemy no great room for triumph. Their chief engineers, and many belonging to the train of artillery, had been active in the remarkable siege and blockade of Prague; others were present at the siege of Egra, and in many skirmishes that had happened in Bavaria and the Upper Palatinate: the taking and re-taking of towns on the Inn, the Iser, and the Danube had likewise furnished them with opportunities of learning the arts and stratagems of war. In a word, the whole French army consisted of veterans, who knew the / whole art of their calling, and glowed with a general's love of conquest; and in point of experience were greatly superior to the confederates: who yet dreaded nothing while under the direction of Lord Stair, and were soon to fight under the eye of the British monarch. However, the two armies did not come to an engagement till the 27th of June, when the great abilities of each commander shone with a particular lustre, the soldiers exerting all their courage, the officers all their skill, and the whole their zeal and affection to those by whom they were employed.

On the morning of that day did the allied army march from Aschaffenberg, without beat of drum, sound of trumpet, or any other ceremony that could give intelligence of their decampment; nor did the bulk of the general officers know where they were to halt: that was a secret entirely confined to the breast of the King, the Earl of Stair, the Duke d'Aremberg*, and Count Nieperg: every thing was done with secrecy and address. The Duke d'Ayen, son to the Marshal de Noailles, was the first to advertise his father of the rout of the enemy; and he, immediately getting up, drew up the disposition of his troops, and appointed the place both of their crossing the Mayne and of the place where they were to draw up in order to wait for the confederates; and this they could easily do without being observed.

It was an astonishment to the army of the allies when first they saw the enemy, or rather when they heard the first report of the great guns from the opposite shore of the Mayne, which was lined with batteries, in order to fire upon them during their / march. The disposition made by Marshal Noailles is cried up as one of the finest ever plan'd by a general: the flower of the troops were posted on the bank of an hollow way, over which the allies must necessarily pass; and these were supported with batteries of cannon of the largest bore, loaded with grape shot. The Duke de Pesguier, who carried the art of an engineer to its utmost perfection, ordered a battery of twelve guns to be planted at the head of the hollow way, in order to enfilade the troops at the time they were engaged with the forces placed in the front: wherever there was the least interruption of the bank in the hollow way, the opening was joined by a redan, and fortified with artillery. By seven in the morning every thing was ready, and the whole snares were prepared. The Duke de Grammont, nephew to the Marshal de Noailles, and who lately espoused his daughter, was placed at the head of this formidable body, with express orders not to stir from his station; and in the mean time the Marshal retired to the other side of the river, in order to draw another party of his troops toward Aschaffenberg, and which might march after the confederates, who in that event would be between two fires, and whose ruin seemed to be inevitable. Experience, numbers, and the use of arms were on the side of the French, nor were they inferior in point of courage and intrepidity.

Never was an army in a more critical situation than was that of the confederates; they wanted provision: the flower of the French, supported

* He had an army of 3000 men belonging to the Queen of Hungary.

by a numerous artillery in their front, an hollow way to pass, at the head of which was a large battery, lay before them; the Mayne was on their left, whose opposite banks were lined with artillery; on their rear stood Aschaffenberg, now in possession / of the enemy, who were marching after them; and on their right lay vast and extended woods, where no provision could be got either for men or for horse: every thing wore a gloomy aspect, and the French generals reckoned the ruin of the confederates to be inevitable: so that their deliverance from so impending a danger, which no less than threatened the personal liberty of a King of Great Britain and his Son, with the intire ruin and destruction of a whole army, may be reckoned one of the most surprising events to be found upon record, either in the annals of this or of any other country.

No sooner had the King and Earl of Stair a view of the position of the enemy, than they rightly judged their plan of operation: to defeat which was a point of delicacy, and required all the art that could be thought of either by prudence or circumspection. The Duke d'Aremberg, at the head of the Hungarians, with Marshal Nieperg, formed one line, with the British infantry, who were placed on the left of the river, where the greatest danger was apprehended, and almost opposite to the gens d'armes and the black musquetaires of France; and to animate the whole, the King rode along the lines, with his wonted sedateness. At the head of the British troops in the lines, was placed old general Clayton, an officer of long experience, having served at the battle of Almanza in the year 1707; the Duke of Cumberland, as major-general, served under him: the generals Honeywood and Campbell were at the head of the second line; and the cavalry brought up the rear. The Earl of Stair, who knew the temper and genius of the French nation, guessed rightly at the enemy's design, and therefore ordered the British troops to advance, with a battery of cannon in / their front, in order to silence those of the French, which were now beginning to play. Fortunately for him Clayton was an officer of experience, and literally obeyed his orders. The cannonading began with fury, and rather increased than diminished: Grammont every moment expected the confederates to pass the hollow way, when he was just ready to begin the carnage; and the Earl of Stair was determined rather to try a passage through a part of the woods in the night-time than to cross the hollow way, in the face of a numerous artillery: or rather he rightly conjectured, that the impatience of the French generals would bring them over to him.

His Lordship's sentiments were just. The Duke de Grammont advanced at the head of the gens d'armes and the black musquetaires, in a menacing posture, with their swords in their hands. The Earl of Stair gave orders not to fire till the colour of the eyes of the enemy could be distinguished: and in this he was partly obeyed; though indeed some regiments fired too soon, and at too great a distance: an inconvenience productive of mischief to those who had committed the rashness; for the enemy marched up with great impetuosity, and almost fired full into the faces of those who were opposite to them: and thus the firing of the small arms begun upon the right, but had not as yet extended along the line, nor yet had become general. By this time the gens d'armes and the black musquetaires were just come up to General Clayton's division, where they halted a little, and each seemed to pause on seeing the order and regularity of the corps whom they were to attack. All at once the Duke de Grammont cracked his whip, which was the signal agreed on, and the cavalry broke in as to a fold with great impetuosity, and with uncommon courage and resolution / rode through the ranks; who, according to orders, had opened from right to left, the better to annoy them. This sudden shock proved fatal to the wing that broke in; the allied troops faced about from every quarter, and poured in their shot upon the enemy; and such as were nearest the horses pierced their sides with their bayonets, and brought them to the ground, which was soon covered with a promiscuous carnage. The black musquetaires of France detached themselves from those with whom they were united, and galloped full along the lines of the confederates, perhaps with a view to divert their attention from annoying the Gens d'Armes, whose ruin and destruction now appeared visible; for almost the whole were either killed or taken prisoners: among which last was a son of the Marquis de Fenelon, who was seized in the last rank of the regiment of Greys. And now the action became general: the firing began from right to left through the whole line: the enemy's batteries were either silenced by a more numerous artillery, or ceased of themselves, for fear of hurting their own men. The Earl of Stair appeared in the thickest places of the firing: in the very heat of the engagement he came to the right, immediately behind the regiment of guards, and looked with as much composure as if he was hearing an account of some friend; he sat about two minutes upon horseback, and in a listening posture: all at once he disappeared with his aids de camp, and on a full stretch galloped toward the left, into the midst of the firing, which every moment increased. The French raised several huzzas, and were answered as they deserved, sometimes by one corps, sometimes by another. 'Come,' says his Lordship, with as much composure as if he had / been at an entertainment, 'drop your huzzas for a few moments; but when I give the signal let the huzza be general through the line, and my life for it the victory is ours.' The aid de camps immediately communicated the orders; and in about three minutes his Lordship took off his hat, waved it in the air, and so the huzza begun, and continued with great loudness. 'If,' said his Lordship, taking a hearty laugh, 'I cannot beat them by firing, I shall beat them by huzzaing.' A vigorous fire, well levelled and full, was poured in upon them: and his Majesty observing an eminence convenient for placing a battery of cannon, seven field pieces were planted upon it, which being discharged into the midst of the French ranks, at a time when they expected no such thing, they began to give ground, and retreat; some over the river, some cross the hollow way, where they were cut down with a terrible slaughter; and one of the bridges having broke down, the carnage was still the more considerable.

Such was the event of the battle of Dettingen, in which the French lost 7000 men, besides 2500 prisoners, with a great many wounded; among whom was the Duke d'Ayen, Marshal Noailles's own son; the Duke de Rochefoucault, and many other general officers. On the side of the allies were killed about 2500, among whom was the brave General Clayton, and many wounded. The Duke of Cumberland received a ball in the calf of his left leg, which when the surgeon began to dress, he said, 'Dress that man's wounds' (pointing to a French officer) 'for he needs more to be sympathized with than I do;' the Duke d'Aremberg was wounded in the breast, with several other officers. All being over, the King dined upon a / cold roasted shoulder of mutton* under a tree, while the Earl of Stair, judging no time to be lost, repaired to the place appointed; but before leaving the field, he wrote a letter to the Marshal Duke de Noailles, in which he informed him, that a number of prisoners having fallen into his hands, they should be taken singular care of, until exchanged or ransomed, and in the mean time recommended the wounded to his protection and generosity. The letter being sent off, the troops moved toward Hanau, the place of their first destination, and arrived about one next morning, greatly fatigued with the battle and the journey, and mightily

* Shoulder of mutton roasted was a favourite dish of King George II.

jaded with an heavy rain, which, from the time they quitted Dettingen, poured down incessantly upon them.

The field being clear, the French general ordered a party to pass over next day to take care of the wounded; those of the allies and their own soldiers were equally regarded. Marshal Noailles gave precise orders as to that particular, which when Lord Stair heard, he wrote him a letter of thanks, in which were these very words among other polite expressions: 'I return you my most sincere and hearty thanks for the care that has been taken of the wounded among the allies, and shall be sure to testify my regard on every occasion; but indeed so generous a conduct was only agreeable to the sentiments of honour, which I ever entertained of the politeness and humanity of the Duke de Noailles.' These two great commanders now endeavoured to outstrip each other in point of sympathy, no less than they had formerly in point of skill, assiduity, and conduct. Stair caused the prisoners to be properly / taken care of, and to be well used; he knew many of the officers and their relations while at Paris, and having given them instances both of his generosity and tenderness, he sent them back upon their parole; for as there was no actual declaration of war betwixt Great Britain and France, both the King and the British general thought it most advisable to send back a number of troops, who could only weaken them by eating up the provisions of the army, now increased by an addition of 12000 men.

But while the confederates were rejoicing for the signal deliverance they had met with, the troops of France were murmuring for their disappointment, in proportion to the sanguine hopes they had entertained. Every body charged the Duke de Grammont with disobeying orders, and imputed to him the loss of the battle; only the Duke de Noailles said nothing against him; and though robbed of the glory of as fine a disposition as ever was made by a General, and which at once might have put an end to the war, he accused nobody, he complained of nobody, but barely contented himself with writing a long and elegant letter to the French monarch, in which he insisted on the absolute necessity of keeping up a strict and regular discipline among the troops.

The End of the FIRST BOOK. /

THE LIFE OF WILLIAM DUKE OF CUMBERLAND.

BOOK II.

CONTENTS.

An Account of the Earl of Stair*'s leaving the Army, – the Intrigues of the Court of* France, *– the Arrival of the Chevalier at* Dunkirk, *– the Duke of* Cumberland*'s Advancement, and the Campaign in* 1744, *– Character of Count* Saxe *and Count* Lowendahl, *– the case of Marshal* de Belleisle, *and the melancholy Death of the Emperor* Charles VII.

THE confederates, by their victory at Dettingen, and junction with the Hessians, were now in a condition to assist their friends, and prescribe laws to their enemies: they had profited by the mistakes of the Duke de Grammont, and now had only to improve the victory in a manner suitable to the address and conduct with which they obtained it: however, from some disagreement / among the commanders, it was not improved properly. Instead of marching directly for Francfort, and seizing the Emperor, and the regalia of the empire, they continued hovering about Hanau in a state of inactivity; and even at this time the superiority of the Earl of Stair's conduct and sagacity appeared in its lustre; for profiting by the example of the armies of France, who mouldered away insensibly, in consequence of their being crammed together in small towns and villages, or the German stoves, he took care to have the troops cantoned in the adjacent country, where they might lie comfortably, suffer nothing from the foulness of the air, nor from the nauseous stench that might be occasioned from a multitude; or, in other words, care was taken to preserve them from distempers, occasioned by contagion and infection; and the serjeants had particular orders to examine narrowly into the state and condition of the soldiers under their immediate inspection, and to report the same to the General officers. The clean were separated from the unclean, and all were properly encamped. In the mean time the officers both of the Confederate and French armies had an opportunity of taking a party of pleasure into different places of the country, and many of them repaired to Francfort, a neutral city, where they had an opportunity of seeing the new Emperor, who had retired thither. Among these commanders were the Marshal de Noailles, and the Earl of Stair, who had occasion to see him, and to observe a distinguished patience under the most cruel mortifications; his hereditary dominions being laid waste by the Pandours, Sclavonians, and other Austrian irregulars; the armies of his allies being wasted and consumed by the patience, address, and courage of his enemies, he himself deserted / by Broglio's army, which defended his capital, and at last reduced to the miserable situation of having neither money nor credit to support a brilliancy of grandeur, which this gaudy pomp of his new titles would require.

Every thing looked dismal on his side; he was without money, without credit, and without friends; experience had shewn him that nothing was to be expected from any junction with the armies of France; Marshal Broglio and Count Seckendorff scarcely agreed in any one article or plan of operation, and the inferior officers, both French and Bavarians, were daily fighting duels, and engaging with each other in single combat. The French troops were so diminished by sickness and desertion, or so reduced by the sword and by famine, that instead of entertaining thoughts of carrying him in triumph to Vienna or Prague, they found themselves obliged to return, in order to defend the frontiers of France against two armies, one commanded by Prince Charles of Lorraine, and the other by the King of Great Britain, and both of them victorious. In three campaigns the French had sent above 120,000 men into Bavaria and Bohemia to the Emperor's assistance, and of these only one fourth part returned with M. de Broglio, who, on the repeated complaints of his Imperial Majesty, was sent into banishment. A poor satisfaction indeed to a man, whose country was, for want of good troops and strong towns, rendered desolate by a devouring and irregular enemy.

The Earl of Stair, who certainly had the glory of his country always in his eye, penetrated into the real state both of the Emperor and of France, and judged it expedient to avail himself thereof; for this purpose he proposed a plan of operation, which he laid before the King his Master, but / submitted it to the perusal of none other. The plan was for returning a second time upon Marshal Noailles' army before it was replaced with recruits, and after this, marching over the Rhine, and carrying the war into the enemy's dominions. In this he adopted the opinion of the Carthaginian general; and rightly judging that the power of France could never be totally abolished by victories and conquests over them in another country, he proposed to transfer the theater of action within her own dominions.

Whatever regard his Majesty King George had for the opinion and sentiments of the Earl of Stair, yet he thought the affair too serious to be entered upon without further deliberation, and consulting the other generals. Accordingly he called the Hanoverian and British generals together, to his own head-quarters, where the question was debated in his presence, and where the officers gave their opinions freely and without reserve. The most part of the British officers were of the Earl of Stair's opinion: they were for improving the victory, and for passing directly the frontiers of France. The Duke of Cumberland was no less desirous of this than Lord Stair himself; and, tho' naturally bashful in speaking, as the sons of Mars generally are, yet he spoke some minutes upon the subject with uncommon sagacity and judgment. However, the Austrian, the Hanoverian, and Hessian generals were of different sentiments, and their opinion prevailed: a circumstance extremely fortunate for France, as at that time she lay open almost on every side to the invasion of a victorious enemy.

These disputes, which in a manner saved France, soon occasioned a real concern in the whole confederate army, but particularly among the British troops on account of their loss of the Earl of Stair, / who, in August after the battle, quitted his command. So much was that nobleman respected and beloved, that a mutiny was apprehended; and the more so as the private men and inferior officers could but shrewdly guess at so sudden a resolution. His Lordship's talent was impenetrable secrecy. The wife of his bosom, tho' a lady of the greatest honour and true generosity of heart, knew no more of his Lordship's secrets than the child that was unborn; and he laid it down as a maxim never to consult a general, other than by a general conversation, except in the case of an extremity. He only told his secrets to a pug dog, which he named Walpole, and to him in a familiar way he said, as he was going up stairs to bed; 'Ah, Walpole,' snapping his fingers, 'you and I shall not be intimate for the future: you take too much the advice of the Hanoverian generals, and these are not masters of their business.' He went that night to bed, and the next morning (viz. August 16th) set off for Worms, leaving a line to his Majesty; in which, after wishing him all possible success in his undertakings, and a happy issue out of all his troubles, he informed him, that he intended to repair to his plough. His baggage was sold off, and he himself repaired to the Hague; where in a formal speech, at his audience of leave, he informed their High Mightinesses of the particular regard which he ever bore to their Republic in general, and to the several members in particular whereof it was composed. However, one significant expression dropt from him, which discovered the cause of his appearing there at that time: 'It is but natural that Sovereigns should employ such as are most agreeable to them.'

The removal of the Earl of Stair was not more melancholy to the confederates, than it was fortunate for the affairs of France; whose ministry now began to take fresh measures for embarrassing their enemies: a war with Great Britain was evidently foreseen; and the King of Sardinia was expected to join therein. In a word, France was soon to be attacked by the forces of Austria, of Great Britain, of Holland, and of Savoy. To oppose which confederacy Louis XV. ordered several men of war to be fitted out at Brest; and, having time to breathe, he increased his land forces, and sent about twelve thousand men to the assistance of Don Philip, third son to the King of Spain, and who then commanded an army for the defence of the Milanese and the Mantuan. To encourage his troops he prepared to head them in person; and, to hurt his enemies the more sensibly, he had recourse to the same expedient which his great grandfather had in the midst of his greatest extremity.

The Pretender to the Crown of England had ever since the decease of James II. at St. Germains, anno 1701, had his eye upon the British throne, and oftener than once had attempted the recovery of it. No less than three different trials were made in his favour: the first in the year 1707, when, by the vigilance of the British fleet, the whole squadron from Dunkirk was either dispersed or taken: the second was in the year 1715, when a very formidable army was mustered, consisting of the most valiant and brave among the Highlanders, who have always been looked upon as a martial people; and were at that time conducted by officers of reputation and address, many of them having served in the British, the Dutch, the French, the Swedish, and the Russian armies: a third was in the year 1719, when they were suppressed by General Wightman, at Glenshiel. 'Tis surprizing that the Duke of Berwick, a general of great reputation / in France, in Spain, and in Italy, should not have assisted him, or have appeared in his favour, if he really thought him to be the son of King James. The unhappy fugitive had watched every opportunity, but never appeared properly in the field. It was in consequence of his being acknowledged King of England by the Courts of Versailles and Madrid that he espoused Princess Clementina, grand daughter of John Sobieski, King of Poland, by whom he had two sons; whose courage and great accomplishments his friends did not fail to propagate through Britain and Ireland. The eldest, named Charles, and who was born the 20th of December 1720, was honoured as Prince of Wales by the Pope and the people of Rome from his infancy: the Court of France cast her eye upon him, as one fit for serving her purpose: some of the disaffected in Great Britain and Ireland soothed his hopes, and no less than seven persons* entered into an association for bringing him in, and had already applied to the Court of France for assistance. The Grand Monarch sent them word, that he had their King's interest as much at heart as they had: the Cardinal de Fleury applauded the scheme, but hesitated about the method of putting it in practice. For his Eminence easily foreseeing a war, only wanted to make use of the Chevaliers on a more proper and critical occasion: for this purpose he strove to gain time, and artfully insinuated, that a body of Swedes, as being Protestants, were more likely to win upon the people of Great Britain than any corps of Roman Catholics whatever. Indeed the scheme was laid with great secrecy and address: 1500 men were to land at Inverness, and / to be joined by the clan of the Frazers, and such others as Lord Lovat, by force, insinuation, and subtilty, could procure. The like number was to land in the West Highlands, near the Isle of Mull, and to be joined by the Camerons, the Macdonalds, and other poor ignorant people in those remote places. All of these were to join and march southward, while a body of 14 or 15,000 were to land upon the coast of Kent, and as near the city of London as possible. The conspirators were

* James Drummond, commonly called Duke of Perth, Simon Lord Lovat, Donald Cameron of Lochiel, William Drummond of Bochaldee, &c.

sanguine in the matter; and yet the backwardness of the Earl Marshal to enter into any scheme with Lord Lovat, together with a suggestion of the Cardinal only delayed the execution of it; and the Cardinal dying in the beginning of the year 1743, made it intirely drop, till a more convenient season. The battle of Dettingen was no very favourable incident, and yet it did not a little contribute to spur on the Court of France to supply the Adventurer; whom two things tended still to animate the more: the disgust taken by the Earl of Stair, at not being allowed an absolute discretionary power, and the death of John Duke of Argyle and Greenwich, were motives not to defer any longer: his imagination suggested no difficulty; though every day the government was more firmly established, and the Royal Family became daily more endearing than ever: Great Britain and Ireland resounded with the elogium of their Monarch, the Royal Family was yearly increasing, the then Prince of Wales behaved in such a manner as every day to procure the greater veneration and regard: the fame of the Duke of Cumberland reached to the East and West Indies; the enemies of his family could hot help admiring his courage and magnanimity: he was on the field of battle created one of the Knight Bannerets; and in the / December following was made colonel of the first regiment of guards. There was a perfect good understanding between the King and the Privy Council: the Parliament was hearty in granting such supplies as might protect the trade of the subject, and assert the dignity of the crown. There was indeed some jars among the ministry, as generally happen in all limited monarchies, each side desiring to be uppermost; but both were equally interested for their Sovereign's cause.

One would have thought that such unfavourable circumstances would have preponderated. John Murray of Broughton, who was afterward secretary to the young Chevaliers, remonstrated against his making any attempt, whether secret or open, until a more considerable number of friends could be brought over; but all to no purpose: he was determined to try the fortune of war. His Father had given him a charte blanche to act as he pleased, and he signed a commission of regency on the 23d of December that year.

Having obtained this appointment he set out from Rome on the 9th of January 1744, without communicating his intentions. On the 13th he arrived at Genoa, in the disguise of a Spanish courtier; and next day, being attended by a single domestic, he embarked for Antibes, and soon arrived at Paris.

The Court of France observed a profound silence in the whole affair, even in the midst of the greatest preparations to convey him to the English coast. No less than twenty-six men of war had been equipped at Rochfort and Brest, without a single officer belonging to their admiralty knowing or imagining their destination: and, to cover the real design the more, a report was spread, that the squadron was intended to force a passage through the straits / of Gibraltar, and to join the Spanish fleet at Toulon; where the English squadron, under Admiral Matthews, had blocked it up. In the mean time twenty ships of war, having on board four thousand land forces, with arms and ammunition, loosed from Brest, and soon arrived between the isles of Ushant and Sorlingues, where they were joined by five more from the port of Rochfort.

This formidable fleet entered the British channel, and divided into three squadrons; the strongest, which consisted of fourteen ships, sailed with a fair wind toward Sandwich on the coast of Kent; the second took its station between Calais and Boulogne; and the third proceeded toward Dunkirk. Count Saxe, a natural son of Augustus I. King of Poland, and who had learnt his first rudiments in the art of war at the battle of Gadebush, anno 1712, was the officer appointed to command that expedition. On the 1st of March he embarked at Dunkirk with nine battalions, and the next day M. de Chaila went on board with six more.

The adventurer was in the same ship with Count Saxe, when for the first time he beheld the coast of England, which the pilot reckoned to reach in about eight hours; but a sudden storm arising, and the wind chopping about, the transports ran foul of each other; they were thrown upon the French shore, where a great many soldiers were drowned in attempting to land from them. Such as survived were much disheartened with the disaster, and some even construed it as ominous of what afterward ensued; only the Chevalier himself was steady and undaunted: his ambition would not let him balance things in a proper manner; he frequently declared that he would try his fortune, though unattended and alone. In this flattering himself that the English would be captivated / with his person, which his friends gave out to be so noble and majestic, that he wanted nothing to be admired, but to be seen; nothing to be joined by numbers, but to set up his standard. Indeed, had the troops been landed while our forces were abroad, the country would have been put into very great confusion; the sea only hindered the execution of his hazardous project; and in the interim an account of the expedition had been received at London almost about the time when the troops were embarking at Dunkirk.

The King of Great Britain communicated his intelligence to both Houses of Parliament, where the same occasioned an uncommon astonishment and surprise, which they expressed in their loyal addresses, and a full promise of standing by him with their lives and fortunes; they even extended the act of the 2d of King William, and the 2d of George I. making it high treason to correspond with the Pretender, to have any connection or correspondence with the son, and passed an act, making it high treason for either to land in Britain, or any of the dominions thereunto belonging: every person began to arm, and to discover their loyalty; the throne was crowded with addresses from every quarter; the militia were armed; and every thing was put in the best posture of defence.

It was surprising that the authors of a conspiracy, to overturn so mild and easy a government, were not instantly detected; some indeed were taken up, but they knew nothing of the matter; and such of them as lived in the remote parts of the Highlands of Scotland were scarcely suspected. Lord Lovat, the spring and primum mobile of all, kept fair with the government, even / when spiriting up the Highlanders to rebel, and firing them into the exercise of arms.

The year 1744 was productive of as great events through Europe, as any of the preceding. The combined fleets of France and Spain were defeated off Toulon by the British fleet commanded by Admiral Matthews; an event which determined the French King, without any further ceremony, to declare war on the 15th of March, both against Great Britain and Hanover, and on the 26th of April against the Queen of Hungary herself. The arms of France forced a passage over the Alps into Italy under the Prince of Conti, to join the troops of Spain and Naples against those of the Queen of Hungary and the King of Sardinia, who now had joined openly with her. The marches and countermarches of the respective forces of these several powers only tended to shew the skill and address of the commanding officers, but not to put an end to the war, which they rather fomented by desolating the fine valleys of the country, and living upon the rich and opulent cities at free quarter. Great Britain and France, without hesitation or reserve, squandered their money in supporting the powers at war; the one by her fleets, the other by her fleets and armies together: nor did the mischief stop here; for the flames of war continued to rage in Germany with more fierceness and violence than ever.

The crown of Great Britain exerted herself with uncommon vigour; she augmented her subsidies, and raised no less than 12,498,055 l. for the service of that year: her fleet in the Mediterranean ruined the trade of Provence, and hindered the French troops from infesting the coast: the troops which fought at Dettingen were recalled back to Flanders, and these being joined to the Flemish and Dutch / regiments, formed at the opening of the campaign an army of about 60,000 men, commanded by Field Marshal Wade, an old officer, bred under the Duke of Marlborough, and well acquainted with every part of Flanders: he was a sanguine man, easily provoked, violent in his passions, and addicted to revenge. The Duke d'Aremberg had the command of the Queen of Hungary's troops; he was a pupil of Prince Eugene, served under him against the Turks and French, and contributed not a little to the success at the battles of Belgrade and Dettingen, and in both was wounded. The Dutch were commanded by Count Maurice of Nassau, a descendant of the celebrated Prince Maurice of Nassau, one of the three brothers, to whom the United Provinces were indebted for their grandeur and liberty.

The French King was resolved to make the campaign in person, and chose to appear in Flanders with Marshal Noailles, rather than in Alsace among the troops commanded by Marshal Saxe, or upon the Rhine, where Marshal Coigni defended the passage of that river against Prince Charles of Lorrain with an army of sixty-one battalions, and one hundred squadrons: he judged that in the two last, the war would only be defensive, whereas every thing was disposed for making it offensive in the Austrian Netherlands; but in this he was mistaken, for it raged with uncommon violence every where. The passing of the Rhine by Prince Charles was the occasion of two battles and two sieges, in which was spilt a deluge of blood; Alsace was ruined by the Bavarians, the French, and the Austrians in their turn; and in Flanders the towns of Ypres, Menin, Chartray, and Friburg, successively fell into the hands of the French, the Confederates not being able to oppose them. /

This inability did not proceed from a want of power, but from a want of harmony between the generals; the Duke d'Aremberg judged himself superior to Marshal Wade, in consequence of being more nobly descended; the Dutch were actually temporizing, and many of the States having large estates in France, were afraid to provoke the Grand Monarch; add to this, that General Wade was no favourite with the soldiers, in every thing the reverse of the Earl of Stair, whose liberality was not inferior to his valour, and whose coolness and experience the armies both of France and of the Confederates sufficiently knew. In short, the allied army this campaign fought no battle; on the contrary, they were the unconcerned spectators of one place after another falling into the hands of the enemy, whose King, from many popular acts, such as raising the pay of the private men, taking care that they should eat as good bread as what he himself used at his own table, became so respected and beloved, that they wanted nothing but orders to enter upon the most difficult plans of operation under his direction and command. His new acquisition of strength by the King of Prussia declaring once more in his favour, with some late successes obtained by the Infant Don Philip and the Prince of Conti in Italy, tended still more to encourage the armies and people of France, whose affection to their monarchs has been always remarkable, though never more conspicuous than now.

The King of Great Britain, from his usual penetration and sagacity, easily foresaw that a general of Marshal Wade's complexion and character was unfit to command a body of troops that were to be employed against an army under the direction of a Prince, who was adored by his subjects. His / late recovery from a dangerous fever, which at once threw the whole kingdom into tears, now raised their thankfulness and gratitude; and his carrying the Dauphin tended to endear him the more.

The several armies of France were at that time commanded by the ablest generals, who had no emulation, but that of outdoing each other in the service of their King. The inhabitants along the Rhine and in Alsace were more in the French interest than in that of the Austrians, or any other among the confederate powers. Every body of their forces was a corps of veterans, to whom the most public-spirited of every nation resorted, in order to learn the art of war.

But of these different armies, none was better appointed than that which the King himself honoured with his presence; the command of it was given to Count Maurice of Saxony, who about this time was created a Marshal of France; the King's aid de camps were mostly general officers, who had headed armies, and distinguished themselves in the field; the

Marshal de Noailles, the Duke de Richlieu, and the Duke de Boufflers, were among the number of these; the bulk of the French army was made up of the flower of the national troops of France, or of the choice bodies of foot and horse raised in foreign countries; the three regiments of Royal Suedois, each consisting of 1200 men, were complete, as were the Swiss guards, and the Irish brigades, then making a body of 8000 men among the best disciplined and most formidable troops in Europe; the Scots regiments were full, and Marshal Saxe had with him a corps of 3000 men, chosen from the chief families in Saxony, remarkable for tallness, and skilled in the whole art of war; some Danes came over with / Count Lowendahl, natural brother to Christian VI. of Denmark.

This Count Lowendahl had been trained up to war from his youth, the first rudiments of which he learnt at the battle of Helsinburgh, where General Count Stembock cut the Danish armies to pieces in the year 1711; he likewise witnessed the various scenes and operations that happened in the year 1717, when Charles the XIIth had the pleasing triumph, in the midst of his misfortunes, of seeing the fleets of four nations sheering off, without daring to make a descent upon Schonen, where he lay with an army ready to receive them. He went afterward into the Muscovite service, where he took Oczakow, and by a close application to literature, he acquired a thorough knowledge of the Latin, French, Spanish, and Italian tongues; and having become a great proficient in offensive and defensive fortification, he thought proper to offer his assistance in the service of France, where he was received with open arms, and where from the superiority of his character he was admitted to the rank of a Lieutenant-General; and Europe itself has heard with astonishment of the rapidity and glory of his conquests.

Such was the French army that was to oppose the Confederates; and to make them still more formidable, they were supported by a numerous train of artillery, conducted by a corps of no less than 5000 men, many of whom understood the practice of gunnery, and most of the private men were either smiths, masons, braziers, or founders, trades extremely necessary toward working of guns, and executing the practical parts of fortification.

It was indeed a difficult task to find out a General capable of dealing with the enemy, when supported with such uncommon advantages, and under the / eye of their sovereign: no British General was thought equal to it, except the Earl of Stair, and he was disgusted. It is true, that in February 1744, he went to court on hearing of an invasion from Dunkirk, and was created Field Marshal of all the forces in England; but he did not chuse to go abroad, unless with an unlimited command. In this situation of affairs the Duke of Cumberland was thought of, as the most popular among the soldiers, and the most likely to compose any difference that might happen between the Austrian officers and those of the States General; however, he was not all at once named, for the armies on both sides were in their winter-quarters.

The resolution of declaring him Captain General being taken, and communicated to him by the King, he applied more than ever to the study of such things as were most likely to qualify him for the high and important charge. His guardian, Stephen Poyntz, has more than once declared, that when he had the honour to call upon him, which he had full liberty to do every day, he always found his Highness busied in some thing or other belonging to the military sphere. Sometimes a map of Flanders, or a plan of some important fortress, lay upon the table, and immediately before him; at another time Monsieur Vauban's Fortification, at a third the Chevalier Folard's Commentaries on Polybius, at a fourth the Military History of Charles XIIth, of Prince Eugene and the Duke of Marlborough. Every officer from the colonel to the ensign had ready access to his Highness: he threw himself in the way of the soldiers; and if at any time he saw them hovering about, he himself would speak to them. He frequented Woolwich and St. James's Park: in the former of which he viewed the artillery, and was / present at all the experiments; and in the latter he delighted in seeing the soldiers mustered, and go through the several evolutions of the military exercise. By these and such other methods he became a proficient in the art of war, and so well acquainted with Flanders, that he almost knew every single village and rivulet in any of her provinces. He likewise endeavoured to get all possible intelligence from such foreign soldiers as were in England; which soon happened to his wish, in consequence of Marshal Belleisle's arrival there.

That brave officer had been seized by an Hanoverian bailiff or magistrate at an inn, just as he and his brother were changing horses at a borough called Elbingrode. The domestics of the two brothers endeavoured to rescue them, but in vain; for the bailiff got assistance in a moment, and, being a man of resolution, he took care to have them conducted to an inn, where, notwithstanding the politeness with which they were treated, yet they were taken such care of, that an escape was impracticable. An account of the affair coming to London, orders were sent for bringing the Marshal to England: where he was treated with all imaginable respect, had the palace of Windsor assigned for his residence, and had eighty pounds a day appropriated to support his dignity. The Court of France complained of this step as a violation of the law of nations, of the privilege of ambassadors, and of the constitution of the empire, he being a prince thereof, and actually an embassador to the Emperor and to the Court of Prussia at the time when he was taken. Many memorials were presented upon it, and the person of the ambassador was required, as sacred; but these were answered with / clearness and precision. It was urged, that the Duke de Belleisle was a prisoner, as being taken on the territory of a Prince against whom his master, the French King, had actually declared war, both as King of England and Elector of Hanover; that he carried on the war with rigour and severity against their ally the Queen of Hungary, whose states he had desolated, and whose beautiful city of Prague had been ruined and depopulated by his means: that according to themselves he was, when taken, going in quality of embassador from one of the Queen's enemies to another; and it would be strange to screen a person who had so notoriously fought against the friends of England and Hanover, under the specious pretence of being a prince of the empire, whose states he was instrumental in throwing into the most terrible convulsions: that in quality of a prince of the empire he must be looked on as a prisoner of state, and in quality of a Marshal of France he must be considered as a prisoner of war. As to the place of his confinement, it was no matter whether the same was to be in Hanover, in England, or in the dominions of the House of Austria. He was in reality an officer and subject of a prince who aimed at the destruction of these, and who in any event had made a wrong choice to fix upon a prince of the empire, as an engine to set her in a flame. In this case the opinion of Grotius and other civilians might be advanced: but I don't chuse to dwell further on a subject already so much exhausted. However, I cannot but acknowledge my regret in being obliged to differ in the whole of this affair from M. de Voltaire's opinion: for whom, on account of the generosity of his sentiments, and the unbounded goodness of his heart, I have for a long time / entertained the utmost personal honour and regard.

But while the Courts of Versailles and London were carrying on a paper war about the law of nations, Marshal Belleisle was regaled in England; where nothing was omitted that might alleviate his situation. He was shewn the paintings at Hampton Court and at St. James's; the tombs in Westminster Abbey, the yard and dock at Woolwich, and the very curiosities in the Tower. He was entertained and regaled by many of the nobility, such as the Dukes of Portland and St. Albans, and by Archibald late Duke of Argyle; and seemed to delight much in the company of this last nobleman; who, being of a turn of mind like the Marshal himself, entertained an equal veneration for him. They discoursed by an interpreter upon the arts of modelling, of gunnery and fortification. The Duke shewed the Marshal several models of his own contrivance, watches and clocks of his own construction and make: and, as the Duke de Belleisle supported academies at Vernon, in Normandy, for improving in all these different branches of knowledge, it was no wonder that two such great and illustrious souls turned to each other as it were by instinct; should demand a quick alliance, and burn with a reciprocal friendship. Happy for his Royal Highness; he delighted always in the company of the learned, and never appeared better pleased than when returning from the conversation of two such great and eminent persons.

The time drew near when he was to cross over into Flanders, and to take upon him the command of the army there. He was on the 20th of March declared Generalissimo, and next day took the oaths requisite in the House of Peers to qualify himself / for so distinguished a station; which being over, he embarked at Gravesend on the 4th of April, and landing at Helvoetsluys on the 6th, he proceeded to join the Confederate army, which then appeared to be in high spirits, and to be properly appointed. The several regiments were complete; for the towns and villages in Great Britain had increased greatly during so long a peace, that the demand for peopling our colonies in the East and West Indies was not so loud, as it has been since that period, so it was easy to recruit the troops out of these; for no sooner did the young men hear that his Royal Highness was to have the command of the army, than they run at the tuck of the drum, and proffered their service. The old Marshal Konigsegg was at the head of the Austrians, and Prince Waldeck commanded the troops of the States General.

No sooner did his Royal Highness appear among them, than the whole army, Austrians, English, and Dutch, raised the loudest acclamations and huzzas. He was on horseback, mounted on a fine Yorkshire hunter, which added to the dazzling splendor in which he appeared, not in the gaudy foppery of dress and costly attire, but in the amiable gentleness of a serene composure, that was legible in every feature of his countenance.

Here he learnt that the French army was already in the field; that the command thereof was given to Count Saxe in preference to the Marshals of France, notwithstanding they were natives of that kingdom, and older officers than he. Such a conduct did not proceed from any superior merit in Marshal Saxe, but from a superstitious notion that no French General had been fortunate against the Confederates during the last war of Louis XIV. /

Marshal Saxe being fixed in the command, did every thing in his power to cherish the good opinion which his new master had formed of him on account of his services, which, for the last three years and an half, he had been continually doing for the glory and interest of France, and for promoting the advancement of Charles Albert Elector of Bavaria to the Imperial diadem.

In the month of November 1741, he joined the French army, then under the Elector of Bavaria, in its way to Prague, the capital of Bohemia, and was the first to scale the town. In this personal act of valour, sufficient to give the world an exalted opinion of his bravery, he set an example to the troops of Saxony, then consisting of 20,000 men, and under his immediate command. He was in the fiftieth year of his age, a time most fit for a General to exert himself, as being in the meridian of his genius, though not of his bodily strength, which an irregular and intemperate manner of living had greatly impaired. Indeed he was naturally given to amours; his father the King of Poland was, for his amours and gallantries, remarkable all over Europe, and his mother the Countess of Koningsmark, a Swede by birth, was no less conspicuous. This commander, who, before his constitution was broke, possessed the same extraordinary strength of body as his father, the same gentleness of disposition, an equal generosity of heart, and the same innate valour, was still more accomplished and skilful. From his reputation, and the interest of his father, he had been chosen Duke of Courland by the unanimous voice of the nation; but Russia having deprived him of the benefit of this election, he comforted himself for his loss in the service of France, and / in the social pleasures of that nation, to whom his merit and personal accomplishments were not as yet sufficiently known; he had indeed proffered his service to Great Britain, but Sir Robert Walpole did not think fit to accept thereof. His understanding was quick and piercing, and his words were substantial and significant; for being one day accused by some persons about the King of Prussia of having entered into one of these trifling quarrels, which generally set the commanders of allied armies at variance, he contented himself with this reply to the charge, 'Those who know me will allow, that I am much fitter to enter the lists with an enemy, than to spin an intrigue.'

He had preserved the dignity of his reputation and character both in Alsace and Flanders, where during the last year he had covered the sieges of the several towns and citadels that had been conquered by the armies of France; he reduced old Marshal Wade to such difficulties, that he knew not what to do, outwitting him almost in every motion which he made. The study of war had engrossed his attention, even in times of peace; to a profound theory he added great practical knowledge; he was possessed of the most brilliant and distinguishing qualifications that can in any way constitute a General, such as patience, wisdom, vigilance, secrecy, the art of knowing properly when to postpone, and when to execute a project. From an uncommon quickness of apprehension, he could discern things all at once; his presence of mind and wonderful foresight were so perspicuous and distinguishing, that he was never at a loss for resources, even in times of the greatest calamity and distress. The officers most acceptable to him were those of the same disposition / and character; a spirit of affection and zeal was from him communicated into the inferior officers, and from these transfused into the minds of the private men, many of whom were irritated on account of the miseries of the late Emperor to exert themselves both to revenge his catastrophe, and to conquer the English army, which, if once done, their imagination suggested that there soon would be an end of the war.

That Prince, the sport of fortune, and the engine of France to set the empire in flames, was, about the latter end of the year 1744, become still more unfortunate. Happy before his connection with the Court of Versailles, his dismal situation rose only from the time of his elevation to the Imperial throne; nature had even been more unkind to him than fortune; a complication of acute disorders filled his days with bitterness, and at last carried him to his grave; he had the gout and stone at the same time; his sufferings, and the losses daily sustained by his subjects, made his maladies return with redoubled fury upon him, for he died at Munich at the age of forty-seven years and an half, at a time when he was neglected and despised in the empire, except by the King of Prussia, who was his ally from no other motive, but on account of an innate hatred to the House of Austria, and his having received lately one million four hundred thousand florins from the Court of Versailles. He was pursued by Prince Charles of Lorrain, and died, apprehensive lest the Queen of Hungary should again compel him to leave his capital. His case, however, may be a lesson to Princes, not to aspire at a throne upon the strength of another potentate, and may convince them, that the highest degree of human grandeur / may lead to the utmost pitch of infelicity. From the opening of his body, in which his lungs, his liver, and his stomach, were found to be mortified, it was concluded by his physicians, that he must for some months have lived in continual pain.

The death of the Emperor did not more whet the resentment of the French and Bavarians, than it excited the indignation of the House of Austria, and her allies, who now plainly saw, that the intention of France was only to desolate the other states of the Empire and of Flanders by a destructive war, as they had already done by the Electorate of Bavaria. The most Christian King had even some difficulty to find out a candidate to supply the late Emperor's room; he could not with any degree of honour proffer the Empire to the young Elector of Bavaria, he being then but seventeen years old: he therefore cast his eyes upon the King of Poland, Elector of Saxony; but he refused it, from the consideration of his being unable to sustain at one and the same time the weight of the Polish and Imperial diadems. The example of the Elector of Bavaria confirmed him in the maxim, 'not to lose certainty for hope;' for as he was not powerful enough of himself, to carry his point against the Great Duke of Tuscany, he might soon be driven like the last Emperor from his capital. He absolutely refused the proffer, and joined in a closer alliance than ever with Great Britain, and the Queen of Hungary, whose husband's claim upon the Imperial throne he now favoured as much as before he had endeavoured to divert it.

Never was greater emulation among two contending armies, than between the forces commanded by Marshal Saxe, and those under the

/ command of his Royal Highness the Duke of Cumberland. They prepared against each other with uncommon address and endeavour, as the individuals of either army thought that on the event of a battle the fate of their respective Sovereigns, their own future repose and tranquillity, with the safety of their wives, their children, their country, and their all depended; and this prepared a way for fresh and uncommon adventures.

The End of the SECOND BOOK. /

THE
LIFE
OF
WILLIAM
DUKE of CUMBERLAND.

BOOK III.

CONTENTS.

The French *King joins the Army in* Flanders, – *the Battle of* Fontenoy, *with the Surrender of* Tournay, – *the personal Accomplishments and Character of the Earl of* Chesterfield.

Louis the XVth, commonly called Louis Le Bien Aimé, having resolved to finish the conquests in Flanders, set out on the 6th of May from Paris, and that night arriving at Douay, he received, just as he was going to bed, a courier from Marshal Saxe, informing him that the Confederate army was approaching, and would soon be in sight; and though this intelligence was ill founded, as the Allied army lay safe at Moulbray till the 9th, yet it tended to promote that alertness / and spirit, which would soon become so necessary.

The French Monarch, who had the cause in which he was engaged no less at heart than his own personal character and reputation, which so much depended upon the issue of the ensuing campaign, said to the officers and aids de camp, 'There shall be no time lost; I will set out to morrow morning at five o'clock, but do not disturb the Dauphin.'

The next morning he set out by five, and arrived toward two in the afternoon at Pont-a-Chin near the Scheld, within reach of the line of circumvallation formed about Tournay. The Dauphin, who had been apprized, was there in time, and attended his father when he went to reconnoitre the ground designed for the field of battle. As they passed along the lines the air resounded the joyful acclamations of the soldiers, who now became more animated than ever; many of them had been some way or other personally known to him during the campaign of last year; and in a particular manner the engineers, and those belonging to the artillery: however, his presence did not more encourage his own troops, than it fired the forces of the Allies into a desire of coming to blows. The States General, though frequently slow in their operations, were yet the first to give orders for an engagement. Tournay, one of the eyes of France, and which contained a garrison of 12000 men, was in danger of falling into the hands of an enemy, who looked upon the same as his property. The other generals were for delivering Tournay, and so the operations proceeded; and what not a little tended toward determining the Duke of Cumberland, was the intelligence which he procured of the strength and situation of the enemy, not only from deserters, / whose information is frequently false, but from gentlemen of real honour and integrity.

Among the different persons who undertook the arduous task of a spy, none executed their commission with more address, and real advantage, than William Earl of Hume, and Captain Andrew Robinson, then Colonel of the Grenadier company in the third regiment of guards; the latter was a man of learning and ability; be had been bred up in the literary way, and by being a travelling governor, acquired such a competent knowledge of the French tongue, as to speak it fluently; he was likewise well acquainted with Brabant and Flanders, and from conversing with old settlers, he knew particularly the method of acting in that character; his countenance was far from being agreeable, and his person seemed to be much like that of a Brabanter, meagre, hollow, and distorted, and yet he was about this very time near being detected. Happily for him the serjeant on duty was an Englishman, and a deserter; he observed the ginman with his cask of gin, and wrangling with some soldiers about the quantity they had taken, and for which they had not properly paid; the man's heart was touched with compassion. A report that a spy was in the camp now circulated among them; the soldiers threatened to confine him to the main guard, and to have him brought before a commanding officer. The ginman seemed to consent; in which case his fate would have been inevitable. While in this situation, the serjeant assured them, that he was a poor countryman, servant to a boor, and who had for many years sold gin through the provinces of Holland and West Frizeland, and desired he might be let go. The men were persuaded, and agreed to the proposal; they left him and the serjeant together, / when the latter informed him, that he knew him perfectly well; that he was Captain of the Grenadier company, and begged of him to make the best of his way to the camp. 'But pray,' continued he, 'think on me when you shall be safe in the Allied army; for my misfortune happened in consequence of the severity of a superior officer, and a youthful amour; and if you can assure me of being welcome to my former appointment, I shall quit this service the first opportunity, and give his Royal Highness the best information in my power*.' All of which was agreed to, and in time was punctually fulfilled; and so grateful was the Captain, afterward General Robinson, that he allowed the man four shillings a week so long as he lived. The Earl of Hume was indeed more fortunate, notwithstanding his face, his person, and his make, were entirely English, and that he wore an artificial dress; among which a pretended beard, the better to disguise him. He was indeed a hero, a nobleman in every respect; his aspect was comely and noble, his person graceful and amiable, and his qualifications as a soldier were in every respect unquestionable and great.

In consequence of the most sure and undoubted intelligence, the Confederate army marched the 9th from Moulbray, and encamped that evening with the right at Bosignies, and the left at Moulbray, within a little more than musket shot of the advanced posts of the enemy.

His Royal Highness, with some other Generals, went directly to observe their position, and advanced so far, as easily to discern several of their squadrons, which were separated from the Confederate / by a country divided by a little rivulet on the left thereof; and by underwood, copses, and hedges, which they had filled with their Pandours and Graffins, supported by several little squadrons drawn up on a plain, which rose by an easy ascent to within a little distance of their camp, which was situated at the top of that rising, beginning at Antoin, leaving the village of Fontenoy in their front, and extending itself toward their left near a large wood, which lay beyond the village of Vezon towards the center of the right of the Allies. This village was also possessed by the enemy, and covered by small squadrons placed at short distances from each other.

* He had gone through such another adventure a little before the battle of Dettingen.

As it was impracticable to get into the plain, which lay between the French camp and the defiles, without first driving the out-parties from all their little posts, it was resolved to put off the attempt till next morning. Accordingly on the 10th six battalions and twelve squadrons, with 500 pioneers, six pieces of cannon, and two haubitzers, were commanded from each wing for this service, which was performed with great ease, the enemy having been driven every where to the very top of the rising near their camp, where they were drawn up in one body, as well to cover the dispositions making behind that eminence, as to observe the motions of the Confederates. His Royal Highness, the Marshal, and the Prince of Waldeck, rode into the plain, and after examining the ground, they brought back the troops to the camp in the evening; and in the mean time left strong detachments at the posts that had been taken, and which might facilitate the attack which was resolved on next morning. As the engagement at Fontenoy cannot be reckoned so much a battle, as the storming of a camp or a citadel, so it will not be improper to take a view of what the enemy were doing, in order to fortify themselves within these devouring inclosures, where it is to be observed, that the presence of their King was of the utmost importance to them; for on the evening before he discovered an unusual chearfulness and gaiety, and the conversation turning upon the battles at which the Kings of France had been present, he said, 'That since the battle of Poictiers*, no King of France had his son with him in an engagement; that none of them had ever gained a signal victory over the English, and he hoped to be the first.' And indeed to obtain it nothing was left undone that possibly could be effected; every height was fortified, and the ground where the battle was expected to happen was encircled with batteries. All which must be reduced, or at least silenced, before the Confederate army could come to blows with the French, who were all night working upon their entrenchments, and wherever the ground was level, they either cut ditches cross it, or joined the villages between which the open ground lay with redans of earth, and these were fortified with cannon. Marshal Noailles himself directed some of these; three redoubts were raised on the level ground interjacent between Fontenoy and Antoin, and these were furnished with three batteries of cannon, one of eight pieces, the other two of four; and besides

* The place where Edward the Black Prince took King John and his son prisoners.

these precautions, a masked battery of six sixteen pounders, was planted so as to take in flank any enemy that might attack the village of Antoin.

There was a piece of ground about three quarters of a mile long, which had a gentle ascent between the woods of Barri and Fontenoy, and this / was flanked by a strong redoubt at the verge of the former of these, and on which the guns were fixed in embrazures; another was planted at the extremity of the village of the latter, and in such a manner as to form a cross fire sufficient to stop the efforts of the most intrepid enemy.

If the Confederates should attempt to pass through the wood of Barri, they would have met with another redoubt furnished with cannon; if they made a greater circuit they had entrenchments to force, and must have been exposed to two batteries that had been fixed on the high road to Leuze. Thus was the ground on every side turned to the best advantage possible; every redoubt and every battery was properly supported by troops, who knew their business, and were well acquainted with war. About one hundred pieces of cannon were planted upon these different redoubts and batteries, and M. d'Argenson himself, with M. de Saxe, visited them, to see that they were in good order, and if all had arrived.

With respect to the position of the French troops beginning from the bridge of Calonne, where the King and Dauphin were stationed, there was no one part left naked. The infantry were in the front, the horse in the second line, and the gens d'armes and carabineers were stationed behind the corps of reserve. This was a new practice of Marshal Saxe recommended by Chevalier Folard, to secrete from an assailant's view such troops as are most famed for bravery, against whom every enemy directs the flower of their own forces.

Such was the disposition of the French army, and such was the spirit of the combatants of which it was composed; and now the hour was approaching when the fate of Europe itself was to be determined: for had the French King been defeated / the siege of Tournay would infallibly be raised, and perhaps the troops of France would have insensibly mouldered away; her allies would have receded from their engagements, and probably turned their arms against her: whereas if the Confederates were repulsed, it would be no more than a disappointment easily to be compensated by the treasure of Great Britain and Holland, and by the numerous swarms of soldiers to be found in the hereditary dominions of the House of Austria.

On the 11th of May, N.S. his Royal Highness the Duke of Cumberland put himself at the head of the English and Hanoverians about two o'clock in the morning; and when near the Wood of Barri he halted a little, sat on horseback, and saw the troops pass before him. He appeared extremely sedate and composed, smoothed some of them upon the shoulder, and said, 'These men look very well, and seem extremely fitted for the business on which they are to go.' Here he was informed, that there was a fort* mounted with cannon, in which 5 or 600 men might be lodged, and which might annoy the troops greatly if they advanced. Without hesitating a moment he ordered Brigadier General Ingolsby with four battalions, among whom was the regiment of Highlanders, and with these four pieces of cannon, six pounders, to attack the same sword in hand, whilst the Prince of Waldeck, with the Dutch troops, should attack the village of Fontenoi, as he had undertaken to do.

The battalions advanced with spirit, and the Highlanders run up to the very mouth of the cannon with incredible swiftness; but, to their astonishment, they found the place moated round. There / was a small causeway, about six feet broad, which they crowded upon to cross over; but in their way the cannon on the rampart were levelled against them, and they were obliged to retire, with the loss of 1 captain and 1 ensign, with 30 private men, killed; 1 captain, 2 ensigns, 2 serjeants, and 86 private men, wounded; 1 serjeant and 12 private men taken prisoners. The other battalions, disheartened by the fate of this resolute corps, retired without attempting any thing further. This unfortunate beginning did not in the least alter the plan that had been laid down. The cannon of the English and Hanoverians were placed in such a manner as to answer the fire from the different batteries of the enemy, and some moved forward with the lines as they advanced. By one of these batteries the first redoubt of the Wood of Barri was silenced, a regiment of the French guards put into great disorder, and their colonel, the Duke de Grammont, was killed by a cannon ball of three pounds, which struck his horse in the shoulder. Count Lowendahl, who was near him, was in an instant covered with blood; a piece of flesh, which flew off with the shot, fell into his boot. 'Have a care,' said the Count to the Duke, 'your horse is killed:' 'And I too,' replied the other; and so expired. The cannonading continued on both sides till eight in the morning with great vivacity, and the English

* This was the fort d'Eu, so called from the corps that defended it

troops seemed to be gaining ground: they encompassed the village of Fontenoy, and attacked it on every quarter: they even threw some bombs into it; one of which fell before the Marshal Saxe, just as he was speaking to Count Lowendahl.

The Dutch troops advanced afterward towards Antoin, and the two attacks were equally well supported: and though the flying batteries of the / enemy were silenced, yet those in the redoubts continued to play with great execution and briskness. The British troops were thrice obliged to give over the attack at Fontenoy, and the Dutch were forced twice to retire from before Antoin. At the second attack almost a whole Dutch squadron was swept away, there being only fifteen men left: from which time the forces under Prince Waldeck acted but faintly, and at a distance. However, the British ardour increased with the danger: they not only attacked Fontenoy, but likewise a redoubt near a place called The justice of the lady in the wood, near which the French King and his Son stood, surrounded by the aids de camp, and attended by about 120 men for a guard. The British cannon played briskly on this redoubt, and the shot from the small arms reached beyond it: a domestic of the Count d'Argenson having been wounded in the forehead by a musket-ball a considerable way behind the King; who, having his eye every where, gave orders that the villages which were attacked should be properly supported: for, after directing some regiments to move towards Fontenoy, and to play upon the flank of the troops which attacked it, he himself moved towards the side of Antoin, at the very time when the Duch were renewing the attack upon it. The cannon balls fell round him and the Dauphin; an officer, named M. d'Arbaud, was covered with dirt from the rebounding of a ball, and the King himself, with those about him, were daubed therewith. He only fell a-laughing, and said to the colonel of the artillery, 'Put up these balls, and send them back to the enemy: I will have nothing belonging to them.' His orders were obeyed; and soon the Dutch began to slacken their fire and to retire. /

Things continued in this situation till about half an hour past ten o'clock, when the Duke of Cumberland took the resolution of forcing his way between the reboubts of Barri and Fontenoy, which was scarce a full mile over. In this attempt he had a deep hollow way to pass, exposed to the fire of the redoubts, and on the other side of the hollow way was the French army. How unfortunate for him that the redoubt attacked by General Ingolsby had not been carried! as in that case the fire on its ramparts would have been turned against the enemy, and have facilitated the advancing of their own men into the field. But notwithstanding this, his Royal Highness put himself at the head of the British and Hanoverian troops, having under him Lieutenant General Sir John Ligonier, the Earl of Albemarle, Lieutenant Generals Howard, Durour, and Handasyde. The first three were upon the right, and the second on the left of the line, well supplied with cannon, which they dragged along with them; but not with horse or dragoons; as there was not room to march them: and, to encourage the troops still more, the Earl of Crawford was chief Aid de camp and Lieutenant General of the day.

One cannot without being moved conceive an army of brave men (about 30,000) marching between two devouring batteries, which kept an incessant fire upon them, and galled their flanks in a terrible manner, whole ranks dropping down to the right and left: however the cannon which they brought with them answered briskly in their turn; they pressed forward, still filling up their ranks; and, wedged in the firmest array, they passed the hollow way without being disordered.

They were formed in three lines, each of them four men deep; and in this posture advanced boldly, / with six field pieces in their front, and six more in the middle of their lines; they were now advanced to within 150 yards of the left of the enemy, where were placed four battalions of French guards, with two battalions of Swiss guards at their left, the regiments of Courten and Albeterre to their right, and further on the King's regiment, which lined Fontenoy the length of the hollow way.

From that part where the French guards were posted to where the English were forming it was a rising ground. The officers of the former said to each other, 'We must go and take the English cannon.' And accordingly they ascended to the top with their grenadiers: but when they got there, behold! a whole army before them. The cannon and some platoons were fired upon them, which brought very near 60 of them to the ground, and the remainder returned to their ranks in the greatest disorder.

In the mean time the British infantry advanced, and the French guards with the regiments just now named moved forward to meet them. When within thirty yards of each other, the British officers saluted the French, by taking off their hats. The Count de Chabannes and the Duke de Biron advanced forward, and returned the compliment. Lord Charles Hay, brother to the Marquis of Tweedale, and colonel of a company in the third regiment of guards, and afterward a major-general, cried out in French, 'Gentlemen of the French Guards give fire.'

The Count d'Antroche, then lieutenant of grenadiers, made answer, with a loud voice, 'Gentlemen, we never fire first; fire you first.' Then Lord Charles said to his men in English, 'Fire.' Accordingly they made a running fire; that is, they / fired in platoons, in this manner, that when the front of a battalion four deep had fired, another battalion made its discharge, and then a third, while the first were again loading. The line of French Infantry was extremely thinned; so that, as they could not return the platoons, they did not fire: their ranks were pretty distant, and not at all supported by any other body of infantry: besides, their eyes were surprised with the depth of the British corps, and their ears were stunned with a continued fire. 19 officers of their guards were wounded at this first charge, 95 soldiers killed upon the spot, and 285 wounded; as were 11 Swiss officers, 145 of their private men, and 64 were killed. Colonel de Courten, his lieutenant-colonel, 4 other officers, and 75 private men, dropped down dead; 14 officers and 200 men were dangerously wounded, as the cannon fired grape shot. The first rank being thus swept away, the other three looked behind them, and seeing only cavalry, at the distance of 600 yards, they dispersed. These indeed came on in a menacing posture, brandishing their swords, and the horses lashing their flanks with their tails; but they were miserably cut off by the guards, who gave them their fire in platoons, and brought them in heaps to the ground, tumbling on each other. In this manner the troops under his Royal Highness advanced gradually, as if they were performing their exercise. So happy a beginning compensated for the loss sustained from the artillery of the masked batteries, and extremely encouraged the men; who were now exceedingly caressed by their superior officers.

Thus the troops under his Highness pierced beyond Fontenoy and the redoubt. But, by reason of the narrowness of the ground, they were formed from the lines into an oblong figure, a solid body / of foot, unshaken from its weight, and still more so from its courage and intrepidity. The regiment of Aubeterre moved, with the Duke de Biron at their head, to meet them: but M. de Biron had an horse shot under him at the first discharge: M. Luttaux, who came from Fontenoy, where he had been hurt by a splinter, received two mortal wounds; 100 soldiers were killed, and 200 were wounded. The Duke de Biron, at the head of the King's regiment, presented himself at the little distance from the left flank of this compacted body: on which the third regiment of guards advanced some paces towards him, and gave so close and regular a fire, that 3 captains were killed, 15 were wounded, and 12 lieutenants, with 79 of the private men; and at the same time 266 lay dead upon the ground. The regiment de la Couronne, being a little way behind the King's, likewise proceeded forward, to stop the career of the victors; but its colonel the Duke de Havre, the lieutenant-colonel, all the staff-officers, with 37 subalterns, were wounded, so as to be obliged to quit the field; and the first rank, consisting of 260 soldiers was overthrown. The regiment of Soissonois advancing after that of la Couronne, had 14 officers wounded, and lost 130 soldiers. The regiment of Royal, with that of la Couronne, was still more roughly handled; for the British soldiers were after every fire improving in the art of levelling their pieces, and became more and more spirited: 6 of the officers of the Royal were killed, with 136 soldiers; 32 officers with 509 soldiers were wounded.

Had the Dutch troops under Prince Waldeck taken the same resolution as the British under his Royal Highness, the French army would have been inevitably ruined; or could the British cavalry, so terrible to those of France, have appeared, the / like event would have happened. The former only attacked redoubts, to no purpose (an error which lost the battle of Pultowa to Charles XIIth) and the other did not care to advance without being commanded. General Campbell, who headed them, was killed, and the other officers did not chuse to take too much upon them; so that the infantry were left to act by themselves: and, as they could not separate into small divisions, the enemy had time to rally the shattered reserve of the several regiments, whereof one after another had been overthrown. The Duke de Biron rallied his own regiment and some grenadiers, in the hollow way, that lined Fontenoy, and made a brisk discharge upon the flank of this compacted body; those of the King's regiment, of la Couronne and Aubeterre, entrenched themselves behind the dead and wounded, which lay in heaps before them: the French and Swiss guards were rallied by the Count de Babonnes toward the redoubt of Eu; but could only form one battalion, the rest having been either killed or wounded. These sheltered themselves under the cannon of the redoubt, having no stomach to advance against the British infantry; who still kept firm and close, and was continually gaining ground. They found the tents standing, and even took the very kettles as they were boiling the soldiers victuals, which instantly were seized.

Marshall Saxe saw the countenance which they wore, and did what he could to stop their progress; but in vain. But whether from the acute pain occasioned by his illness, which impaired his usual penetration and judgment, or from some other fatality, he certainly committed mistakes not to be pardoned even in an ordinary officer.

Three regiments of horse, under the Count d'Etrees, attacked the British infantry, now flushed / with success, and breathing revenge for the loss of their brave comrades, but to no purpose: a regular and well supported fire overturned the several small detached bodies which successively presented themselves. The Marshal, who was in the hottest place of the action, rode up with full speed to bring on the second line of cavalry: the regiments of Noailles and Penthievre fell on the front with intrepidity, while the Marquis de Vignacourt rushed with his squadron upon their flank. The British soldiers opened from right to left to let them come in; and, afterward closing upon them, cut them in pieces, except fourteen troopers, and the Marquis himself, who endeavoured to break through. Of these eight were afterward killed and six taken prisoners. In this daring adventure the soldiers run their bayonets up to the muzzles of their fusees into the sides of the enemies horses; and one private man forced his bayonet with such violence into M. de Vignacourt's leg, quite through the boot, that he was obliged to let go his piece: the horse, having received several wounds, ran away with his master; while the but-end of the musket trailing on the ground, widened and tore the wound, of which he died soon after.

The Count d'Argenson, son of the secretary at war, charged with his regiment de Berri, at the very time when that of Fiennes was marching up. He advanced three times to the attack at the head of a single squadron. The regiments de Brionne, de Brancas, and de Chabrillant rallied, and returned to the charge: but all these different bodies were repulsed one after another, and driven back with prodigious slaughter. All the general officers kept riding from one brigade to another. The regiments of the Colonel-general, of Fiennes, with the Croats, suffered much; that of the Prince de / Clermont endured still more; twenty-two of their officers having been wounded, and of the Croats twelve. The staff-officers were in motion: M. de Vaudreuil, major-general of the army, the same who commanded afterward at Guadaloupe, rode every minute from right to left. Four quarter-masters were wounded, as was the Count de Longaunac, aid major-general; and the lieutenant-general d'Ache had his foot shattered by a ball.

The further the British infantry advanced it became the deeper, and of consequence the better able to repair the continual losses sustained from so many different attacks: it still marched on, close and compact, over the bodies of the dead and wounded on both sides, seeming to form one single corps of about 16,000 men.

A great many troopers were driven back in disorder as far as the place where the King and the Dauphin were posted; so that these two Princes were separated by the crowd that came tumbling upon them.

During this disorder the brigades of the life-guards, who were in reserve, advanced of their own accord against the British infantry; but were received with the same running fire, and overturned. Four squadrons of the gens d'armes, who arrived that very instant from Doway, charged immediately, notwithstanding their fatigue and an uninterrupted march of twenty-one miles; but they were received in the same manner; as was the regiment of carabineers, a corps of no small reputation and character.

Marshal Saxe, though extremely weakened with fatigue, was still on horseback, riding gently in the midst of the firing. He passed pretty near the front of the British infantry, to observe what passed on the left, toward the Wood de Barri, where they / were going on in the same manner as on the right, endeavouring, but in vain, to put the infantry in disorder. Opposite to their left were the British guards; the French regiments presented themselves one after another, while the British facing about, on every side, and placing their cannon properly, and always firing in divisions, kept up a constant and running fire, whenever they were attacked, which soon overthrew the enemy, and then they remained immovable and ceased to fire. The Marshal at that time observing a regiment engaged with the British guards, and which stood immovable even while whole ranks were dropping down, asked what corps was that? And being told that it was the regiment de Vaisseau, commanded by M. de Guerci, the same who was afterward the French ambassador at London, he cried out, 'Admirable indeed.' Two-and-thirty officers of this regiment were wounded, and one-third of the soldiers were either killed or rendered unfit for action, The regiment of Hainault did not suffer less: their colonel was the son of the Prince de Craon, governor of Tuscany; the father served in the troops commanded by M. Konigsegg, and his sons were in the armies of France;

this young man was killed at the head of his troops, the lieutenant-colonel was mortally wounded near him, as were 19 of the officers, and 260 of the private men lay dead upon the spot.

The regiment of Normandy advanced, but they had as many officers and soldiers wounded, as that of Hainault. Some Irish brigades fell next upon the flank of the British infantry, but Colonel Dillon was killed, with 13 other officers, and 56 were wounded.

Marshal Saxe then returned by the front of the British line, which at this time had advanced three / hundred yards beyond the redoubt of Eu, and Fontenoy; in which last they had exhausted their ball, and now answered the fire of the assailants only with gunpowder. The corps of artillery stationed there had been very roughly handled; M. de Brocard, lieutenant-general of the artillery, and many officers of the ordnance, were killed, and a great many more were wounded.

The Marshal, finding things in this situation, earnestly desired the Duke de Harcourt, whom he accidentally met, to go and beseech the King to remove further off. At the same time he sent orders to the Count de la Marck, who defended Antoin, to quit that post, and to draw off the regiment of Piedmont. Victory now seemed to declare for the Confederates; the French were bringing back their field-pieces from every side, and were just upon the point of removing the artillery from the village of Fontenoy, though a supply of ball was come; they had even begun to send off the train. The Marshal's intention was to make his last effort against the British infantry, which, notwithstanding the repeated attacks of the enemy, still appeared to be of the same depth as at the beginning; for from the time of crossing the hollow way between Fontenoy and the Wood of Barri, their loss was but very inconsiderable, the attack being only made by cavalry, and these almost overthrown so soon as they appeared: every thing wore the aspect of victory; the enemy thought so, and accordingly prepared for a retreat, and the Dutch stood ready to take possession of Antoin the moment the enemy quitted it, and so did the troops employed in the attack of the village of Fontenoy. The Marshal's earnest entreaty was intimated to the King, who had hitherto stood firm and undaunted, notwithstanding the British / troops were in the middle of the ground which his own had so lately occupied, but he refused to comply.

The French generals now held a tumultuous kind of council around their King, who was pressed, in the name and for the sake of France, not to expose his person any longer. At this very instant arrived the Duke de Richlieu, lieutenant-general of the army, who served as aid de camp to the King; he was come from Fontenoy, and had been reconnoitering the British infantry: he had charged them with the regiment of Vaisseaux, and with the life-guards; he had also caused M. Billett to advance with the gens d'armes, and these stopped the victors, who began to halt, as many of the men had shot all their complement of gunpowder, in order to be supplied, which they were from the cartouches of the slain that lay before them. Having thus rode about on every side without being wounded, he presented himself quite out of breath with his sword in his hand, and all covered with dust. 'Well Resce,' says Marshal Noailles, (this was a familiar expression used by that officer) 'What news do you bring us, and what is your opinion?' 'My news,' replied the Duke, 'is, that the victory is ours, if we have a mind; and my opinion is, that we immediately bring four pieces of cannon to bear upon the front of the enemy, while this artillery throws it into disorder; the King's household and his other troops will surround it; we must fall upon them like foragers, and I will lay my life that the day is ours.' 'But Fontenoy,' said they, 'is in the hands of the enemy.' 'I come from thence,' says the Duke, 'it holds out still.' 'We must see,' replied they, 'whether the Marshal has not designed this cannon for some / other use.' He answered, 'There is no other to make of it;' he was convinced himself, and persuaded the rest. The King was the first who approved of the important proposal, and every body else joined in the opinion. He gave orders therefore that they should instantly go and bring four pieces of cannon; twenty rode away directly on the errand, when Captain Issards, of the regiment of Touraine, perceiving four pieces which they were carrying back, he gave notice of it immediately, and that very evening he had the cross of St. Louis.

They were pointed by M. de Senneval, a lieutenant of the artillery, just opposite to the front of the British line, and only waited to move forward. The Duke de Richlieu, being mounted on a fresh horse, galloped off at a full stretch to give orders to the King's household to march, and these were put in motion in a moment. The Prince de Soubise assembled the gens d'armes under his command; the Duke de Chaulnes did the same with his light horse; four squadrons of the gens d'armes advanced at the right of the King's houshold, having the horse grenadiers at their head, and the musquetaires immediately before them; they all drew up in order and marched, and the cannon followed the center. The French troops rallied on every side, and crowded toward this moving line, which they increased every moment. The Count de la Marck, by the persuasion of the Duke de Biron, returned to his post at Antoin just as he had quitted it; and Marshal Saxe coming up at that instant approved of Biron's opinion. Here being informed of the King's resolution, and the disposition of the troops, he acquiesced therein; and after ordering the regiment of Piedmont back to Antoin, he moved, notwithstanding his weakness, / to the right and left, and toward the Irish brigades, strictly charging all the troops he met on his way not to make any irregular charges, but to act in concert.

While he was with the Irish brigades, attended by M. de Lowendahl and Lord Clare, the Duke de Biron, the Count d'Estrees, and the Marquis de Croisy were together on the right, and had a full view of the lines; the King's regiment, those of Aubeterre and Courten were on that quarter, with five squadrons of Penthievre's regiment; the squadrons of Fitzjames, Noailles, Chabrillant, Brancas, and Brionne, advanced with their respective colonels, though they had received no orders; and there seemed to be a perfect harmony between their movements, and all that had been proposed by M. de Richlieu. Lord Clare marched up with the Irish, the regiment of Normandy, the French guards, and a battalion of Swiss, advancing higher up toward the redoubt of Eu. All these moved at once, and from their appearance seemed to form a solid body of 40,000 men, 30,000 of which were infantry; the Irish marched against the front of the British infantry, and the guards a little higher up toward their left. Nothing now retarded them but a hollow way, on the brink of which the troops opened from right to left to let forward the four pieces of cannon, which began to fire with great briskness when within an hundred yards of the first line; they made two discharges, and thinned the ranks. Lieutenant General Ligonier, the moment he saw them make this motion, caused the troops to open every where from right to left. The enemy in the mean time plunged into the hollow way, and under cover of the cannon advanced firing almost muzzle to muzzle, and then falling upon the British infantry with screwed bayonets, / the regiment of Normandy broke into one of these openings; the carabineers followed, and seemed with success to be piercing through the first ranks: however, they were disordered; but rallying in the very midst of the lines that were pressed on every quarter, they had more time than otherwise they would have had. The Irish pressed forward and widened the breach; the carabineers mistaking these for a part of the British guards, they having the same uniform, fired upon them. The Irish cried out, *Vive France:* but in the confusion they could not be heard, so that some of the Irish were killed through mistake.

The King's houshold followed the impression that had been made in the front, the cavalry pressed it hard upon the left flank, by bearing upon them with the breasts of their horses. Some of the boldest among them charged sword in hand, and others charged pell-mell with the guards and musquetaires. His Royal Highness did all he could to animate his troops, who were extremely fatigued with so long a service; but it was impracticable to stand against artillery, and the fresh troops of an enemy, who crowded from every quarter: whole ranks were cut down, so that a retreat was resolved on. The British forces repassed through the way they came, and were not pursued by the enemy; for these wanted now to expose them to all the fury of the batteries, which certainly would have torn them to pieces, had not the Prince of Waldeck and M. Konigsegg kept them in play. A retreat being now resolved on, the Earl of Crauford had the conducting of it. Accordingly they hastily retreated the same way they came on; and here they were preserved in a very singular manner. A body of the enemy's troops having lodged themselves among some copses opposite to the village / of Fontenoy, there was no firing from that quarter; but all at once, as the British troops came up, those in ambush rose up and fired full in the flank of the retreating infantry, who yet faced about, formed in a moment, and attacked the assailants with their fire and with screwed bayonets. The enemy was soon overthrown and fled; the bulk of those who forced the troops over the hollow way saw it, and yet durst not march forward; they beheld the menacing countenance of the cavalry, and did not chuse to proceed beyond the shelter of their batteries; but advanced no further than the top of the ascent near Fontenoy, where they called, *Vive le Roi de la France;* and so returned. In the mean time the infantry of the Confederates were regaining their ranks, and marching off; the horse moved after them in the rear, with three Hanoverian regiments under Major-General Zastrow. Some of the gens d'armes, who had advanced beyond the rest, pushed forward and attacked them; but the corps commanded by Zastrow gave them so close a fire, that several of the horses returned without riders, and trampled upon many of the wounded men, who might have recovered, had it not been for this unlucky accident. Very little of the baggage of the allies was taken; that was left at Bruffoil, and the baggage of his Royal Highness was transported to Aeth, where that afternoon it arrived, as did himself with the British troops about three in the morning. The only advantage gained by the enemy next to the repulse itself, was a number of cannon, about 47, which the contractors abandoned in the time of the engagement; and these they added to the train of artillery, to be employed in the reduction of Tournay.

Such was the event of this battle of Fontenoy, in which the enemy had about 15,000 men killed, / and 20,000 wounded; among whom were many of the princes of the blood, who, with the flower of their troops, were destroyed; and though they kept possession of their camp, yet the resolute and unparalleled efforts of the Allies, particularly of the British infantry led on by the Duke of Cumberland, were so great, that they never wanted to face them in the open field during the course of the war.

On the side of the Allies were killed about 4041 men, and 629 horses. Of twenty regiments of foot, there was not one who did not lose considerably; the three regiments of guards, by being exposed to the repeated attacks, and sometimes to the batteries of the enemy, obtained the highest honour and reputation. Out of some companies no less than 35 were missing when they mustered before the Duke's quarters; and here occurred a small incident, which shewed the real disposition of his Highness's heart, and how much the same was subject to be impressed with sentiments of compassion and humanity. One of his aid de camps informed him that the guards had misbehaved; he seemed to hear the account with some emotion, and continued to harbour a bad opinion of them, till next morning, when they came to the parade in the area immediately before his lodging, the gentleman in waiting informed him that his Highness's guard was come to do duty: 'What!' replied he, 'are they of the regiment of guards?' The gentleman answered, 'they were:' 'What!' said his Highness, 'they are not the King's guards, they are black guards;' and so walked toward the window to look at them. Being surprized to see men from the different regiments, he paused a little, and asked the meaning of it; on which he was told, that on account of their loss the whole / three could not make one complete. This seemed to startle him; he looked upon them with visible concern, spoke to several among them, and even was observed to shed tears; and from that time never entertained the aid de camp with the same degree of confidence or regard as before.

Among the number of the killed was Lieutenant-General Sir James Campbell, whose leg was shot off by the patella of the knee about the beginning of the engagement; the ball that struck him came from the village of Antoin, just as they began to attack it. He was carried out of the field, and saw without emotion the leg cut off, without saying any more than this; 'My dancing will henceforth be over:' a prediction which was soon fulfilled, for he died some hours after, only lamenting that he could not live to see the happy event of that glorious day. Major-General Ponsonby was killed by a cannon ball just as he was leaning on his pike, and taking a pinch of snuff, on their first halting, after putting to flight the front of the enemy; the Earl of Albemarle, afterward ambassador in France, was rode over, and bruised; Major-General Howard was wounded in four places; the Brigadiers Churchill and Ingolsby, the Lords Ancram and Cathcart, aids decamp to the Duke, were wounded also; five Colonels were killed outright, among whom was Colonel Carpenter of the guards; Colonel Duroure of Bligh's regiment was wounded, as were the Lieutenant-Colonels Lord Charles Hay, Waldgrave, Whitmore, Kennedy, and Lord George Sackville, with above 300 inferior officers, many of whom died afterwards of their wounds. The Hanoverians lost, between killed, wounded, and prisoners, about 1762; there were of the Dutch, between killed and wounded, about 1544; and the Austrians / lost 830; so that the whole loss on the side of the Confederates amounted to 8177 killed, 8000 wounded, and 2000 taken prisoners.

In consequence of this repulse the siege of Tournay proceeded with vigour, and without interruption; for on the day after the battle there was a discharge of 160 pieces of cannon and 40 mortars against the town, in token of the victory; the place was every day more and more closely invested, so that on the 12th day Baron Dorth, the governor, found himself obliged to surrender the fort into the hands of the besiegers, and the citadel soon yielded. The French King himself was present at the gate as the garrison marched out, and with great humanity enquired the names of the several regiments as they passed by; and to shew his complaisance to the States General, he permitted the garrison to retire, upon condition of not serving against France for a year; and to be still more polite, he ordered the prisoners that had been taken at the late battle to be set at liberty.

His conduct to the British prisoners was quite otherwise: they were closely confined. His Royal Highness wrote to Marshal Saxe about the matter, desiring that they might either be exchanged or ransomed, according to the cartel settled at Francfort, anno 1741, to which the Count wrote an answer to this purpose, That charity and humanity engaged his Majesty of France to give orders, that the English and Hanoverian prisoners should be taken care of*; but that he would keep them in his prisons, forts, and citadels, until the King of Great Britain / did him justice with regard to the arresting of Marshal Belleisle and his Brother, who were still detained in England, contrary to the faith of the cartel: That, not having the same reasons of complaint against the States General, his Majesty had ordered the Dutch prisoners to be set at liberty.

The chief advantage gained by the French was, that they were at more freedom to attack the fortresses in Flanders; which, to the ruin of their own armies and finances, they have so frequently over-run: but this was the boundary of what they could do. In every other respect their affairs were but indifferent. The great and ample supplies granted by the British Parliament towards carrying on the war, the advantages gained by the British ships at sea, the rapid progress of Prince Charles of Lorrain on the Rhine, notwithstanding the efforts of the Prince of Conti to oppose him, the accommodation between the Queen of Hungary with the young Elector of Bavaria, who now joined the enemies of France, the resolution of the States of Holland, and their engagements for settling the proportion of expence and forces to be employed against their common enemy, could not fail to counterbalance the small advantage which only the forts and encampment about Tournay had given them.

This disposition of their High Mightinesses was in a great measure owing to the address and superior ability of Philip Dormer Earl of Chesterfield, who had a little before appeared at the Hague, as ambassador extraordinary and plenipotentiary from the King of Great Britain. His Lordship was a man of deep penetration and judgment, cool in his passions, deliberate in his actions, and vigorous in executing his schemes. He had once been ambassador to the same Court before, and, having / cultivated an intimacy with several of their leading men, he had the fairer opportunity of improving that acquaintance to the good of the Sovereign whom he represended; and his words had the more influence on them. For in a memorial which he delivered to the Deputies, with whom he had held a conference, he expressed himself in these nervous and pathetic terms, in which he exposed the delusive conduct of France, without so much as mentioning her name. 'Let crafty policy,' said he, 'employ the

* Scarce were the British troops retired, when a parcel of maroders, English, Irish, and Scots renegadoes, stript the dead and wounded, which when the French King heard, he ordered the whole either to receive back their own clothes, or others in their stead.

most seducing artifices, to cover its ambitious designs; let it put every spring in motion to deceive your confidence*, or at least lull you into a fatal security; true friendship, such as that which unites the King my master with your High Mightinesses, despises those artifices, and abhors these indirect means: it is simple, and its language is the same.'

'The close union of the two nations is neither the effect of some transient views, nor the fruit of accidental conjunctures; but a right consequence of our reciprocal and invariable interests. Nature pointed it out to us, in placing us as she has done; and the uninterrupted experience of almost a century, does not permit us to be ignorant, that our mutual prosperity depends upon our union.'

The States of Holland at that time could not help observing the strength and vigour of his arguments: they were convinced, that Germany, Italy, Bohemia, and Flanders were the theatres of blood and slaughter through the policy and ambition of the Court of France. Ghent submitted without / resistance; and Ostend, which once had formerly endured a siege of three years, now holds out but three days against Count Lowendahl. The state of Flanders was indeed more alarming than either the progress of the Prussian armies in Silesia, or of the united forces of France and Spain upon the territories of the Republic of Genoa. But to check their progress the British and Dutch armies were recruited with men and horses, ammunition and provisions; nor were the enemy capable of interrupting the timely supplies: for the regiments were soon filled up. The behaviour of his Royal Highness was every day more and more engaging: for, despising fatigue, he would think nothing of setting out about ten at night to view a piece of ground that had been recommended to him for an encampment. The strict discipline enjoined to be observed by the soldiers could not fail to promote respect and veneration from the boors, notwithstanding the innate clownishness and peevish disposition, so visible and general in these. Not to say, but irregularities were committed by some of the military in the places where the Allies were cantoned; but, wherever there was any proof, the complainer had an ample satisfaction. In a word, things were, towards the beginning of July, so well recovered, that the Confederate army was ready to fight the enemy upon equal terms; and towards the latter end of that month an agreeable piece of news arrived, which not a

* Alluding to a speech of M. de Fenelon, March 19, 1744, in which he told the States General, that his master had in the year 1721 thwarted the design of the Court of Vienna to establish an East India Company at Ostend

little contributed to animate the troops, and to give the country people an high opinion of the power of their masters.

Every person has heard of the Isle of Cape Breton, which, lying near to the entrance into the river of St. Lawrence, almost commands the fisheries upon the Banks of Newfoundland. Sir Peter Warren was the person who achieved this / important conquest. He appeared before it on the 28th of April, and by a close siege, in which he prevented all succours from coming to the enemy, he reduced it on the 16th of June thereafter.

The news of this important acquisition arriving at London on the 20th of July, caused an universal satisfaction and joy; and addresses of congratulation from every quarter. It was sent in a letter by an express to the Duke of Cumberland, who read over the contents to the general officers as soon as he received it, and it was by them communicated to the private men. Aeth was illuminated, conduits were prepared, and ran with wine, and the artillery fired. A grand entertainment was prepared, to which the general officers were invited, and had the honour to dine with his Highness; the subalterns dined at another table, and the private men had the broken victuals, and plenty of wine for regaling them.

As they sat at table his Highness was observed to be more than ordinarily chearful, and to take occasion to represent the singular advantage that would accrue to the nation from a conquest so important in itself and so prejudicial to the enemy*, that ten repulses at Fontenoy were not so hurtful to Britain as the losing of Cape Breton was disadvantageous to France.

This opinion of his Royal Highness seemed to be the same with what the Court of Versailles had formed of the matter: she now more than ever endeavoured to embarrass the King of Great Britain, by obliging him to recall his forces out of Flanders; that by thus taking off the greatest obstacle / to her ambitious views, the other might follow of course, and she might act with impunity. She had recourse to the favourite project of setting the Pretender on the throne of England; a scheme so grand at first appearance, that posterity will find it difficult to give credit to the suddenness of the enterprize, or to believe the several occurrences that attended the bold and daring adventure.

The End of the THIRD BOOK. /

* It yielded to France yearly a revenue of 1,400,000 l. sterling, and was a nursery for seamen to her fleets.

THE LIFE OF WILLIAM DUKE OF CUMBERLAND.

BOOK IV.

CONTENTS.

The Rise of the Rebellion 1745, – *a Description of* Scotland, – *the Pretender's eldest Son arrives at* Edinburgh, – *his Manifestoes,* – *and the Battle of* Preston-pans.

AMONG the several attempts in favour of the Pretender to the crown of Great Britain, there were none conducted with such address and secrecy, as that which broke out in the summer of the year 1745; and what is no less wonderful than true, some who had engaged in the association to promote his advancement, were never very remarkable for secrecy and reserve.

The principal among the conspirators was Simon Lord Lovat, a nobleman of a crafty turn of mind, / and who experienced the vicissitudes both of good and bad fortune in the early part of life, and in his more advanced years. When but young he committed a rape upon his aunt-in-law, the Lady Dowager of Lovat. To screen himself from justice, he roamed about the Highlands and Western Isles of Scotland, and at last retired into France. During this period of his exile he became perfectly well acquainted with the nature of the people inhabiting these remote parts. As his mother was a daughter of the Laird of Macleod, and his grandmother a daughter of Sir Donald Macdonald of Slate, so his misfortunes only furnished him an opportunity of cultivating a correspondence with the different families of these two chieftains, and the other heads of the clans. While in France he had occasion to be acquainted with the several orders among the Jesuits, and embracing the Roman Catholic religion, he cherished all her tenets, but none more than those of dissimulation and perfidy to heretics; for though he lived and died a Roman Catholic, yet he frequently endeavoured to get himself elected as a member of the General Assembly of the Church of Scotland, and took the oaths once and again to King William, to King George I. and II. in whose reign he was Captain of an independent company of Highlanders for fifteen years; when in the year 1736 General Wade having detected the iniquitous methods by which he enriched himself, and imposed upon the government in the most flagitious and oppressive manner*; and observing the backwardness with which / his corps went through the several evolutions of the military exercise, with the uncouth and tawdry condition in which they appeared, he, in consequence of being lieutenant-general of the King's forces in Scotland, broke the company, and took away the commission of their captain: at which Lovat was so much enraged, that from that day he meditated no less a revenge than that of dethroning the King; in which event General Wade and other officers would be involved in the catastrophe and change.

To bring this about he proposed and signed the association formerly mentioned, sent it to France, where it was approved, and a promise was given to support it. The old Chevalier was so pleased with it, that he thanked him by a letter under his own hand, promised to pay all the debts upon the estate of Lovat, to create him Duke of Beaufort and Frazer, and Lieutenant-General of the Highlands.

The pompous title of Duke of Frazer, instead of Lord Lovat, the high and distinguishing station of Lieutenant-General of the Highlands, instead of being Captain of an independent company of Frazers, flattered the ambition of the man, who, notwithstanding he was in the 74th year of his age, yet expected before his death to be the greatest subject of the nation, in consequence of having restored *the King!*

Full of resentment against the government, and big with the hopes of titles, riches, and distinguished appellations, he applied in good earnest to entice the subjects from their allegiance, and to fire them into an inclination to arms. As the people are poor, ignorant, and born with a military genius, so the task became the more easy. His circumstances were

* His company, as he gave out, consisted of 120 men, besides officers and pipers; but on enquiry it was found that he had pocketed the money, and only remitted a small part of the corn or carriage-service to his tenants for appearing at the reviews.

abundantly opulent; for during the / fifteen years in which he retained the command, he saved almost *9 l.* every day. At Edinburgh he set up his chariot; his house at Castle Downie was daily frequented, and his visitors were hospitably entertained. He told them stories of what happened long ago among the Highlanders, magnified the superior advantage of the broad sword and target above the gun and bayonet, ridiculed the custom of bestowing commissions upon children and boys; and, to crown all, he interpreted prophecies and dreams. His age was an advantage to him, as it furnished him with a pretext of telling them, without being suspected, fabulous tales about their forefathers, the connections of these with each other, with the neighbouring clans, and with his clan in particular. In fine, he denominated them his cousins, and usually dismissed them with the appellation of children and friends. He had kept up a correspondence with the Court of St. Albano from the time of the association; and now on the repulse of the Allied army from before Tournay, he looked with impatience for an invasion.

The young Pretender was at Rome when he first heard of the disappointment which his Royal Highness the Duke of Cumberland had met with; his flatterers magnified the disaster, and threw the whole blame upon the British commander; they charged him with being the cause of the Allied army engaging that day, though that step was entirely owing to the Prince of Waldeck: it was easy to persuade a man who thirsted after power, and aspired after a crown. The ambitious young man set out from Rome on the 16th of June, and, arriving at Paris by the way of Avignon, he had again conferences with the disaffected there, and with Lord John Drummond, and some officers of / his regiment, who had come on purpose to meet him concerning the method of his procedure; and to be more secure, he wrote a letter to John Murray of Broughton, informing him that he intended soon to set out for Scotland, and desired that his friends might be ready to join him upon his landing. The letter was transmitted to Perth, Lovat, Lochiel, and others, who all (except Perth) were absolutely against his landing at that time. Murray wrote him the opinion of his friends; but before the arrival of the letter the hasty adventurer was set out.

He went to Port Lazare in Britany, and there hired a small vessel, in which he embarked only with seven persons, and upon the 15th of July landed in South Uist, where his encouragement was far from being answerable to the expectations which he had conceived; old Clanranald, the chieftain of the Macdonalds in that part, was over in Arisaig, dissuading his followers there to join in any enterprize; Macdonald of Buisdale, Clanranald's brother, being on the spot, remonstrated against it with all the eloquence he was master of. The young men breathed the same spirit of acrimony and resentment, and the Lady Clanranald became the most sanguine in the cause. After some altercation and argument, it was settled that he should repair to the continent; and in case the chieftains there should set up his standard, he might depend upon being joined by the clan under the command of her second son.

This being settled, he accordingly sent back the vessel, and in an open boat set sail for Ardna-murchan, / from whence he intimated his arrival to his friends. Cameron of Lochiel, and his brother the Doctor, were the first to repair to him; and appearing greatly surprized at seeing him, they earnestly besought him to return; on which, with some emotion, he took out the French King's obligation to support him, and said with no little warmth: 'If you will not set up my standard, deliver me up to the Elector of Hanover; for since I am arrived among you upon your own invitation, I am determined not to return.' To which Lochiel replied, 'I must say your Highness uses me ill, to think I could be guilty of delivering you to the Elector; I shall join you, as my honour is engaged; but remember I tell you, that your hasty procedure will render your scheme abortive, and prove the ruin of your friends.' The principal heads of the clan were of opinion that the project was impracticable, and threatened to confine their chieftain, notwithstanding the cordial affection which they bore him; however, the remonstrance was in vain: that very night it was agreed to set up his standard* next day at Glenphillin, provided Lord Lovat approved of it; and in the mean time Dr. Cameron rode away to his Lordship with the news.

Though this nobleman did not applaud the Pretender's impatience, yet he gave it as his opinion that the standard should be set up: he promised to send out his own clan, and even head them himself, so soon as his infirmities and sickness were removed. The Doctor returning with Lovat's answer, the standard was erected at the place appointed, to which many of the country people came in; the / Macdonalds of Glengary, Keppoch, and Clanranald, with the Maceans of Glencoe, and some of the Maclauch-

* It was a square piece of red silk fixed to a long staff, with a white standard in the middle, and this motto, *Tandem bona cause triumphans, The good cause at last triumphing.*

lans crowded to it; such was the abject and miserable slavery under which they groaned. With this little army he marched to Fort William, where he encamped, and from thence proceeded southward: they were regimented after the manner of regular troops: the pay of the private men was 8 *d. per diem;* and when a party of the Macdonalds of Keppoch's family surprized seventy new raised men of Sinclair's regiment, he granted the booty, viz. 50 *l.* to themselves. And here it will be proper to give a character of those principally concerned.

William Marquis of Tullebardin, who had been attainted in the year 1715, was one of the seven that attended him from France. He was no soldier, no statesman, and his frequent misfortunes, with a three years imprisonment for debt in Paris, had so broken his constitution, that he was very unfit for the design whereon he came: however, he was abundantly popular, and in that situation prevailed on a number to join him. General Macdonald, a lieutenant colonel in the Irish brigades, Sir Thomas Sheridan*, and Mr. O'Sullivan; Mr. Mechel, who was his gentleman; Mr. Kelly, a man deeply involved with Dr. Atterbury, bishop of Rochester, and a Guinea black attended him likewise.

In his way to the south country he was met by several of his friends, such as James Drummond, commonly called Duke of Perth, John Murray of Broughton, and Stuart of Ardshiel; men abundantly brave, but ignorant of the art of war. And indeed it is to be observed, that he had not one / good officer along with him: his dependance was upon his own stratagems, Sullivan's schemes, and the bravery of the Highlanders, or the alertness of those who should join. And here an account of the Northern part of the United Kingdom may be expected.

That part of the united kingdom, called Scotland, is about 240 miles long, and 200 broad: not but in some places it is broader†; but I only speak of it at a medium. It contains 940 parishes, and the inhabitants of these amount to the number of 1,500,000 persons, the clergy, women and children included. The country abounds every-where with rivers, which yield prodigious quantities of excellent salmon; its extended coast from south to north is one continued white fishery, and its southern and western, is no less remarkable for herrings, which sometimes draw great numbers of

* This man's spouse had suckled the young Pretender, which was the reason of his being knighted.

† The northern point of Caithness is distant from the Mull of Cantire 240 miles. /

people from every quarter. Many rich mines of coal, of iron and of lead are to be found within the bowels of its mountains. The southern parts are productive of wheat, and yield excellent pastures. How unhappy for the Adventurer to expect an army from those, and at the same time to take the most unlikely method to procure it. He came among them with a crowd of Highlanders; people no less disagreeable to the well-peopled counties in the lower part of the kingdom, than the Sclavonian Pandours are to the citizens of Vienna, or the superstitious Laplanders to the inhabitants and burghers of Stockholm. Their dress, though the nearest to that of the old Romans, was no way agreeable to the people of the south of Scotland; and yet the Chevalier, though born in the middle of Italy, had one made for him, and put it on.

This popularity in the remote parts did him no service as he advanced. Indeed some of the name of Macgregor, a clan who had been outlawed for robbery and murder ever since the year 1430, joined him in his way to Perth; but in this place he might begin to guess at his unhappy situation.

If we take a view of North Britain, it may be ranged under four divisions. The eastern, which extends from Berwick upon Tweed to Edinburgh; the western, which begins there, and, passing along the Forth, reaches to the utmost limits of Argyleshire; the southern, which proceeds from Edinburgh to Solway Forth; and the northern, which, according to some, stretches from the Forth to the Orkneys.

No person acquainted with the southern division can have the least doubt of the loyalty of its inhabitants. Scarce can one among a thousand be found in those parts in the least tinctured with Jacobitism. Out of the shires of Roxburgh and Selkirk, which contain about one hundred thousand inhabitants, only three were concerned in the rebellion: two of whom were delirious, and the third had been carried over into Spain in his infancy. Out of Annandale was only one. His misfortune arose from his situation: he was a prisoner for debt when the Pretender arrived at Carlisle: the prison doors were set open: the prisoners joined him; but embraced the first opportunity of quitting his service: they all left him at Penrith. From Kircudbright, Wigtoun, and Lanerk were none; from the shires of Berwick and Haddingtoun were three, and from Peebles were only two; so far as I could find upon the strictest enquiry. And these districts put together contain about six hundred thousand inhabitants. /

Between the southern and western division lies the shire of Edinburgh; which being a place of public resort, especially the city, cannot be free from disaffected people. However, the Loyalists are by far the most numerous: and this county, including the metropolis, contains about one hundred thousand inhabitants.

From Edinburgh we may pass to the western district, which includes the shires of Linlithgow, Galloway, Stirling, Dumbarton, Renfrew, Air, Bute, and Argyle; the inhabitants of which may be about four hundred thousand: and have generally been so remarkable for their true revolution principles, that no people have endured more hardships under a tyrannical government than their forefathers. The clans, the ancestors of those who lately appeared in arms against the government, were brought from the isles, and remote places of the kingdom, to live upon free quarters among them. The memory of the havock and desolation caused by them, was not wholly obliterated.

Out of the most wealthy of the western shires there was not a single man in the Pretender's army. On the contrary, many of them appeared in arms for the Government.

We cannot indeed say so much for the loyalty of the inhabitants in the northern division: yet the spirit of disaffection has greatly abated even in these counties, where the same was most notorious and palpable. We shall give a short sketch of these, that the reader may better understand the state and genius of the country: and though I cannot be of opinion, that the shire of Fife, so remarkable for her antient heroes of old, and for her industrious inhabitants at this time, is a part of the north division, yet I must begin with it, as it is / the first county that occurs after crossing the Forth.

The shire of Fife, in proportion to its extent, is full as populous* as any in England, Middlesex only excepted. It abounds with all the necessaries of life, and enjoys many natural advantages. There are inexhaustible mines of coal and pits of salt; of which the Fordel coal is the most intire and cleanly, and burns more brightly than the best Newcastle coal. The natives are devoted to trade and manufactory. Scarce ten persons joined the Highlanders from her populous districts. On the contrary, many armed against them. Passing from Fife we enter the shire of Forfar, where the people, though generally averse to Presbyterian government, were not averse to his Majesty King George; the people of property are to a man well affected,

* It contains 200,000 inhabitants.

and the commonalty so devoted to labour and an industrious way of life, that they want to live in peace and in quietness. Many of them withstood the most awful threatenings to join the Pretender's standard.

Though the counties which lie beyond the Esk, the utmost boundary of the shire of Forfar, may be branded with disloyalty more than their neighbours, yet it is very remarkable, that out of the shires of Kincardin, Aberdeen, Bamff, Murray, and Nairn there were not eight hundred who joined the insurgents. The shire of Inverness was the next where the bulk of them has brandished their arms. The Isles had augmented the rebellious corps; about two thousand from Perthshire crowned the head of the rebellious standard, and a few from Rossshire and Cromarty supported it. And even in these remote places were to be found numbers / of persons extremely well affected: as in the shire of Sutherland, which is exceeding poor; and in the shire of Caithness, which, though the remotest in Scotland, is yet so plentiful, that I doubt if there be a county in the King's dominions which abounds more with the comforts and necessaries of life, and whose natives are more given to hospitality.

Happy for the Pretender that he had known the country. He was deceived by others, and indeed he deceived himself: and yet his schemes were hitherto so successful, as not a little to animate such as had joined him.

His chief encouragement proceeded from the little resistance which he met with from the King's forces. 'Tis indeed true, that they were too far off to attack the corps that first set up his standard. The real services done him by Sir John Cope, the then lieutenant-general of the King's forces in Scotland, were beyond the most sanguine expectation of his friends. That officer had never taken care to support the grandeur and dignity of a commander in chief. Being of a phlegmatic temper, he was ready to discover an uncommon degree of fire and warmth upon trivial occasions. I have seen him come to the Court of Justiciary*, in order to kill a tedious hour, but in a dress far below that of an ordinary gentleman, and almost unattended. Unmoved at the hints which might have arisen in the mind of a man of the least sagacity, he did nothing in consequence of the seizing† Sir Hector / Maclean and Bleau of Castlehill; nor did he

* The highest in Scotland.

† June 5th 1745. This Sir Hector was the son of Sir John Maclean, a chieftan who had taken up arms against King William and against King George I. He was an officer in the French service, came over to Scotland with letters wrote in French, and in short hand. The very circumstance of his hiding the letters, when apprehended, was a sufficient suspicion.

exert himself to get the troops together, although sollicited thereto by the officers of state, and by the Earl of Hume: though Sir Duncan Campbell sent an express to Edinburgh, with an account that the Pretender was landed, yet he did not march so soon as he might have done. In short, the Adventurer was eighteen days openly in the country before Cope began to stir; and even after he had begun his march with the forces, who it must be owned were but about 1500 foot, mostly new-raised men, supported with only six pieces of cannon, he by his motions gave them all the time and intimation they possibly could wish for: and, as if afraid that they should not have proper intelligence, he at Daalnacardach, where the extended desart between Athol and Ruthven begins, drew up his men, made them fire their pieces in the air, in order, as he gave out, to see if they were fit for action. This done he marched forward toward Dalguiny, where he was within six miles of the Insurgents; and here in a council of war his opinion prevailed, neither to march against the enemy, who was ill armed and not supported with cannon, nor yet to return and stop their progress into the low country. He passed by them, and thus left them a free and open passage to march, if they pleased, to the metropolis.

When the Chevalier was informed of this false step of the General, he seemed to be elevated with a joy which he was at no pains to conceal; and, drinking Cope's health in a bumper of brandy, he said, 'If all the Usurper's officers act like him, I shall soon be at St. James's.' From that day the two armies widened their distance: the Royalists proceeded to Inverness, and the Highlanders advanced to Blair of Athol, and from thence to / Perth, which the Chevalier entered in triumph, and ordered his manifestoes to be proclaimed.

While in this place, he was joined by some people of desperate fortunes, such as Mercer of Aldie, Oliphant of Gask, and Sir John Wedderburn; but, to his great misfortune, the gentlemen of Fife quitted their own houses, sent their plate to the castle of Edinburgh, and laid the strongest injunctions upon their tenants and dependants not to join the army of the young Chevalier.

Of the number of these brave gentlemen was Lieutenant-general Philip Preston, then governor of the castle of Edinburgh, an officer of great experience, and whose behaviour had been every way agreeable in the wars of Queen Anne; the gentlemen of the name of Anstruther, and Sir Robert Henderson of Fordel followed their cousin General Preston's example.

This Sir Robert is the lineal representative of a very antient family, not only connected in blood with the first and greatest in the county, but linked to them by the more strong and lasting ties of friendship, correspondence, and a generous deportment. The bravery of this family has been displayed in foreign countries, their distinguissied merit has shone in several reigns, and their loyalty stands untainted: many of its branches have been regaled in Sweden, in Denmark, in Germany, and in France. One of them was commander of the first Scots guard* that was established in France; a corps to whose fidelity the sacred persons of their kings were entrusted. Another of the descendants contributed greatly to gain the battle of Lutzen, on which depended the Protestant cause. / Nor is he himself the unworthy son of such famous and renowned ancestors; for not to insist upon the most amiable disposition, and the most endearing generosity of heart, he has had eyes to see what lay hid from ages, goodness to improve it to the best advantage, and a spirit to carry it into execution for the public utility; he has, on his own charges, built an harbour, at a place† which had not so much as a name! And future ages cannot fail gratefully to remember the man who did so much for preventing shipwrecks, for saving a number of lives; and who in the period when the Government could best distinguish her friends from her enemies, set the most bright and striking example of loyalty to his fellow subjects; for in that whole county there was not a single man of the least property who joined the young Chevalier: which might be the reason why his friends and followers treated the country people there with the greater harshness and severity, for being now in Perth, they began to spread themselves by detachments into the adjacent villages.

On the 7th of Sept. a party of Clanranald's regiment entered Dundee, proclaimed the Pretender, searched the town for arms, horses, and ammunition, and levied the public money. In this excursion a ship with gunpowder was seized: it was carried up the Tay to Perth, and there unloaded for the Pretender's service. Other parties visited the towns‡ of Fife, where they rifled the merchants shops; and, carrying the goods to the Pretender, he ordered that the same should be restored to their respective

* It took its name from a company of young gentlemen who accompanied Margaret, Princess of Scotland, when she went to be married to Lewis XII. 1430.

† Capernaum.

‡ There are in this county fourteen large corporation towns, besides many extensive and populous villages.

owners, on their paying the third part of their price. The noblemen and gentlemens houses / were visited by them; money was demanded with impunity, arms and ammunition were laid hold on, the cattle were driven from the parks and inclosures, while the corn and the straw of the farmer and labourer were seized. All was in confusion from these proceedings, and the country was drowned in amazement and surprize.

Such was the situation of the Chevalier's affairs, when General Cope, after a stay of five days at Inverness, for refreshing his men from the fatigues they had endured, thought of the necessity of marching southward. He had indeed concerted means with Duncan Forbes, president of the court of session, for using such means as might be of the greatest efficacy for hindering the Adventurer's army from being recruited, which was so far prudent and wise. In other things he acted without thought, and fell into the mistake of despising the enemy, and of declaring his contempt to the gentlemen who proffered their service to the Government. He called the Highlanders a raw banditti; without considering, that the bulk of his own soldiers were raw new-raised men: nor did he so much as thank the people who offered to join the King's forces.

On the 4th of September he set out for Aberdeen, where, according to his own desire, there were transports ready to conduct the troops under his command to Leith: and, though the poor people of the districts through which he passed did every thing in their power to support the spirits and courage of the soldiers, and the noblemen and gentlemen did whatever could be expected toward rendering the march agreeable to him and the officers, yet he ordered the encampment to be fixed amidst the ripe standing corn, contrary to the remonstrances both of the proprietors and of the / soldiers themselves. In this march Captain Munro accompanied him, with two hundred of his name.

On the 11th of September, the day the Chevalier set out from Perth, the army arrived at Aberdeen; where they halted till the 15th, when they embarked on board the transports, that had been sent to bring them up. They sailed for Leith; and, entering the Forth on the 17th, they had information, that the Pretender's army had got possession of Edinburgh, where his manifestoes had been proclaimed: an account which determined him to divert his course to Dunbar, where that night the forces were disembarked, in order to march as soon as possible against the enemy; who, in consequence of the fatal steps taken by the King's officers, had made a surprising progress.

For having intelligence of the sailing of the transports to Aberdeen, and of the march of the troops from Inverness, they set out from Perth on the 11th, and on the 18th forded the Forth at the Frew, where Colonel Gardiner's dragoons made a shew to oppose them; had Gardiner been in his vigour, as formerly, he might with his single regiment have prevented their passing over; had the dragoons alighted, and marched with two pieces of cannon, which might soon have been brought from the castle of Stirling to the brink of the river, it is scarcely possible to imagine that the insurgents, without artillery, and even without arms, would have attempted it; many of them had only pitchforks, and were without firelocks: however, the Colonel was valetudinary; fame had magnified the number of the enemy, and he did not chuse to run any hazards; he retired before them to Edinburgh, and they followed but slowly after him. The fruitless parade made by the citizens only tended to animate the insurgents, and to furnish / them with arms. The citizens, in an amazement, called a council upon what was proper to be done; every one spoke as he pleased; the disaffected magnified the danger, and filled the friends of the government with fear; the soldiers of the city guard were the most abject and most paltry of wretches; Maitland their officer, who died mad, was an infamous bankrupt, addicted to drunkenness and hypocrisy, a coward, and unacquainted with discipline. By protracting the time in sending out deputies to the Chevalier, and receiving messages from him, the night was turned, and the morning began to appear. A coachman, who had carried one of these deputations, was urgent to get out of the town. At his earnest entreaty the port was opened, and the Clan Cameron instantly rushed in, seized on the centries, and marching directly to the guard-house, they laid hold not only of the arms belonging to the town-guard, but also of all that they found in the hands of the volunteers and trained bands; a very fortunate circumstance indeed for them, and which paved a way for the easy victory that was gained on the fourth day thereafter.

Before five in the morning both the city and suburbs were occupied, and they began to supply themselves with such necessaries as they wanted; clothes, linen, shoes, and bonnets, were prepared for their use, and the armourers rubbed up their weapons; the generality of them were in very ragged attire, having only a short coat of coarse tartan, a pair of plaid hose much worn, reaching scarce above the calf of the leg, their plaids and bonnets in the same condition.

By eight in the morning the adventurer arrived at Duddingston, having fetched an half compass about the city for fear of the guns from the castle, / and about nine he entered the palace of Holyroodhouse, Perth riding on his right, and Lord Elcho, who had joined him the night before, on his left hand; the multitude huzzaed as he passed along, and he seemed extremely well pleased with his reception. He was a slender young man, about five feet ten inches high, of a ruddy complexion, high nosed, large rolling brown eyes, long visaged; his chin was pointed, and his mouth small in proportion to his other features; his hair was red, but at that time he wore a pale peruke; he was in an Highland habit, with a blue sash wrought with gold coming over his shoulder, red velvet breeches, a green velvet bonnet with a gold lace round it, and a white cockade, which was the cross of St. Andrew; he wore a silver hilted broad sword, was booted, and had a pair of pistols before him: his speech seemed to have more of the English than the Scottish accent, and no way painful and distorted, as that of a foreigner generally is.

Before closing this account I cannot but declare, that if an officer of the Duke of Cumberland's spirit had been there with one single well appointed regiment, he would have dispersed them. But where is such an one as his Highness? One of far less abilities than he might have routed them.

Every thing having succeeded so well, the Chevalier's first care was to publish his father's and his own manifestoes: the heralds were seized, and proceeded to the cross in their robes, with a trumpeter blowing a trumpet before them; and while the Clan Cameron surrounded the cross in three divisions, the doors and windows were crowded with spectators of the unusual scene; the following manifestoes were read over, which, however well understood by the spectators, sure I am the fortieth / man of the encircling guard did not know a single sentence of them.

His MAJESTY'S *most gracious Declaration.*
JAMES R.

JAMES VIII. by the grace of God, King of Scotland, England, France, and Ireland, Defender of the Faith, &c. To all our loving subjects of what degree or quality soever. Greeting.

Having always borne the most constant affection to our ancient kingdom of Scotland, from whence we derive our royal origin, and where our progenitors have swayed the sceptre with glory, through a longer succession of kings than any monarchy upon earth can at this day boast of, we cannot but behold, with the deepest concern, the miseries they suffer under a foreign usurpation, and the intolerable burdens daily added to their yoke, which become yet more sensible to us, when we consider the constant zeal and affection the generality of our subjects of that our ancient kingdom have expressed for us on all occasions, and particularly when we had the satisfaction of being ourselves among them.

We see a nation always famous for valour, and highly esteemed by the greatest of foreign potentates, reduced to the condition of a province, under the specious pretence of an union with a more powerful neighbour. In consequence of this pretended union, grievous and unprecedented taxes have been laid on and levied with severity, in spight of all the representations that could be made to the contrary; and these have not failed to produce that poverty and decay of trade, which were easily foreseen to be the necessary consequences of such oppressive measures. /

To prevent the just resentment which could not but arise from such usage, our faithful Highlanders, a people always trained up and inured to arms, have been deprived of them: forts and citadels have been built and garrisoned, where no foreign invasion could be apprehended, and a military government has been effectually introduced, as into a conquered country. It is easy to foresee what must be the consequences of such violent and unprecedented proceedings, if a timely remedy be not put to them; neither is it less manifest, that such a remedy can ever be obtained, but by our restoration to the throne of our ancestors, into whose royal hearts such destructive maxims could never find admittance.

We think it needless to call to mind how sollicitous we have ever been, and how often we have ventured our royal person, to compass this great end, which the divine Providence seems now to have furnished us with the means of doing effectually, by enabling our good subjects in England to shake off the yoke under which they have likeways felt their share of the common calamities. Our former experience leaves us no room to doubt of the chearful and hearty concurrence of our Scots subjects on this occasion, towards the perfecting the great and glorious work: but that none may be deterred, by the memory of past miscarriages, from returning to their duty, and being restored to the happiness they formerly enjoyed, we, in this public manner, think fit to make known our gracious intentions towards all our people.

We do therefore, by this our royal declaration, absolutely and effectually pardon and remit all treasons, and other crimes hitherto committed against our royal father or ourselves: from the benefit of which pardon we except none, but such / as shall, after the publication hereof, wilfully and maliciously oppose us, or those, who shall appear, or endeavour to appear, in arms for our service.

We farther declare, that we will, with all convenient speed, call a free parliament, that, by the advice and assistance of such an assembly, we may be enabled to repair the breaches caused by so long an usurpation, to redress all grievances, and to free our people from the unsupportable burden of the malt-tax, and all other hardships and impositions which have been the consequences of the pretended union, that so the nation may be restored to that honour, liberty, and independency, which it formerly enjoyed.

We likeways promise, upon our Royal word, to protect, secure, and maintain all our Protestant subjects in the free exercise of their religion, and in the full enjoyment of all their rights, privileges, and immunities, and in the secure possession of all churches, universities, colleges, and schools, that conform to the laws of the land.

All this we shall be ready to confirm in our first parliament, in which we promise to pass any act or acts that shall be judged necessary to secure each private person in the full possession of his liberty and property, to advance trade, to relieve the poor, and establish the general welfare and tranquillity of the nation: in all such matters we are fully resolved to act always by the advice of our parliament, and to value none of our titles so much, as that of *Common Father of our People,* which we shall ever shew ourselves to be, by our constant endeavours to promote the quiet and happiness of all our subjects. And we shall be particularly sollicitous to settle, encourage, and maintain the fishery and linen manufactory of the nation, which we are sensible may be of such advantage to it, and / which, we hope, are works reserved for us to accomplish.

As for those who shall appear more signally zealous for the recovery of our just rights, and the prosperity of their country, we shall take effectual care to reward them according to their respective degrees and merits. And we particularly promise, as aforesaid, our full, free, and general pardon to all officers, soldiers and sailors, now engaged in the service of the usurper, whether of the sea or land, provided that, upon the publication hereof, and before they engage in any fight or battle against our forces, they quit the said unjust and unwarrantable service, and return to their duty: in which case we shall pay them all the arrears that shall be at that time due to them from the usurper: we shall grant to the officers the same commissions they shall then bear, if not higher; and to all soldiers and sailors a gratification of a whole year's pay, for their forwardness in promoting our service.

We farther promise and declare, that the vassals of such as shall, without regard to our present declaration, obstinately persist in their rebellion, and thereby forfeit all pretensions to our Royal clemency, shall be delivered from all servitude they were formerly bound to, and shall have grants and charters of their lands to be held immediately of the crown, provided they, upon the publication of this our declaration, declare openly for us, and join heartily in the cause of their country.

And having thus declared our gracious intentions to our loving subjects, we do hereby require and command them to be assisting to us in the recovery of our rights, and of their own liberties: and that all our subjects, from the age of sixteen to sixty, do, upon the setting up of our Royal / standard, immediately repair to it, or join themselves to such as shall first appear for us in their respective shires; and also to seize the horses and arms of all suspected persons, and all ammunition, forage, and whatever else may be necessary for the use of our forces.

We also strictly command all receivers, collectors, or other persons, who may be seised of any sum or sums of money, levied in the name or for the use of the usurper, to retain such sum or sums of money in their own hands, till they can pay them to some person of distinction appearing publicly for us, and demanding the same for our use and service, whose receipt or receipts shall be a sufficient discharge for all such collectors, receivers, or other persons, their heirs, &c.

Lastly, We do hereby require all sheriffs of shires, stewards of stewartries, and their respective deputies, magistrates of Royal boroughs, and bailies of regalities, and all others to whom it may belong, to publish this our declaration at the market-crosses of their respective towns and boroughs, and there to proclaim us, under the penalty of being proceeded against according to law, for their neglect of so necessary and important a duty.

Given at our Court at Rome the 23d day of December 1743, in the forty-third year of our reign.

J. R.

JAMES R.

WHEREAS we have a near prospect of being restored to the throne of our ancestors, by the good inclinations of our subjects towards us; and whereas, on account of the present situation of this country, it will be absolutely impossible for us to be in person at the first setting up of our / Royal standard, and even some time after; we therefore esteem it for our service, and the good of our kingdoms and dominions, to nominate and appoint, as we hereby nominate, constitute and appoint, our dearest son CHARLES Prince of Wales, to be sole regent of our kingdoms of England, Scotland, and Ireland, and of all other our dominions during our absence. It is our will and intention, that our said dearest son should enjoy and exercise all that power and authority, which, according to the ancient constitution of our kingdoms, has been enjoyed and exercised by former regents. Requiring all our faithful subjects to give all due submission and obedience to our regent aforesaid, as immediately representing our Royal person, and acting by our authority. And we do hereby revoke all commissions of regency granted to any person or persons whatsoever. And lastly, We hereby dispense with all formalities, and other omissions that may be herein contained, declaring this our commission to be as firm and valid, to all intents and purposes, as if it had passed our great seals, and as if it were according to the usual stile and forms.

Given under our sign manual and privy signet at our Court at Rome the 23d day of December 1743, in the forty-third year of our reign.

(L.S.) J. R.

CHARLES P. R.

BY virtue and authority of the above commission of regency, granted unto us by the King our Royal father, we are now come to execute his Majesty's will and pleasure, by setting up his Royal / standard, and asserting his undoubted right to the throne of his ancestors.

We do therefore, in his Majesty's name, and pursuant to the tenor of his several declarations, hereby grant a free, full and general pardon for all treasons, rebellions, and offences whatsoever, committed at any time before the publication hereof, against our Royal grandfather, his present Majesty, and ourselves. To the benefit of this pardon we shall deem justly intitled all such of his Majesty's subjects, as shall testify their willingness to accept of it, either by joining our forces with all convenient diligence, by setting up his Royal standard in other places, by repairing for our service to any places where it shall be set up; or, at least, by openly renouncing all allegiance to the usurper, and all obedience to his orders; or to those of any person or persons commissioned or employed by him, or acting avowedly for him.

As for those who shall appear more signally zealous for the recovery of his Majesty's just rights, and the prosperity of their country, we shall take effectual care to have them rewarded according to their respective degrees and merits; and we particularly promise, as aforesaid, a full, free, and general pardon to all officers, soldiers, and sailors now engaged in the service of the usurper, provided that, upon the publication hereof, and before they engage in any fight or battle against his Majesty's forces, they quit the said unjust and unwarrantable service, and return to their duty; since they cannot but be sensible, that no engagements, entered into with a foreign usurper, can dispense with the allegiance they owe to their natural sovereign. And, as a farther encouragement to them to comply with their duty and our commands, we promise to every such officer, the same, or a higher / post in our service, than that which at present he enjoys, with full payment of whatever arrears may be due to him at the time of his declaring for us, and to every soldier, trooper, and dragoon, who shall join us, as well as to every seaman and mariner of the fleet, who shall declare for and serve us, all their arrears, and a whole year's pay to be given to each of them as a gratuity, as soon as ever the kingdoms shall be in a state of tranquillity.

We do hereby farther promise and declare, in his Majesty's name, and by virtue of the abovesaid commission, that, as soon as ever that happy state is obtained, he will, by and with the advice of a free parliament, wherein no corruption, nor undue influence whatsoever, shall be used to bias the votes of the electors or elected, settle, confirm, and secure all the rights, ecclesiastical and civil, of each of his respective kingdoms; his Majesty being fully resolved to maintain the Church of England as by law established, and likewise the Protestant Churches of Scotland and Ireland conformable to the laws of each respective kingdom, together with a toleration to all Protestant Dissenters; he being utterly averse to all persecution and oppression whatsoever, particularly on account of conscience and religion. And we ourselves, being perfectly convinced of the reasonableness and equity of the same principles, do, in consequence hereof, farther promise and declare, that all his Majesty's subjects shall be, by him and us, maintained in the full enjoyment and possession of all their rights, privileges, and immunities, and especially of all churches, universities, colleges, and schools, conformable to the laws of the land, which shall ever be the unalterable rule of his Majesty's government, and our own actions. /

And, that this our undertaking may be accompanied with as little present inconveniency as possible to the King's subjects, we do hereby authorize and require all civil officers and magistrates, now in place and office, to continue, till farther orders, to execute their respective employments in our name and by our authority, as far as may be requisite for the maintenance of common justice, order, and quiet; willing and requiring them, at the same time, to give strict obedience to such orders and directions as may from time to time be issued out by us, or those who shall be vested with any share of our authority and power.

We also command and require all officers of the revenue, customs and excise, all tax-gatherers of what denomination soever, and all others who may have any part of the public money in their hands, to deliver it immediately to some principal commander authorized by us, and take his receipt for the same, which shall be to them a sufficient discharge; and, in case of refusal, we authorize and charge all such our commanders to exact the same for our use, and to be accountable for it to us, or our officers for that purpose appointed.

And having thus sincerely, and in the presence of Almighty God, declared the true sentiments and intentions of the King our Royal father, as well as our own, in this expedition, we do hereby require and command all his loving subjects to be assisting to us in the recovery of his just rights, and of their own liberties: and that all such, from the age of sixteen to sixty, do forthwith repair to his Majesty's Royal standard, or join themselves to such as shall first appear in their respective shires for his service: and also seize the horses and arms of all suspected persons, and all ammunition, / forage, and all whatever else may be necessary for the use of our forces.

Lastly, We do hereby require all mayors, sheriffs, and other magistrates of what denomination soever, their respective deputies, and all others to whom it may belong, to publish this our declaration at the market-crosses of their respective cities, towns and boroughs, and there to proclaim his Majesty, under the penalty of being proceeded against according to law, for the neglect of so necessary and important a duty. For as we have hereby graciously and sincerely offered a free and general pardon for all that is passed, so we, at the same time, seriously warn all his Majesty's subjects, that we shall leave to the rigour of the law, all those who shall from henceforth oppose us, or wilfully and deliberately do or concur in any act or acts civil or military, to the lett or detriment of us, our cause or title, or to the destruction, prejudice, or annoyance of those, who shall, according to their duty and our intentions thus publicly signified, declare and act for us.

Given at Paris the 16th of May 1745.

C. P. R.

It is needless to take up the reader's time in a confutation of these papers, or of those of the 22d of August, the 9th and 10th of October 1745, as this has been so frequently and so judiciously done: 'They were,' said Sir William Young, 'an abridgment of the many scandalous libels*, calumnies, and falshoods published against this constitution and government,' and were, in obedience to an order of the House of Peers, with / the hearty concurrence of the Commons, burnt by the hands of the common hangman.

The resolution of the Two Houses of Parliament is too important not to be inserted here, especially as the same was not the effect of a sudden transport of passion, but of the utmost deliberation and coolness; for on the 6th of November they were read in the House of Lords, when a committee was appointed to consider them, and to prepare a commentary upon them, which was to be communicated to the House of Commons, who were desired to come to a conference in the Painted Chamber at three o'clock in the afternoon of next day; the desire was agreed to, a number was named, and met the Lords at the time appointed; and the resolution being laid before the whole, it was unanimously confirmed and ratified. The tenor of which is as follows:

Resolved,

'By the Lords Spiritual and Temporal, and Commons, in Parliament assembled, that the two papers respectively signed James R. and dated at

* See Lord Lovat's Trial, p. 16.

Rome the 23d day of December 1743, and the four printed papers signed Charles P. R. dated respectively the 16th day of May 1745, August the 22d 1745, the 9th day of October 1745, and the 10th day of October 1745, are false, scandalous, and traitorous libels, intended to poison the minds of his Majesty's subjects; containing the most malicious, audacious, and wicked incitements to them to commit the most abominable treasons; groundless and infamous calumnies and indignities against the government, crown, and sacred person of his most excellent Majesty King George II. our only rightful and undoubted sovereign; and seditious and / presumptuous declarations against the constitution of this united kingdom; representing the High Court of Parliament, now legally assembled by his Majesty's authority, as an unlawful assembly; and all the acts of parliament, passed since the late happy revolution, as null and void; and that the said printed papers are full of the utmost arrogance and insolent affronts to the honour of the British nation, in supposing that his Majesty's subjects are capable of being imposed upon, seduced or terrified, by false and opprobrious invectives, insidious promises, or vain and impotent menaces; or of being deluded to exchange the free enjoyment of their rights and liberties, as well civil as religious, under the well-established government of a Protestant Prince, for popery and slavery under a Popish bigotted Pretender, long since excluded by the wisest laws made to secure our excellent constitution, and abjured by the most solemn oaths.'

Resolved,

'By the Lords Spiritual and Temporal, and Commons, in Parliament assembled, that, in abhorrence and detestation of such vile and treasonable practices, the said several printed papers be burnt by the hands of the common hangman, at the Royal Exchange at London, on Tuesday the 12th day of this instant November, at one of the clock in the afternoon; and that the sheriffs of London do then attend, and cause the same to be burnt there accordingly.' These orders were punctually obeyed, amidst the repeated acclamations of a prodigious multitude.

The declarations being read, which sufficiently pointed out the intentions of the adventurer, and / the spirit of his party, he next day sent to the magistrates of Edinburgh a paper, requiring, on pain of military execution, 1000 tents, 2000 targets, 6000 pair of shoes, and a proportionable number of white iron cantines, against the 23d; all which was furnished at the time appointed.

Next day an order was read over the cross, 'requiring all the inhabitants of the city and suburbs, and of the county of Mid-Lothian, to give up at their own expence the whole arms and ammunition in their custody, under pain of being deemed as rebels, and treated as such.' This order was likewise obeyed, and to strengthen himself still further, a drum beat up for soldiers in the Pretender's name: whoever could raise 40 men was to be made a captain, and whoever could bring 20 men into the field was to have a lieutenant's commission. This encouragement had its effect also; for many raw and unexperienced young men, of no prospect or fortunes, had commissions given them: but indeed there was not a proportionable number of private men; all wanted to be officers; they were anxious about preferment, and desirous to command.

Among other advantages reaped from getting possession of the city of Edinburgh, that of obtaining the printing-houses was not the least: one Drummond had already printed his declarations, and now the news paper, known by the name of the Caledonian Mercury, was by its conductor, James Grant, a Roman Catholic, moulded to his mind. The Chevalier was represented as another Charles XII. of Sweden, with this superior difference, that the former was more cool and deliberate than he. When the King's Speech came out, though as fine a one as ever came from a throne, it was commented on, and called 'The / Elector of Hanover's Speech to his pretended Parliament.'

While the flame of rebellion was burning with unusual fierceness, and while the flashes thereof daily increased, Cope was at Dunbar joined by the volunteers of the city of Edinburgh, and by two regiments of dragoons under Brigadier Fowkes, who had lately come from England to command them.

The Earl of Hume, with other noblemen and gentlemen, did every thing in their power to render his expedition agreeable; they furnished the troops with every thing necessary, and procured intelligence of the enemy's motions; nor indeed were these behind them in that particular, for on the very night of their debarking, one John Stuart, commonly called Roy, from the redness of his hair, mingled with the country people, and in the habit of a farmer counted them as they stepped on shore, or advanced to the place of rendezvous. This Roy Stuart was extremely well adapted to any undertaking, however arduous or desperate: he had been a serjeant in one of the independent Highland companies, afterward quarter-master in the regiment of Greys, and at this time captain of grenadiers in Lord John Drummond's battalion; he had carried on the correspondence between the Pretender and Lord Lovat, and now in hopes of making his fortune, he went on board a ship from Holland, landed at Harwich, and without stopping, arrived in the camp of the adventurer.

As Cope had resolved to beat up the Pretender's quarters, so he set out for Haddington on the 19th, the very day on which the insurgents were strengthened by 350 of the name of Grant from Glenmoriston. At Haddington the army was received in the most affectionate manner, not only by the / towns people, but by those of the adjacent villages; and being extremely well accommodated, they next day marched westward to meet the enemy, who that very morning had set out from Edinburgh to give battle to the King's forces. These, to their great misfortune, instead of marching to the Esk, and planting a battery of cannon upon the bridge thereof, halted on a corn field near Prestonpans, in order to wait for the enemy. Here they were regaled by the country people, and dined plentifully; but scarce was dinner over, when the Chevalier appeared with 2500 men, but without any kind of artillery, on the side of a hill, directly to the southward of them. Both sides raised an huzza, and now was the time for Cope to attack, while it was the business of the enemy to wait patiently till the twilight, if not till the dawn of the morning: the latter was what actually happened; for after spending a night of silence, about three in the morning they crossed through some inclosures, and coming upon the flank of Cope's lines, they attacked them with hideous acclamations, gave them a full fire all at once, and then run in sword in hand. The dragoons, startled at the noise, fled off all at once, and disordered their own infantry, which at this time was overpowered: the onset was so sudden, that in less than a minute the rout was total, and the carnage became terrible indeed, the Highlanders pursuing the poor soldiers with unspeakable fierceness and antipathy; many of them being cut in pieces as they were clambering over some inclosures for their lives; others were overtaken, and cut in the most inhuman manner by broad swords and Lochaber axes, the authority of the officers being unable to restrain their rage. /

In this battle about 360 of the King's troops were killed, among whom were the pious Colonel James Gardner, five captains, and one ensign.

There were about 500 wounded, among whom were Lieutenant-colonel Whitney, and Major Bowles of Hamilton's dragoons. The fate of this last worthy gentleman was every way deplorable: they had cut him cruelly in eleven different places, and perhaps would have finished him, had not O'Sullivan accidentally come by, when the Major said to him, 'Sir, you seem to be an officer and a gentleman, pray don't suffer them to use me so cruelly, for you See I am disarmed.' The Master of Torphichen was treated in much the same manner. About 83 officers were taken prisoners, and several of these were wounded or hurt, with about 1150 private men: all the rest being either killed or wounded. And this with little loss on the side of the Pretender's army; of whom there were only two captains, one lieutenant, and one ensign killed, with about forty private men, and eighty wounded. The artillery, consisting of six pieces of cannon and two cohorns, fell into their hands, as did all the tents, the military chest, with Cope's baggage, and the equipage of the other officers. Four thousand and ninety pounds were only found in the military chest, the rest being secured in the Fox man of war, or at Haddington; which was the only prudent step that had been taken during this inglorious campaign. The dragoons lost no more than fifty, including killed, wounded, and prisoners. And thus was an army of about 1624 foot, mostly raw men, and but raised in the summer before, with two regiments of dragoons, destroyed almost in the twinkling of an eye, meerly through the sullen behaviour and headstrong obstinacy of a general officer; who rode to Lauder / with the shattered part of the dragoons, and from thence proceeded by himself to London, to be the messenger of his own disaster. On the 29th he appeared at St. James's, where the eyes of the whole court were fixed upon him; and the King coming into the drawing-room said, 'Well Cope, I have heard lately much about you. Has there been a battle?' Being answered, with a profound reverence, 'there has;' his Majesty replied, 'I see you are safe and sound; but what's become of my men?' To this he was incapable of giving a sensible answer; which the Sovereign observing, he turned upon his heel, and, with a visible concern, directed his discourse to another person; and never after consulted him in any plan of operation. While Cope was at London, the living witness of his own shame, and while the wounded, who had escaped from the enemy, carried the dismal marks of a brutal fury in the numerous and inhuman cuts they had received, the Chevalier was at Holyrood-house, increasing his party and forwarding his cause.

The consequences of a battle are not to be judged of, from the number of the slain, or from a passage that may be opened to a fortress which one army was desirous to besiege, and another wanted to relieve. More substantial advantages flowed from the defeat of the King's troops at Preston: almost the arms of the whole body of foot and of the volunteers, with several firelocks and broad swords belonging to the dragoons, fell into the hands of the victors, and these were distributed among the recruits, whom the Marquis of Tullibardin was sending up to them. The whole of North Britain was now in their power. Officers were chosen to act in the Pretender's name: tho' indeed none would undertake to act, except in the / places where there was a force sufficient to enjoin the orders: and this might be one of the reasons of his delaying to march into England. Parties were sent into different places to collect the public money, and to take up any arms that had been secreted. The goods in the custom-house of Leith were sold by auction; and in some places the land-tax was brought in: though it must be owned, many of the officers of the revenue quitted the kingdom, and carried off the money that was in their hands, to be delivered to those who had a better right to receive it. Five thousand guineas were raised from the citizens of Glasgow, and about as much from the gentlemen in the neighbourhood; whose bureaus were broke open, and repositories forcibly pulled down.

Such was the behaviour of the party whom he sent out; nor could he with all his address and policy palliate their conduct. A proclamation to make no rejoicing for the late victory, as it had been obtained by the blood of his Majesty's subjects, was highly extolled by his friends; while the following declaration opened the mouths of his enemies, but particularly the clergy, whose affection to the Government shone at this time with a surprizing lustre.

CHARLES *Prince of* Wales, *Regent of* Scotland, England, France, *and* Ireland, *and the Dominions thereunto belonging;*

WHEREAS we are informed, That several of our subjects, as well clergy as laity, in our antient city of Edinburgh, and neighbourhood thereof, did associate and take up arms against us; and that many of them fled from their houses, lest they had been prosecuted, and made examples of, as their crimes demerited: /

And whereas we have nothing at heart but the good of all our subjects, how much soever deluded by the prejudice of education or mistaken interest; and being always disposed, as a true father of our country, to display that mercy and tenderness natural to us, and the distinguishing characteristic of our family:

We do therefore, in his Majesty's name, hereby grant a full pardon to the persons associated as aforesaid, for all treasons, rebellions, and offences whatsoever, committed by them at any time before the publication of these presents, whether against our Royal Grandfather of blessed memory, his present Majesty, or ourselves, dispensing with the generality hereof, and admitting the same to be as effectual, to all intents and purposes, as if all their names had been herein set down. Provided always, that the persons aforesaid present themselves within twenty-four days after the publication hereof, to our trusty and beloved counsellor John Murray of Broughton esquire, our secretary, or any one of our council appointed for that purpose, at our palace of Holyrood-house, or where else we shall be for the time, with a declaration that they shall live for the future as quiet and peaceable subjects to us and our government, otherways these presents to be of no effect to them. Given at our palace of Holyrood-house, the twenty-fourth day of September, and of his Majesty's reign the forty-fifth year, 1745.

CHARLES, P. R.

By his Highness's command, Jo. Murray.

This declaration, which had for his own sake been better let alone, was productive of nothing advantageous to him; nor was the protection offered to the banks, if they would return from the / castle to their former business. His popularity in declaring, that if his scheme succeeded, 'Scotland should he his Hanover, the palace of Holyrood-house his Herenhausen,' was not believed: the bulk of the people were of the complexion formerly mentioned. Let the fewness of his followers, even after a regular army had been destroyed, speak their loyalty. And a fruitless attempt to reduce the castle of Edinburgh, by cutting off all communication with the country, tended to confirm them the more in their affection to the Government.

This daring enterprize, to which he was so unequal, was the occasion of the garrison's firing several cannon, for keeping the avenues clear: and yet it is observable, that no cannon were fired until General Guest, the then commander of the forces, had intimated, by a letter, his intention to the magistrates of the city; which when they carried to the Chevalier, he sent them the following reply, wrote by his own hand:

'Gentlemen,

'I am not a little surprized at the inhuman orders of the commanders of the castle of Edinburgh, and which, they say, they received from the Elector of Hanover. If he looked upon you as his subjects, he would never require of you what he knows to be out of your power to grant. It is impossible to prevent inconveniencies in cases of this nature; but I shall take care to have all sufferers indemnified, as soon as the public tranquillity is restored, and in the mean time shall make full reprisals upon the estates of all those who are abetters of the German Government.

C. P. R.' /

This chimerical blockade lasted but three days, when they laid hold of a packet from London, directed to the garrison of the fort, to spare the city as much as possible; but to keep the avenues clear, till the force destined for its relief should arrive among them. The Chevalier, to be before-hand with this gentle and pacific order, caused the following proclamation to be pasted up in the public places of the town.

'C. P. R.

'The Prince Regent taking into consideration the many murders committed upon the innocent inhabitants of the city of Edinburgh, has of his innate clemency, the distinguishing characteristic of his family, yielded to the supplications of the distressed, and considering that justice ought to give place to mercy, when the good of a people require it, he therefore takes the blockade off the castle, and commands, upon his part, all hostilities to cease.'

He ever affected to treat the person of his Majesty King George with indignity; and no sooner heard of the Parliament being summoned to meet Oct. 17th, than he emitted a declaration, discharging the same, and next day published his last manifesto.

CHARLES *Prince of* Wales, *&c. Regent of the Kingdoms of* England Scotland, France, *and* Ireland, *and the Dominions thereunto belonging: Unto all his Majesty's Subjects, of what degree soever, Greeting.*
CHARLES P. R.

As soon as we, conducted by the Providence of God, arrived in Scotland, and were joined by / a handful of our royal father's subjects, our first care was to make public his most gracious declaration; and, in consequence of the large powers by him vested in us, in quality of regent, we also emitted our own manifesto, explaining and enlarging the promises formerly made, according as we came to be better acquainted with the inclinations of the people of Scotland. Now that it has pleased God so far to smile on our undertaking, as to make us master of the antient kingdom of Scotland, we judge it proper, in this public manner, to make manifest what ought to fill the hearts of all his Majesty's subjects, of what nation and province soever, with comfort and satisfaction.

We therefore hereby, in his Majesty's name, declare, That his sole intention is to re-instate all his subjects in the full enjoyment of their religion, laws, and liberties; and that our present attempt is not undertaken in order to enslave a free people, but to redress and remove the encroachments made upon them; not to impose upon any a religion which they dislike, but to secure them all the enjoyment of those which are respectively at present established among them, either in England, Scotland, or Ireland; and if it shall be deemed proper that any further security be given to the established church or clergy, we hereby promise, in his name, That he shall pass any law that his Parliament shall judge necessary for that purpose.

In consequence of the rectitude of our royal Father's intentions, we must farther declare his sentiments with regard to the national debt: that it has been contracted under an unlawful government, nobody can disown, no more than that it is now a most heavy load upon the nation; yet, in regard that it is for the greatest part due to those very subjects whom he promises to protect, cherish and defend, / he is resolved to take the advice of his Parliament concerning it, in which he thinks he acts the part of a just prince, who makes the good of his people the sole rule of his actions.

Farthermore, we here in his name declare, That the same rule laid down for the funds, shall be followed with respect to every law or act of parliament since the revolution; and in so far as, in a free and legal parliament, they shall be approved, he will confirm them. With respect to the pretended union of the two nations, the King cannot possibly ratify it, since he has had repeated remonstrances against it from each kingdom; and since it is incontestible, that the principal point then in view, was the exclusion of the Royal Family from their undoubted right to the crown, for which purpose the grossest corruptions were openly used to bring it about. But whatever may be hereafter devised for the joint benefit of both nations, the King will most readily comply with the request of his parliaments to establish.

And now that we have, in his Majesty's name, given you the most ample security for your religion, properties and laws, that the power of a British sovereign can grant; we hereby for ourselves, as heir apparent to the crown, ratify and confirm the same in our own name, before Almighty God, upon the Faith of Christian, and the honour of a Prince.

Let me now expostulate this weighty matter with you, my father's subjects, and let me not omit this first public opportunity of awakening your understandings, and of dispelling that cloud, which the assiduous pens of ill-designing men have all along, but chiefly now, been endeavouring to cast on the truth. Do not the pulpits and congregations of clergy, as well a your weekly papers, ring with the dreadful / threats of popery, slavery, tyranny, and arbitrary power, which are now ready to be imposed upon you by the formidable powers of France and Spain? Is not my Royal father represented as a bloodthirsty tyrant, breathing out nothing but destruction to all those who will not immediately embrace an odious religion? Or, have I myself been better used? But listen only to the naked truth.

I, with my own money, hired a small vessel, ill provided with money, arms, or friends; I arrived in Scotland, attended by seven persons; I publish the King my father's declaration, and proclaim his title, with pardon in one hand, and in the other liberty of conscience, and the most solemn promises to grant whatever a free parliament shall propose for the happiness of a people. I have, I confess, the greatest reason to adore the goodness of Almighty God, who has, in so remarkable a manner, protected me and my small army through the many dangers to which we were at first exposed, and who has led me in the way to victory, and to the capital of this ancient kingdom, amidst the acclamations of the King my father's subjects: why then is so much pains taken to spirit up the minds of the people against this my undertaking?

The reason is obvious, it is, lest the real sense of the nation's present sufferings should blot out the remembrance of past misfortunes, and of the outcries formerly raised against the Royal Family. Whatever miscarriages might have given occasion to them, they have been more than atoned for since; and the nation has now an opportunity of being secured against the like for the future.

That our family has suffered exile during these fifty-seven years, every body knows. Has the nation, during that period of time, been the more happy and flourishing for it? Have you found / reason to love and cherish your governors, as the fathers of the people of Great Britain and Ireland? Has a family, upon whom a faction unlawfully bestowed the diadem of a rightful Prince, retained a due sense of so great a trust and favour? Have you found more humanity and condescension in those who were not born to a crown, than in my Royal forefathers? Have their ears been open to the cries of the people? Have they, or do they consider only the interest of these nations? Have you reaped any other benefit from them, than an immense load of debts? If I am answered in the affirmative, why has their government been so often railed at in all your public assemblies? Why has the nation been so long crying out in vain for redress against the abuses of parliaments, upon account of their long duration, the multitude of place-men, which occasions their venality, the introduction of penal laws, and, in general, against the miserable situation of the kingdom at home and abroad? All these, and many more inconveniencies must now be removed, unless the people of Great Britain be already so far corrupted, that they will not accept of freedom when offered to them; seeing the King, on his restoration, will refuse nothing that a free parliament can ask for the security of the religion, laws, and liberty of his people.

The fears of the nation, from the powers of France and Spain, appear still more vain and groundless. My expedition was undertaken unsupported by either: but indeed, when I see a foreign force brought by my enemies against me, and when I hear of Dutch, Danes, Hessians, and Swiss, the Elector of Hanover's allies, being called over to protect his government against the King's subjects, is it not high time for the King my father / to accept also of the assistance of those who are able, and who have engaged to support him? But will the world, or any one man of sense in it, infer from thence, that he inclines to be a tributary Prince, rather than an independent monarch? Who has the better chance to be independent on foreign powers? He, who with the aid of his own subjects, can wrest the government out of the hands of an intruder: or he, who cannot, without assistance from abroad, support his government, though established by all the civil power, and secured by a strong military force, against the undisciplined part of those he had ruled over so many years? Let him, if he pleases, try the experiment, let him send off his foreign hirelings, and put the whole upon the issue of a battle; I will trust only to the King my father's subjects, who were or shall be engaged in mine and their country's cause: but, notwithstanding all the opposition he can make, I still trust in the justice of my cause, the valour of my troops, and the assistance of the Almighty, to bring my enterprize to a glorious issue.

It is now time to conclude, and I shall do it with this reflection. Civil wars are ever attended with rancour and ill-will, which party-rage never fails to produce in the minds of those, whom different interests, principles, or views, set in opposition to one another; I therefore earnestly require it of my friends, to give as little loose as possible to such passions; this will prove the most effectual means to prevent the same in the enemies of our royal cause. And this my declaration will vindicate to all posterity the nobleness of my undertaking, and the generosity of my intentions.

Given at our palace of Holyrood house, the 10th day of October 1745. C. P. R.

By his Highness's command, J. Murray. /

This declaration, condemned by Parliament, was followed by 'An address to the army and people,' wrote by S. Sheridan, in the most insinuating and persuasive manner; and as it is the duty of a skilful physician to lay open the most dangerous wounds, that the same may be more speedily and effectually cured, so it is the duty of a faithful historian, or of an honest man, that best of characters, to give a genuine narrative of such arguments as an invading party use, to the intent the same may be answered in due time, and that a remedy may be prepared if an incident of the like nature should happen again.

That great politician and artful reasoner, after insisting upon what is laid down in the Pretender's manifesto, observes, that, of all crimes, parricide is of the deepest dye! And that of the several species of it, none could come up to that of dethroning and torturing a king; which last, the keeping him from his right must necessarily imply; a crime, continued he, unknown to the Heathens, and at which, 'Pilate, the Roman governor, cried out with horror, *What, crucify your King?*' On this he dwells for two pages; then proceeds to remove the objection raised against the reality of his Master's birth, whom he calls, 'the most accomplished gentleman in Europe;' he insists upon the depositions of the several maids of honour to the queen dowager Katherine of Portugal, and others, with regard to it, and puts the question, how such a base thing could enter into the heart of a man? But, proceeds he, 'What has the youth (meaning the Adventurer) done against you, a youth adorned with such charms, that he wants nothing to be admired but to be seen?' Then he shews, that the preservation of the Protestant religion under a Roman Catholic King is not / impracticable; as in the case of the subjects of Saxony, and those of the Palatinate; he then reflects upon the present Royal Family, and puts the question, 'Have they not been cyphers since ever they came among you, and the very ridicule of those over whom they govern?' So concludes, 'with beseeching them to return to their allegiance, that they may not henceforth be a proverb among other nations for having expelled their King; whose ancestors were the foundation, whence they and theirs had derived their titles, their honours, and their arms.' To these I shall only make the following answer.

Parricide is certainly a crime of the deepest dye, and that of dethroning a King is of the worst species; and I wish that neither Sheridan, nor any of his cabal, had been guilty of such an intention: but no definition of parricide, that implies guilt with regard to King James, can be applied to us, unless his own abandoning a throne upon the peoples praying for a redress of grievances, can be called by such a terrible and odious name; far less indeed can it be applied to the case of the Pretender, who never was in possession, and who, if the real son of the abdicated James, must, according to the laws of reason and revelation, have the forfeiture of his father entailed upon him. Tho' parricide is a crime sufficient to excite the astonishment of a Heathen, yet Pilate, by sitting in judgment, and trying our Saviour, whom his accusers called 'King of the Jews,' is a demonstration, that he thought kings themselves were accountable for their conduct; or, in other words, he judged, that both kings and subjects were to be balanced in the scales of the law.

The oaths of the witnesses concerning the birth of the Chevalier, and of the maids in particular, / shall not be weakened by me; one thing is certain, these incomparable ladies have said so little upon the subject, that it is astonishing they should be named; nor is it a new thing, to find a spurious breed of pretenders to a crown, in the Scots, English, or other annals; for no less than two have appeared in Sweden, since the death of Charles XII. As to the accomplishments of the old Chevalier, I can say nothing, except from his manifestoes, and in these I presume will appear the charms of his Son. As to the consistency of enjoying the exercise of the Protestant religion, under a Roman Catholic King, let it be considered, that the example of the King of Poland, is truly the worst he could think of, since that monarch, and his father, like other crowned heads, only professed the Roman catholic doctrines to qualify themselves for a throne. The same thing, though in a less degree, could be observed of the Elector Palatine; and, of late, we have seen that the Brother of the Duke de Deux Ponts has commenced a Roman, to gain the favour of the Court of Versailles, since he is out of all hopes of ever enjoying the Crown of Sweden. His reflections upon the Royal Family are surely ill grounded, and as the eyes of Europe in general, and the British nation in particular, are open, they must easily see, as clear as noon-day, the malignity and wickedness of the ungenerous aspersion.

Nothing now hindered his advancing into England except the conduct of Lord Lovat, whom they were solliciting by frequent letters to join them: but that nobleman was not willing to throw off the mask and to appear openly. He had been a rebel in his heart even in the year 1715; but did not join the Pretender's standard because one Mackenzie of Frazerdale, who had married the heiress of Lovat, headed the clan, to the exclusion / of him, as he was the heir male of that family. He indeed staid at home, but no sooner did the news arrive that the Duke of Argyle had defeated the rebels, than he mustered up those very men who had appeared at the battle of Sheriffmuir against the Royalists, and at their head he joined those in arms for the government.

At this time he imagined, that he might play the same game: his scheme being to send out his son and his followers, while he himself remained at home, big with the hopes of being rewarded for their services if successful; but that his son only should be the sufferer if the undertaking failed.

The most earnest intreaties openly to throw off the mask were to no purpose: he contented himself with writing letters full of the most fulsome flattery. And indeed his pretext was the more plausible, as the twenty companies of independent Highlanders had now been raised, and appeared openly for the Government; and that the Earl of Loudon had arrived in a ship from London, to take upon him the command of that corps. Toward the latter end of October the Adventurer resolved on decamping. He was convinced that he had received all he could expect from the north part of the kingdom, and that nothing was to be done in the other districts, and therefore prepared to set out for England: where, from the first moment of his public appearance, every proper step had been taken to defeat his intention and design.

The End of the FOURTH BOOK. /

THE LIFE OF WILLIAM DUKE OF CUMBERLAND.

BOOK V.

CONTENTS.

The State of England, *– the Preparations against the Pretender, – the Association at* York, *– his Royal Highness puts himself at the Head of the Forces, – the Route of both Armies.*

THE Pretender having decamped from Holyrood-house, and sent his troops by different roads into England, did on the 8th of November cross the Solway Firth with an army of 5520 men, supported by 13 pieces of brass cannon 12 pounders, which he had received from France, besides those taken at the battle of Preston-pans: he had plenty of ammunition, and had no doubt of being properly supplied with provision in a more opulent country, abounding with every convenience, and where the harvest had been remarkably plentiful. /

If we take a view of England and Wales, we may say with great certainty, that it contains more inhabitants than any district of the same dimensions in the known world: there are almost seven times the number of people in these than there are in Scotland, though the extent of the country is but one sixth part more; a plain demonstration that South Britain is by far the finer country, and at the same time a convincing proof not only of the small encouragement given to the latter, but of their own lethargic idleness to cultivate the fisheries, since a right improvement of these would soon set the northern upon an equal footing with the southern division.

The whole of England lies in such cherishing and wholsome climates, that the ground itself is productive of their liberty: no nation possesses more real advantages, whether we consider the fertility of the soil, the temperature of the air, the preciousness of its mines, the abundance of its forests, the tallness of its trees, the capaciousness and safety of its harbours, the splendor and magnificence of its cities, the cleanliness of its villages, the largeness of its cattle, the comeliness and beauty of its men, some of whom are as remarkable for improving in the sciences, as others have been conspicuous for a martial spirit, and admired for bravery and conduct. The Duke of Cumberland was born in her bosom; nor is it one of her least glories to have given birth to so great and illustrious a son; happy and independent in herself, but still more so, if she knew the art of contentment, and was not ready on every occasion to be hurried into schemes destructive of her true and lasting interest: could we suppose a crowd of Spaniards to settle in it, their descendants would in time work out the moroseness of their disposition; / whereas should an English colony settle in Spain or in Africa, the offspring of these would gradually be of the same dull genius with the natives, and become devotees to a superstitious and gloomy religion.

But England is not more happy in her natural advantages, than in her constitution and government both in church and state; which to erect was the work of ages, and at the expence of an immensity of blood and treasure. During the desolating civil wars between the Houses of York and Lancaster, the natives of England might be said to be tillers of the ground, and in bondage to their superiors; so that whenever a battle was gained, be victor who will, the commons were sure to be slaves; but when the Two Houses were united in the person and family of Henry VII. then was a cessation from domestic broils, the people began to look about with more ease, and the fruit of their enquiry was freedom, which soon formed them into a commercial state. Sensible of their advantages, they began to send representatives to parliament from among themselves; and from this origin that constitution arose, which has been the glory of every Englishman, and which they apprehended the rebellion was calculated to overturn.

The regency in the King's absence, upon being assured of the Pretender's landing, issued out a proclamation setting 30,000 *l.* on his head, which when he saw, he answered it by a counter-proclamation, which we shall here set down.

Lochergag, August 22, 1745.

WHEREAS upon setting up our Royal standard, for the recovery of our just right to the throne of our ancestors, we were not a little / surprized to find that the Elector of Hanover had not only contrary to the moderation of Christian Princes, but even to humanity itself, given an encouragement to parricide, by setting 30,000 *l.* upon the head of our Royal father, or our own, and so make us fall a sacrifice to the hands of bloody and cruel men, as our great grandfather King Charles I. of glorious memory had done near a century ago: this is therefore requiring all our liege subjects to endeavour to take the Elector of Hanover dead or alive, if he should venture to land in any of the King's dominions, and they shall receive a reward of 30,000 *l.* in consideration of so good and important a service.

Signed CHARLES, P. R.

By his Highness's command,

JOHN MURRAY.

It is needless to add any thing to the observations on this placart, further than that it was printed on the same type, the same letter, and the same size as the manifestoes formerly named. As the rebellion continued to increase, they dispatched a courier to Hanover with the important news; his Majesty, without hesitating a moment, set out for his regal dominions, and on the 29th of August came to St. James's.

Scarce had he arrived, when addresses came in from every quarter; the merchants and trading part of the city of London associated, at the hazard of their lives and fortunes, to fight for their religion and liberty, and in defence of the King's person and government; men of property of all ranks and orders crowded in with liberal subscriptions for raising forces, beyond the example of former times, and uncompelled by law. The admirals / and captains in the navy agreed to levy a regiment of foot, for paying which they appropriated their own salaries; the proprietors of the Prince Frederic and Duke privateers gave a loan to the King of 700,000 *l.* which was their share of some rich prizes, to be repaid as the parliament should direct; the clergy formed their hearers by precept, and excited by example to exert themselves in support of the crown, their own liberties, and the reformed religion; the Bishops of Oxford, Hereford, Worcester, Bristol, and Durham, with Dr. Potter, Archbishop of Canterbury, wrote circular letters to the inferior clergy of their dioceses, enjoining them to rouse up and to cultivate in their respective parishes a spirit of loyalty and affection; and Dr. Herring, the Archbishop of York, who afterward filled the see of Canterbury, rode night and day to bring the nobles and gentlemen of the ridings in that extensive county to a meeting at the castle of York, where he made a pathetic harangue to promote an association.

A SPEECH made by his Grace the Lord Archbishop of York, *at presenting an Association entered into at the Castle of* York, Sept. 24, 1745.

My Lords, Gentlemen, and Reverend Brethren of the Clergy,

I AM desired by the Lords Lieutenants of the several Ridings, to open to you the reasons of our present assembling; and as the advertisement, which has called us together, is in every body's hands, and the fact now speaks itself too plainly, a few words will be sufficient on the occasion.

It was some time before it was believed (I would to God it had gained credit sooner) but now every child knows it, that the Pretender's son is in Scotland; / land; has set up his standard there; has gathered and disciplined an army of great force; receives daily increase of numbers; is in possession of the capital city there; has defeated a small part of the King's forces; and is advancing with hasty steps towards England.

What will be the issue of this rapid progress must be left to the Providence of God. However, what is now incumbent upon us to do, is to make the best provision we can against it; and every gentleman, I dare say every man in England, will think it his wisdom and his interest to guard against the mischievous attempts of these wild and desperate ruffians.

But the great mischief to be feared, which ought to alarm us exceedingly, and put us immediately on our defence, is the certain evidence, which every day opens more and more, that these commotions in the north are but part of a great plan concerted for our ruin. – They have begun under the countenance, and will be supported by the forces of France and Spain, our old and inveterate (and late experience calls upon me to add, our savage and blood-thirsty) enemies. – A circumstance that should fire the indignation of every honest Englishman. If these designs should succeed, and popery and arbitrary power come in upon us, under the influence and direction of these two tyrannical and corrupted Courts, I leave you to reflect what would become of every thing that is valuable to us!

We are now blessed with the mild administration of a just and Protestant King, who is of so strict adherence to the laws of our country, that not an instance can be pointed out, during his whole reign, wherein he made the least attempt upon the liberty, or property, or religion, of a single person. / But if the ambition and pride of France and Spain is to dictate to us, we must submit to a man to govern us under their hated and accursed influence, who brings his religion from Rome, and the rules and maxims of his government from Paris and Madrid.

For God's sake, gentlemen, let us consider this matter as becomes us, and let no time be lost to guard against this prodigious ruin. To your immortal honour be it spoken, you have considered it; and are now met together to call in the unanimous consent and assistance of this great county. This county, as it exceeds every other for its extent and riches, so it very naturally takes the lead of the inferior ones. And it will be extremely to our credit, give courage to the friends of the best constitution in the world, damp the spirit of its enemies at home (if any such can be conceived in Britain at this dangerous crisis) and be an instruction to those abroad, that there is still spirit and honesty enough among us to stand up in defence of our common country. This will be the use of an unanimous and hearty declaration of fidelity to our country, and loyalty to our King. But the times, gentlemen, call for something more than this! Something must be done, as well as said. – And the fund for our defence, already begun, and now to be proposed to this great assembly, will, it is hoped, from reasons of public example and public safety, meet with the hearty concurrence of every individual that composes it. And at the same time that your hearts go along with the association, your hands will be open to support the necessary measures of self-defence.

As to you, my Reverend brethren, I have not long had the honour to preside among you; but from the experience I have had, and what I have / always heard of your honest love to your country (if you permit me to say so) I will be your security to the public, that you will decline no pains to instruct and animate your people; nor expence, according to your circumstances, to stand up against popery and arbitrary power, under a French or a Spanish government. – We scorn the policies of the Court of Rome, have no interests separate from the people, but on every occasion, where our country is concerned, look upon ourselves as incorporated with the warmest defenders of it; or, if we do desire to be distinguished, it will be by our ardor and zeal to preserve our happy constitution.

Let us unite then, gentlemen, as one man, to stop this dangerous mischief, from which union no man surely can withdraw, or withhold his assistance, who is not listed into the wicked service of a French or Spanish invasion, or wholly unconcerned for the fate of his bleeding country.

May the great God of battles stretch out his all-powerful hand to defend us; inspire an union of hearts and hands among all ranks of people; a clear wisdom into the councils of his Majesty; and a steady courage and resolution into the hearts of his generals!

Scarce had his Grace finished his speech, when the whole assembly unanimously agreed to enter into an association, the tenor whereof is as follows.

The ASSOCIATION.

WHEREAS there is now a horrid and unnatural rebellion carried on in Scotland by Papists, and other wicked and treacherous persons, countenanced and supported by the old and inveterate enemies of our country, and the religion and liberties thereof, the crowns of France and / Spain, in order to dethrone his present Majesty King George, the only rightful and lawful King of these realms; and having subverted our religion, laws, and liberties (which God forbid) to set upon the throne a Popish Pretender, a dependent and a slave to those tyrannous Courts: We the Lord Archbishop of York, Lords Lieutenants, Nobility, Deputy Lieutenants, Justices of the Peace, Clergy, Gentlemen, Freeholders, and others of the county of York, whose names are subscribed to this writing, and every of us, being of opinion, that in times so full of danger and treasonable practices as these are, an union of our hearts and forces will be most conducing to his Majesty's safety, and the public good of our country, do voluntarily and willingly bind ourselves every one of us to the other jointly and severally, in the band of one firm and loyal society, and do hereby promise, that with our whole powers, bodies, lives and estates, we and every of us will stand by and assist each other in the support and defence of his Majesty's sacred person and government, and will withstand, offend, and pursue, as well by force of arms, as by all other means, the said Popish Pretender and traitors, and also all manner of persons, of what state soever they be, and their abettors, that shall attempt, act, counsel, or consent to any thing that shall tend to the harm of his Majesty King George, or of his Royal Highness the Prince of Wales, or any of their issue, or to the subversion of his Majesty's government. And we do by this instrument declare, that no one of us shall, for any respect of persons or causes, or for fee or reward, separate ourselves from this association, or fail in the prosecution thereof during our lives.

Dated at the castle of York the 24th day of September, in the year of our Lord 1745. /

Every freeholder engaged for a year's valued rent of his estate, and in a short time about 33,000 *l.* was paid down; some went so far as to raise companies, among whom was William Thornton of Cattel, who paid and clothed a company of 70 men, whom he denominated the Yorkshire Blues. The northern counties followed the example of York, and the Dissenters, following the steps of the church, contributed according to their capacity; indeed they were equally interested in the important affair, the church of Rome having almost the same antipathy against them all. The doctrines of the churches of England and Scotland were nearly the same, though these differed widely in their discipline and worship, as Dr. Blair, one of the Prebendaries of W – r, certainly must know, since he came under the most sacred engagements to the Presbytery of Dunbar never to deviate from the latter, and has since bound himself under the strongest ties to adhere to the former. As no other occurs to me who came under obligations to both churches, I therefore have in a manner appealed to him, hoping he may speak truth at times.

The Quakers furnished woollen waistcoats to enable the troops to go through their winter campaign. The Roman Catholics, apprehensive that in the event of the Pretender's success their estates and properties would become a prey to foreigners, declared their aversion to a change. On the theatre was revived the tragedy of Perkin Warbeck*, in which was exhibited a lively picture of the desolation and havock caused in England, when he / marched into that kingdom with some Scotch forces then under the command of their King†.

The nobility and gentry sollicited for liberty to be allowed to raise forces; the Lord High Chancellor Yorke, and Mr. Onslow, Speaker of the

* Said to be Duke of York, and son to Edward IV. anno 1497.

† James IV. who afterward married King Henry the VIIth's eldest daughter.

House of Commons, set the example; the Duke of Montagu, Master-General of the Ordnance, raised a regiment of foot and another of horse; the Duke of Bedford raised one in London, and another in Bedfordshire; the Dukes of Bolton and Ancaster, with the Marquis of Granby, levied each a regiment of foot, as did the Earls of Halifax, Berkley, Cholmondely, and Edgcumbe; the Viscounts of Falmouth and Harcourt; Lords Gower and Herbert. In short, about 15 regiments were raised, and so properly stationed, that the friends of the Pretender were deterred from rising in arms. The judges, counsellors, and attornies at law, surrounded the throne, solliciting to be permitted to hazard their lives for their country, and to raise forces at their own expence for its protection.

The city of London put their militia in order, and commanded that of Westminster to hold themselves in readiness to march; and on the 10th of September the Lord-Mayor and Aldermen waited on their Sovereign with an offer of their service, declaring, 'That upon every occasion they were ready to sacrifice all that was dear and valuable to them in defence of his Majesty's person and family, and in support of the happy constitution both in church and state.' On which six regiments were raised, who abjured the Pretender, and took the oaths to the government; the Court of Lieutenancy followed the example; the merchants protested their loyalty; the universities of Oxford / and Cambridge presented addresses, while the other towns through the kingdom, like the members of the body influenced by the head, followed the example of the metropolis, and the trading part of the nation followed the steps of the London merchants.

The four battalions of guards were augmented, and on the 5th of September a proclamation was emitted against Papists and Nonjurors, to take effect after the 19th. An advertisement was published from the war-office, offering 6 *l.* bounty-money to every able-bodied man, five feet seven inches high without shoes, under thirty years of age, if before the 24th of September he would list in the guards. On the 18th orders were sent to the several counties of England and Wales to raise the militia, and arms were distributed among them; and on the 14th a proclamation was issued out, importing, that every man, who from that time till January, should inlist in any regiment of horse, foot or dragoons, was to receive his discharge in two years, if the same was required. On the 23d the regiment of Scots Greys arrived at Gravesend from Flanders, as did the three battalions of the foot guards, the foot regiments of the Major-Generals

Pulteney, Howard, Braag, Johnson; Brigadiers Douglas and Cholmondely; and Colonel Sowles. All these had been in the late battle at Fontenoy; and though extremely thinned in the late engagement, as constituting a part of that body, which headed by the Duke of Cumberland had pierced between the redoubt of Fontenoy and the Wood of Barri, yet they were now recruited, and their complements were full. His Royal Highness directed their rout, and even accompanied them to within 20 miles of Ostend, when again he returned back to the army. /

On the 26th about 1500 merchants, traders, and proprietors of public funds agreed to take Bank notes in payment of their debts, to the intent that the specie might circulate among the troops. On the 9th of October, the day when the Venetian ambassador made his public entry with great magnificence, the trained bands began to mount guard at the Royal Exchange, and other public places; and though they continued twenty-four hours on duty, till relieved by some companies from the six regiments, yet they did not complain. On the 10th the Tower Hamlets mounted guard at Whitechapel Bars, at Wellclose-square, and on Tower-hill; and on the 17th the parliament met, notwithstanding the following charge to the contrary:

CHARLES *Prince of* Wales, *Regent of* Scotland, England, France, *and* Ireland, *and the Dominions thereunto belonging;*

CHARLES P. R.

WHEREAS we are certainly informed, That the Elector of Hanover has taken upon him to summon a Parliament to meet at Westminster, on Thursday the seventeenth of this instant October; we hereby warn and command all his Majesty's liege subjects, whether peers or commoners, to pay no obedience to any such summons, and not to presume to meet or act as a Parliament at the time and place appointed, or any other; the so doing by any authority but that of the King our royal Father, since the setting up of his standard, his Majesty's gracious pardon offered for all that is past, being an overt-act of treason and rebellion: but if, notwithstanding this our declaration, any number of persons shall presume to meet in either house, and act there as members of a lawful Parliament, / they cannot but be sensible that no right or privilege of Parliament can avail to justify what they say or do in such an unlawful assembly. And for those of his Majesty's subjects of this his antient kingdom of Scotland, whether peers or commoners, who shall, contrary to these our express commands, presume to sit or vote as aforesaid, as soon as the same shall be verified to us, the transgressors shall be proceeded against as traitors to their King and country, and their estates shall be confiscated for his Majesty's use, according to the laws of the land; the pretended union being now at an end. Lastly, We hereby strictly enjoin and command all his Majesty's faithful subjects, of what rank and degree soever, to pay no obedience or regard to any act, vote, order, or resolution, that may be published in the name of both houses, or of either of them respectively, as they shall answer the contrary at their peril.

Given at our palace of Holyrood-house, the ninth day of October, one thousand seven hundred and forty-five.

CHARLES P. R.

By his Highness's command, J. Murray.

Both houses being met, for but few of either were absent, the King in his speech informed them, 'That the open and unnatural rebellion, which had broke out, and was still continuing in Scotland, had obliged him to call them together sooner than he intended,' – 'That the wicked and daring attempt in favour of a Popish Pretender to his Crown, headed by his eldest Son, carried on by traiterous and desperate persons, and encouraged by his enemies abroad, required the immediate advice and assistance of his Parliament; / that the unanimity shewn by his subjects had given him the firmest assurance that they were resolved to act with a spirit becoming a time of common danger.

'I have,' continued he, 'through the whole course of my reign, made the laws of the land the rule of my government, and the preservation of the constitution in church and state, and the rights of my people, the main end and aim of all my actions. It is therefore the more astonishing, that any of my Protestant subjects, who have known and enjoyed the benefits resulting from thence, and have heard of the imminent dangers these kingdoms were wonderfully delivered from at the happy Revolution, should by any arts and management be deluded into measures, that must at once destroy their religion and liberties, introduce Popery and arbitrary power, and subject them to a foreign yoke.' He declared himself sensibly affected with the extraordinary burthen which the attempt must bring upon his faithful subjects: and concludes with assuring, that the interest of him and his people was always the same; and that whoever heartily and vigorously exerted themselves in the national cause, might depend on his favour and protection.

Next day, the Lords presented their address, in which, after the usual introduction, they declared, that they 'wanted words to express the just indignation and abhorrence rising in their breasts, at so wicked, traiterous, and desperate an attempt in favour of a Popish Pretender to his crown, whose groundless claim they had unfeignedly abjured, and whose principles and designs they did, from the bottom of their hearts, detest and abhor; then very gratefully acknowledged his / paternal regard for the laws; that they were resolved to hazard their lives and fortunes in defence of his sacred person and government, and that they would concur in all such measures as might most effectually conduce to extinguish the rebellion, to deter any foreign power from presuming to support it, to restore the tranquillity of his government, and to add strength to that excellent constitution which the flagitious attempt was intended to subvert.'

The Commons presented an address in terms to the same purpose, assured him of having 'his hands strengthned by effectual supplies, for supporting his sacred person and government, which from every consideration, human and divine, they were bound to defend.'

On Monday the 21st, they impowered the King to secure and detain such persons as he should suspect of conspiring against his person and government. And, on the 4th of November, no less than 1,298,000 l. 4s. 9d. was granted for paying 49,229 effective men, for the year 1746: they likewise voted 64,365 l. 18s. for paying the fifteen regiments formerly named, for 122 days from the time of their being raised, with 13,176 l. 10s. for the pay of two regiments of horse, for the same time and in the same way; and 35,252 l. 10s. for maintaining the twenty independant Highland companies for 361 days: and upon the 24th the King was impowered to raise the English militia.

There were now 36,000 regular troops in the kingdom, commanded by gallant officers, who had given signal instances of their valour and intrepidity; and, what not a little animated both army and people, his Royal Highness the Duke of Cumberland was among them. His Highness had on the 14th of October left Brussels, and on the 18th arrived / at St. James's. The troops which he ordered to follow landed on the 25th. They consisted of four troops of Sir John Ligonier's dragoons, the detachment of the foot guards which served at Ostend, Lieutenant-general Sinclair's battalion of foot, the foot regiments of Lieutenant-general Harrison, Major-general Husk, and Lord Harry Beauclerc. On the 27th Prince Henry Frederic was born, on which the Parliament complimented the King, as they did on the 30th, being his birth-day. It was kept in England with uncommon gaiety: and perhaps the drawing-room at St. James's was never fuller. It was likewise observed in every part of Scotland, except where parties of the enemy were stationed: the garrison of the castle of Edinburgh observed the different parts of rejoicing with uncommon splendor and shew: the union flag was displayed, at twelve o'clock a round from her guns was discharged, and these were answered by the ships in Leith road, and by vollies from the small arms of the garrison drawn up upon the platform.

Every place was put into the best posture of defence; the garrison of Berwick was reinforced by eight companies of Price's foot, just as they landed from Flanders, and five companies of Ligonier's were ordered by General Handasyde to be stationed in Holy Island till further orders. In a word, England was now become a seminary of soldiers, actuated by the spirit of their Sovereign, who declared in council, That if the rebellion continued, he himself would march at the head of the troops in person. And in the mean time an army was ordered to the north, over which Field-marshal Wade was appointed to command.

That officer moved from Doncaster on the 21st with the British infantry, and with the Swiss regiments whom the States of Holland had, conformable / to treaties, upon the requisition of the British ambassador, sent over to the King. Newcastle upon Tyne was the place appointed for the rendezvous. The forces marched thither from twenty different quarters, and about the 28th they, on a muster upon the Moor of that town, amounted to 14,000 men, with a large train of artillery.

The Marshal resolved to wait here; both to observe the motions of the enemy and to protect the coal mines, which if once seized by the Insurgents would be of the utmost disadvantage to the Royal cause.

From this place he caused a proclamation to be made, and afterward to be inserted in the newspapers, 'That those of his Majesty's subjects inhabiting the Highlands of Scotland, and others, who have been seduced by the menaces and threatenings of their chiefs and superiors to take arms, and enter into a most unnatural rebellion, should be objects of the Royal mercy, if they would return to their habitations, on or before the 12th of November; but if they slighted this offer, they were to be punished according to the demerit of their crimes.'

This voluntary proffer did not meet with a suitable return: the chiefs were too much involved: the Pretender was too ambitious; and two-thirds of his army could neither read nor write. Gracious declarations were attributed to a reigning panic occasioned by the defeat at Preston-pans; so that, depending on the weakness of the King's troops, especially in the time of winter, and on their own superior alertness, they entered England on Friday the 8th of November. The whole army was now together, and after scouring the country for two days, the Pretender marched at their head to the Moor of Carlisle, where he waited for his cannon / and the remainder of his forces; who brought him the mortifying news, that thirty-four of their waggons had been seized by a party of the Dumfries militia-men, in arms for the Government: a piece of news which however disagreeable, yet did not hinder his sending Geohegan, a French officer, with the following summons:

CHARLES *Prince of* Wales, *Regent of the Kingdoms of* England, Scotland, France, *and* Ireland, *and the Dominions thereunto belonging:*

BEING come to recover the King our father's just rights, for which we are arrived with all his authority, we are sorry to find that you should prepare to obstruct our passage: we therefore, to avoid the effusion of English blood, hereby require you to open your gates, and let us enter, as we desire, in a peaceable manner; which if you do, we shall take care to preserve you from any insult, and set an example to all England of the exactness with which we intend to fulfil the King our father's declarations and our own: but if you shall refuse us entrance, we are fully resolved to force it by such means as Providence has put into our hands, and then it will not perhaps be in our power to prevent the fatal consequences which usually attend a town's being taken by assault. Consider seriously of this, and let me have your answer within the space of two hours; for we shall take any further delay as a peremptory refusal, and take our measures accordingly.

Nov. 10, 1715. Two in the afternoon.
For the Mayor of Carlisle.

This menacing letter was answered from the cannon on the ramparts. The Chevalier, who had / marched to Brampton Muir, eight miles east of Carlisle, in order to give battle to General Wade, or to waste and consume the forces under that officer by marches and countermarches, or to surprize them in the night-time, as opportunity offered, was not a little touched at the refusal; he sent back a small party on the 13th with some fascines and scaling-ladders, made of the wood cut in Corby and Warwick Parks, and toward sun-set these arrived near the town. Next morning they broke ground within 300 yards of the Scots gate, but were driven off by an uninterrupted fire from the batteries; however, this disheartening circumstance did not counterbalance one more encouraging, and which arose from a thick mist, which then darkened the atmosphere. Under favour of it a trench was dug toward the English gate, as the most defenceless; the insurgents advanced the works, and Perth, the conductor of the siege, wrought in his shirt as the meanest labourer; Carlisle was attacked in three places at once, which being discovered on the sky clearing up, the centries in surprize spread a consternation among the inhabitants. Many people leaped over the wall, which is about six feet high, and five feet broad, and crossed the ditch, which is of the same breadth with the wall; these generally escaped, though some fell into the hands of the enemy. The militia being shut up in a town, where they were fatigued with a continual watching for seven days and seven nights together, and the inhabitants almost killed with the apprehensions of a massacre, desired a meeting. The Mayor, Aldermen, and Citizens convened, with Colonel Durand, Governor of the castle, to consult about the proper methods to be taken in this extremity. The Governor's opinion was, that the place might hold out, but he was overpowered / by the multitude; the terror of the Highlanders storming the town sword in hand in the night-time, had already filled them with the most killing apprehensions, it was resolved to surrender the place. Accordingly a white flag was hung out, which the enemy observing, the intended assault was laid aside, and deputies came out with a proposal of terms; they were told that the town should enjoy her liberties, but that the provision and ammunition should be delivered in the case they were in; and in the mean time a message was sent off to the Chevalier, who answered, 'that he was not to do things by halves, he must have both the castle and the town, or neither of them.' The garrison of the former were, by the faithful Durand, almost prevailed on to stand a siege; but, upon after-thoughts, about 320 out of 400 men deserted in one night, and some of these who remained were unfit for action, so that the governor was oblige to withdraw. Things being thus situated,

Perth, who was afterwards made governor, took possession of the town and castle in the Pretender's name about ten in the morning of the 15th. His declarations were proclaimed with great solemnity, and he himself made his entry on the 17th, escorted by the Elphinstone troop, then commanded by Arthur Lord Balmerino, who appeared for the first time as an officer, and Colonel of the life-guards. Here were found provision for three months, arms for a numerous militia, and near 200 horses with proper furniture; and in the castle were 1000 stand of arms, with many of the swords of the Highlanders taken at Preston, anno 1715: all which, with 100 barrels of gunpowder, and many valuable effects belonging to the country people for several miles round, were secured. /

And here Perth performed a piece of generosity, which could not fail of gaining an universal esteem. From his frequenting the horse races at York, Newcastle, and Black Hamilton, he became acquainted with almost the whole gentlemen of Cumberland, and the adjacent counties, so that when he came to receive them in the market-place, there was a continued embracing one after another of the prisoners for near half an hour; they were invited to dine with him, and after being properly regaled, were dismissed upon their parole. Some gentlemen of these parts have told me, that though they looked upon this step of Perth as inconsistent with the character of a soldier, yet it was a signal instance of his politeness and humanity, for they were suffered to retain their arms! Indeed he had no reason to be ruffled in his temper, as the besiegers lost no more than one Dalton an engineer, an Irishman, who was killed, and a private man, who was wounded.

These suceesses, in themselves equal to a victory, were still heightened by the slowness of Marshal Wade's motions; that officer, instead of stationing himself half way between Newcastle and Carlisle, had continued at the former place, notwithstanding he had intimation of the Pretender's rout by an express next day after their quitting Edinburgh. He did not decamp till the 16th, and then Carlisle was in the hands of the enemy; the Dutch troops were a drawback upon his motions, and would not march when directed: these had come over only for the sake of form. The French ambassador at the Hague remonstrated against their being sent over to England, under pretence that they were included in the capitulation of Tournay, and were not to fight directly or indirectly against the crown of France for a year. Some memorials passed upon / this subject, and the troops in the mean time were transported; England was pleased with their arrival, and France was pacified with their inaction; for during the whole time of their continuance, they were not so much as engaged in a skirmish, or the least accidental rencounter.

On that day the Major-Generals Howard and Oglethorpe, with the Brigadiers Cholmondely and Mordaunt, marched at the head of the infantry in excessive cold weather amidst an intense frost and a falling snow, which lay three feet deep upon the ground. About eight at night they arrived at Ovington, through roads terribly broken and full of ice, in which some of the foot of the last column had dropt through fatigue, and might have perished, had not the Major-Generals Huske and Oglethorpe hired countrymen with lights and carts to bring them up. In this service they were employed till nine next morning, when the forces continued their march for Hexham, which the first line entered about four in the afternoon, and the rear at midnight. Here the Marshal, having intelligence of the fate of Carlisle, resolved to return, and on the 22d arrived at Newcastle through roads almost impassable, and with an army spent with fatigue.

The magistrates received them with a becoming sympathy; the malthouses, public halls, and other empty buildings, were warmed and fitted up, while such as appeared to be most jaded were quartered in private houses, and entertained at the proprietor's charge. Here they continued two days, and on the 24th began their march southward in quest of the enemy, who, after leaving a garrison of 450 men at Carlisle, had about ten in the morning of the 20th set out for Penrith, where and at Shap they halted till the 22d, when they marched for / Kendal, advanced to Lancaster on the 24th, and reached Preston on the 26th, proclaiming their leader in every town amidst the acclamations of the multitude. Here the Chevalier, who hitherto marched on foot, mounted on horseback, and surveyed the passes and bridge of the town, taking with him such as had been there in the year 1715, when the Earls of Derwentwater, Nithisdale, Wintoun and Carnwath, with almost their whole forces, were taken prisoners; and here, as in other places, they collected the cess, the land-tax, and excise, with the other branches of the public revenue.

The neighbourhood of the enemy filled the western counties with surprize and astonishment, and the towns began to provide for their safety; the city of Chester, the key into Wales, was by the care of the Earl of Cholmondely put into a posture of defence, and its bridge broken down. The inhabitants of Liverpool secured their valuable effects in the ships then in the road; which precautions had such an influence, that on the 29th the enemy turned eastward to Manchester, where their cavalry arrived by ten in the morning, and the Pretender at the head of his infantry about two in the afternoon. Next day they beat up for volunteers, when some Roman Catholics and Nonjurors engaged with them, but no person of rank or distinction came in: however, they formed the Manchester regiment of horse, whose livery was blue clothes, hangers, a plaid sash, and white cockade: they made free with the best horses they could find, and beat up for recruits as they advanced. The Colonel of that regiment was the unfortunate Francis Townley, a gentleman of great courage and activity, but who, through the misfortunes of his family, had gone to serve in the armies of France. Their quarter-master was one Thomas / Cappoch, a Presbyter of the Church of England, who was soon declared Bishop of Carlisle; an unhappy preferment for him, as it brought him to a fatal end, which every wretch, who, on the prospect of a piece of bread, swerves from his solemn engagements never to deviate from the discipline and worship of one church, who has impowered him to preach the Gospel, ought to meet with. It is no wonder that villains of this stamp should shake off all the ties binding on a scholar, in order to use the arts of circumvention, and, like a bailiff's follower, turn a man out of his bread, and fix himself in it. Poor Cappoch was hanged, drawn, and quartered. At Manchester the bellman was sent about with orders to all such as had public money to bring it in, and in the evening he intimated that the place should be illuminated; which last being partly complied with, was of good service to the rear of the army, as it was night before they could enter.

On the 1st of December a party of them made a feint of marching to Stockport, and another westward to Knotsford, having crossed the Mersey in different places, though then very rapid and swollen by the rain. The cavalry forded it, while the foot and artillery passed over bridges of plank and of poplar. In the mean time the Pretender arrived at Macclesfield with 3000 men, and the artillery came in about two in the afternoon. Next morning the van was sent to Congleton, where they received intelligence that the main body of the King's army, consisting of 12,700 men, mostly veteran regiments, and among them three battalions of the guards, commanded by his Royal Highness the Duke of Cumberland, was at Newcastle under Line, nine miles south west of them. /

For on the 16th of November his Majesty had ordered three regiments of horse, two of dragoons, and fifteen of foot, to march into Lancaster to observe the motions of the enemy. They marched by the way of Barnet, Dunstable, and Wooburn, through roads almost impassable, and rendezvoused at Stafford on the 26th of November, when Sir John Ligonier was appointed to take upon him the command. As they advanced the Duke begged of his Royal father to be permitted to put himself at the head of the forces. His request was granted, but with difficulty. The King told him, 'William, I grant your desire, but pray take care of yourself; for this young man is not a fool with whom you have to deal: learn this lesson from your father, never to despise an enemy.' A salutary advice, worthy the most solid wisdom, and which the Duke so well observed, that he did not commit one single oversight during the whole time of his command. On the 26th he set out from St. James's about one o'clock in the morning, and in three days arrived at Stafford, between which place and Tamworth the army was cantoned. He no sooner appeared among them, than the air resounded with the most joyful acclamations.

Here getting intelligence that the enemy intended to march for Congleton, he ordered that part of the cavalry, which was posted at Newcastle under Line, to retreat till the infantry should come up, and the two bodies being joined here, he drew them up on Stonefield, expecting the enemy would come that way: but on information that they were marching further east, he caused the army to move to the south east, the better to intercept them. The roads and avenues were properly secured, and the day was somewhat dark; circumstances very favourable for him, as by means of these advantages / he would have been up with the enemy, being within three miles of them: and now there might have been an end of the matter, had it not been for a turnpike-man, who first informed the Pretender's party, that the Duke was advancing upon that road, and within three miles of them, and therefore directed them to turn off to the left hand. His directions were followed, and in about an hour after the Duke came up with the troops, when the turnpike-man assured him that the enemy had marched to the right, and were but two miles distant; whereon his Highness set out more eagerly than before, and in his way saw a lieutenant of Johnson's regiment lying among the whins, miserably mangled, and a little further on, six others in the same situation. He had marched two miles before discovering the cheat, and so returning the same way, he ordered the turnpikeman to be brought before him. The unhappy fellow made no defence for himself, further than that he did not want a battle should happen near his abode. An excuse of so little weight in itself, that the whole general officers insisted on putting him to death, which was done instantly; he was carried to a tree, and hanged on the bough thereof, which overshadowed the road.

This done he marched to Coventry with all his horse, and two battalions of foot, having ordered the remainder to encamp on Meriden Common, where the flannel waistcoats (the gift of the Quakers) were arrived. This step of his Royal Highness entirely disconcerted the plans and measures of the enemy, for turn which way they will, the troops were alert to attack them.

The Pretender having intelligence of these motions, and of the alacrity of the King's army, marched his van to Ashburn, and the main body / of his forces to Leek, and all of a sudden turned to Derby, which he entered on the morning of the 4th, with 450 horse, and 2300 foot; the rest, in order to appear more numerous, continuing to enter till late, when their artillery and baggage did arrive.

The suddenness of their approach surprized the people of the town, who retired in such confusion, that the clerk in a hurry left upon a bureau the roll of those who subscribed for sums in the government's service. The paper falling into their hands, the different quotas and public money were rigorously collected, and at night was held a council of war; in which the question was, Proceed forward, or Retreat? The reasoning was tedious and long, but nothing then was concluded. Next day after dinner the question was resumed; the Chevalier was so eager upon fighting, that he was ready to cry. Clanranald and Clunie Macpherson joined him; but Lord Pitsligo and the other leaders were unanimous against it. 'I am told,' said Pitsligo, 'that the Elector is to raise his standard at Finchley Common, and the advantage of being in possession of London is known from the case of Edward IV. Should we fight the Duke of Cumberland, the fortune of war is doubtful; should we pass him, which may be done, yet we have another army to encounter before we arrive at St. James's; in case of a defeat, we shall be exposed to the rage of the country people. Let us not then bring certain destruction upon ourselves, and an indelible stain upon the Scottish nation, who, when unanimous, never marched so far as we have done; we will conduct you back (turning to the Chevalier) and by an honourable retreat secure that safety, and that character, of both / which the rash adventuring forward bids fair to deprive us.'

This reasoning was just; for in case they did escape the Duke, they would be put between the fire of his army, and that formed under the eye of the Earl of Stair, which was composed of the guards, Lord John Murray's old Highland regiment, two troops of Ligonier's horse, and the remains of Sir Robert Rich's regiment of dragoons, with those of Lieutenant-General Halley, who on the 1st had arrived in the Thames from William-stadt. The associated regiment of the law, for the defence of the Royal family, and the preservation of the constitution in church and state, made up of the gentlemen of the gown, under the command of Lord Chief Justice Willes, entered here upon the first rudiments of a winter campaign; there was a large train of artillery, consisting of 33 field pieces, and 48 covered waggons, 20 chests of arms, and 240 matrosses, under the direction of Captain Speedwell, an officer of 55 years experience. The Lieutenancy of London directed, that two regiments of the trained bands should be out every night, and one in the day-time, and several wealthy citizens enlisted as volunteers in the first regiment of foot guards, while all the public and private effects of the city began to be packed up, to be safe against the worst of events.

But the difficulties he had to encounter on land were no less discouraging than his disappointments; for some of the transports from France had been driven back, and others taken, as on the 25th of November the Soleil privateer, on board of which was Mr. Charles Radcliff and his son, 11 captains, 10 lieutenants, and 60 private men. The crew were sent to Dover castle, and the remaining prisoners distributed in the several men of war of / Admiral Vernon's squadron; but the officers were conducted to the Tower, where apartments were fitted up for them, young Mr. Radcliff being taken for the second son of the Pretender, now Cardinal Steuart, who was then in France amused with promises.

On these and other accounts the whole were brought into Pitsligo's sentiments; however, they artfully concealed their designs, by rubbing up their arms, as if intending to fight, while a small party was detached to the Trent, to repair the bridge that had been broke down, and to lay others for passing over the troops, as if they designed to march forward to their adherents in London, who, in expectation of their approach, had privately dropt the Pretender's declarations at St. James's upon the parade, while others, less prudent, were for malicious expressions taken into custody, and received an arbitrary punishment for their ill-timed zeal; however, they continued in high spirits till the arrival of an express that their friends had retreated; on which the cannon sent to the camp returned, the King's advancing to it was deferred, the orders given to the troops were countermanded, the day duty of the trained bands was discontinued, and the volunteers were dismissed. These had passed in review before the King and Earl of Stair through St. James's Park, with their wives and children before them, to signify that all was at stake; and that they were determined to fight *pro aris et focis*.

On the 6th of December, at ten of the morning, after several feints, the rebels began their march from Derby, with their cavalry in front, and 13 pieces of cannon in the center; some seeming to move to Loughborough, entered that place, and plundered it of what was valuable, while others / kept on the Ashburn side. When about a mile from town they halted till near four, and then went off, their carriages being on full trot, and their foot almost running. While here, not content with their former demands, they sent a party to require a large sum of money, which by force they obtained.

Notwithstanding this device, which kept their true intent a profound secret, yet that very night the Duke had an account of their march. By three next morning he put himself at the head of all the horse and dragoons, and 1000 volunteers mounted till the foot should come up, and sent expresses every where to the militia to intercept them; but this could not be so easily done, as these had hitherto retired before them, and because their motions were so quick and uncertain, their designs so intricate and dark.

However, the places on which they were supposed to have an eye, were put in a posture of defence. The Duke of Richmond, the Marquis of Granby, the Earls of Cholmondely and Warrington, with the Lord Gower, repaired to Chester, to stop their advancing into Wales, while the Liverpool battalion of 700 men were ordered to take post at Warrington. These picked up about sixteen stragglers, who afterward were sent to different gaols. A thousand new raised foot were dispatched to Newcastle to prevent their coming there, or if they came to keep them in play till the troops should come up. These, and indeed the whole militia, were very eager in the service of the government, and willing to fight the rebels; but their leaders being men of experience, considering that they could not be defeated without the loss of some useful lives, they were referred to a more able avenger, who, with his cavalry and foot, / mounted on horses supplied by the country people, was now in full pursuit of them.

On the 8th they were at Macclesfield, and next day at Manchester, where they levied 16000 l. and committed 13000 *l.* of damages. On the 10th they marched to Wigan, and on the 11th to Preston, where they halted the 12th. On the 13th they made the longest march during this chase, and arrived at Lancaster, where they halted the 14th; but having intelligence that the troops were gaining ground of them, they continued their flight from the Duke, who about eleven of the night of the 10th arrived at Macclesfield from Litchfield with two regiments of dragoons, having marched about forty miles in two days through terrible roads, by Uttoxeter and Cheadle; and about an hour after the foot arrived, being provided with horses by the gentlemen of Staffordshire. After four hours repose they began their march for Manchester, which they entered upon the 12th amidst repeated huzzas, bonfires, illuminations, and other demonstrations of joy. By three next morning they were in motion, and marched so hastily, that the van reached Preston about four hours after the rebels had quitted the town; the first who entered were the Georgia rangers, soon after a party of the Duke of Kingston's horse, commanded by Lieutenant-Colonel Mordaunt, and the Captains Lord Byron and Lord Robert Manners. It was here General Oglethorpe joined the Duke's army with 1000 horse, which were composed of St. George's dragoons, the Duke of Montagu's horse, and those of Marshal Wade.

That officer had on the 24th of November marched by the way of Durham, Darlington, and Richmond, in order to cover Yorkshire. On the 28th he was at Pets-Bridge, whence he moved to / Wetherby, where his troops halted the 5th of December, and received their bread from Leeds, as also shoes, stockings, and flannel waistcoasts from London; from Wetherby he turned eastward to Ferry-Bridge, where the arrived on the 9th, as did the cavalry at Doncaster. It was at this place that accounts were brought of the retreat of the enemy, for intercepting of whom Wade resolved to march by the way of Wakefield and Hallifax into Lancashire; but getting intelligence that they had slipt him, he marched back with his foot in several divisions; and that they might be under cover every night by reason of the freezing winds, the chilling frosts, and almost continual snows, he took the rout of Northallerton, Darlington and Durham, and arrived at Newcastle on the 20th of December, having detached General Oglethorpe, as is already observed. The troops under him had marched from Doncaster, and in three days made about 100 measured miles over snow and ice, either to come up with the enemy, or to join the Duke of Cumberland, by whom that march was literally paralleled.

The rangers were immediately sent after the enemy, who had halted at Lancaster on the 14th, till the whole of their troops should come up. By two in the afternoon they got a sight of the rebels rear, and two of them riding beyond the rest were taken prisoners.

That day, about ten in the forenoon, Perth, who thought nothing of riding down three horses in a day for intelligence, reached Kendal with an hundred hussars, and whence, after halting for a little refreshment, he went on; but as the rear of his corps was entering upon the bridge, some country people being there at market mobbed them. One of them was killed by a musket from a window, / and two taken prisoners. On this the party faced about, when as many as the bridge could give room to fired upon the mob, of whom a shoemaker and ostler were killed, on which they dispersed, after the rebels had discharged a general volley, but at too great a distance to do harm. This being over they posted to Shap, where on the 16th they arrived.

The day after the affair at Kendal the whole body of the rebels came into that town, where hearing that one of their hussars was slain, and two taken prisoners, they breathed nothing but revenge; the cess and public money were demanded, under penalty of the severest execution. With the utmost difficulty could the magistrates pacify the chieftains, by representing the innocence of the inhabitants, and that in a public market offenders must be unknown. As Lochiel came at last to understand the matter, the contributions were abated, though a great sum was levied; and on their departure their last rank plundered some houses, stript some people of their shoes, and attempted to fire a lodging, but the match did not take. On the 16th their main body marched for Shap, but the rear-guard halted at a farm four miles from Kendal, to prepare small carts for carrying their ammunition, which could not be got forward over steep hills, and through a bad road, upon their four-wheeled waggons, that were mostly broken down. Next night these arrived at Shap, while the bulk of them marched with the young Adventurer to Penrith, where in the evening they were joined by the rear-guard.

While General Anstruther is advancing from Coventry to London with Colonel Sowles and Skelton's regiments of foot, which composed the first division of his Royal Highness's army, while Marshal / shall Wade is marching his troops in different divisions toward Newcastle upon Tyne; and while the army is forming upon the Kentish coast, where a descent was apprehended, the Duke came up with the enemy upon the 18th at night with his cavalry, after an uninterrupted march of ten hours.

The rebels, being continually alarmed by the approach of the light horse, had sent a party through Lord Lonsdale's parks of Lowther, thinking to find some of these who had harrassed them about his house, as he was Lord Lieutenant of the county of Cumberland. Some of them were seen, but then at too great a distance to receive any loss. In their progress they took a running footman belonging to his Royal Highness, and a gentleman of the county, whom they called an officer: from these they were informed, that the Duke was within a mile of them with about 4000 horse and dragoons, besides light horse and militia; on which they abandoned Lowther hall to make a stand against him. Accordingly Lord George Murray, who always commanded the rear-guard, took possession of the village of Clifton, a mile to the north of Lord Lonsdale's seat, upon the high way to, and two miles short of Penrith; he sent Colonel Roy* Steuart's regiment and Clunie's battalion to the bottom of the moor, while the Macdonalds of Keppoch stood at a little distance to wait the event; they fortified themselves behind three hedges and a ditch. It was now about an hour after sun-set, when the King's troops appeared upon the open moor with their leader, who directly ordered 300 of Honeywood's dragoons to dismount, and march forward to attack the enemy. They advanced to / the very brink of the ditch, when the rebels fired from behind the hedges, and killed a few; on which the troops fired some platoons, and then retired a few paces. The enemy taking this for the beginning of a flight, crossed the ditch with incredible swiftness, and rushed on with sword and pistol in hand, but were so well received, that some of them lay dead upon the spot. The dragoons, who had drawn their swords, were now ready to pay them in their own coin. The shouts began, the clashing of swords was heard; some of the rebels swords broke

* In Irish red, so called from his infancy for the redness of his hair.

upon the steel caps which the cavalry commonly wear, on which they drew their daggers, and fought with great obstinacy for an hour; when observing the resolution of the forces, they returned with as much precipitation across the ditch, as at first they came on, and with full speed carried the consternation to Penrith, where the body of their army, with the artillery and baggage, was arrived. Such was the skirmish at Clifton, in which about twelve of the dragoons were killed, and twenty-four wounded, among whom were Colonel Honeywood, Captain East, and the Cornets Owen and Hamilton. On the side of the rebels were slain about twenty men, and seventy taken prisoners, among whom was Captain George Hamilton of Redhouse, who then commanded in the absence of Roy Steuart; he had fallen upon the ground by some accident, and recovering himself, was just sitting up, when an hussar coming by, struck him upon the vertebræ of the neck, so that he fell back, with these words, 'Oh, I am killed!' The hussar dismounted, took his money out of his pocket, with his watch, and then left him, till the country people, who had known his severity, tied up his head with an handkerchief, and delivered him a prisoner; he was / mounted upon an horse, with his legs tied below its belly, and directly sent to gaol. As the rebels, who had not advanced, carried off their killed and wounded on the other side of the ditch, the same could not be certainly known; they gave out that they only lost twelve men, who run up the moor; whereas his Royal Highness wrote to the King, that seventy of them were taken prisoners, besides those who were wounded and killed. The only thing the enemy had to boast of, was, that they took some broad swords from the dragoons; but from the best information, I find these only amounted to seven, which were taken up as they first leaped over the ditch, when the troops retired, or were seized from the wounded officers formerly named.

Being driven from the village, and come to Penrith, a council of war was held, where Roy Steuart was for marching back, and surprizing the dragoons in the night-time, or by day-break next morning, before the foot had arrived; but Lord George Murray was not for diminishing the forces by skirmishes, but for pursuing their rout, and joining Lord John Drummond, who had landed from Dunkirk with a regiment of 600 men at Montrose. He was afterward joined by a like body of the Duke of Gordon's vassals, then under his brother Lord Lewis, the Frazers under the Master of Lovat, the Farqhuarsons under Francis Farqhuarson of Monaltry, the Chisholms of Strathglass under the chieftain's youngest son, two battalions of the Mackintoshes raised by the Lady Mackintosh, whose husband was a Captain in the service of the government. These were commanded by Macgillivray of Drumnaglass, one of the branches of the Catti; in all about 2500 men. /

Next day their whole army marched for Carlisle, where that night they arrived, and next morning, being the Chevalier's birth-day, he was complimented by the officers, and his army drawn up upon the moor in battalia, where they continued under arms till about twelve o'clock, giving out, that they were resolved to fight the Duke's army before the arrival of the artillery; but on hearing that the foot and artillery were fast approaching, they drew off with pipes playing and colours flying, leaving at Carlisle a garrison of about 400 men, consisting chiefly of the English that joined them, and some few Scots under the command of John Hamilton, the Duke of Gordon's factor, with a proper train of artillery, and a promise of returning with greater force in eight days.

By two o'clock they came up to Langtown, where they crossed the Esk, then about four feet deep, and not very rapid, as the tide was in. The cavalry entered the water with the hussars in front, and the Pretender in the center, with a boy belonging to Cappoch behind him. When half way through, he observed two people giving way, and seizing them by the hair, cried out in Irish, Coaer, Coaer, Help, Help, and so these were relieved; Perth, being better mounted than the rest, crossed the water several times, and brought off a person every time he went. The infantry, with Lord George Murray at their head, arrived safe to the other side, by keeping hold of each other, according to the direction of the country people, and of some drovers who were among them.

Scarce were they in Scotland, when they divided into parties, the Chevalier with 4000 marching to Annan, and the other of 2500 to Ecclefechan, where they rested. Next day Lord Elcho was sent with 500 horse to Dumfries, where he levied the / excise, and imposed on the town a contribution of 2000 *l.* and a thousand pair of shoes; seized 9 casks of gunpowder, all arms public and private, horses and horse furniture, while the private men among them committed above 4000 *l.* damages in the country, by plundering houses, robbing people on the highway, stripping others of their shoes and body clothes. Near 1100 *l.* was instantly paid by the magistrates, who, on remonstrance, were told that they might be glad their town was not laid in ashes, considering their association, and seizing of their waggons.

Next day the Pretender, the French ambassador, Perth, Lochiel, Clanranald, Cappoch and Glengary, went by the way of this pillaged town, while the Marquis of Tullebardin, Lord George Murray, Lords Ogilvie, Nairn, and Pitsligo, took the Moffatt road. They intended to march to Edinburgh, but hearing that General Guest had caused an intimation to be made from the pulpits, that he designed to keep the town out against them, till the arrival of the troops, they directed their rout to Glasgow, and in their way stopt at the castle of Douglas, where the Duke of that name behaved in a manner every way becoming his great and illustrious ancestors. The bulk of the private men were lodged in and about town, while the Chevalier with his guards and general officers repaired to the castle, hoping to prevail on the Duke to join, but in this they were greatly disappointed; for his Grace of Douglas was of the same sentiments as in the year 1715, when he accompanied the Duke of Argyle to Sheriffmuir, and with some of the principal noblemen* in the kingdom charged as a volunteer at the head of the cavalry.

The first who came to his Grace found him in a plain room, and homely dress, sitting before a fire, near which was a table whereon were placed seven silver watches. On their entering, he said, 'Do any of you want to take a watch?' And so touching one with his fingers he added, 'Take a watch, take a watch: here is variety.' Accordingly three of them took watches, while others demanded his money and his arms: 'It is not,' said he, 'the custom of a Douglas to deliver up his arms; but what cash I have about me shall be yours:' so rifling his pockets, he laid down his money† upon the table, which being soon snatched up, the keys of his bureau and other repositories were loudly called for. 'No keys,' said the Duke, 'I have; no keys will I give. Desire my cousin Perth to speak with me.' Accordingly Perth came in, attended by some of the chieftains, among whom were Lochiel and Dr. Cameron. These, understanding what had past, began to make an apology, by setting off the justice of their cause, and proceeding to remonstrate upon the glory that would accrue to his Grace's family, if he would join the righteous heir to the

* The Duke of Roxburgh, the Earls of Rothes, Haddington, Loudon and Leven, the Earls of Islay, who received two wounds, and Archibald Douglas, Earl of Forfar, who received twenty-two. /

† According to my information 100 l. twelve pound of which was in silver.

crown; they even went so far as to proffer to introduce him to the P – , or to bring the P – into the room to him. To which the Duke replied, with some emotion, 'I neither want to see him, nor that he should see me! Don't tell me of heirs and pretenders to the crown, I might put in for my own claim*.' / So addressing Perth, 'I thought,' said he, 'Perth, you knew me better: you might have come to me yourself.' Then, turning to Lochiel, he added these very words, 'You, Sir, have it in your power to take me prisoner, but you have it not in your power to make me assist or acknowledge any heir or pretender to the crown. I lie under obligations to no Prince, except to him who sits upon the throne; and to him I am bound by indissoluble ties of gratitude.' Having so spoke he turned upon his heel and retired, with all the dignity and air of a Douglas. There was an universal pause, the chieftains looked wistfully at one another; and, being struck with the resolution and firmness of the man, they not only desisted from troubling him further, but saved his house from being plundered; however, the army drank plentifully of his Grace's liquors, seized upon the arms which they found, and among these the sword which the great Sir James Douglas used at the terrible battle of Bannockburn, and at sixty-two more encounters, including those in Spain and in Palestine. But whether from the inability of any one man in the Pretender's army to wield the weapon, which had contributed so much to fix the independency of Scotland, and to pull down the followers of Mahomet, or from the reverence which many of them bore to the venerable name of its first owner, certain it is, the sword was sent back, and deposited in the place from whence it was taken.

Finding little encouragement at Douglas they proceeded forward to Hamilton, where, meeting with the other body of their troops, they continued two nights, the Chevalier and his officers lodging in the palace, as the Duke of Hamilton was at Lisbon, for the recovery of his health, which, through riot and irregularity, had been miserably impaired. / After regaling themselves, their van set out for Glasgow on the 25th, and next day the Pretender followed with the main body. They indeed made a most dismal appearance, being very much jaded with their winter campaign, and chagrined at their not being joined by numbers of the English, as they expected: however, for their comfort, they had the news

* William Earl of Douglas was a candidate for the throne against Robert II. the first King of the name of Stuart, anno 1370, and his Grace was descended from Margaret Tudor, eldest daughter of Henry VII. of England.

of the landings in the north country. The Chevalier received letters from his Brother, acquainting him, that the Courts of France and Spain had acknowledged his title, and had resolved to support him: and, to crown all, the French ambassador took on his public character.

The End of the FIFTH BOOK. /

THE LIFE OF WILLIAM DUKE OF CUMBERLAND.

BOOK VI.

CONTENTS.

The Siege of Carlisle, – *an Account of the Clergy of* Scotland, – *with the state of Affairs there,* – *the Conduct of Admiral* Vernon, – *and the Battle of* Falkirk.

THE Duke of Cumberland not being able to pursue his advantage at Clifton through grounds covered with snow, roads broken with ice, and darkness which was the greatest difficulty, rested his troops that night, and next morning set out for and entered Penrith with all his forces: here were to be seen the melancholy vestiges of revenge; four shops having been broken, vast quantities of goods carried off, some thrown into the streets, torn and destroyed, as a punishment to the owners, for being concerned in the riot at Kendal / on the Saturday before; some of their neighbours having informed against them. From the sight of this dismal scene, he began his march on the 21st for Carlisle, which he reached about one in the afternoon, and, at a mile's distance, surrounded it: Major-general Bland investing it on the Scots side, with St. George's dragoons, and three hundred of Bligh's regiment, to prevent any passage over the bridge of the Eden; Major Adams in the suburbs of the English gate; Major Meiric at the Irish gate, and Lieutenant-colonel Sir Andrew Agnew at the Sally-port, with 300 men: the Duke himself rode round the place, though sometimes balls lighted within a yard of his horse's head, as the garrison fired upon all in their view.

Mr. Townley, the commandant, ordered the guns to be mounted upon the walls, the houses within reach of the batteries to be burnt, and several chevaux de frize to be fixed at the gates and entrance of the city, to prevent the approach of the horse. He was for making sallies on the King's troops, but in this last he was opposed.

His Royal Highness observing the posture of the city, and that it might cost some lives to take it by assault, without proper artillery, sent to Whitehaven for some battering pieces; accordingly, four of eighteen pounders arrived upon the 24th, and six of the same size upon the 25th. No sooner were these up, than the Royalists began to erect batteries, notwithstanding a continued fire from the walls, and by the 28th one of six pieces was finished, from which they play'd upon the four gun battery of the town; but next day the firing ceased, for want of shot, till towards evening, when a fresh supply arrived, and the fire being renewed with great briskness for two hours, caused the utmost consternation among the inhabitants, who in / the most supplicant manner appeared before the commandant, beseeching him to think of preserving their lives; he went directly to Hamilton, governor of the castle, to consult what was proper to be done. A capitulation was proposed, to which Hamilton agreed; two letters were immediately written, and a man sent with them; who being brought to the Duke by an advanced party, delivered the one directed to his Royal Highness, and the other for the commander of the Dutch troops, supposed to be with the army, signed Geohegan, 'Commander of the French artillery, and of the French garrison that was at, or might come to Carlisle, for defence of the town and citadel.' The contents were to summon the Dutch officer to retire with his troops from the English army, under pretence of the capitulation of Tournay.

The night of the 29th was spent in raising a new battery of three eighteen pounders, which was compleated by the morning; when the old battery fired a platoon, as an earnest of what was to follow; this menacing aspect soon intimidated the garrison, who directly hung out a white flag, and called over the walls, that they had two hostages ready to be delivered at the English gate which is on the opposite side. On this, Lord Bury and Colonel Conway were ordered to deliver the two following messages in writing;

'I. His Royal Highness will make no exchange of hostages with rebels; and desires they will let him know by me, what they mean by hanging out the white flag?

'II. To let the French officer know, if there is anyin the town, that there are no Dutch troops, but enough of the King's to chastise the rebels, and those who dare to give them any assistance.' /

In about two hours they brought a written paper, signed by 'John Hamilton, in the name of himself, and of all the officers and soldiers of the garrison,' informing, 'that the white flag was hung out on purpose to obtain a cessation of arms, and to know what terms his Royal Highness will be pleased to give them upon surrender of the city and castle of Carlisle:' to which they received this declaration, signed by the Duke of Richmond, Lieut. General.

'All the terms his Royal Highness will or can grant to the rebel garrison of Carlisle, are, That they shall not be put to the sword, but be reserved for the King's pleasure.'

The terms were agreed to, the governor and principal officers surrendered, after sending a paper recommending themselves to the King's mercy, and begging the intercession of his Royal Highness. On this Brigadier Bligh took possession of the town with 400 of the foot guards, 700 marching foot, and 100 horse, who patroled the streets in the night-time.

Next day, December 31st, the Duke entered Carlisle on horseback, amidst the blessings of the citizens, and the acclamations of the country people, who had conceived such an opinion of him, that upon his first appearance they flocked in with provisions, tools, and other necessaries, yea, and contributed with their own hands to advance the works against the town. They were enamoured to see the city restored to her King, to herself, and to them; while their satisfaction was crowned with seeing such things as were forcibly or otherwise taken away exposed to view, that all might receive their own on proving their property.

In the mean time the garrison was confined in the cathedral, and a list of their names and designations given in; but by a special order were neither / stript of their money, nor their clothes; for said his Highness, 'They will need these during their confinement.' There were here of English Colonel Townley, 5 captains, 6 lieutenants, 7 ensigns, 1 adjutant, 93 non-commissioned officers, drummers, and private men, with the quartermaster Cappoch, chaplain to the Manchester regiment, who was to be no longer Bishop of Carlisle.

Of the Scots, Governor Hamilton, 6 captains, 7 lieutenants, one of whom, James Nicolson of Perth's regiment, broke the capitulation by endeavouring to escape, which circumstance, at his trial, not a little militated against him; 3 ensigns, 1 surgeon, 256 non-commissioned officers, drummers, and private men.

Of French, Sir Francis Geohegan, a captain of Lally's regiment, 1 serjeant, with 4 private men, Colonel Strickland, of no regiment, and Sir John Arbuthnot, a captain in Lord John Drummond's. There were found six guns of one and half pounders, three of four pounders, one octagon, all with carriages, four cohorns, and two royals, all of brass.

His R. Highness, after having walked round the walls, and viewed the fortifications, was conducted to the same house, and laid in the same bed, where formerly the Pretender lay; and getting up as usual by three in the morning, had the pleasure about six hours after, of seeing not only the general officers and soldiers, but the nobility and gentry, yea, and multitudes, who from all quarters repaired to him. The city of Edinburgh sent four deputies, among whom was Mr. Patrick Haldane, late Sollicitor for Scotland, a gentleman of great learning and peculiar address, to congratulate him on his success, and to intreat him to honour her with a visit, if he came to Scotland. They were introduced / by the Earl of Panmuir, received in the most gracious manner, and had the honour to dine with him, when he drank to the prosperity of that town, and of the adjacent towns; his deportment while here was every way princely and serene; he encouraged the people to persevere in their loyalty, and to apply to their daily business, for said he, 'there is nothing to fear;' when speaking of the Highlanders, 'he lamented that so much bravery should be misemployed, and even wished they would disband in time, before the forces, whom he here took occasion to commend, were too much provoked against them, and their shattered remains should fall into the hands of offended justice.' After settling matters, and leaving the command of the troops destined for Scotland to General Hawley, he set out on the 2d of January for London, where his presence was necessary for curbing any invasion, which at that time was expected, notwithstanding the following precautions.

A proclamation was issued out December 6th, for putting the laws, particularly the act of parliament of the 27th year of Queen Elizabeth, and another of the 3d of King James I. and VI. in execution against Jesuits and Popish Priests, and promising a reward of 100 *l.* for every such person after conviction, within London, Westminster, the Borough of Southwark, or within ten miles round those places. Upon the 11th a Priest, and his landlord for harbouring him, were confined in Newgate for remaining in London beyond the time appointed.

Upon the 12th advice came, that an embarkation of troops was carrying on with great expedition at Dunkirk, where already were most of the vessels for that purpose, and that furniture was shipped / on board for 1000 horses. In two days a proclamation was published, commanding the wardens, sheriffs, mayors, lieutenants, justices of the peace, and other officers, to cause the coasts to be carefully watched, all cattle, and every other thing that might be serviceable to the enemy after landing, to be removed; alarm posts were fixed; the several guards were ordered to be in readiness to march upon the first notice of any tumult or insurection in London or Westminster; the signal was firing seven half minute guns at the Tower, which were to be answered by the like number in St. James's Park; on hearing of which every officer and soldier of the six regiments of the city militia, and the two regiments of the Tower hamlets, were to repair with their arms, and a sufficient quantity of powder and ball, to their respective places of rendezvous, on pain of being punished as deserters. Signals also were settled on the coasts of Sussex and Kent, whither 4000 foot and 2500 horse were dispatched; the same was done on those of Essex and Suffolk, whither 3000 foot, and 1000 horse had repaired, by putting out flags in the day-time, and lights on the tops of the steeples and castles in the night, so that notice of an invasion would be at the Tower and St. James's Park in a few hours. The Lords of the Admiralty ordered all the men of war at Portsmouth to put to sea, and took up 50 merchant men to be armed for cruizing in the channel.

Admiral Vernon, whose name for the taking of Porto Bello, anno 1739, had once resounded throughout Europe, with Commodores Smith and Boscawen, were already at sea, each with a strong squadron. The Dover privateers had voluntarily gone to the Admiral, in order to receive and follow his instructions; on which he wrote them a letter / from on board the Norwich in the Downs, dated December the 10th, assuring them, that he would take care to reward every one's services, and endeavour to procure from the crown an ample consideration for their zeal.

Upon the 12th two of those Dover ships fell in with eight transports bound from Boulogne for Dunkirk, under convoy of a French man of war of 22 guns, to take troops on board; they seized three of them, sent one of them that night to the admiral in the Downs, and the other two to Dover next morning. Upon the 19th they fell in with about sixty sail, mostly fishing boats and small vessels from Dunkirk, bound, as they supposed, for Calais or Boulogne, to take in troops. Near the first place they drove seventeen of them on shore, blew up one, sunk two, and brought three away, two of which were directly carried into Dover, but the third was lost in that bay. All these vessels had some warlike stores on board, such as small cannon, powder, ball, horse colours, clothes, bedding for soldiers, and poles about seven feet long, spiked at each end with iron. Two of less value from Roan to Boulogne were afterward sent in.

The very day that the Dunkirk embarkation met with this disaster, the King sent a message to both Houses of Parliament, 'that he had undoubted intelligence of the preparations at Dunkirk, and other French ports, for invading his kingdoms, and that already a person* had actually landed in Scotland, and emitted a treasonable declaration at Montrose, December the 2d.' That he was come with written orders from the French King, to make war upon the Elector of Hanover, and those who would not assist the / Prince Regent in the recovery of Scotland, England, and Ireland, whose undoubted Title his most Christian Majesty, with the concurrence of the King of Spain, is resolved to support, at the expence of all the men and money he is master of. '†

King George further told them, that 'he had ordered into this Kingdom the 6000 Hessian troops taken into British pay the 11th of June last, by virtue of a treaty with the King of Sweden as Landgrave of Hesse Cassel, the better to prevent the invasion and suppress the rebellion;' and concludes, 'that he has no doubt of their enabling him to make good that agreement, and concur with him in such measures as may best defeat the attempt.'

* Lord John Drummond, Brother-German to Perth.

† He likewise signified in the declaration, that all ships with the Pretender's letter should have free access to trade in every port belonging to either Crowns of the House of Bourbon.

A copy of the treaty being laid before them, an address was drawn up, 'thanking his Majesty for communicating the advices he had received, and for his paternal care in providing for the security of his people, by directing the Hessians to be brought into the kingdom; and assuring him of their making good the expense on that account; and of their readiness, with their lives and fortunes, to support his sacred person and government;' and so concluded with 'declaring their detestation and abhorrence of the impious design.'

Next day the country was alarmed by a letter from Admiral Vernon from on board the Norwich in the Downs, to Sir John Norris, at Deal-Castle, or to the Mayor of Deal in his absence, informing, that great numbers of small embarkations were / brought from Dunkirk, and that several of them were laden with all sorts of military stores: that the Irish troops had marched to Calais from Dunkirk, where General Count Lowendahl, and many other officers, were with a young person, said to be the Pretender's second son; and advising to assemble the neighbouring towns in their defence, promising on his part the cruizers signal, which is a jack flag flying at the top-mast-head, and to fire a gun every half hour, in case the enemy approached.

The Deputy-Lieutenants of Kent published the letter, with a warm invitation for all within twenty miles of the coast to appear in arms on the 22d on horseback in Swinfield-Minis, and to bring two days provision with them. About 4000 people of the adjacent parishes took arms, and brought in pick-axes, shovels, and other necessaries.

Notwithstanding these advices, many were of opinion, that the preparations about Dunkirk and its neighbourhood were only to amuse; for Captain Gregory of the Norwich reported, that upon taking a view of Dunkirk, there were but five or six vessels in the road, and very few in the harbour. Commodore Knowles, afterward Governor of Jamaica, informed the Admiralty, that he had stood within half a mile of the piers head of Boulogne, and within two or three of Calais; that in the harbour of the former there were not sixty of all kinds, the largest of them a galliot hoy, whose gaff was much higher than any of the other vessels mast heads; and that there was not a single one which had a topsail yard rigged aloft; that within the pier of the latter there were three or four topsail vessels, the rest, about thirty, being only galliots or fishing-boats. From these reports we may judge, whether the fears of a French landing were / ill or well founded? Which ever was the case, the enemy, on finding how the scale was turned, gave over their alarms.

For the troops were cantoned conveniently along the coast, and the Duke was returned from the chace to St. James's, where on the morning of the 5th, being Sunday, he arrived in perfect health, was at chapel, afterward in the drawing-room, and did not appear in the least fatigued, though he had not been in bed for three days, his countenance being as vigorous and lively, as if he had not gone through a winter's campaign in the midst of snow, ice, and other hardships. The whole Court appeared very gay on the occasion, and every one seemed to take a particular pride in paying him their compliments.

Besides these cantonments, and the forces that were to encamp at Finchley, there were two armies, one under General Wade at Newcastle, and another, who had served so well under the eye of his Royal Highness, composed of the regiments of Lieutenant-Generals Ligonier, Richmond, Sinclair, and Albemarle; Major-Generals Howard, Skelton, and Bland; Brigadiers Semple, Douglas, and Bligh; Artillery, Lesley, Bernard, and Roper's, Brigadier-Majors; Colonel Sowle's and Colonel Johnson's regiments; besides Gower's, Montague's, Halifax's, Granby's, and Cholmondely's new raised regiments of foot, each consisting of 824 men, Montague's and Kingston's new levied horse, containing each 273; together with Major General Oglethorpe's body of 1000 horse, with which he had been detached from General Wade, who was no sooner at Newcastle, than he sent 1000 of his best infantry, and 500 horse to the assistance of the Duke, who, to keep up an harmony among all ranks, never failed, as in the case of the gentlemen and inhabitants / of Whitehaven, and of the few who rose under the Duke of Portland, to return his hearty thanks in writing, for their commendable zeal in the cause of their country.

But the gloomy prospect of meeting with too warm a reception after landing, was not more discouraging than the landing was precarious and uncertain; for Vernon, whom the French then as much dreaded as the English loved and admired, was at sea with 11 ships of the line, from 70 to 16 guns, 15 small tenders, privateers, and customhouse sloops, leaving proper squadrons under the respective commanders, at the places where attacks were apprehended.

But further, the British nation were not single in defending King George's title to the crown, by covering the sea with fleets, and guarding the coasts with numerous forces; for Europe, except France and Spain, declared for it.

Christian VI. of Denmark, more united by interest than blood, or the recent tie of marriage betwixt his son and the British Princes Louisa, who since died in childbed, proffered not only the 12000 troops in British pay, but all his forces, if they could be carried over. The old King of Sweden, that intimate acquaintance of our Kings George I. and II. rightly judging, what was the case of King George to-day might be his on the morrow, declared his abhorrence of the impious attempt, contrary to the faith of treaties; and though King of a people naturally lovers of the British nation, but through policy in the interest of France, yet he let out the troops of his Landgraviate in support of our King; and it is remarkable that many Swedes served among them. The same might be observed of the King of Poland, who, notwithstanding he had one daughter married to the Dauphin / of France, another to the King of Naples, and had his brother Count Saxe, whose incredible strength of body was not so great, as his bravery and gallantry of mind, a Mareschal of the French armies; yet suddenly he clapt up a peace with the King of Prussia, under the mediation of King George, that the former, with the House of Austria, might be at more liberty to act in support of his right. The Prussian Monarch, tho' frequently so docile as to march his army by the direction of the Court of France, and receive his 1,400,000 florins, offered his whole army to his Royal uncle. The Empress of Russia, tho' raised to the throne by the intrigues of the House of Bourbon, yet, pressing the steps of her father Peter the Great, proffered a quota of troops to be employed as the Court of Britain should direct. For these and other reasons, France left England to extinguish the rebellion now driven into Scotland, where several vicissitudes of good and bad fortune had in the Pretender's absence attended the Royal cause.

For no sooner had the rebels left that Kingdom, than the oeconomy of the different places was restored as much as possible, only the Court of Session did not sit, which made it necessary to frame an act of parliament, securing every person's right, and importing, that the time of the troubles should not be detrimental in any action.

The clergy now returned to their several congregations, recommended loyalty to their King, and a regard to their country.

The Presbyterian church of Scotland is founded upon the plan of M. Calvin, a Frenchman; with this difference, that whereas he reformed from the church of Rome, they have reformed from him. The Westminster Confession of faith is the standard by which they go: in their worship they neither / use liturgy, nor notes; and in their discipline, there is no subordination of officers among them. They have synods, instead of diocesan bishops; and their assemblies supply the place of convocations of the clergy in England. At that time some of their private ministers were loose in their morals and vicious in their lives: and yet there were many men of probity and conscience among them. Mr. Kinloch and Mr. Wallace were eminent for piety and learning: the hospitality of Principal Campbell, of the college of Glasgow, was remarkable and great: the prudence of Mr. Ramsay, minister of Kelso, of Mr. Kirk at Dornoch, and of Mr. Brown at Selkirk, was universally admired. These and some others whom we could name might have adorned any church. But indeed those in the most lucrative places were too obnoxious to the censure of the enemies of the government. Wishart, the Principal of the college of Edinburgh, was addicted to the grossest and most sensual voluptuousness, a man of little learning, and of still less piety and religion. Gowdie, the Professor, was a dull man: and established there only that he might be enabled to discharge his debts: he was obstinate to the highest degree, and so trifling, that he wasted the time of the students upon such topics as, the perpetual virginity of the Virgin Mary, and whether or not Adam was the first man; and so devoted to the old Scottish words, that he has used them in his most elaborate discourses; a man without learning, without sympathy, and without feeling for his fellow creatures: however, with all his faults, both he and Wishart were intirely devoted to the Government: nor do I believe that his Majesty has in the whole circle of his dominions, more faithful subjects, more cordially affected to his person, family, and government, than the national / church of Scotland. The masters of the universities were generally men of probity and skill, and the masters of schools were very harmless and laborious men, extremely well skilled in classical learning.

The commission of the Scots assembly published a warning to the people, and the inferior judicatures followed their example.

The masters of the university at Edinburgh returned, and on the 21st began to teach in their respective halls, being now secure, as General Roger Handasyde, in Sir John Cope's place, had arrived from Berwick upon the 14th with Colonel Price's and Ligonier's regiments of foot, Hamilton's and Gardiner's dragoons. The night they entered was one of the most boisterous that has been observed, and proved fatal to several ships; among whom was the Fox man of war of 20 guns, which perished with her crew. Her wreck some time after was thrown in nigh Dunbar, where was found and decently interred the corpse of Captain Beaver, who had so well defended the passage of Kinghorn during the stay of the rebels in the Lothians. His skull was terribly fractured, and his eyes eat out of his head, he having, as was apprehended, been dashed against some craigs by the violence of the waves; his whole body was miserably disfigured, and had it not been for his legs, which were remarkably long, he could not have been distinguished.

On the 13th the Lords of Justiciary, attended by the freeholders of the counties of Merse, of East and Mid-Lothians, entered the city on horseback, and passed through the street then crowded with spectators. They were met by the late magistrates at the cross, and loudly huzzaed by the people. Thence they proceeded to the Parliament / Close, where alighting, they advanced to the house, and being seated, Andrew Fletcher of Miltoun, then Lord Justice Clerk, informed them, 'That he and his brethren, conscious of their duty to their King, their country, and themselves, laid hold of the first opportunity of returning to this capital, to endeavour with their help to restore peace, and revive the civil government; to shew to the world how little accession the southern parts of Scotland had to the recent calamities, from which they were lately delivered; that Marshal Wade had ordered a body of troops to march for protection of this city, and the adjacent country from insults; that if the present troubles did not subside, provision should be made against any future disturbance; that the heritors of every parish should make up lists of the able-bodied men in their respective lands proper to be entrusted with arms; that these were to be delivered to the respective sheriffs, to be transmitted by them to the persons appointed by the King for that purpose; that application should be made to the established church for their assistance in that affair.'

The sight of these was very agreeable upon the anniversary of the battles of Preston and of Dumblain thirty years before; the castle fired a round from her great guns, and the music-bells played tunes suitable to the occasion. The methods proposed were complied with. A new subscription was opened by the city of Edinburgh for raising 1000 foot for his Majesty's service, and persons by advertisement were invited to sign; gentlemen and clergy, some of whom headed their parishes, and acted the soldier, appeared in numbers; and in a short time a sufficient sum was paid down; the drums beat through the city for recruits, and such / as had listed formerly, but had been obliged to disband on account of the rebels, were now desired to repair to their duty, when they should enter into the pay of 4 *s. per* week without discount. In a short time 400 men enlisted, and were daily trained in the Parliament and College Close by such as had skill.

The 18th of December was by a Royal proclamation, dated November 12th, to have been observed as a day of humiliation and fasting; but by an unlucky circumstance it was kept at Edinburgh and many other places rather as a festival; for on the Monday before, a false piece of intelligence, that the Duke had attacked the rebels at Lancaster, and totally routed them, being published in the Evening Courant, the symptoms of grief gave place to those of joy; the clergy preached the news from the pulpits, and exulted in the event.

The family of Argyle have ever been patrons of liberty. John the second Duke of Argyle promoted the union of the crowns, and defeated the rebel army in the year 1715, when the present Duke, a nobleman of the utmost politeness and humanity, was his aid de camp. At the breaking out of the rebellion 1745, Archibald the third Duke of Argyle, a nobleman who shone among the sons of genius, was of signal service to the Government. He had been at Rosneath, one of his family seats, and getting one of the Pretender's letters into his hands*, and information concerning another, he shewed the same to Mr. Craigie, the then Lord Advocate, who only laughed at the matter; adding, that nothing could be apprehended from seven persons: to which his Grace replied, 'On account / of the fewness of his numbers the more is to be feared: and,' with a smile, 'the number seven is frequent enough among the Romans.' The matter was likewise laughed at by the Marquis of Tweedale, and other officers of state: which when his Grace observed, he refrained from coming to the privy-council, till sent for, and then he readily told his mind; and wrote to his principal gentlemen to be ready in the service of their country.

The militia of Argyleshire were soon mustered, the act of parliament against any number of Highlanders rising in arms being suspended: and happy had it been for many poor people that the same had sooner been

* The Pretender had caused many letters to be wrote, which he signed; but referred to Murray of Broughton to direct them to whom he pleased.

done. Arms and warlike stores were shipped off from Liverpool for their use; and the present Duke of Argyle, then General Campbell, set out from London, to take upon him the command of these levies.

That officer had on the 4th of November arrived in the Thames with his regiment from Flanders, as did those of General Handasyde, Brigadiers Skelton, Bligh, Mordaunt, and Semple, with the Highlanders. All these officers, from the moment of their landing, were busied in the service of the Government; but none more than General Campbell, who arrived at Inverara on the 31st of December, with a commission to raise 3400 men, which was soon effected. The private soldiers had full pay, but the officers only half. One party was stationed at Campbelltown in Kentire, to prevent any invasion from Ireland, and to overawe the disaffected clans scattered through the shire: the camp was formed at Inverara, whence detachments were sent out to protect the country. One of these, of 300 men, attacked a squadron of the Macgregors, put them to flight, killed two and took seven prisoners. Garrisons were put into the castles along / the coast, and the remainder only waited an opportunity of joining the regular forces.

So laudable an example was soon followed thro' the western counties. The city of Glasgow raised a regiment at her own expence; which was provided with arms from the castle of Edinburgh, and put under the command of the Earl of Hume. The town of Paisley levied a corps of 210 men. The shire and town of Renfrew armed, under the Earl of Glencairn; as did the inhabitants of the respective counties, under their immediate Superiors and Lords. The same spirit of loyalty spread through the eastern and southern parts of the kingdom, while the storm raged in the north, and several unhappy people were carried down the stream of rebellion.

Some small detachments of French troops dropped in with their privateers; and, on the 30th of November, Lord John Drummond arrived at Montrose, with 600 men, 15 pieces of cannon, some of which of 18 pounders; these animating the party, they marched to Perth, where they formed a camp, to which some people of desperate conditions actually repaired.

Among the number of those was Lord Lewis Gordon, a petulant and refractory young man; the late Earl of Cromartie, a nobleman who in the heat of liquor was prevailed on to join. When at Inverness he proffered his service to Sir John Cope, who not only refused it, but slighted his Lordship's Son so far, as not to bestow upon him a commission in a regiment of Highlanders then raising for the Government: a circumstance which however trivial in itself, was yet made an handle of to stir up a man who had never been remarkable for judgment or sagacity, during the course of his life. /

Such a powerful appearance in the north, under the Viscount of Strathallan, who had been left by the Pretender to secure the landings from France, at last prevailed on the Frazers to espouse the cause, in which their Chieftain had been so long and so deeply involved.

The Earl of Loudon, being then in the country, told Lord Lovat, that he had as much against him as would hang every Frazer in his district; and the Lord President of the Court of Session dissuaded him by letters, to the utmost of his power: the former went to his seat of Castle Downie, planted cannon against it, and carried old Simon in a chaise to the prison of Inverness; out of which in three days Frazer of Gortuleg delivered him; for carrying a bundle of straw into his room, under pretext of forming an easy bed for his Lordship, he stripped him to his shirt, rolled him in the straw, carried him out on his shoulders, and that night conducted him to Gortuleg; where he kept up a treasonable correspondence with the Pretender and his principal followers.

This powerful party soon lorded it over the friends of the Government; a great body of whom was routed at Inverury by Lord Lewis Gordon on the 22d of December: the Monros and Macleods, with Mr. Maitland the sheriff, were defeated by an handful of men.

An impotent attack or a faint resistance is the greatest service that one enemy can do to another; the latter of which happened at Inverury, and at once determined the fate of that vast tract of ground interjacent between the Forth and the Spey. The public money was raised: the farmer and the proprietor were taxed in an arbitrary manner; the cattle and carriages of the labourer were seized, and the landings from France were supported. / Lord Loudon could not spare any men from his camp to regain the superiority; he and the President had sufficient business on their hands, to thwart the stratagems of Lovat, and to hinder recruits from going to the enemy: and indeed in this they acted their parts so well, that Sir Alexander Macdonald, who could command 800 followers, with above 5000 others, were retained in their allegiance and duty.

But, notwithstanding all their advantages, their communication with the lower parts of Scotland was cut off, by a squadron under the command of Admiral Byng, and sometimes their reinforcements from Dunkirk were taken: as on the 25th of November, when the Lewis privateer of Dunkirk was taken by the Milford man of war, and in it 106 men, 330 stand of arms with bayonets, as many broad swords, with a great number of saddles and other furniture for horses. To balance this loss to the Chevalier, the Hazard sloop of war fell into the hands of the French, who carried her to Dunkirk, and converted her into a privateer, to which they gave the name of the Prince Charles Snow. She three times carried troops, money, and ammunition, for the use of the enemy, and at a critical juncture fell into the hands of her first owners, who restored her to her service and name.

Such was the condition of Scotland when the Pretender entered it, and by his presence threw the balance into the scale of his party. At Glasgow they were supplied with every thing necessary, such as tartan, broad cloth, linen, bonnets, and shoes: the city was assessed in ten thousand pounds, and the army lived upon free quarter. Paisly and Renfrew, with the other adjacent counties, were assessed in sums beyond their ability: and as the people of Lismahagoe had been, in a particular manner, zealous / against his cause, the same was burnt to the ground. In short, the Highland army spread themselves from the Clyde to the Forth, obliging the regular forces to withdraw to Edinburgh, opening to themselves a communication with their friends in the northern counties. The young Chevalier wrote a letter with his own hand to Lord Lovat, confirming another that had been signed by three of the principal chieftains, earnestly begging he would pull of the mask, and take upon him the sole command as generalissimo.

After a repose of nine days, he set out on the 4th of January for Stirling, taking hostages with him for payment of the money exacted from the city: they soon got possession of Stirling; but the castle there held out against them. General Blakeney, the governor, refused to treat with them any other way than from the mouths of his cannon; and they had got no artillery fit for carrying on a siege; that article was supplied by Lord John Drummond, and was transported on a brig which they had seized; the Pearl sloop of war not being able, on account of the shallowness of the water, to prevent it: nor could they hinder the troops from Perth and Montrose, on account of the fire of the batteries that had been erected on either shore by the enemy, from joining the main body of the Pretender's forces.

Things being in this situation, the army of Marshal Wade was ordered to march into Scotland, to perfect what his Royal Highness the Duke had so well begun; and the command thereof was given to Lieutenant-general Henry Hawley, an officer of experience, tho' but indifferently beloved by the private men. He had been a Lieutenant colonel in Evan's dragoons at the battle of Sheriffmuir, a circumstance which promoted this choice more than / the rigour and severity for which he was but too remarkable. The officer next to him was Major-general John Husk, a gentleman who knew Scotland well, having been quartered with his regiment of Welch fusileers in the Canongate of Edinburgh about ten years before. He was exceedingly well beloved both by the forces and by the people of the country.

The sending of Wade's army was extremely well judged, as that under his Royal Highness had gone through so severe a campaign. Perhaps no English army ever marched in so rigorous a season, and never did troops go more chearfully through danger and fatigue. It must be owned, that they had uncommon encouragement: the King sent each soldier two pair of shoes on his own charge; the Prince of Wales remitted to them 500 *l.* the citizens of London sent them 12,000 pair of breeches, 12,000 shirts, 10,000 woollen caps, 10,000 pair of woollen stockings, 1000 blankets, 12,000 pair of knit woollen gloves, 9000 pair of woollen spatterdashes: the Duke allowed them 10 *l.* every day out of his private purse, to enable the private men to pay the landlords of the inns where they might dine, or be quartered over night; but the generality of the inn-keepers refused to take any money from them, and the country people furnished them with horses. Notwithstanding the march must be supposed to be fatiguing; to men who sometimes entered a town about eleven at night and were obliged again to be in arms by three in the morning; yet

No toils were painful that could danger show,
Nor climes unlovely that contain'd a foe.

The troops destined for Scotland set out by detachments, and by different roads: some took the / rout of Haddington, others that of Lauder, and a third marched by the coast road, through Dunbar by North Berwick; finding every where the most hearty and cordial reception. At every place where they halted they were supplied from a fund appropriated for the purpose: each soldier had a pound of beef, a pound of bread, two-thirds of a quartern of gin or brandy, and a bottle of ale: and the farmers for thirty miles round brought their horses to help them forward. By the 10th of January the whole had arrived at Edinburgh, where they were joined by Gardiner's and Hamilton's dragoons, Price's and Ligonier's regiments of foot, the Glasgow and Paisley militia, which with those of the Lothians amounted to 4000 men, well armed, well cloathed, and hearty in the Government's cause.

On the 13th of January General Huske marched with the foot regiments of Monro, Cholmondely, Price, Ligonier, and Batterau, the Glasgow militia, Gardiner's and Hamilton's dragoons; and next day the regiments of Price, Barrel, and Pulteney marched by the way of Borrowstonness; and on the 15th were followed by Flemings, Blakeney's, and a battalion of Sinclair's. They all rendezvoused on the 16th at Falkirk, where, next day, they were joined by 1300 of the Argyleshire militia. They indeed made a very noble appearance, and amounted to 8000 men: two-fourths of which knew their business very well, and the far greater part had served under his Royal Highness at the battle of Fontenoy. In short, nothing but management was wanting to bring things to an effectual and speedy conclusion.

General Hawley, having followed the army the day after the last division had quitted the city, and brought with him Cobham's dragoons, fell into one / of these mistakes which since the days of Sampson have been accounted fatal to a commanding officer.

Scarce was he at Falkirk, when he received a message from the Countess of Kilmarnock, desiring the favour of his company. An invitation from a Lady so remarkable for wit and gaiety, could not be refused. Hawley went up to the Callendar, where he was entertained with great politeness and decorum, and the morning of the 17th proving rainy, she made a posset for him with her own hands, to fortify him against the damp and the cold; he continued at the Callendar till between twelve and one in the afternoon, notwithstanding the frequent expresses brought him, that the enemy was in the neighborhood. At last one of these was so importunate, that the General resolved to depart, and yet the ascendancy of the Countess was such, that she prevailed on him to dine before setting out; and in the mean time the troops in the camp sat down to dinner also; but before it was ended the Highland army was observed to move up the hill, and to extend themselves upon it, at the distance of a mile south-west from them; for Lord George Murray, brother to the Duke of Athole, who was that day the chief commander, had artfully placed the standard at the Torwood, where it continued standing, till the Highlanders were just entering the ground they intended for the field of battle. About two hours before, General Huske had, through a glass, discovered their colours at four miles distance, directly west of his camp: on which he formed the army, to prevent a surprize; but could not march forward, either to the heights whereon was the battle, or toward the standard, without orders from the superior officer.

The Royalists looked at each other with impatience and astonishment, gazing for Hawley, but / Hawley was not to be found. Toward three o'clock he appeared all at once, and observing the enemy on the brow of the hill, he put himself at the head of the cavalry, who advanced with great resolution and swiftness sword in hand, the infantry following as fast as possible, and huzzaing as they approached. Unhappily for him the enemy was duly prepared; for just when the horses were within three yards of their lines, they gave so close a fire, that men and horses promiscuously tumbled down; some indeed broke through their ranks, but these opening, every one of them was either killed or taken prisoners; while the major part turned about their heads, and scattered with great impetuosity and vehemence, in spite of their riders, who did every thing possible to retain them. They returned upon the flank of the Glasgow militia, which they greatly disordered; the confusion spreading insensibly, four regiments out of six, that composed the first line, were hurried down the stream, and the rout had been general, had not Brigadier Cholmondely stopt it, at his division; for wheeling with Barrel's and Ligonier's foot, the Old Buffs, and a battalion of the Scots Royal, these advanced some paces with a good aspect, and the enemy began to hasten forward; but that division commanded by General Huske gave them so close and full a fire, as made them halt without proceeding further. Unhappily for the troops, Colonel Cunningham of the train, had fled off without planting the artillery, and the conductors had run away with their horses. A violent storm of wind began to blow full in the face of the Royal army, wet their clothes and their cartridges, so as to render them incapable to proceed, as the flints would not strike, the powder would not burn, and the twentieth gun was not fit to be discharged. Both armies looked at each / other, the Highlanders being unwilling to move for fear of an ambush, and in hopes of surprizing them next morning, as they had done by Cope at Prestonpans. General Huske saw into the extent of their design, and therefore moved off, with drums beating, colours flying, and the other signs of a brave and resolute behaviour, and joined the shattered runaways, who by this time had been rallied by Sir John Mordaunt, as were the dragoons by Colonel Francis Ligonier. They all advanced to Falkirk, where, for fear of a surprize, it was agreed to march that night to Linlithgow, as it was not safe to stay in the neighbourhood of a resolute enemy, without cannon, or any other kind of artillery. This being settled, the Argyleshire militia drew up at the bottom of a park dyke, and along their line the troops defiled, till all were passed, and the militia forming, brought up the rear. They advanced that night to Linlithgow, viz. six miles, the wind and rain still continuing, and next night the whole came to Edinburgh in such panic and surprize, that I really believe one thousand desperadoes could at that time have cut the whole army to pieces. One thing is certain, that if ever the Highlanders wanted a day fit for using their swords, it was the 17th of January 1746, when they were so much assisted by a storm, and the bad management of the officer commanding against them. It is true, that on the field of battle the two men, who had the Pretender's cause most at heart, were that day the ruin thereof. When his cavalry first began to pursue on the separating of the dragoons, Roy Steuart cried out, 'Gentlemen, keep your ranks, these are only Cope's dragoons, you have the battle yet to fight;' and when Lord John Drummond, another aid de camp, observed the Royal Scots to wheel, he called / out to the troops, who were upon the point of running down upon them, 'that regiment behaved admirably well at Fontenoy, pray keep your ranks;' and so they desisted: but what was still more, Lord Kilmarnock proffered to conduct them through some inclosures, by which they could get sooner to Linlithgow than the Royalists; but in this he was not believed.

Such surprizing escapes were attributed by some to the immediate hand of Providence, without considering the mean by which the interposition thereof so signally appeared. If my heart does not deceive me, no man is, or at least ought to be, more convinced of the reality of a superintending Providence than I am. And on that day it was visible indeed! but visible as it was, let us trace out the mean by which the same wrought so powerfully in behalf of the King's army.

When the enemy saw that the Royalists were gone, they began to march, both to secure the baggage of the troops, or to attack them at

Falkirk, as they saw opportunity. Cameron of Lochiel, with his two battalions, entered the west end of the town, just as the rear of the King's army was marching from the east, and Falkirk is not above three quarters of a mile long. At this very instant he was told, that the Argyleshire militia brought up the rear; an event which not a little startled him, and all at once made him become pensive and thoughtful. By his mother, a sister of Sir Duncan Campbell of Lochnel, he was related almost to all the officers of the Lorn battalion*. By his Lady, a daughter of Sir James / Campbell of Achinbreck, he was connected with all the officers of the Kilmartin battalion; and these were the militia who were there. Many of his own officers were closely connected with them likewise, not only by blood, but by correspondence, neighbourhood, and traffic. He was only in the rebellion from a false principle of honour, and from passing his word to Lord Lovat in an unguarded moment; he could not think of fighting hand to hand with men for whom he had a thorough kindness, and the most sincere and affectionate regard. The other officers, observing a sort of backwardness in him, without considering the prevailing motive, gave over all thoughts of a pursuit for that night; contenting themselves with seizing upon Hawley's baggage (among which was the very post chaise that had carried him to Scotland) with that of the general officers, nay, of the whole army; for neither soldiers nor officers retained any thing but their arms.

Such was the battle of Falkirk, in which the King's army were repulsed, but not broken, and in which the enemy made so little of their advantage. On the side of the former 250 were killed, among whom were Colonel Sir Robert Monro, the Lieutenant-Colonels Whitney, Biggar, and Powell, three Cornets of horse, thirteen Captains, and two Lieutenants, 300 were wounded, and about 230 taken prisoners (but these were mostly of the Glasgow and other militia) with Captain Thornton, and seventeen of his Yorkshire blues. He continued among them for some days, when William Henderson, a merchant, contrived his escape, by secreting him in a chest, and keeping him close in / that repository, even while the rebels were in the room in quest of him.

On the side of the enemy about fifty were killed, but none of note, and as many wounded; among whom were Lord John Drummond and Lochiel; one Major Macdonald was taken prisoner. He had seized upon

* To my certain knowledge above twelve of these were his first cousins; among whom was Colonel Dugal Campbell, who was my pupil for two years, whose brother was killed at Culloden on the side of the government, and who was afterward member of parliament for the shire of Argyle.

one of the dragoon horses after his rider had been killed, and mounted on horseback. The horse, on hearing the drum beat to arms, in consequence of Ligonier's rallying the dragoons, run off with the major into the midst of them without halting. Finding himself in a net, he began to act as one of the Argyleshire militia; but General Huske detected him as an impostor, and had him directly secured. He was afterward hanged, drawn, and quartered at Carlisle.

Never was a body of forces of such undoubted bravery and reputation repulsed with so small a loss, and never was a victory improved to so little advantage; and yet the poor country continued to bleed for a time, in consequence of the strange and unaccountable event, which was indeed the more surprizing, as it was believed at St. James's that the rebellion had breathed last, and the public tranquillity had been restored.

The End of the SIXTH BOOK. /

THE LIFE OF WILLIAM DUKE of CUMBERLAND.

BOOK VII.

CONTENTS.

The Arrival of his Royal Highness in Scotland, – *the Retreat of the Pretender's Army,* – *the Operations of the* Hessians, – *the Passage of the* Spey, – *and the Battle of* Culloden.

WHEN the news of the battle of Falkirk first reached London, it raised an universal surprize; for removing which the Duke himself set out on the 25th, by two in the morning, for Scotland; where he arrived about three in the morning of the 30th, attended by James Duke of Athole, the Earl of Albemarle, Lord Bury, Lord Cathcart, and some other officers. The citizens of Edinburgh on the night before had expressed their joy for the coming of their Deliverer, by the most splendid illuminations, the ringing of bells, / and other demonstrations of gladness; and altho' the day was immoderately cold, yet multitudes went out to meet him.

No sooner had he arrived than he sent notice to the general officers, to come to him by eight in the morning, and to bring with them such accounts as were requisite with regard to the situation of the forces; whose numbers by this time had been recruited by the arrival of the dragoons of St. George, and of General Bland, with the Duke of Kingston's horse, and the foot regiments of Colonel Campbell and Lord Semple: a military chest, escorted by a party of St. George's dragoons, towards paying the army, came in; as did sixteen pieces of cannon from Newcastle, in order to replace the ten which had been lost at Falkirk; and with these came a sufficient quantity of stores, with 40 gunners and matrosses to work them. Every thing was put into the best posture imaginable; only some severities had been used by Hawley, which tended to discourage those under his command. Many of the private men were whipped in a terrible manner; the shrieks and cries of their wives and children were too piercing to be related. Four dragoons were hanged at one time, in the Grass-market, about noon, and continued on the gibbet for twenty-four hours: two were to suffer on the morning when his Highness arrived; but the sentence was respited, and they were received into their own corps.

At the time appointed the generals waited on him, with an account of what was past: and these threw no blame on each other. Hawley's conduct was approved; and yet it was judged, that he was more proper to obey than to command. Brave, bold Huske accused no body; he complained of no body, and wanted only to crush the insurrection, / and to restore the public tranquillity. While the general officers were in the room with his Highness, the Nobility and such Lords of Session as were in town went to congratulate him on his arrival. About one o'clock the Ministers of the Presbytery of Edinburgh, and such others of that profession as were in the place, went in a body to welcome him; and lastly came the Masters of the University, with the college mace carried before them: all had the honour to kiss his hand, and met with the most gracious reception.

This being over he walked down stairs, to view the sixteen pieces of cannon in the Close, and upon the spot where the Pretender's had stood before. As he came out of the gate, the drums ruffed, a loud and continued *huzza* ensued. He walked along the cannon, placed in two parallel lines, scarcely taking his eye from off them, and looking all the time majestic and serene. This being over he returned to the room, the same in which the Pretender had lodged before, sat down to dinner, with his officers, and then began to concert the operations of the army. – The result of the consultation was, that the troops should march next day, by four in the morning: the orders were secretly intimated; and never did more chearfulness appear among a body of men: for, repining at Hawley's severity, they looked upon his Royal Highness as their deliverer and friend. Some soldiers who had after the battle of Fontenoy been compelled to list in Lord John Drummond's brigade, embraced the first opportunity of deserting, and gave the King's troops the best intelligence in their power:

their services were ingratefully received by General Hawley, but now were properly acknowledged.

At the time appointed the troops were in readiness to march. About half an hour past four in / the morning they set out in two columns, consisting of fourteen battalions of foot, the Argyleshire militia, and the dragoons of the Viscount Cobham and of Lord Mark Ker. General Huske led the van, and the artillery brought up the rear. About nine his Highness set out in a coach, that had been sent him by the Earl of Hopton, a nobleman so well affected to the Government and so well disposed, that he sent twelve guineas to every foot regiment, and twenty-five to the Argyleshire Highlanders. And here his Highness acted every way like a soldier: for, as the report of the guns in Edinburgh Castle could in a clear day be heard at Stirling, so he wanted that no intimation should be given to the enemy: and, as a further precaution, Ligonier's and Hamilton's dragoons were ordered to patrole along the roads leading westward. Coming up with the troops at about seven miles distance, his Highness put himself at the head of the Royal Scots, and, as he passed along the lines, earnestly expressed himself in these terms: 'Gentlemen, there is a near prospect of a battle, and if there is any person here who is unwilling to engage, pray let them speak freely, and with pleasure they shall have my discharge: nor shall their quitting the service be ever thrown out as a reflection upon the country to which they belong.' The whole answered with repeated shouts and acclamations; and the two soldiers pardoned that morning were the first to raise the huzza. That night eight battalions marched to Linlithgow with the Duke, and Sir John Mordaunt with six to Borrowstonness; the dragoons to the adjacent villages, and the Argyleshire men in front towards the Avon. Next day they were put in motion by four in the morning, and at the west end of the bridge were drawn up in order of battle, in which / they marched toward Falkirk, and were joined in their way by the dragoons, the militia, and by Brigadier Mordaunt's division: about ten in the morning they entered Falkirk; but, to their astonishment, no enemy was near them.

By this march of the troops the siege of the castle of Stirling was raised. It had not been very hard pressed, on account of the unfitness of the enemy, and the resolution of General Blakeney to hold out to the last. He answered the summons of the Pretender in very pertinent terms: 'That he was always looked upon as a man of honour, and that the Rebels should find he would die so.' The cutting off all communication with the town did not dishearten the garrison, then consisting of 600 men. Two batteries, that had been erected under cover of some woolpacks, were dismounted by the fire of the garrison; and these suffered no inconvenience except in the breast-work of the rampart, a small part of which was beat down. Stirling was delivered before she was aware, and the Castle was relieved before she knew that the Duke of Cumberland was arrived. The enemy moved off their baggage on the 31st in the morning, with about twenty pieces of cannon, having spiked up some others; and endeavoured to set fire to a magazine of powder, which had been laid up in the church of St. Ninian, to prevent its falling into the hands of the troops: however the train missed, and the noble fabric of St. Ninians might have been standing, had it not been for seven stragglers, who lagged behind, went to the church in quest of prey, and in expectation of some houshold furniture that had been hidden there in great quantities: a private man called Macintosh came to the window, and, at the desire of a French engineer, fired a pistol thro' it. The shock was sudden; the powder / blazed; the plunderers, the incendiary, the seats and roof blew up in the air, and the stones flew about the church-yard, struck some of the towns people, while the whole were stunned at the terrible convulsion. The report was heard for many miles round: the Duke's army rightly judging it to be an indication of a retreat, Brigadier Mordaunt was sent forward with the dragoons and the Argyleshire militia to harrass them, but they were gone too far: and the enemy looked upon it as an attack upon one of their parties. They had already crossed the Forth, and now redoubled their flight toward Crief; where, holding a council of war, they separated into different bodies, and appointed Inverness to be the place of their rendezvous. Their scheme was to make the country as serviceable to them as possible; to collect the public money, and to take up provisions; and to favour the landings from France. The greater part, with the Pretender at their head, took the road of Perth, where they threw the swivels taken out of the Hazard sloop into the Tay, and nailed up thirteen pieces of brass cannon, of eight and twelve pounders. Here they subdivided, Lord George Murray taking the rout by Dundee, Montrose, Aberdeen, Bamff, and Elgin of Murray, while the Chevalier and the principal clans advanced by the way of the Blair of Athole; where after staying five days they continued their march to Ruthven of Badenoch; the barracks of which they blew up: and finding a man, called Riddell, who was carrying letters to Lord Loudon, which he had secreted between the soles of his shoes, the poor fellow was taken up and hanged. From this place they proceeded to Agymore, where the Grants of Strath-Spey entered into a neutrality with them, neither to fight for or against them. Hence they went to Inverness, where Major George / Grant, the governor, gave them little trouble; for, contrary to the advice of Mr. Thomson the gunner, and of Lieutenant Graham, of Guise's regiment, he surrendered the fort, upon no other condition but that of saving his own baggage; while that of the officers and private men was permitted to the enemy. There were in it about 100 of the name of Grant, many of whom listed with the enemy, or were permitted to depart by the interest of friends.

When all was over the Pretender came from Castlehill into the town, and had the pleasure of seeing the chief place and principal fort in the north in his hands. By this conquest he acquired 12 pieces of cannon, 16 barrels of powder and ball, besides other ammunition and military stores, 100 barrels of beef, and 500 bolls of oatmeal. A governor was directly appointed, however shortlived was his command; for the outworks and body of the place were soon blown up. A strange delusion indeed! to destroy a castle which gave lustre to the town, and on which the government had expended 50,000 *l.* but thirteen years before.

On the very day when the fort surrendered, the van of the party which had taken the coast road came into the town, and the other divisions successively arrived, making the most of their march; for having met with two Spanish privateers at Stonehive, they took 100 chests of arms out of them, besides a large quantity of powder and ball, which Roy Steuart took particular care to transport safe to Inverness, which was from this time denominated the head quarters.

The rebel army being got together, detachments were sent every-where to secure provisions, and to keep the country in awe. Every shire and district was visited by such as seemed best acquainted therewith; / the Camerons and Macdonalds of Glengary were sent to Fort Augustus and Fort William; the former fell into the hands of the enemy, with Major Wentworth the governor, and three companies of Guise's regiment, a ball having fallen into the powder magazine. The fort was turned into a place of confinement for the troops which they could not transport*, and so

* Many prisoners were sent to Dunkirk in the privateers that carried troops and ammunition into Scotland.

continued till the 13th of April, when the whole barracks, on which the government had expended 30,000 *l.* were blown up. The garrison of Fort William was more fortunate; and notwithstanding the town was burnt, yet Captain Scott the governor took such care of the fort, that he disputed every inch of ground with them, and obliged them to retire with the loss of their batteries, which consisted of the artillery taken from Sir John Cope at the battle of Prestonpans, and two large mortars. We cannot pass over this account of the prisoners, who fell into their hands, without taking notice of a fact, which does not a little illustrate the spirit of the party. Such of the soldiers of the garrisons of Inverness and Fort Augustus, as were confined in the former, were put into a church, and there stript of their clothes, in order to bestow them upon the recruits that were coming in. Fortunately for them one Fleming, the Marquis of Tullibardin's gentleman, came by, and saw their distress; the men complained of their hardships, and he was prevailed on to intercede in their behalf. Their clothes were soon ordered to be restored, which indeed they had better have wanted, for many of them listed with the Adventurer, and soon came to an untimely end; perhaps the party wanted to cloath the Frazers, / who now crowded in with impunity. Before this time many of them refused, till Macdonald of Barisdale, and young Frazer of Inneralachy, carried the bloody cross among them, and threatened to burn them in their own houses, if they did not take up arms and rebel.

Lord Cromartie was sent into Rossshire, as the bulk of his estate lay there; and Macdonald of Barisdale was dispatched after the Earl of Loudon, and the militia under his command. Happily for his Lordship the fire from the garrison prevented their crossing the bridge after him; they were obliged to ford the Ness a considerable way nearer the mouth of the harbour, and all the time the Royalists were gaining ground, and had passed the ferry of Kessoch before their pursuers could arrive at the shore thereof. This obliged Barisdale to march about five miles higher up, to cross at Beulie, and from thence to follow his pursuit. The next day he came in view of them about three in the afternoon, and certainly would have committed a most dreadful havock, had it not been for the Vulture sloop of war, whose head just appeared within the Sutors* of Cromartie, as Barisdale and his corps were seen upon the brow of the hill; the

* A corruption of the Greek word Σωληρες, Deliverers, because when once a ship is within these, she is safe from the most violent storms.

loyal militia huzzaed, and made every other signal for the Vulture to come near, but they had no boats to send off to her: the signals were known, the sloop came as near as possible, and fired three cannon toward the hill; three of the corps fell by the shot, several were wounded, and the remainder returned the way they came. In the mean time the Loyalists were transported into Rossshire on board the Vulture's boats, and other small craft as they / could find on the opposite shore. They proceeded in their rout to Sutherland, where they encamped at Dornoch, the only town in the county. In this manner they acted in the shires more immediately in their power, and continued to send out parties every-where, even within a day's march of the grand army, where no preparations were neglected to bring matters to a final conclusion.

For no sooner had his Royal Highness got rid of the compliments of the city of Glasgow, and the deputies from the adjacent villages and towns, than he set out from Falkirk to Stirling, which he entered amidst the loudest acclamations and huzzas, that were answered by three rounds from the cannon of the fort. It was indeed no wonder, for the common people of that part of the kingdom are in a particular manner devoted to Presbyterian church government, which the Pretender would never ratify; and to heighten their satisfaction, the Duke was attended by a crowd of prisoners, who at the late battle had fallen into the hands of the enemy. He only staid here till the 4th, when the arch of the bridge, that had been blown up by General Blakeney for retarding the progress of the enemy, had been repaired. That day the army marched, and proceeded to Crief, where they arrived next morning, while one party turned to Castle Drummond, seized the Dutchess of Perth, and another turned to Strathallan, and took the Viscountess, both of whom were escorted to the Castle of Edinburgh, where on the 11th they were closely confined, there being the strongest suspicion that the former had prevailed on her son, and the other on her husband, to join the Chevalier. Next day the troops advanced to Perth, where magazines of provision were laid in. Here the noblemen and gentlemen of the adjacent counties waited on him, / as did the ministers and the deputations from the towns. He received them all in a very princely and becoming manner, and then returned to business, from which no visits could divert him. Detachments were instantly sent out to secure the passes; Sir Andrew Agnew was dispatched to Dunkeld with 500 of the infantry, and 120 of the Argyleshire militia; Lieutenant-

Colonel Leighton was sent with a party of 500 men to Castle Menzies, in order to prevent the excursions of the enemy. Here he continued till the 18th, when he set out for Edinburgh, attended only by Lord Cathcart, and some few servants, in order to confer with his brother-in-law the Prince of Hesse-Cassel, who had lately arrived from Holland with a body of 5000 men.

These troops had been hired from Frederic King of Sweden, in consequence of an agreement concluded at London with the Hessian Envoy. His Swedish Majesty was to receive the annual subsidy of 150,000 crowns while the treaty existed, and 250,000, if they should be dismissed before the determination of it; they were to receive the same pay as the national British troops, were only to be employed in Great Britain, or in support of her Allies in the Low Countries; the charge of their transportation both coming and going should be defrayed; eighty crowns were to be paid for every horseman that should be wanting, and thirty for every foot soldier. In consequence of this agreement they repaired to Williamstadt, where on the 5th they embarked on board thirty-six transports, and under convoy of four men of war arrived at Leith about five o'clock at night of the 8th.

A very proper and timely supply, especially as the Dutch troops had been recalled, in order, as was given out, to prevent the incroachments of / France upon their barrier; nay, so very pressing were the States General, that even while the Pretender was in England they not only made a requisition of the auxiliaries which they had sent over, but also of a body of British troops to protect them. His Highness of Hesse received the same honours as his brother-in-law, and his corps was cantoned in the best and most commodious manner; they were really very fine troops, cloathed in blue, with white livery, whose shape was varied for distinction sake; their hussars, about 500, looked extremely well, wore scimitars of a great length, which hung by a cord tied round their bodies; their horses were long-tailed, of a strong make, and generally black, of a much less size than those of the British army, but more durable and fit for use; they were mostly Swedish, or of that brood, which is reckoned the most serviceable in the northern nations.

The Royal Brothers having met and consulted together, the result of their conference was, that the British army was to march to Aberdeen, and the Hessians to Perth, and from thence to Blair of Athole, in order to stop the return of the enemy, and to hem them in upon every quarter. The plan was followed, and the Hessians, with the Earl of Crauford at their head, advanced to Blair with only two men killed, and one wounded, by some random shot that had been directed against them from behind bushes and copses of wood.

His Royal Highness being returned to Perth, he on the 20th put the troops in motion in four divisions; two of them took the road of Cowpar of Angus, whither two battalions of foot and 250 horse had marched six days before; another directed their march to Dundee, the artillery followed, and by the way of Forfar and Brechin arrived on the / 22d at Montrose with the main body of the army. Here the magistrates behaved in a very handsome manner; they in a body complimented his Highness, and very hospitably entertained the troops; the officers were regaled in the best houses of the town, while every soldier had either rum or brandy, and a biscuit for their refreshment.

At this place a court-martial sat for the trial of some officers, one of whom was broke for rifling the house of Mr. Oliphant of Gask, notwithstanding that gentleman was in the rebellion. On the 24th his Highness emitted a proclamation for such as had returned with their arms, or such as had any of their effects to bring them in, those who had been assisting to them, and lurking about the country, to give in their names and places of abode to the next magistrate or minister of the church of Scotland, and entirely to submit to the King's mercy.

This voluntary condescension had not the effect that could be wished, merely owing to the same causes that had defeated the intent of M. Wade's declaration from Newcastle; and what was still a further hindrance, the few inhabitants in that county, who had taken up arms, had either been killed in skirmishes, seized at Carlisle, or were in the camp at Inverness, where the private men were kept in ignorance of what was doing, and the officers were both afraid and ashamed.

On the 26th his Highness set out for Aberdeen, where on the 28th he arrived with the troops; the magistrates went out to meet him, and ushered him into the city, which he entered amidst repeated and accumulated huzzas; the masters of both colleges stood before the gate welcoming him in, and next day waited on him, as did the clergy, who were all most graciously received; the principal / noblemen and gentlemen came to pay him their compliments; the Duke of Gordon, the Earls of Aberdeen, Kintore, and Finlater, with the Lords Braco, Forbes, and Strichen; and at last the Laird of Grant, with 100 of his name. This step was looked upon by the rebels as a breach of the neutrality; Lord Nairn was sent into Strath-Spey with the regiment of his name to remonstrate against it, when he was told that an handsome retinue attending their chieftain was no substantial infringement of the bargain; Nairn admitted the apology, and being not only regaled with his party, but supplied with a considerable quantity of provision for the camp, he retired with all possible satisfaction.

While at Aberdeen his Highness acted in so princely and amiable a manner, that friends and enemies were obliged to confess the superiority of his genius, and the most distinguishing abilities. He daily rose at four, reviewed his troops, appeared at entertainments, walked the streets with his officers, and established hospitals for the sick; he likewise sent out parties to scour the country, one of which, consisting of 200 foot and 80 horse, marched up the Don to Braemar to seize upon the rebel magazines, and to recover the booty of the southern counties, which lay concealed there. The clergy were very assisting in this expedition, as they conducted the detachment to the shallows and fords of the river, and directed them to the hidden caverns, where the magazines and valuable effects had been secreted. During this search none but actual rebels were molested, nor were any goods seized, except such as had been forcibly taken away; for when some soldiers went to a gentleman's house and robbed it, the officer was tried, and broke by a court-martial; another was served in the same manner for taking six guineas from a merchant of / Aberdeen, as a reward to preserve his shop from being rifled. In a word, nothing was wanting to animate the troops, and to protect the country on the part of his Royal Highness.

Of the different parties sent out from the camp, none met with the least disaster, except a small detachment belonging to the Earl of Albemarle.

That nobleman had been sent to a place called Strathbogie, the ancient seat of the family of Gordon, and with him General Bland, having under his command the regiments of Barrel, Price, Cholmondely, and the Scots Royal, Cobham's dragoons, Kingston's horse, and 60 men of the Lorn battalion. Just about this time Roy Steuart and Major Glascoe had come down with an intent to penetrate as far as possible. His Royal Highness had an account of their design before his Lordship had got half way to the place appointed; on which he sent Colonel Conway, one of his aids de camp, to Inverurie, with orders to General Bland to march forward to attack them. Bland was in motion in a moment, he joined the foot regiments in their way from Old Meldrum, and both marched with such alacrity, that they were within half a mile of the enemy before they were discerned. The rebels then waiting dinner, fled off immediately; only some of their hussars drew up upon the green, and made a shew of standing upon the defensive; but this was only to favour the retreat of the foot. They withdrew with great dexterity to a place called Westerton, at a mile's distance, and there halted until a party of the Argyleshire militia appeared in their front, and a squadron of Kingston's horse were observed to ford the Devron below them. This determined them to file off. The Royalists pursued to the top of the hill of Cairnie, but there stopped; only the Marquis of Granby, Colonel / Conway, and other volunteers advanced a few yards further, and fired some pistols, but the fire was not returned; for Roy Steuart's intention was to decoy them into the middle of a party, who had been there laid in ambush, but he was disappointed.

Some few days after Roy Steuart contrived another scheme for seizing upon 30 of Kingston's horse, and 50 Argyleshire Highlanders, at a place called Keith, within six miles of the Spey. These had marched to the hill above Castle Gordon, but retired for fear of being overpowered. The enemy, taking them for an outguard of a much greater body, set out after them about ten at night, and arrived by one in the morning. The avenues to that town were stopt; Major Glascoe came up to the centry, who said, 'Who's there;' 'A friend,' replied the other, 'of the Duke of Cumberland,' and directly seized him. The man was disarmed, and a pistol held to his breast, threatening immediate death if he cried; two others were served in the same manner: fortunately one of the sentinels fired and gave the alarm: all was confusion at once: Kingston's horse were all taken, except five, with two men and a cornet; a party of the Highlanders were seized in their beds, except twelve men, who retired into the church-yard, and fired from it: however, these were soon overpowered, and driven into the church, out of which they fired, and received the fire of the enemy through the windows; seven of the party were killed, and five wounded. In short, only one escaped to the Earl of Albemarle, who dispatched an express to Aberdeen; the Duke sent him two battalions, and ordered out Brigadier Mordaunt with three others, and four pieces of cannon, to Old Meldrum, to be near to support his Lordship. /

This successful attempt upon Keith was the very foundation of their not pursuing a design still more ample and extensive; for Roy Steuart had laid a plan for surprizing the Earl of Albemarle in his head quarters: fortunately for his Lordship one Macaty, a schoolmaster at Glass, got intelligence of it, and communicated the same to the camp. The troops were kept in readiness, and under arms, so that the enemy did not come forward; however, by watching and impatience the men became weary and fatigued; they had watched for three days and three nights together, and about twilight of the third day the man again brought information that the enemy was drawing near. His Lordship of Albemarle did not believe him, and therefore speaking to him in a manner different from his usual politeness, he ordered him to be sent to Aberdeen, where he received 500 hundred lashes for wilfully giving false intelligence; he was likewise disciplined at Old Meldrum and Strathbogie, and then dismissed with orders to tell the rebels, that the King's troops were prepared for them. Hawley was the occasion of this severity: 'For,' said he, 'his design is to ruin the army through want of sleep, and then to bring the enemy upon them.' This indeed was the design of Roy Stuart, but not of the poor man. Notwithstanding his hardship, Macaty gave no hurtful intelligence to the enemy: and yet these heard of the punishments he had undergone, and of the message sent by him. Overawed with the alertness of the King's troops they kept near the Spey, at the distance of twelve long miles from Albemarle's quarters, from whence, as from them, there were sent out patroling parties, to get the best information possible of each other's progress. /

Though these incidents might have diverted the enemy, yet it could not effectually have prevailed on them to lay aside the design of surprizing the troops in the night-time. Secretary John Murray, who about this time fell sick of a cold, was the person who altered the method of their proceeding, and advised to fortify the banks of the Spey, and to wait the Duke's army at this place.

The river of Spey is one of the most rapid in Europe; by experiment it is found to run at the rate of fourteen miles in an hour, and for the space of thirty miles, meandring through a fertile country; it empties itself into the sea, a little below Garmouth, a small village famous for being the landing place of King Charles II. anno 1650. No river in Britain is so swelled by the rains and the snows. The hidden caverns in Galloway don't fill the Tweed, the heights of Breadalbane do not send such a supply from their melted snows into the Forth, lake Tay and its adjacent eminencies do not so fully replenish the river of its name, the Dee does not receive such a quantity of water from Braemar, nor the Don from the hills of Innercauel, as the Spey does from the mountains of Badenoch and the impetuous streams that run into it; and its narrowness, being about forty yards over at a medium, contributes to the velocity of its flow. For fifteen miles it rolls with great force, and only in three places are fords to be found. Cromdale is the highest; the ford of Achainanie is about eight miles lower down, and hither Roy Steuart was sent with 700 men draughted from different corps, and two pieces of cannon. Nine miles lower was the ford of Bellie, over-against Gordon-castle, and near the mouth of the river. Lord John Drummond had the direction of the batteries to be fixed there. These were ordered to be placed upon two eminences, / so as to flank each other within the reach of cannon shot. The rapidity of the river and sleepness of its banks gave them the greatest encouragement; but in this they deceived themselves, as in other things: for Lord John was no engineer, and the batteries, notwithstanding the remonstrance of the Secretary, were neglected. The Pretender was at a distance, busied about other things: he was receiving recruits in great numbers from among the different branches of the Catti, and from the western parts of Rossshire, as also several supplies from abroad: at times he affected to be gay, paid visits through the country, and once declared his curiosity to see a salmon caught with a rod upon the water of Beuly. His parties were not come in from the excursions on which they had gone out. A battalion of the Athole men had been sent to Cushiville and Cainachan: these surprized a small party of the Argyleshire militia; but could make no impression upon the quarters of the Hessians or of the Earl of Crawford. Another party had gone to Sutherland, where the very advantage which they obtained turned out to the detriment and loss of their cause.

Every person has heard of the notable scheme contrived and executed by Perth in person, for surprizing the Sutherland militia, and dispersing the corps under the Earl of London's command. For this purpose he got together about forty large boats, on board of which he put a body of 1500 men, draughted from the different divisions of their grand army. By means of a thick fog he, on the 20th of March, set off from Burghhead, and crossing the Firth, landed with the greater part below Dornoch, and sent about 200 men to surprize the out-guard at the Kittle, three miles to the westward: the bulk of the militia was seized in a moment; / only some few escaped, to be messengers of their own disaster: and the Earl of Loudon, being at the pass of the Bonar, to observe Barisdale, who was on the opposite side of the water, could give them no assistance. Sutherland fell into their hands, and a communication with the plentiful county of Caithness was now opened: the detachment sent to the Kittle came to Dornoch, and spread desolation, as they had done in Rosshire before. All were treated alike, provided they were for the Government. The clergy were visited without distinction. Those of Eastern Ross were at that time, for the most part, truly amiable men: those of Sutherland were not inferior in point of candour and other Christian virtues: however no distinction was made; the amiable and endearing Mr. Kirk, minister of Dornoch, was treated more cruelly than Daniel Monro*, minister of Tain, though this last was an uncouth man, a monster of impiety, wickedness, and ill-nature: the former had lodged the Earl of Loudon, and this was all his crime; they violently thrust him down his own stairs, so that the innocent honest man was much bruised; and yet not one impatient word dropt from him.

However, vengeance pursued them; for, on leaving him and recollecting the generous openness of his comely and venerable countenance with the silver colour of his grey hairs, they quarrelled with each other, and from words came to blows, by which many of them were maimed: and indeed it is no wonder that their consciences, however callous and obdurate, should upbraid them for an insult upon a gentleman by birth, more so by his education and prudence, and a favourite of Heaven, / for his amiable and endearing deportment: a Nathaniel indeed in whom there was no guile: a truly good man; whom, from the frequent accounts given by the best of preceptors†, added to my own experience, I knew to be almost the best and most valuable of mankind; whether we consider him as a gentleman, a minister, a parent, an husband, or a friend.

While the enemy is spreading over Sutherland, and Lord Cromartie's son was riding into Caithness, where his success in raising men was nothing, but where he took up a considerable quantity of meal for the Pretender's use, the Earl of Loudon retired to Strathnavern, where he

* He was afterward turned out of his church for fighting, and other immoralities.

† Mr. John Henderson, master of the grammar school of Nairn, a truly divine man, and who understood classical learning as well as any man in Europe.

had an immediate opportunity of doing a more substantial service to the Government, than if he had continued undisturbed in his camp.

For, on the 25th, the Prince Charles Snow had run ashore, on the shallows near Tonge Bay, after an engagement of five hours with the Sheerness man of war. Her men and money were landed that night, and next morning they set out: however they had not gone far, when eighty-six of Lord Loudon's militia and about an hundred of Reay's men fired upon them from some eminences: six of the enemy were killed upon the spot, and as many wounded; the remainder became disheartened, and surrendered with the money and the arms they were carrying with them. They were conducted on board the Sheerness, whose Captain took possession of the prize, in which were found fourteen chests of pistols and sabres, thirteen barrels of powder, besides ammunition and military stores, with 12,500 guineas in cash: all which, except the / cash, were conducted to Stromness in Orkney, whither the Captain sailed on the information received from the prisoners, who were about one hundred and twenty, including soldiers and sailors, with twenty officers. At Stromness twelve ships were relieved, and a privateer of fourteen guns, that had laid an embargo upon them, was taken.

As the Pretender's party was now in possession of the country, a visit was expected by Lord Reay, who embarked with the treasure and the prisoners: and, arriving at Aberdeen on the 6th of April, he gave such an account to his Royal Highness, as intirely determined him to decamp, in order to give battle to the enemy before they should be joined by the embarkations carrying on at Dunkirk, as he learnt from the prisoners, or by others who might be dazzled by the glittering appearance of his good fortune.

Every thing being got in readiness, the army marched on the 8th of April, and, by the way of Old Meldrum and Bamff, arrived at Cullen upon the 11th, where he was joined by the Earl of Albemarle's battalions, and next day proceeded to the Spey. His Highness with General Huske led the van, which consisted of fourteen companies of grenadiers, the Argyleshire militia, and all the horse, with two pieces of cannon, which were immediately planted upon a ground that commanded the ford over which the army was to cross. As Lord John Drummond had not expected his Royal Highness at that time, so the batteries were not finished, and the opposite shore was but slightly guarded; and such as were there, fled off with precipitation on seeing Kingston's horse enter the water, and galloped off to Elgin with the news.

The van being come to the river, his Highness was the first to enter the water at the head of the / horse, who forded it a little above Garmouth, while the grenadiers and Highlanders passed somewhat higher up: the infantry waded over as fast as they arrived. And though the water was very cold and up to their middles, yet they went on with great chearfulness. Thus the whole got over, with no other loss but that of one dragoon and four women, who were carried down by the stream.

The troops were cantoned that night on the banks of the Spey, and next day proceeded to Elgin, the party who had deserted the Spey keeping at a proper distance before them. It was Sunday, and the people were just coming out of church: they crowded about the Duke with uncommon alacrity and gladness, pouring out their blessings upon him, and even reckoned themselves happy if they could but kiss his boot: he held out his hands to them in the most condescending and gracious manner, and with great affability asked some women, as they thronged upon him, 'Will you give me a share of your brose*?' He was invited to step into the town, and to take a little refreshment; but he excused himself in the most princely manner, by telling them that he was a soldier, and upon his march. So truly amiable was his deportment, and so winning his behaviour, that the people could not but admire him. At a mile's distance the army halted and dined, the Duke's table being the head of a drum; from thence they marched to Alves, and next day set out for Nairn. The Duke on his way gave a singular instance of his humanity and real goodness of heart. About half a mile from Forress is the water of Findhorn, over which the troops were to pass; in the middle thereof, one of the carriage horses dropt down, and the waggon stuck fast in the bed of / the stream. Hawley came up immediately, and fell to lashing the waggoner; the cracks of the whip sounded in the ears of his Royal Highness; he turned about, clapped spurs to his horse, rode into the water, and checked Hawley for his impatience: 'Fye upon it, Hawley, to use any person so, the man is my friend, and do you not see that he is assisting us;' so turning to the man he directed him to loose the harness, and to free the horse from his incumbrance: his orders were obeyed, and so without further trouble all was set right as before. Hawley became every day more hated, and his Highness increased in favour with the army, who looked upon him as their father, their deliverer, their ornament, and friend; that night they

* From the Greek word βρωσις, meat.

came to Nairn, within twelve miles of the enemy: Perth continued at the end of the bridge till Kingston's horse came within an hundred yards of him, and then galloped off at a full stretch, never halting till he was at Inverness, where the Pretender had but only the night before heard of the Duke having passed the Spey.

Next day being the anniversary of his Highness's birth, the troops rested; but by a particular order, they were not allowed to observe it otherwise, than that every private man had half a pint of rum and a biscuit given him. These were supplied from the transports which kept pace with them; however, in every other place, except where the Pretender prevailed, it was kept as a jubilee; in some towns the Adventurer was hanged in effigy, which, with a skirmish that happened at Golspie in Sutherland, was an omen of the stunning blow, which next day he received.

The Earl of Cromartie and his son, with some officers, being at Dunrobin on a visit to the Countess of Sutherland, who was in a different interest / from her husband, had the curiosity to see one Dr. Vanhoven perform some feats of activity: while his corps was marching to the Little Ferry, he was taken up with his diversion; the servants of the family apprized a party of the Sutherland militia, who were at a small distance from them. Poor Cromartie had in Lochroom issued forth the most horrid and execrable orders, such as to hang men at their own doors, and burn their houses, if they did not join the Pretender's standard; and in this place several very cruel things were done inconsistent with humanity. The Macgregors and Barisdale's corps were in the country, and there was little provision to be found; Cyderhall, the most elegant house in the shire, was burnt, and in it a granary of meal; the house of Kintredwell was also set on flames, as was another at Kilgour; incidents that could not fail to provoke.

During the time of his Lordship's diversion, the militia got together, and contrived to surprize him; Barisdale was on the other side of the ferry: he had none with him but the poor men whom he had forced from their own houses, and who were poor inoffensive innocents. These marched in a body, and were near two miles from Dunrobin when his Lordship set out. As he came to the brook of Golspie, a party of twenty-six men fired upon them from a church-yard; their horses startled, and directly returned; the party pursued them, but on coming to Dunrobin they found only shut doors; on which one Mackay desired access, and being told that every person who appeared in view was to be fired upon:

'What!' says Mackay, 'fire upon one man,' a phrase which he so frequently uttered, that the gate was opened, and he was let in. Accordingly he was carried up stairs to Cromartie, and insisted on his surrendering; so going / down again, he told the centry that his master had surrendered himself, and that it was needless to stand out any longer: he delivered up his arms and the keys, and some of his party coming up on a signal given, they were put in possession of every thing. In the mean time those who had marched forward were attacked and broken; they fled to the ferry, where they were made prisoners; Cromartie, with his son, Lieutenant-colonel Kendal in the Spanish service, and nine other officers, were conducted in their boots to an island in Brora Water, and from thence were carried on board the Hound sloop of war, which, on an express concerning the event, had loosed from Cromartie, in order to take them in. All this time Barisdale was marching toward the Bonar, in order to join the Chevalier, who now prepared for a stand.

From the flight of his men having intelligence of the Duke's approach, he called in his out-parties, and drew them up in the street of Inverness on the 14th, and then marched at their head to the Parks of Castle hill and Culloden, where they encamped that night, and next day drew up in order of battle upon Drumossie Muir, with their batteries placed to the right and left of them, and one of four pieces in the center; they were in high spirits, all hearty and well. Towards nine at night they discovered some uneasiness, to remove which the Pretender proposed, in a council of war, to march forward, and surprize the Duke's camp in the night-time. Accordingly they set out about ten, in two columns; that on the right was conducted by himself, and that on the left by Perth; they marched in the most silent manner, orders being given for no man to speak above his breath. By three in the morning the right column was within two miles of the Royalists, and could hear / the centries call and answer to one another, 'Is all well?' 'Yes, all is well.' Here they halted upon a large heath for the second column for half an hour, but the troops thereof had mistaken their way; so that by the time they came in sight, the morning dawn began to appear, and one of Kingston's horsemen was observed by an out-party to gallop full speed toward the camp; by which it was concluded that their arrival would soon be known. A dejection of spirit was now legible in their faces; and the Pretender was heard to say, 'D – n it! Are my orders still disobeyed?' They turned about, the rear became the front, and so they returned and came up to their former ground about eight, and rested upon their arms, to ease them from the fatigue they had gone through.

There is not a part in this whole expedition in which the truth is so hard to come at, as whether the Pretender did well or ill not to attack the Royalists in their camp. The fact is represented literally as it was; and from this we may safely conclude, that if the Pretender, who depended so much upon stratagem and surprize, came really in quest of a coffin or a crown, it was not like a soldier to proceed without a full resolution to engage before returning. The corn-fields about Nairn were not more advantageous to the Royal army than the common, whereon the action happened. The troops were not intrenched, and the dawn of the morning is known to be the fittest for startling horses. Charles XII. of Sweden, to whom his friends have so frequently compared him, would not have marched back without trying the fortune of war; nor yet would the Duke of Cumberland, notwithstanding all the precautions that had been taken, /

For his Highness on the night before rode round the camp, and surveyed all the avenues leading thereto; the men were drawn up in order of battle, with the cannon in the front, and the horse in the rear; three regiments were drawn up about his own quarters, which were in the house of Mr. Rose of Kilravock, a gentleman of great humanity and good-nature, and a sincere friend to the Government. Parties were appointed to patrole for three miles round, I mean from the water of Nairn to the Firth; by the first of which his Highness was secured on the left, and by the latter his rear was protected: as I know the ground, so I can speak the better upon it. Several gentlemen have declared, that if the enemy had attacked, they would rather have been in a worse situation than at Culloden. Be that as it will, certainly every possible method was taken to prevent a surprize, and his Highness not only visited the parts, but spoke to the officers to encourage the private men; he rode along the lines with a chearful countenance, and said: 'My brave boys, we have but one march more, and all our labour is at an end; sit down at your tent-doors, and be alert to take your arms.' He was answered with the strongest protestations of loyalty, and retired to his lodging, where he supped with his general officers, and appeared exceeding chearful during the whole time. Several of the clergy crowded into the room, some to give intelligence, and others out of curiosity; but he desired them to go home, and assist the troops with their prayers. This being over, he composed himself to rest, but without taking off either his boots or his clothes, till about three in the morning, when getting up on his feet, he directly walked down stairs, and coming to the front was agreeably surprized to find the whole in battalia / and under arms, which had been done in about two minutes after the first alarm from one of the patroling parties. Without hesitating a moment, he ordered every soldier a glass of brandy, a biscuit, and a little cheese, and so the army set out in four columns in pursuit of the enemy. The three lines of foot, each of five battalions, were broke into three from the right; the artillery followed the first, and the cavalry made the fourth upon the left; and though a storm of hail drove full in their faces, yet still they advanced. They had marched about eight miles before the enemy was perceived: forty of Kingston's horse and the Highlanders, led by the Quarter-master-general, had the first view of them at two miles distance, making a motion to the left of the army, who instantly turned their faces from the west in order to front them. In this position they continued some minutes, till observing those whom they had espied to retire to their main body, they put themselves in their former posture, which they kept till within a mile of the enemy, where again they formed as before.

It was not till eleven o'clock when the two armies got a full view of each other, that the rebel chiefs entered seriously into a council. Lord George Murray, Lochiel, Roy Steuart, and almost all the chieftains were against fighting that day: however Boyer, the French ambassador, and the officers of the brigades insisted upon it. Stapleton even went so far as to say, that 'the Scots were always good troops till things came to a crisis.' An expression which fired them so much that Lochiel has declared oftner than once, 'that he did not believe there was an Highlander in the army who would not have run up to the mouth of a cannon, in order to confute the odious and undeserved aspersion.' / And in this temper of mind where they when the Duke was within a mile of them. Their cannon were fired, to let such as had fallen asleep know that the King's army was advancing: they were awakened by the noise; the Pretender galloped from the house of Culloden, as did the M. of Tullibardin, and the parties run in to their respective battalions.

Both armies were now ranged in order of battle: the Royalists (about 8500 men) extending from right to left were drawn up in two lines. The first was composed of the regiments of the Royal Scots, Cholomondley, Price, Royal North British Fusiliers, Monro, and Barrel; the second was made up of the regiments of Batterau, Blakeney, Howard (alias the Buffs) Fleming, Blyth, Semple, Ligonier and Wolf. There was a corps of reserve, from whence the Duke ordered Pulteney's to the right of the Royal, the better to cover the enemy, who before this much outlined the troops: there was a morass on the right, which secured them from a surprize on that side, and the dragoons under Generals Hawley and Bland were, with 150 of the Highlanders, ordered to the left, in order to fall upon the right flank of the enemy; the other part of that corps being left to guard the baggage behind the whole.

The rebel army, consisting of 9000 men, stood formed in three lines; the first was composed of the Athole battalions headed by their respective Colonels; that of the Marquis of Tullibardin, Lord Nairn, Colonel Menzies, Robertson of Blairfitty, and Steuart of Kainachan; next them stood the Camerons, two battalions of Frazers, Mackintoshes, and Macdonalds: Lord George Murray commanded on the right, and Lord John Drummond on the left. Their second line was made up of the Irish brigades, and / seventy of Fitzjames's horse, Lord Lewis Gordon's regiment, with those of Perth, Roy Steuart, Glenbucket, Kilmarnock, Lord John Drummond, and Lord Ogilvie. The Pretender stood with a body of horse behind the whole, almost opposite to the center, but without reach of musket shot. Their lines were distant from each other about five hundred yards, whereas those of the King's troops were not above fifty; the enemy's cannon was placed in three divisions, consisting each of three pieces; that of the Duke, consisting of ten pieces, was planted in five divisions, two being in each. Things being in this condition, his Royal Highness ordered them to advance, and riding along the lines in a very soldierly and comely manner, he called out to them: 'My brave boys, your toil will soon be at an end; stand your ground against the broad sword and target; parry the enemy in the manner you have been directed*, be assured of immediate assistance, and I promise you that I shall not fail to make a report of your behaviour to the King; and in the mean time, if any are unwilling to engage, pray let them speak freely, and with pleasure they shall have their discharge.' These words were uttered with such earnestness, and in so lively a manner, that one would have thought he had already conquered. The whole soldiers gave repeated declarations of their standing by him, and so they advanced.

* They were taught to push over the right arm against the right breast of an antagonist, and mutually to defend each other, by pushing against the man who was engaged with his right hand comrade.

The battle would have begun directly, but one Robert Frazer, the same who had been Secretary to Lord Lovat, by insinuating himself with the corps of the artillery, led them a wrong way; / he conducted them up an hill, and over a marshy ground, in which a wheel of one of the carriages was broken. His Highness, whose eyes were everywhere, ordered a workman to right it, and some more horses to be yoked, in order to draw it through, and a tenant of Kilravock's stepping up, conducted them in the best and plainest road. The army was now within five hundred yards of the enemy, when the morass ended which covered their right; to remedy which, Kingston's horse and sixty of Cobham's dragoons were ordered to supply that deficiency. The day was rainy, and the wind began to rise from the north, and the army endeavoured to keep it on their backs, while Lord Bury, now Earl of Albemarle, was sent forward with some few troops to reconnoitre what appeared somewhat like a battery. His Lordship went on, and their cannon began to play against him; but being ill served and ill pointed, the balls flew over the heads of the whole, except the last rank, where a cannon bullet took a man full below the abdomen, and shot his body off almost by the ilion. The artillery of the King's army was better served; Major Belford attended it there in person, and took care to level the guns so well, that they made lanes wherever they came. The Highlanders did not like the salutation; they came down three times within an hundred yards of the right wing, brandishing their swords, and firing their pistols. The troops kneeled, to receive the fire, as they were directed, the first rank bending on their knee, the second stooping, and the third standing upright; the two last were to fire, but not till the enemy was within thirty yards, and the first was to receive them with their fire, and on the point of their bayonets. Lord John Drummond did all in his power to decoy the Royalists to give their fire at / a distance, that his wing might come in sword in hand; he even walked between the lines with his pike in his hand. The Duke of Cumberland saw into the extent of his design, and was not to be provoked into an unsoldier-like action; in short, the two continued to front each other in this alarming posture, and in the mean while the right wing of the enemy and the left of the King's were closely engaged; for in a stooping posture, covering their head and breasts with their targets, the Athole battalions, the regiment of Mackintoshes and the Camerons, run swiftly upon the cannon, making a dreadful huzza, and even crying out, 'Run ye dogs:' they broke in between the grenadiers of

Barrel and Monro; but these had given their fire according to the general direction, and then parried them with their screwed bayonets: the two cannons on that division were so well served, that when within two yards of these they received a full discharge of cartridge shot, which made a dreadful havock; and those who crowded into the opening received a full fire from the center of Bligh's regiment, which still increased the number of the slain: however, such as survived possessed themselves of the cannon, and attacked the regiments sword in hand; but to their astonishment they found an obstinate resistance. His Highness being on the right, saw them the moment they moved to break in, and ordered the regiments of Wolfe and Fleming to wheel to the left of Barrel's, and attack them in flank, while those of Bligh and Semple, brought up by General Huske, poured in their shot upon the front of them. The enemy could not stand such uncommon efforts, planned in the most judicious manner, and executed with all the intrepidity imaginable. The Pretender saw the Athole battalions advance, and sent one of his aids de camp, / Colonel Maclauchlan of Inchconnell, with orders to the left wing to wheel to the right, and support the impression that might be made, while the second line was to move forward to supply their room. The orders were not delivered, for Maclauchlan's head was struck off by a cannon ball, as he was galloping with them; so that the left retained its former posture. The Duke saw it, and observing through a glass what was doing on the left, he cried out, 'They run, They run! rise up Pulteney's and shoulder.' His words were heard by Lord John Drummond, and such as were near him; they looked about and saw the catastrophe: all at once they threw down their firelocks, and began to give way; on which the right wing advanced some paces, and gave their fire in so close and so full a manner, that the ground was soon covered with the bodies of the dead and wounded, and the cannon being again loaded, these fired into the midst of the fugitives, and made a frightful carnage. In the mean time the dragoons and Argyleshire Highlanders, under the Generals Hawley and Bland, began to break down a dyke to the right of the enemy, who were now flying off in the greatest confusion; and as at their coming on they received a salvo from two pieces of cannon, so at their going off they had a like salutation from other two that were brought up to bear upon them. The dragoons rode in among the fugitives, and hacked them terribly with their broad swords; some had their brains beat out by the horses, so that only few of that wing escaped to the other side of the Nairn, where it was not practicable to pursue them. There was business for the dragoons and Kingston's horse on another quarter; they had already met together in the very center of the ground where the rebels had stood, and from thence / they separated into small parties in pursuit of the unhappy people now flying for their lives. Many of these advanced five miles into the country before they returned; such as took the road to Inverness were more fortunate than those who fled between that water and the Nairn, and yet many of these were killed and wounded: in a word, the rout was total, the victory complete. About fifteen hundred were killed upon the spot, and as many in the pursuit; among whom the Viscount of Strathallan, Col. Maclauchlan, with his Major, and most part of their officers; Colonel Macgillivray and Major Macbean of the regiment of Macintoshes, with all their officers, and most of their private men; Colonel Maclean of Drimnin, with his Major, almost all his officers, and his two sons. About one thousand were wounded; among whom was Macdonald of Keppoch, who died some few days after, with Cameron of Lochiel, and almost all their officers; young Frazer of Inveralachy, a Lieutenant-Colonel; Hugh Frazer, Lord Lovat's Secretary; and many others too tedious here to mention. Brigadier Stapleton died of his wounds some few days after.

The young Pretender, having seen the flight of his men, ordered a house behind which he stood to be set on fire, and by means of the smoke he crossed the Nairn, whither Perth, Lords Ogilvy and Pitsligo, Lord Lewis Gordon, Lord George Murray, with Lord John and Lewis Drummond repaired, with a considerable number of such as had escaped. They all had swords, but few or none of them retained their firelocks: many of them were wounded, and their ears were dinned with the noise of the soldiers, who were tossing up their hats in the air, and calling out, 'Come down ye dogs, and we will cut you in pieces.' / They seemed to be much discouraged, and the Pretender himself was not the last to complain: 'D – n the shipping,' says he: 'there's now no more to be done.' And so parting from his followers he, with some few horse, repaired to the house of Frazer of Gortuleg, in Stratherrick, where Lord Lovat lodged. He was received by his aged partizan with open arms: and his Lordship excused his attendance on account of his infirmities and years. After this he went to bed, and next morning set out for Glengary, where he resided for some time; but daily heard of the surrender of his troops, and the hardships that befel them.

Several officers of note were made prisoners: among whom the Earl of Kilmarnock; who, taking a party of dragoons for Fitzjames's horse, separated from the few that were with him, and came up to them. He was too near before he had discerned his mistake; so that to return was impracticable: Lord Ancram knew him and saved his life, otherwise he would have been cut down. Their artillery, tents, and baggage were seized: Sir John Wedderburn, Colonel Farqhuarson, Major Steuart, five captains, three ensigns, and six inferior officers, such as surgeons and engineers, with nine hundred private men were taken also. And all this with very little loss; there being only fifty killed, and one hundred and twenty wounded. Of the first was Captain Lord Robert Ker, of Barrel's regiment, and son to the Marquis of Lothian: his head was cut, by Major Macbean, from the crown thereof to the collar bone, and afterward he was hacked in pieces; Captain Campbell of Lord Loudon's regiment, Captain Campbell of the militia, and Captain Grosset of Price's battalion: of the second was Lieutenant-colonel Rich, whose right hand was cut off by the wrist, and left almost / cut through above the fingers; he had likewise a deep wound in the elbow: one captain, one lieutenant, and two ensigns of Barrel's were wounded also; one captain of Price's, one lieutenant of Bligh's, one captain, two lieutenants, and two ensigns of Monro's, one captain of Ligonier's, and one captain of Batterau's. The cavalry suffered but little; having only received some random shot from the more obstinate, who at times turned about upon them: Kingston's horse had but two killed and one wounded. Howard's, Cholmondley's, and Batterau's lost but two or three, and Pultney's none. Bligh's sustained some small loss by firing of pistols, and from some of those who run in among them: Semple's, who relieved Barrel's, had a small damage also.

In the mean time the Duke was improving his victory: he rode along the lines, and in a very princely manner heartily thanked them for their good behaviour, which he promised to represent to the King. This done he ordered each man a glass of brandy and a biscuit, and, after receiving the compliments of the nobility, &c. upon his success, he pursued his way to Inverness at the head of his troops. They advanced huzzaing, and were answered by three rounds of the great guns from the ships in the road, who denounced to the people on the opposite shore the account of the event.

His Highness entered Inverness at the head of the dragoons, all bespattered with dirt, covered with dust and with sweat, and his sword in his hand. The bells were set a ringing, and the people gave the signal to huzza; but he moved his hand to give over, and calling for the keys of the prison ordered the doors to be set open and the prisoners to be brought forth: liberty was the first fruit of his conquest: and as the confined men came / down stairs he clapped them upon the shoulder, saying, 'Brother soldiers, you are free:' ordered an entertainment for them, and payment of all their arrears. About four o'clock the whole army came in: they advanced huzzaing, and seemed to be prodigiously pleased: and what tended to heighten the satisfaction was, that from the time of his entering Inverness, prisoners were either brought to him in troops, or else submitted themselves. Scarce was he two hours in town when six French officers, who had not been in the battle, wrote a letter to General Bland, surrendering themselves prisoners of war.

Such was the Battle of Culloden, which the enemies of the Government have so cruelly represented, to the shame and reproach of the illustrious Leader, who, under God, was the chief instrument of the victory. The whole account given of it by Tobias Smollet is one continued misrepresentation. Had the Duke of Cumberland been a favourite with Tobias, he would not have used him so ill: for I am told, that T – s, when a friend, is far from being bad; but, if an enemy, his very tender mercies are cruel. For my part, I never spoke with him, and perhaps never will: though I must own, that from the tenor of his writings, and his account of Culloden field, this character of him seems to be a just one. 'The glory of the victory was' [*not*] 'sullied by the barbarity of the soldiers,' as he says: not one of them was allowed to stoop until all was over, and the dead had been stripped. The soldiers, though provoked by a severe winter campaign, which would even have irritated Tobias himself, were *not* wrought up 'to the most savage thirst of revenge:' they did *not* traverse the field after the battle,' and 'massacre those miserable wretches who lay maimed and expiring:' / and yet many of these, who had been torn to pieces by the grape shot, would have been glad to be put out of pain: *nor yet did* 'some officers act a part in this cruel scene of assassination, the triumph of low illiberal minds, uninspired by sentiment, untinctured by humanity:' *nor yet were* 'a great number of people, who, from motives of curiosity, had come to see the battle, sacrificed to the undistinguished vengeance of the victors*: the vanquished Adventurer' *neither* 'forded the Ness, ' *nor did* 'he retire to the Aird.' He fled to a place of greater safety. 'Detachments' *were not* 'sent out on all hands to hunt down the fugitives, and lay waste the country with fire and sword.' 'Tis true, the houses, *not* 'the castles of Lochiel and Glengary,' both of which I have seen, 'were burnt down;' but it is equally true, that 'every house, hut, or habitation,' '*did not* meet with the same fate without distinction. The inhabitants' *were not* 'shot upon the mountains like wild beasts†,' *nor* 'put to death in cold blood, without form of trial.' *Neither were* 'the women, after having seen their husbands and fathers murdered, subjected to brutal violation, and then turned out naked with their children to starve on the barren heaths.' *No* 'one family was inclosed in a barn, and consumed to ashes. Those ministers of vengeance' *were not* so alert in the execution of their office, that in a few days, there was neither house, cottage, / man, nor beast to be seen within the compass of fifty miles.' *Nor yet was* 'all ruin, silence, and desolation.'

I have enquired into all these things, and find, that on the day of the battle only actual rebels were molested: there was not a house burnt, notwithstanding the field of battle was almost surrounded with those of the Macintoshes, who formed one of the regiments which broke in upon the left wing of the Royal army, except one which was set on fire, to cover the Pretender's flight. One Noble, a weaver, in Failie, at the distance of five miles from Culloden field, met with an accident: for, alarmed with the noise, he had the curiosity to look out, and one of the fugitives, being just at his door, running from two of Kingston's horsemen, these fired; the balls missed the person at whom they were aimed, and one of them struck Noble in the forehead, so that he died directly. I hope Dr. Smollet will not construe this accident as the effect of fore thought, cruelty, malice, and antipathy, by which the curse of the necessitous may cry against one who wickedly, basely, and diabolically contrives, by the venom of his quill, to wound the poor in his family and reputation, and take away the bread from helpless children.

* The Doctor did not inform his readers, that the Rev. Mr. Macbean, father to Colonel Macbean of the artillery, now at Woolwich, had a most narrow escape for his life: as one of the flying Highlanders lifted up his sword to cut him down; but happily a by-stander warded off the blow.

† Perhaps he means Captain Monro of Culcairn, a man well attached to the Government, for want of other instances! or three of the Old Buffs, who were shot as patroling between Fort William and Fort Augustus

However, the sinistrous representations against his Royal Highness arose from the frequent executions that followed the decisive action. Among the number of prisoners were many who had deserted the King's service: Roy Steuart's regiment was formed mostly of these, after the battle of Prestonpans: and, if listing with the Pretender was a fault, certainly many of these were culpable. Three fourths of Lord Elcho's regiments, of Perth's battallion, and of Kilmarnock's corps were from these deserters. Roy Steuart, who had the Pretender's / cause more at heart than any other, came to Saint Anne's yards, behind Holyrood-house, and while a prodigious number of people were walking for curiosity, he spoke to about fourteen of Hamilton's dragoons, and of Major Bowles's troop, as they were desirous to enlist in his regiment. 'Gentlemen,' said Roy, 'you certainly know the business we are upon: there is no force or compulsion upon you: pray lay your hands to your heart. If you join us, you shall be well paid; but if you endeavour to deceive us, you can expect no mercy if ever you should fall into our hands.' They insisted to be received, and he insisted on their digesting the matter before they were sworn. At the very time when Roy was dealing thus with them, a serjeant gave out, that he was sick, and desired to be excused – Roy was so far from being angry, that he ordered him to be taken care of with the other prisoners: he retired, but took notes of all that had passed. These very men were taken in arms with the rebels: and the serjeant, being with the Royal army, swore in these terms before the court-martial. Indeed the fact could have been proved by many witnesses; but the serjeant's testimony hanged them all. They were executed on the common gallows, where two deserters from the Pretender had been hanged some few days before. They were all hung up in one morning, and the executioner stripping them naked, they were suffered to continue exposed for three days. Others were served in the same manner; among whom one Niman Dunbar, who had deserted from the regiment of guards: and, as he was a native of the adjacent county, the thing made the greater noise. What pity that the minutes of the court-martial had not been published: in that event the conduct of the generals would not have been / so much blamed, and that of his Royal Highness would have shone with lustre. Hawley was indeed enraged at the unhappy prisoners: five of whom had taken sanctuary at a place called Petty, about a mile from the field of battle. The evidence for the crown, that had taken away the lives of the first fourteen, likewise destroyed these five. Hawley ordered twelve dragoons to put them to death in the place where they were: these just came at the time when Shaw, the minister, was going up to see them: they were taken out, set against a wall, and shot to death, without further ceremony.

When his Highness came to hear of these frequent executions, he interposed his authority, and commanded that a report should be made to him before executing the sentence: among others one Gordon, who had been a soldier in the third regiment of guards, was brought to his trial, as being an officer in the rebel army. The Duke himself spoke to him: and when his Highness was told, that he (Gordon) had been ill used by his superior officers – that three times another person was made a serjeant when the place properly belonged to him – the excuse was admitted: the man was received back to his own regiment, and is still alive. The clergymen both in Stratherrick and in the Aird, possessed by the Frazers, nine hundred of whom were in arms against the Government, declared to me, that in obedience to the command of his Highness, they intimated from their pulpits, that all persons should be pardoned upon surrendering themselves to them: that the people gladly came in, had certificates of their surrender given them, and these were always sustained. In these districts not one house was burnt, except Castle Downie, the seat of the family of Lovat. I had the same account from the clergy of Abertarff; in which there was scarce / a house burnt, except that of Glengary itself: which indeed was a pity, as it was a handsome building, and beautifully situated upon the side of a lake, out of which both salmon and trout might have been caught from any of the windows by a line. In Lochaber the house of Achnacarrie, belonging to Lochiel, and that of Keppoch Macdonald were also set in flames; but all more by the militia than by the regular forces.

It is a very disagreeable task to balance an account of burnings and plunderings between the Pretender's party and the regular troops; and yet we have in some measure drawn it out. The former was debtor, to the burning of the village of Lismahagoe, the beautiful and stately fabric of St. Ninian's church, the village of Inverlochy, and the houses in Sutherland before-mentioned: they likewise had been debtor, to burning the house of Balnagown, the place which gave title to the illustrious Lieutenant-general Charles Ross, had not Lochiel ordered the fuel, which was piled up to set it on fire, to be carried off, just at the time when it was about to be kindled up. The reader may depend upon what is here said to be true.

I wish sincerely that Smollet may seriously reflect upon his own conduct in many other things, beside the cruel, the false, and the daring aspersions thrown out, in studied terms, upon the illustrious Son of our King; whose disposition to humanity, and whose real goodness of heart, shone every day with more transcendent lustre.

His Highness, on the fourth day following Culloden battle, had the curiosity to dress himself like an ordinary officer, and to walk toward the Castlehill. When just past this place, he observed a man quite pensive and solitary, and, making toward him, began to converse about the state of the / town before the arrival of the army. The man told him, 'that he was a native of the place; that his house was below yonder hill (pointing to it); that he had the honour to bear the King's commission, as you my dear young man do: I was gunner of that castle which lies in rubbish, and which was once an ornament to these parts; the force to reduce it was nothing at all; the officers in the garrison proposed to sally out upon the besiegers, and both Lieutenant Graham and I laid down a method to undermine them, if they proceeded to a sap. All was in vain; the governor was against every thing; his brother vassals (the Grants) had embraced a neutrality with the enemy; he got very good terms for himself, but the rest of the garrison, and I among others, have been stript of our all.' The dialogue continued for two hours; the young officer and the reduced gunner seemed to like each other extremely well: at last a lieutenant passed by, and knowing the officer, he came to him hat in hand, and begun his business with, 'May it please your Royal Highness.' The reduced gunner was struck with the expression, and coming forward almost trembling, he in the most submissive posture begged pardon for not having treated his Highness as his dignity deserved. 'No, no!' replied his Highness, 'My little old man, you have treated me extremely well; from this time you shall be put in your usual pay, and in the mean while I desire you may go to the Secretary's office, and tell them from me, that you must have immediate payment of all your arrears.' On which the two separated, his Highness repairing to his lodging, and Mr. Thomson the gunner, from whom I had the information, to the Secretary's office, as directed. /

That very night the Duke remonstrated with Hawley upon the impropriety of putting so many of the deserters to death, and in the most sympathizing manner insinuated that men were not made to starve: 'You may,' continued he, 'try an officer for surrendering up a fort, when under no necessity to do it, but let not the blood of the poor be spilt profusely.' His instructions were followed: Grant was arraigned before a courtmartial, when the evidence was so strong and full against him, that nothing but the interposition of his Highness could have mitigated the sentence, to declare him unworthy of his Majesty's service ever after.

It was in consequence of the conversation with Mr. Thomson, that his Highness performed an act sufficient to endear him to posterity; and though it turned out to the detriment of Inverness, yet it became a singular advantage to the country.

From the earliest period in the records of Scotland, we find that a castle was always looked upon as absolutely necessary at Inverness, and accordingly it continued upon one spot till the time of Oliver Cromwell, who blew up that fortification, and built another nearer the harbour, still holding it as a maxim, that a fort must infallibly be there. At the restoration Cromwell's fort was razed to the ground, the old one was rebuilt, and continued to be augmented with many out-works and conveniencies at a vast expence to the government, till the 18th of March 1746, when Major Grand surrendered it into the hands of the young Chevalier, who ordered the works to be blown up.

The Duke of Cumberland saw what had been hid from ages; he expressed his surprize that a fort should be built upon a spot commanding no pass or navigable river, and in all respects void of the / advantages that ought to constitute a fortification. He preferred the place which old Oliver had fixed upon; however, the magistrates would not dispose of this small parcel of ground* for less than 25,000 *l.* His Highness rode out with his engineers, and took a view of the coast; and getting the better of the false maxim, that a fort was absolutely necessary at Inverness, he judged, and very truly, that if a fort was built near it, the same might be more for the King's service. He had not rode above eight miles, when he came to a point of land called Arderseir, which lies opposite to Rosemarkney in Rossshire: between these is a gut two miles over, which begins at the great sea that spreads between Norway and the coast of Scotland, and propagates itself for twelve miles without making a safe or commodious harbour, except at Arderseir, where the inlet begins. The proprietor of this obscure place, Mr. Campbell of Calder, was more docile than the magistrates of Inverness; he made a present to his Royal Highness of that large piece of waste ground,

* It scarcely contains two square acres.

near the point, which scarcely yielded pasture for a few sheep in the summer season. All of a sudden five hundred men were set to work; architects, masons, smiths, joiners, and labourers were employed: and while the former were building the fortress, which owed its birth to his Royal Highness, who examined the plan thereof, the latter were occupied in cutting a canal from the sea to the gut quite round it; so that the fortress, which is a pentagon regularly flanked and strengthened by all kind of outworks, is a perfect island, defended by a deep wet ditch toward the country, and on the wings and front / by the sea, which last constitutes a harbour, where the largest ships in the world may lie with safety.

Without the ditch a large and populous village is built, and many considerable merchants have settled in it, for the conveniency of trade and commerce. A road has been cut from Perth to the fort, which is full thirty miles nearer than that known by the name of General Wade's road to Inverness; the whole country is enriched by it; the barracks can contain six thousand men, and in its present situation, is as capable of holding out a siege as any one fortress in Europe.

What man alive could have thought about twenty years before, that the solitary Arderseir would have put on so gay and so brilliant an aspect? Had a genius told the people in that neighbourhood of the wonderful change, they would, like Æneas in Elysium, have been transported with the prospect of what was to come; they would have been overjoyed to think that a beautiful structure, nay, a town to be called for their Sovereign, should rear its head at a place which had not so much as a name*.

He had not spend his time in exercising severities for what was past; his aim was to confute the false calumnies and invectives raised against the crown, person, and dignity of his Royal father, by a moderation and lenity not to be found in ancient times, and scare to be believed in times to come. I have been told by the clergymen in those parts, that no sooner was a certificate produced from any of them of a man's having surrendered himself, than he was at full liberty to carry in all manner of provision to the camp, and was paid in ready money for every single article: for desiring safety, not / revenge, he took nothing from his enemies, except the power of hurting; and even when these came to deliver up their arms, he accepted their submission with an air of sympathy, which discovered rather a concern for their misfortune, than a triumph in their misery: he received Lord

* Hæc tum nomina erunt, sunt jam sine nomine terræ!

Lewis Drummond, the French ambassador, and forty-nine other foreign officers, with great affability: he gave passports to the Pretender's servants, these being all French, and sent off the French prisoners to the number of one hundred and ten, to be exchanged for an equal number of the British forces: he did not assume the power of trying any one of the rebels: he referred these to be tried by the laws of their country. Among others were the Earls of Kilmarnock and Cromartie, with the unfortunate Lord Balmerino, whose case is too singular not to be represented.

His Royal Highness having, the day after the battle of Culloden, issued out a proclamation for all such as had been in arms to surrender themselves to one of his Majesty's justices of the peace, or to a minister of the Church of Scotland, great numbers embraced the golden opportunity, and among others Lord Balmerino. He no sooner heard of it, than he rode directly from Aggimore, and surrendered himself to Sir Ludovick Grant, at the castle of that name. Unluckily for his Lordship the Grants had embraced a neutrality, and his Highness, ever a greater enemy to the cunning of the fox, than the wrath of the lion*, discovered a kind of reserve toward the generality of them; for when their chieftain came into Inverness attended by one hundred and seventy men of his own / and of different surnames, his Royal Highness, though walking by the side of the river, neither went to view them himself, nor did any of his officers go: however, Balmerino was received without informing of his voluntary surrender; his Lordship thought, that it would be more to his advantage to be spoken of by Grant than by him, so the favourable circumstance was not named; and what was still a greater infatuation, he did not so much as mention this in his defence, when he came to be tried.

It must be owned that Grant's conduct in other respects was preposterous; for the Grants of Glenmoriston were through his mistake led into a snare: they entered Inverness, and drew up in the same order as on the Muir of Culloden, armed cap-a-pee, to the number of three hundred; which the Duke observing, he walked up, asking 'What body of men is there!' To which he was answered, 'The Grants of Glenmoriston;' 'To whom have they surrendered,' replied his Highness? 'To me,' says Grant, 'and to none in Britain would they have submitted, except to me.' 'No!' answered the Duke with a pause, 'I will let them know that they are the King's sub-

* By this metaphor Cicero expresses the fraudulent practices of the crafty, and the resolution of the courageous and brave. Cic. Offic. lib. I.

jects, and must likewise submit to me;' and with these words he ordered a regiment to surround and disarm them: they were directly embarked on board the transports, and were next day shipped off for Tilbury Fort, with a clergyman of their name. It is observable, that none of these were tried for their lives; some of them died on ship-board, and the remainder were transported to his Majesty's colonies, where, like others who had been involved in the calamities of their country, they settled, and procured a more comfortable sustenance than if they had remained at home. /

Historical exactness, which is the brightest gem in annals, has obliged me to insist more upon conduct of his Royal Highness, than otherwise I would have done, especially as Smollet has represented 'all to be ruin, silence, and desolation, within the compass of fifty miles,' placing Fort Augustus in the center; and as his words are much stronger than I chuse to insert, I shall refer the reader to them*: however, I must remind him, that Inverness is just twenty four miles from Fort Augustus, and that not a single stone in that town was misplaced by any one in the King's army, notwithstanding several of the rebels were inhabitants there. I could mention Nairn, Forress, Chanory, Rosemarkeny, Ardmucknage, Dalquiny, Fort William, and Morvern, with many other places much nearer to Fort Augustus than fifty miles; but I do not chuse to dwell upon the mistakes of a man, who has so miserably misrepresented the Deliverer of his country; neither is it fair to detract so much from the glory of a conquest obtained over the bravest of men: men inured to victory, provoked to resolution, and drawn up upon ground of their own chusing: the unparalleled bravery of the Highlanders was not confined to the small number of five hundred men, as a certain voluminous author would insinuate†.

Then let the obstinate look into the ocean while it is calm and sooner may they be able to raise tempests there, than to disturb the universal joy that reigns in every British breast since the grand decision. Let the name of the hero be fixed upon every heart, and be remembered with a becoming gratitude; the hero who was the soul of the cause, who look the affair upon himself, and may millions / yet unborn be ready upon every occasion to express their thankfulness to the God of heaven; for raising up so shining an instrument, when they read of the glorious event. The troops which, under the command of Hawley, were broken at Falkirk,

* See Complete Hist. of England, Vol XI. p. 240.

† Complete Hist of England, Vol. XI. p. 236.

intirely routed their conquerors at Culloden, when headed by the Duke of Cumberland.

> *Hark! what a burst of joy*
> *Intones the ecchoing air!*
> *As if an angel from on high,*
> *Had now discharg'd his care.*
> *'Tis he! 'Tis he! the pride of fame,*
> William *return'd the shouts proclaim!*
> William *with northern laurels crown'd*
> William *the hills and vales resound!*
> *What numbers fled, what numbers fell,*
> Culloden's *glorious field may tell,*
> Culloden's *field the muse may fire,*
> *To sing the son, and charm the fire!*
> ODE, Oct. 30, 1746.

The End of the SEVENTH BOOK. /

THE LIFE OF WILLIAM DUKE OF CUMBERLAND.

BOOK VIII.

CONTENTS.

The Disarming the Highlanders, – the Motions of the King's Troops, – the Trial of the Rebel Lords, – and the Wanderings of the Pretender.

THE victory at Culloden gave birth to an inexpressible joy through the extensive dominions of the British empire; not only Europe and Africa, but the two Indies joined in the shout, and gave joyful acclamations. The night after the battle Lord Bury was dispatched with a letter to St. James's, and taking the opportunity of a ship to North Berwick, where he landed on the 21st, he hired horses for London, where he arrived in the morning of the 24th, and delivered his message to the King. The news was declared from the great guns in the Park and in the Tower, and / these were answered by the ships in the harbour, and by vollies from the small arms of the guards drawn up upon the parade. The bells rung incessantly tunes suitable to the occasion, such as Judas Maccabæus, or Britons strike home. At night the bonfires and illuminations were general; and on the Sunday was the most brilliant Court that ever appeared on any other occasion, every one taking a pride to pay their compliments. The Parliament was sitting, and both Houses congratulated their Sovereign upon the defeat of his enemies, and the heroic part which 'his son, the image of his virtues, had, in suppressing that project, upon the ruin of which the constitution was more firmly secured;' and without loss of time conferred upon his Royal Highness the yearly sum of 25,000*l.* in augmentation of the 15,000*l.* which he formerly enjoyed. They wrote him a congratulatory letter upon his glorious success, to which they received a very princely and obliging answer. A run of addresses, like the waves of the sea jostling out each other, crowded about the throne from every quarter; the pulpits and theatres sounded with the praises of our Deliverer; the streets rang with his eulogium; the presses teemed with the recital of his virtues, and the news-papers were filled with his applause; the sons of genius vied in his encomium; in Scotland his friends were so taken with him, that several children were baptized publicly in the churches by the name of CUMBERLAND WILLIAM, as a monument of their gratitude for the blessings they had received through his means; and to crown all, the King wrote him an answer with his own hand, in which were these very words: 'I desire you may give my hearty thanks to the brave officers and soldiers, who fought so gloriously at the late battle; and assure / them no less of my real esteem, than of my constant favour and protection.' All which was directly obeyed: he read over the letter in the midst of the soldiers, and on ending it, he renewed his hearty acknowledgments of their services, and at departing said; 'You, gentlemen, have resisted an attack, which I believe no troops upon earth could have withstood but yourselves; the enemy indeed fought like furies, and you, my fellow-soldiers, have behaved like so many heroes.' He never failed to acknowledge his sense of services done, whether by societies, or by individuals; and with his own hand wrote a letter to the Church of Scotland, thanking them for their affection, loyalty, and zeal. His humanity went so far, that on hearing of the sorrow which the poor prisoners, who had listed for a piece of bread, daily sustained, not so much for what they were to undergo, as on account of having missed the opportunity of fighting under so glorious a commander, he ordered the regiments to be recruited from them; so that of eleven hundred of these, only forty fell by the hands of the executioner: could the strict and indispensible rules of the martial law have been got over, they would all have been spared, in the same manner as the others, who had been involved with the Pretender.

Duncan Forbes, Lord President of the Session, and the Earl of Loudon, being returned, they advised to recruit the foot regiments from among the natives of the adjacent counties; a direction that was complied with, but no new companies were raised at that time, though soon after a full regiment under Lord Loudon was mustered up; and to be still more agreeable, none of the regular troops were suffered to enter into rebel districts: that business was referred to the militia. Accordingly the Argyleshire Highlanders were sent / into Lochaber, Moidart, and Arisaig, and afterward into the isles; their commander, General Campbell, a man of as great humanity and politeness as any officer in Europe, would put an hardship on no man: his officers breathed the sentiments of their general: however, they could not hinder the people of Glengary from firing the house of their chieftain, from an apprehension that the troops were intent upon destruction. The same thing might be said of the Camerons with regard to Achnacarrie, and of the other places which fell at that time; the people of Lochaber and Glencoe, of Keppoch and of Moidart, delivered up their arms, and continued in their own habitations, as did the clans scattered through the western isles; the Sutherland militia were sent into the Aird, and the district of Strathglass, and the Grants into that possessed by the Macintoshes; but with no orders either to plunder or to burn.

Unfortunately for some of those, the people sent in among them pretended that money was due from the proprietors, under colour of which, some of the Grants and Sutherland people seized the cattle upon the premises, and sold them; some to the troops in the camp, and some to graziers, who hastened to be rich.

Among the number of those new graziers were some of these immoral clergymen, who, by the viciousness of their lives, had brought religion into contempt, and opened the mouths of the disaffected; these double dealers were of the names of Grant and of Monro, and among others was one Rose Macinucater, minister of Nairn, a wretch of such uncommon wickedness of heart, that such a one ought never to have been born; one Alexander Shaw in Braemurray, who agreed to rear such as Rose had bought, through the winter, at the rate / of 2 *l.* 10 *s.* for every twenty cows, assured me that most of them died through change of food, and other inconveniencies, so that Rose rather hurt than bettered his circumstances; and to complete his ruin, he died farmer, grazier, adulterer, smuggler, and bankrupt, having left at his death debts behind him to the amount of 2500*l.* and scarce seven farthings in the pound to discharge them. I hope this circumstance will not be attributed to the Duke, or to any of the troops under his command; they had other business, as stragglers were daily coming in, among the number of whom were Hugh Frazer, one of Lord Lovat's secretaries, and Robert Frazer, the other amanuensis. Sir James Kinloch and his brother were seized by the Hessians, as was Ker of Graiden; the Marquis of Tullibardin, and Mechel the Pretender's valet, surrendered to Mr. Buchanan of Drumachail, who committed them to Dumbarton Castle, till an opportunity offered of transporting them to London, where the Marquis was confined to the Tower, and soon died of a flux, the effect of his winter campaign; others gave out that his death was not natural: Kilmarnock, Cromartie, and Balmerino, were likewise imprisoned there.

But the business of the greatest moment was, an account that the most desperate among the Highlanders had got a supply of money from France, and that they had resolved to continue together; for on the 4th of May two French men of war had arrived off the coast of Arisaig, and sailed up Lock Nuay, not knowing the Pretender's disaster. About 35,000 Louisdores were landed from these for the use of his troops; on this a meeting was held among the chieftains, at which Lord Lovat, Lochiel, and Secretary Murray were present: part of the money was distributed, though Murray retained the major / part. Here it was agreed, that each chieftain should raise what men he could, and keep in a body until they could receive proper terms from his Royal Highness. Accordingly they rendezvoused at the head of Lochargeg, where they continued till the 29th of May, when the Duke's army advancing by the road, the scouts brought in such an account of their strength and alertness, as determined them to disperse, and every one to do the best he could for himself.

Being come to Fort Augustus, he expressed some concern at seeing such vast tracts of uncultivated ground, and at the blindness of those who had blown up the beautiful and commodious barracks that had so lately been an ornament to that unfortunate district. From this he marched to Fort William; where not only Mr. Scot, the governor, but every private man in the garrison had the honour to kiss his hand, and to receive his thanks for the gallant defence they had made. He had not been long in Lochaber when Lord Lovat was taken, being discovered by the very persons to whom he had given bread. His Lordship was confined on board the Furnace, and from thence was escorted by a Party of dragoons by the way of Edinburgh and Newcastle to London, where he was confined to the Tower: so that this primum mobile of the rebellion being now in the Government's power, and fifteen of the Pretender's standards, taken at Culloden, being burnt on the 5th of June by the common hangman, his Highness thought all was safe, and set out on the 20th of July for London, where he arrived in six days, to the universal joy of all who saw him. In his way he honoured Lord Breadalbane with a visit, and staid with him a night at Taymouth. The second night he lodged at Stirling; and on the next day dined at New / Leston, the seat of the Earl of Stair; where he was magnificently and nobly entertained. He declined all public acknowledgements; but only received the freedom of some places, as of Edinburgh and Newcastle, in gold boxes.

All this time the Parliament was examining into the rise of the late troubles, and on the 8th of June attainted of high treason forty-six different persons*: appointing them to be prosecuted, unless before the 12th of July they should surrender themselves. None of these suffered; they having either escaped or complied. Among the latter was Secretary Murray, who, thinking to make a merit of bearing testimony against Lord Lovat, proffered his service, to the Lord Justice Clerk for Scotland. His proposal was accepted, and he apprehended by a party of dragoons, who, on the 28th of June, conducted him to Edinburgh, whence he was carried to London; and appearing in the Court of King's Bench in Westminster-hall, he pleaded, that he had dissolved the force of the bill of attainder, by surrendering to a proper officer. The Attorney-general admitted the fact, and the Court having a power, by virtue of a writ of Certiorari to them directed from the Court of Chancery, they made a record of the same.

Upon the 20th of July the Judges sat at Saint Margaret's Hill, where Colonel Townley, Counsellor / Morgan, Andrew Blood, and other officers of the Manchester regiment appeared before them. The trials of the three last were but short, and as Townley's defence of being in the French service was unanimously over-ruled, they were all condemned to die; and on the 31st were hanged, drawn, and quartered at Kennington Common.

Some of the principal Scots Gentlemen were tried there likewise, as Sir John Wedderburn, Hamilton governor of Carlisle, Sir James Kenloch,

* Perth, the Earl of Kelly, the Viscount of Strathallan and his Son, the Viscount of Dundee, Lords Elcho, Nairn, Ogilvy, Lord George Murray, John Drummond, and Lewis Gordon, the Master of Lovat; Mercer of Aldie, Sir William Gordon of Park, John Murray of Broughton, secretary; Glenbucket, Lochiel junior, and his brother Dr. Cameron; Camerons of Torcastle and Dungallan, Clanranald junior, Keppoch, Barisdale, Glencoe, Cluny, Maclauchlan, Mackinnon, Ardsheil, Gask senior and junior, young Carnwarth, and Airth, Roy Steuart, Farquharson of Monaltry, Drumnaglash, &c.

and his brother Mr. Alexander. The case of these two last is too singular to be passed over.

These two Gentlemen had been arraigned before the ordinary Jury; but as the trial promised to be long, and the Court was weary, it was put off till next Day; when the twelve Judges of England sat upon the indictment, and another jury was called, the former being discharged. The counsel for the prisoners moved against the legality of arraigning them before any other jury than that which at first was charged with them; and that by Magna Charta no man was to be arraigned before separate juries upon the same fact. After many arguments pro and con the Judges gave their opinion: and Mr. Justice Wright differed from the whole: for his judgment was, that no other jury had a power to try the prisoners, except that before whom they were first called: so that they were tried, cast, and condemned; but it was thought prudent not to execute the sentence.

The counsel for the crown were Sir Dudley Rider, Mr. Murray (now Lord Mansfield) Sir John Strange, and Mr. Yorke (now Attorney-general.) The witnesses were wretches guilty of the crime of rebellion. The counsel for the prisoners offered to prove some of them to be the most flagitious of / mortals: but in this they were answered by a question put by Sir John Strange: 'Was there,' said he, 'a man of probity or honour in the rebellion?' To which an answer was a matter of delicacy, and so he received no reply. However, the question might have been answered, with great truth, That above a thousand people of real probity and worth were in that rebellion; but that they had done mischief ignorantly, not knowing the English tongue, even in the Scots dialect.

On the 1st of September the assizes began at Carlisle, when three lawyers went from Edinburgh to plead the cause of the prisoners: but their defence, 'That accomplices could not be admitted witnesses in the case of treason,' being soon overruled, the trials were far from being tedious; the return, Guilty, was made in a moment. The gentlemen of the jury were of the militia that had been stationed at Carlisle, when the Pretender came there; so that neither the tenderness nor advice of the Judges could restrain their havock. Here, of one hundred and five, thirty suffered, five were acquitted, and seventy were pardoned. Hence they went to York, where the jury acted with great candour and humanity: but here, as at Carlisle, the evidence was irresistible. Among others came on the trial of two Frenchmen, whose defence was, 'That in the nature of things they could not be construed traitors to his Majesty King George, as being foreigners, and had never sworn allegiance to him.' The plea of the one was sustained; as he had come over with the Pretender's party in the heat of the rebellion: but that of the other was repelled; as a distinction was made, that though he owed the King of Great Britain no natural, yet a local allegiance was due, as the prisoner had come / over under the protection of the Dutch General, who landed with auxilaries in support of his Majesty: on this he was condemned; but, on his way to the gallows, a pardon was brought him. Here, of seventy-four prisoners, thirty-five were condemned, twenty-two of whom suffered by the hand of an Executioner, and fifteen were suffocated in the prison, as they had set fire to the prison door, in order to escape. In short, only seventy-four were put to death by course of common law, for rebelling against a King who had ruled eighteen years according to law*. Whereas six hundred were put to death anno 1685, for taking arms against King James II. or VII. who in five months had violated the first principles of Magna Charta.

But a greater trial than any of these was that of the Earls of Kilmarnock and Cromarty, with Lord Balmerino, before the House of Peers, an indictment being found against them by the Surrey jury. The two Earls pleaded Guilty; but his Lordship denied the charge, on a false apprehension, that no jury could find a bill of indictment, unless it was composed of men in-dwellers in the county where the crime was charged to have been committed; and that the time of his guilt was not properly specified, he having been twelve miles from Carlisle at the time when he was charged to have been there. Both his defences were over-ruled, and the witnesses swore point blank against him. On this they were condemned to die: but before sentence was pronounced, Kilmarnock, with great propriety of accent, set off by the elegance of his person, which might have adorned any assembly, / urged the loyalty of his ancestors, their behaviour at the revolution, and since that period: he appealed to the conduct of his father in the year 1715, at which time he himself bore arms for the Government: he mentioned the behaviour of his son, who bore his Majesty's commission, and on Culloden field had behaved as became him: he told them, he abhorred the thoughts of being pardoned thro' the influence of a foreign Court; that he was far from being considerable among the rebels, and had

* Several were spared through the intercession of the Duke of Cumberland; and perhaps more had shared of the Royal mercy, had not the Dutch ambassador in France wrote a sneering letter to the Duke of Newcastle in favour of them.

no share in any of their barbarities: and so concluded with recommending himself to his Majesty's compassion, and their lordships sympathy.

The Earl of Cromartie's arguments flowed from his own personal distresses: he told their Lordships, that he had involved an affectionate wife, and with her an unborn infant, his eldest son, and eight other innocent children, who must feel their parents punishment before they knew his guilt: 'Let them, my Lords, be pledges to his Majesty: let them be pledges to your Lordships, let them be pledges to my country for mercy; let the silent eloquence of their grief and tears, let the powerful language of innocent nature, supply my want of eloquence and persuasion:– let my remorse for my guilt as a subject, let the sorrows of my heart as an husband, let the anguish of my mind as a father, speak the rest of my misery! Your Lordships are men, you feel as men; but may none of you ever suffer the smallest part of what I suffer.' This being over, the Lord Chancellor Hardwicke, then Lord High Steward, before passing sentence, made a speech, in which, after pointing out the heinousness of the crime of rebellion, especially against a King famous though the world for his mild and easy government, he told them, 'that the death of every person, who fell during / the troubles, was a murder; that the many murders of the innocent soldiers were rather chargeable upon the chiefs the principal, than upon their inferiors and followers, though the instrumental cause; and that the deaths of the criminals, whom justice had overtaken, were only to be ascribed to those who had involved them in the desperate cause.'

As it was foreseen that intercession would be made, it was resolved in council that two of the three should die, the cries for justice being loud and piercing: the interest for the Earls was great, while that for Balmerino was nothing at all; which the King observing, he said: 'Many apply for Kilmarnock and Cromartie, but none for Balmerino; I believe him to be the honestest man of the whole, and must do something for him myself;' which he certainly would have done, had he not laid it down as a maxim never to thwart his Privy Council.

The opinion without doors was, that Kilmarnock's interest would have prevailed in consideration of his ancestors, and the fidelity of his son: add to this, that Lady Charlotte Hamilton, daughter to the Duke who was killed in Hyde Park, was incessant for his Lordship: the fate of the two Earls hung in equilibrio, till the diligence of the Countess of Cromartie turned the scale in favour of her Lord.

That Lady being then with child, went almost to all the nobility and gentry about Court, and at last to the Princess of Wales; and getting ready access, she fell upon her knees, begging, 'that her Highness would have mercy on her, and on her five children' (pointing to them) 'and intercede for her unfortunate Lord.' 'Wait there,' replied her Highness, 'and I shall soon / bring you an answer;' so withdrawing a few moments, she returned with her five children, the eldest of whom (the Princess of Brunswick) was just turned of nine years, and setting them before her, said, 'Pray, Madam, what compassion had your Lord upon my five children and me? It is true, I am not now in your case, but then I was; and God knows what would have come of them, or of me, had your husband's scheme taken place! however, I shall intercede with his Majesty for him:' which that very night she endeavoured to do.

Not contented with this, Lady Cromartie went to Kensington, and at the time of his Majesty's going to chapel, presented a petition to him: he just took it out of her hand, when she fell backward and fainted away; which the King observing only with the last glance of his eye, he ordered her to be taken up, and with his usual sedateness said, 'I shall consider her case;' which he accordingly did, and next morning signed a reprieve for ninety-nine years. This determined the fate of the other two, who suffered on the 18th of August. At going out of the Tower-gate, and hearing the Ordinary say, 'God save King George,' Kilmarnock bowed very reverently; whereas Balmerino taking off his hat, and waving it, cried, 'God save King J – s, and all his Royal family.' From the time that the Earl quitted the gate he attracted the eyes of all the spectators, being about six foot high, cloathed in black, with a bag appended to his hair, and walking in the most decent, serious, and majestic manner; he was attended by Mr. Foster, a dissenting clergyman, a gentleman of real goodness of heart, and endowed with the most extensive good-will to mankind: he had been at great pains both to bring / his Lordship to a sense of his sin, and to be reconciled to the change he was to undergo. Happening to be in the Tower when the warrant came for execution, he contrived to let his Lordship know it in a manner the least likely to create a surprize: he introduced a discourse with General Williamson concerning death, which continuing some minutes, his Lordship said, 'Is the dead warrant arrived?' Being answered in the affirmative, Mr. Foster very properly replied, 'We are all under sentence of death;' and entering upon a serious conversation, his Lordship became quite calm and serene.

Never did two unfortunate noblemen go to a block more different from each other than Balmerino and Kilmarnock, as will appear by the following little incident: the former desired to speak with the latter, which was granted; and then his Lordship asked, if he knew any thing of an order given by the P – on the morning of the battle of Culloden, 'to give no quarter to the Elector's troops on any account whatsoever.' To this Kilmarnock replied, 'that he had heard of such an order since that time, but as to himself he knew nothing of it.' From this the former inferred, that no such order ever had existed, and the latter reasoned that the conclusion was not fair, 'since such an order might have been given, tho' unknown to me.' 'It is,' said Balmerino, 'only an invention to palliate their own murders!' Whether such an order existed by itself is a question; the Royalists roundly assert it; and I think it is substantially to be found in the Pretender's manifestoes*; and it is known that many in the Pretender's army declared, that the soldiers should not meet with such kind treatment as hitherto they had done.

When Kilmarnock appeared on the scaffold, he drew sighs from every heart, and tears from every eye; the executioner himself, tho' he had on him part of the cloaths in which Colonel Townley had suffered, shed tears, and fainted away, till revived by artificial spirits, when his Lordship spoke to him, and gave him five guineas; after which he submitted to his fate, and the executioner severed his head from his body at one stroke, all but a small bit of skin that covers the *obliquus inferior*.

Next came Balmerino, who hitherto was so obscure, that on mounting the scaffold the crowd was at a loss to know the criminal, till he began to prepare for the block: perhaps his chagrin arose from the faint impression which his voluntary surrender had made upon the government: he did not consider that the same was not properly known. But be that as it will, his deportment startled the executioner, to whom he gave three guineas; for on taking the ax out of his hand, and thumbing it, he walked round a part of the stage moving it up and down in his hand, so that the very men attending the sheriff became affrighted, and reproached Jack Ketch for his simplicity: however, no bad consequence ensued, the ax was restored,

* See page 94, line 11–15. /

when the terrified fellow did his business but poorly, not finishing it with less than three blows.

The next sufferer was Mr. Charles Ratcliff, who, by a warrant from the King's Bench, was beheaded on Little Tower-hill for a treason committed about thirty years before: he had behaved insolently to the Court, pleading his peerage, and the privilege of being a subject to the French King; for snatching the hand of one of the jury as these sat upon the identity of his person, he said, 'Here is the hand of a man among the lowest class of mechanics; / Is this a proper person Mr. Lee* for trying a peer?' But upon the scaffold, December the 9th, his deportment was every way composed and serene, and he died a Roman Catholic.

But the greatest trial of all was that of Simon Lord Lovat, whose two Secretaries, with three others of the name of Fraser, and John Murray of Broughton, appeared against him. One Chevis deposed, 'that his general discourse for many years had been in favour of the Pretender's person and interest; that he had cursed the reformation for introducing a false religion, and the Revolution for involving Great Britain in an immense load of debt; that he drank confusion to the Royal family under the masked expression of, *The white horse and all the generation of them*; that his Lordship and Roy Steuart had diverted themselves with poetical compositions in Erse, of which they tried a translation† sufficiently expressive of a real wickedness of heart.' Murray had given up his letter to the Pretender, another to Lochiel, a third to himself, a fourth to the Marquis of Tullibardin, and two to his own son the Master of Lovat. Robert Fraser swore to his writing these letters, and that they had been dictated word for word by his Lordship, produced duplicates of such as had been worn or effaced, and gave in two letters received from the Master, one from the Pretender, with one signed by Lochiel, Cluny, and Murray, earnestly praying he would throw off the mask, and join openly; and at last Sir Everard Falkener swore to a letter received by his Royal Highness the Duke of Cumberland. From these it appeared clearly, that he / had been the life and soul of the Pretender's cause for many years, the chief promoter of that rebellion so lately suppressed; and that he had sent out his son with nine hundred Frazers into it. The speech of Sir William Young at opening

* The Lord Chief Justice.

† When that Charley shall come o'er,
There shall be blood and blows in good store.

the indictment is among the most nervous to be met with upon this or any other occasion: 'When I look to the prisoner at the bar, I am moved with pity for his infirmities and years*:– but, my Lords, had his scheme succeeded, such of your Lordships as had escaped with your lives, when fighting for your religion and liberties, would have been arraigned at that very bar before a body of mock peers, who would have rejoiced in your sufferings!' It is imagined, that if the Pretender had prevailed, Lovat would have been tried for high treason.

On finding him guilty, the Lord High Steward, before passing sentence, made a speech, in which he said, that it had been happy for his Lordship, if the terrors of the law had retained him in his allegiance, when his oaths and his engagements were too weak ties to bind him: he observed, that the foreign enemies of Great Britain were not so forward to invade her, as her own degenerate and unnatural sons; that whether this backwardness proceeded from the little dependence to be had on so false a set of men, or from the great improbability that a general infatuation should all at once seize the people of Great Britain, so as to make them renounce their allegiance to a Protestant King, who reigned in justice and with mercy, and declare for a Popish Pretender, long since abjured by the most solemn oaths, in either case, continued he, France was in the right; for what faith could be put in so detestable a crowd of parricides? After / mentioning his being a Roman Catholic in private, and a Protestant by his oaths to the government, he proceeded to lament the situation of the people in the remote parts of Scotland, who, in consequence of an abject subjection to their chiefs and superiors, must be compelled to take up arms, and be forced to rebel against their lawful Sovereign. Now, said he, we know the disease, and can better apply a remedy†; and having remarked that the Protestant Succession was not an empty name, but something real and essential, he concludes with these words: 'Your Lordship has led a life of craft, dissimulation, and perfidy; but the sentence which I am to inflict upon you, will soon send you to a tribunal, where no disguise nor artifice can avail you.'

April the 9th he was led to the scaffold, and behaved in the same manner as at Kirkhill, or at Beaufort, speaking in English, in Latin, and in French by turns: he told the sheriff that he was glad he had fallen into

* He was near eighty.

† There was an act of parliament soon afterward, abolishing the vassalage, and declaring the people free: the same thing had been done before the union of the two crowns, but the people, knowing no language but the Erse, were ignorant of it.

such good hands, and that he must obey him even *in articulo mortis*. He then repeated these admirable words of Ulysses out of Ovid; lines which he had pronounced on many occasions.

> *Nam genus et proavos, et que non secimus ipsi*
> *Vix ea nostra voco!*

> *The deeds of long-descended ancestours*
> *Are but by grace of imputation ours,*
> *Theirs in effect!* /

Whether he meant this of the Pretender, or of his own son, is not determined, nor have we any thing to guide our conjecture, except the next elegant phrase out of Horace:

> *Dulce et decorum est pro patria mori –*

> *'Tis a becoming and a pleasant thing for a man to die for his country.*

So giving ten guineas to the executioner, he desired him to do his business well, and added smiling, 'If you mangle me, and I lift up my head, I shall be very angry.' This being over, he was led to the block by two yeomen of the Tower; and as he walked along said, *Je meurs un fils indigne de l'Eglise Romaine*. His head, notwithstanding the shortness of his neck, was, by one full, well-aimed, and strenuous blow, severed from his body. Soon after this an act of indemnity passed, in which were but few exceptions.

The hardships of others concerned in the rebellion were great: Strath-Spey was the place to which Roy Steuart and some of the most guilty resorted. Sir William Gordon of Park and others retired into Sutherland, from whence many of them fled over to the Orkneys and Shetland, and from thence into Norway and Sweden. Their native country was the least asylum to the fugitives: the northern counties of England yielded no refuge; and in Scotland the informations were continual. Their only sanctuary was London, and thither did crowds of them repair. Some plied as day-labourers, some went abroad, and others entered into academies under fictitious names. Watts, who had begun an academy in the year 1716, being returned / from strolling up and down France and the West of England, did, at the Christmas 1746, set up an academy in the Parish of St. James. His masters at first were either Irish or French, and all Roman Catholics. The oldest of his boarders was the grandson of a man who had been killed on the side of the rebels at Sheriffmuir, his brother had carried the bloody-cross among Lovat's tenants, and was killed at the battle of Culloden. He himself breathed all the spirit of the party, and seemed to have dipt his tongue in gall. Another had assumed the surname of his mother, and had been one of the Pretender's life-guard. Unhappily for me, I had been sent up in June 1747, to be one of his assistants, little knowing of his bankruptcy*, less of his ignorance (the man being incapable of declining his name in any language) and still less of the people he entertained. My History of the Rebellion was disagreeable to them, as were the two Sapphic Odes on his Royal Highness the Duke of Cumberland. Though I had brought up the impression, yet I was not allowed to publish it, for fear of giving offence. Dr. Blair, who succeeded me December 23d that year (at a time when I had not the remotest apprehension of a successor) might perhaps be more agreeable at that seminary, as his name had not then appeared in public. Possibly Blair had been recommended to Watts by R. Freebairn, the man who was printer to the Pretender's army at Perth anno 1715. To my certain knowledge he frequented Coffee Blair's house: and it is an undoubted truth, that he was of singular service in recommending boarders to Watts from among the disaffected in North Britain. In a word, / Blair was better acquainted with London than I: he had been in it for years before, and he must certainly know best what past between Watts and him. – I have frequently thought, that a Bishop of a Diocese ought, out of compassion and mercy to the rising generation, to look into the practice and principles of those who set up academies and schools: for I have always observed an hidden Jacobite to be a man void of honour, probity, and conscience.

Whatever were the sufferings of others the Pretender himself underwent little more than what might have been expected. It is surprising that a young man of any degree of sagacity could not foresee, that London would be his only sanctuary. I have been told, he was in that metropolis in the year 1751, and it is generally believed, that he was in Westminster-hall on the 22d of September, and saw the Coronation-dinner about ten years afterwards. One thing is certain, he shifted and roamed through the Highlands and Islands for five months; during which time he was almost in continual alarms.

* Thirteen pence halfpenny in the pound: a plausible scheme for bettering his circumstances would make him do any thing.

From Gortuleg, where he had slept the night after the battle, he on the next day retired to Glengary-house; and from thence rode to Ruthven of Badenoch, where Lord George Murray had discharged his followers, and bid every man shift for himself. The inhabitants there had been of his party, but were not at the battle; and these entertained him for five days, in the remotest parts of the district. After this time there was no great encouragement to stay there, as the Macphersons had, in obedience to the proclamation of his Royal Highness, surrendered to Blair, the clergyman of Kinguissie: he thought it more safe to retire into the country of the Camerons, as nearer the sea, in case he should be too closely pursued. Accordingly / he repaired to Achnacarrie, where Lochiel was lying ill of the wounds he had received; and here continued till the time the Argyleshire Highlanders marched into Lochaber. Lochiel, being a man of spirit, urged him to do something for retrieving his affairs; but to no purpose: he had been greatly chagrined at his disaster, and declined appearing any longer in arms. From this he retired farther toward the sea, and put up in the house of Macdonald of Kingsborough, where a party of Kingston's horse had almost surprized him. Some of these informed me, that they frequently had a sight of him at a distance, such as on an opposite side of a morass, a lake, or some such security. Enraged at this disappointment they seized upon Macdonald, as he had conducted him out of the house by a secret passage, even at the time when they were rummaging the several rooms of the dwelling, in quest of him. I saw Macdonald as they were escorting him into Edinburgh, and was present when he was confined there. How unfortunate for the Fugitive to be absent when the French ships landed the money on the 4th! These carried off Perth, Lord Elcho, Lord John Drummond, and many other officers. From Kingsborough he went to the dwelling of Colonel Macdonald of Barisdale, who seemed at first not to shew the same regard as hitherto: however, in a short time he became more obsequious than ever, and began to lay down a variety of schemes, either for supporting him by force, or for extricating him by a timely escape out of all his hardships: but in this he was acting deceitfully; for he had already been with Hawley, and had agreed to get the Stranger delivered into the hands of the Government; but in such a manner as to reflect no dishonour upon himself. The Fugitive and his guardian S. Tho. Sheridan, who / was still with him, began to harbour some suspicion of the man, which increased the more, as he went out one morning, as he said, to kill a deer; but in reality to inform the garrison at Fort Augustus, that the Pretender was safe in his house. A party set out the moment they received the information, and certainly would have seized him, had not he and Sheridan beheld them, from an eminence, advancing to the house where they had been lodged. On this they hastened toward the head of Loch Sornard, almost opposite to Fort William, where a servant of Cameron of Callard procured them a boat, which carried them down by the Back of Lismore, and, doubling the point of Morvern, sailed with them pretty far through the Sound of Mull. As it was night they put in at Cambusnaguael; where, meeting with an hearty country gentleman, and a devotee of the Church of Rome, they were properly refreshed; and, as the gentleman could not prevail upon them to stay with him, or divert themselves about Mingrycastle, by hunting in the woods, they at night crossed the Sound to Morenish, hoping they might find a vessel to convey them out of the British dominions; but in this they were disappointed: and yet his forlorn condition could not hinder Sheridan from looking narrowly into the natural advantages of the Harbour of Tobermorry, which has so much attracted the speculation of the curious.

Tobermorry* Harbour, in the Isle of Mull (a part of the Duke of Argyle's estate) is perhaps one of the finest and most commodious in Europe. It lies within seven miles of the Western Ocean; is sheltered by the high grounds of Morenish, which almost form a very large segment of a circle about / it, and the deficiency of the curve is supplied by a small island called Calva (belonging to the same Nobleman) about which the sea ebbs and flows. The water to within two yards of the shore is of a depth sufficient for ships of burden to ride in safety. The ship of the Duke de Medina Celi, the Admiral of the Spanish Armada, was sunk here in the year 1588, and in it was the treasure (computed at three millions of crusadoes) inevitably lost. Experiments have been made oftener than once for getting up the wreck, but to no purpose: and I remember very well, that in the year 1737 Captain Roe, whose skill in using the diving-bell was universally acknowledged, staid there five weeks in quest of the prize. The men who were let down saw the vessel whole and intire; only covered with kelp and other sea weeds: and near the stairs of the cabin a sword was discerned lying, with the handle and scabbard almost intire. What

* In Erse, Tober mor Ri, the great King's well, or the great well of the King. There are some fine springs near it.

pity it is that the sons of genius and contrivance could not devise some wooden frame for fishing up this ancient wreck; which, if once found, would much more than compensate all the toil and labour that might be used therein: the depth of the water there not being above fifty yards. I many times have wondered that the harbour of Tobermorry had not furnished an embellishment for the poem of Timora or of Fingal, especially as the scene was Morvern, almost opposite to it. This poem of Fingal is preferred by some to the incomparable Æneid of Virgil.

Whatever asylum Tobermorry might have given the Pretender in the year 1588, it was a very improper place for him now; and therefore he retired directly to Mackinnon's house at Muesnish, hoping that as the lady was sister to Clanranald, she might in some measure contribute to his escape: but in this / he was mistaken, for neither the gentleman nor his spouse were at home: so, resolving to lose no time, he hastened to the boat, and passing by Maclean's Nose, an high promontory, he sailed out into the ocean, and in a few hours landed at Eagg; the proprietor of which Mr. Maclean entertained him hospitably. Here he might have continued some days, but, afraid of a discovery, he sailed over to Canna, a small island belonging to Clanranald; and which, from its situation, had a very extensive prospect; so that no ship could come from any part of the compass without being descried at a considerable distance.

After staying here about ten days, he crossed over to South-Uist, where he was received by the Lady Clanranald and her daughters, who seemed to discover a sympathy toward him, tho' the inhabitants were desirous he should be gone, as they were apprehensive of a visit from some of the King's ships, as had happened both at the Revolution, and in the year 1716, and even at this very time: he had not stayed here above eight days, when he went over to Barra, an island lying at the foot of South-Uist, and separated from it by an eddy: he was advised to go over to Ireland with Sir Thomas Sheridan, who assured him of his knowing the country well, and laid down the most probable means of escaping into France from some port of that kingdom.

The arguments of Sheridan could not prevail with him to pass over into Ireland, where the Parliament had set 50,000 l. upon his head. The Earl of Chesterfield was that year Lord Lieutenant, and he had by a mild and popular administration* secured / the people so firmly to the Government, that both Roman Catholics and Protestants seemed to be reconciled; and the ports were so narrowly watched, that there was not landing there. The Chevalier knew this, and his imagination figured the danger to be more than it really was; so that he and Sheridan parted with mutual embraces, the latter giving a full and absolute promise, that as soon as possible a ship should be sent to carry him over; and commending him to his good fortune, the one put to sea, and the other returned to Clanranald's house.

It was now the beginning of June: daily accounts were arriving of the surrender of those concerned with him; the King's ships were upon the coast, but did not land; they only contented themselves with throwing some few balls among the houses and sheep-folds, but at too great a distance to do any great mischief.

It does not appear from the History of Scotland, that ever a body of men entered South-Uist in an hostile manner since the time when the Danes forded it over the Hebrides, anno 1050, till this very period. His Royal Highness the Duke of Cumberland was the person to propose it, and General Campbell the officer to undertake the execution of the plan which his Royal Highness had laid down. The Argyleshire militia had marched through Lewis, Harris, and North-Uist, and were upon the frontiers of South-Uist before the unhappy fugitive had an account of their being near him. Fortunately for him one Mrs. Flora Macdonald, daughter to Capt. Hugh Macdonald, who had been an officer in the French service, undertook to carry him through the midst of those who were in search of him: he put off his own clothes, and assumed the low dress of a menial servant running / at the horse foot. Upon coming to the small eddy that separates North and South Uist, the servant became more affrighted for fear they should accost him in Erse, a language which he did not understand: they did indeed speak to him in that tongue, but Miss Flora told them that he was a servant from the low country: she conversed with them, took the matter upon herself, and was actually believed. He continued in Miss Flora's service for twenty days, when a discovery being made that the servant was the Pretender himself, the search became more violent; and Miss Flora falling into their hands just about four hours after she had parted from

* Upon the New Year's Day of 1745 the Countess of Chesterfield appeared in a new suit of clothes, every single article of which was of the Irish manufactory.

him, and had left him with a friend, she made a full discovery of all that she knew about him, and directed to the very place where he was. Fortunately for him one of the servants came in and told, that a party of the Argyleshire militia was advancing; and this filled him with the most dismal apprehensions: there was no remedy, but to put on womens clothes; and in this dress he passed for a cousin to the landlady of the house, and even witnessed the search that was making for him: there was not the least observation made upon the Mistres's cousin, further than that she was extremely tall. Miss continued in her clothes for four hours; but upon the party going away in quest of their prey, the Pretender assumed his former habit, and going out, he took a private road by himself, without trusting any person: for two days he wandered in this way, and on the morning came to a fisherman, who had some fish; the stranger was hungry, and one being near who knew him, he was entertained with some broiled fish, and such bread as is used in these parts. On going off he offered a Louisdore; but the people told him, that the search for him was brisk, and / if any money was found upon them it might raise a suspicion; and so he departed. For fourteen days he continued in this forlorn state, the militia seeking for him on all sides, and frequently coming to the very place which he had but just quitted. Mr. Campbell, who was sent to take up the arms both of the enemies and friends of the Government, has told me, that he has frequently been upon the opposite side of the hill from him, and at other times in a small boat just off the shore where the militia was marching.

As the search became every day hotter, in consequence of the information given by Miss Macdonald when under examination*, he retired over to the Isle of Sky, hoping both to find friends there, and that the search would be somewhat abated. He generally set off in the night-time, and continued either at sea through the day, or else upon the top of some mountain, whence he could have a view of the adjacent country. While in Sky he one day accidentally met with a man, whose name was Neil Mackinnon, and he carried him to the house of one of his relations, where he was properly refreshed, but did not discover who he was. The common people of that island are among the most courteous to strangers of any in the kingdom; the destitute fugitive observing him to be very ready to oblige him, he informed who he was: the man was struck with the mat-

* She was conducted up to London, and confined in a messenger's house in Dartmouth-street, Westminster.

ter, and therefore conducted him to the house of Capt. Mackinnon, to whom he was personally known: that very night some strangers came to the house, which raised the more circumspection. The Captain informed a younger brother of the matter, and it was concluded that he should be put to bed, / and a woman's clothes to be laid over his upon the chair that stood near; and this was the second time he ever had recourse to the expediency of a woman's habit. After passing ten days in Sky, he went over to Raarsa, where he continued tolerably safe, and shifting his abode, crossed to the continent of Kintail, where one day he went into a house to have some refreshment, but the landlord, named Macra, declared he would entertain none, except such as he knew. This being the case, the fugitive strolled over the Highlands of Rossshire, came down by the district of Strathglass, and from thence into Lochaber, where the search had entirely abated, and here he continued near the seaside, but never above one night in an house, till the 12th of September, when a ship from Boulogne entered the bay of Barisdale, and the Captain having a letter from Mr. Butler, an Irish gentlemen, and a merchant at Boulogne, he was prevailed on to come to an appointed place, and to have an interview with the Captain, who delivered him another letter from Sir Thomas Sheridan; by which, and other circumstances, being convinced of the integrity and uprightness of the man, he went on board, and coasting by the back of Ireland, the vessel sailed toward Brest in Picardy; but being met by one of his Majesty's men of war, the ship was obliged to crowd sail, and make all possible haste to Morlaix, where he landed to the astonishment of all who saw him, as he brought nothing but the shattered remains of his constitution, to point out his own ambition and rashness, and to shew the power of our King's son, whose name had already been a terror to the armies and council of France.

The End of the EIGHTH BOOK. /

THE LIFE OF WILLIAM DUKE of CUMBERLAND.

BOOK IX.

CONTENTS.

The State of the Ministry in Great Britain *in the Year* 1746, – *the Character of Mr.* Pitt, – *the Arrival of his Royal Highness in* Holland, – *a Body of* Russians *are taken into* British *Pay* – *Character of the Prince of* Orange, – *the Battle of* Lafelt, – *and Peace of* Aix la Chapelle.

THE Adventurer having failed in the enterprize, on the event of which no less than the fate of Europe depended, the British nation was left in full freedom to prosecute the war with more vigour than ever against all her enemies.

The factions of the Earl of Grenville and of the Duke of Newcastle, that had distorted the Privy Council in the beginning of the year, were so far united, that there was an emulation which should outdo each other in promoting the cause of their / country. The former nobleman was a person of great address, and of long experience; he had negotiated a peace between Denmark and Sweden, and between Sweden and Russia, in the years 1719 and 1721; while Lord Lieutenant of Ireland he had done things, which the natives of that kingdom will ever keep in the most grateful remembrance. he had been appointed Secretary of State in the beginning of the year, but in three days resigned his employment; the Duke of Newcastle, who had spent a vast fortune to promote the advancement of the family of Hanover to the throne, had the seals restored to him; his brother Henry Pelham, and such as were more closely connected with him, likewise came in; and to gain the more favour with the public, some gentlemen, whose abilities had begun to shine in the House of Commons, were introduced into a share of the administration.

Among the number of these was William Pitt, Esq; a gentleman who, ever since the time when he appeared against the seamens bill, which enabled every petty constable to search houses at his pleasure, under pretext of seeking for mariners, had now arrived at a great pitch of reputation and character: he was thoroughly acquainted with the different interests of the several Courts of Europe: he has been at one time or other in every metropolis, well skilled in the French tongue, and no stranger to the genius of France in general, or to her ministry in particular; a man of as fine wit and parts as ever had a seat in Parliament, of profound secrecy and readiness of wit, of such persuasion and eloquence, that his very attitudes were so many significant symbols to strengthen his arguments; like Cato he was always last in his own care; like him moderate in private life. In everything / he fixed upon an end to be attained, and never lost sight thereof; he traced out things to their first and natural source; a sincere lover of justice*; a strict observer of truth and decorum; and after Parliaments have heard him with astonishment, exposing the foibles and unmeaning practices of a ministry, too ready to run into the measures of our enemies; by a smoothness of persuasion no less prevailing than that of any orator which ever Greece or Rome produced, did he break down the fences of opposition, level the bulwarks of corruption, and burst the barriers of party: by mere force of argument does he describe the advantages or disadvantages arising from any measure under consideration, and with such propriety, that one would be apt to imagine he was rather reciting a narrative of what was past, than laying open a probability of what was to come. This gentleman was appointed Vice-Treasurer of Ireland, and in a short time after he was made Paymaster General of the forces, and admitted to be a member of the Privy Council.

In consequence of this union among the parties, every ally was supported in a manner suitable to the engagements that Great Britain had contracted; for besides the subsidies granted to the King of Sweden, Landgrave of Hesse Cassel, they granted 300,000 *l.* to the King of Sardinia,

* Justitiæ cultor, rigidi servator honesti,
In commune bonus. LUCAN. PHARSAL. 1. 2.

400,000 *l.* to the Empress Queen of Hungary, 410,000 *l.* for maintaining 18,000 Hanoverians, 33,000 *l.* to the Electors of Cologne and Mentz, and 500,000 *l.* in a vote of credit to his Majesty; the whole charge of that year being 7,250,000 *l.* raised by the land and malt tax, annuities raised / on the additional duties on glass and spirituous liquors, a lottery, a deduction from the sinking fund, and Exchequer bills chargeable on the first aids that should be granted by the next session of Parliament.

Though much of these subsidies had been laid out in suppressing the rebellion, yet there was still a sufficiency for enabling Great Britain to humble the pride of those who had contrived and supported it.

To wound France in her very vitals, it was resolved to send a body of troops into Britany. In September 1746 the inhabitants of Rochelle and Rochfort saw a fleet of sixteen ships of the line, and eight frigates, besides bomb ketches and storeships, appear upon their coasts. The object of this expedition was (according to them) 'to destroy Port l' Orient, and with it the French East India Company, to master Port Louis, to lay Britany under contribution, to excite the Calvinists toward Rochelle, Languedoc, and Dauphiny, to a revolt; and all this at a time when the British fleets were preparing to attack the different settlements of France in Asia and America, and depended upon making themselves masters of Naples, after bringing Genoa under the yoke;' things far from being improbable, as the Austrians were masters of Italy, and that Great Britain had hardly any more enemies at sea.

General Sinclair landed with 7000 men on the 2d of October, at a place called Polduc, without opposition, and among these was the new-raised Highland regiment, the first corps from North Britain that had ever entered France in an hostile manner. From thence he advanced to Plemur, and encamped on an eminence, which commanded L'Orient and Port Louis; but for want of artillery / did not attack the place till the 8th, when he intimated to the inhabitants, that unless they surrendered they were to expect all the inconveniencies arising from a storm; the commander of the militia agreed to his terms, but afterward retracted; and in the mean time the wind chopping about, Admiral Lestock made a signal to give him notice of it, upon which the General drew off the troops, reimbarked at Plemur, then made a descent upon the little Isle of Quiberon, where they burnt a man of war, and would have continued longer upon the coast, but the sea there is shallow, and the winds blow fiercely at that season of the year, so that they sailed for Ireland: however the French may jest at this expedition*, yet it shewed that Great Britain could spare troops, even to annoy her enemies upon their own coasts, at a time when she kept them at bay in Flanders and Brabant, where the French got no real advantage, notwithstanding the immensity of treasure expended in support of prodigious armies; even the victory at Rocoux was of little significance to them.

The British troops at that time were commanded by Sir John John Ligonier, and lay between the village of Warem and Rocoux; and though they could not hinder the siege of Namur, nor prevent its being taken by M. Clermont, yet they kept the French so far in motion, as to stop the rapidity of their conquests, and oblige them to contract their bounds. On the 1st of October the Confederate Generals resolved to decamp, and Marshal Saxe was determined to harrass them; for this purpose he brought up the whole of his army, and that enormous artillery cast in the founderies of Vernon, under the eye of M. de Belleisle; with these / he had battered the walls and works about Brussels and Namur: some pieces of 48 pounders were loaded with cartridge shot to begin the engagement. As the Allied army began to draw off, this enormous artillery fired upon them; the Confederate Generals hastened out of their reach, and the French cavalry began to pursue; but the Earl of Crauford turned about with the British horse, and attacking the enemy sword in hand, drove them back to their ranks with prodigious slaughter, then returned and joined the other part of the army. In this manner the battle continued for about four hours, when the French halting, the Allies pursued their march to Maestricht, where they encamped safe under the walls of the town. Their loss was about 4000 men, besides 1000 prisoners, most of whom were wounded; they likewise left behind them 30 pieces of cannon, merely for want of horses to carry them off. The French lost a much greater number, and among others the Marquis de Fenelon, nephew to the immortal Fenelon, Archbishop of Cambray, besides a great number of officers; whereas the loss of the Allies consisted in private men, particularly the Hessians, who had served so well in the expedition to Scotland.

Encounters like these at Rocoux tended only to inflame the enemies of France. The Dutch, more cordially united than ever, resolved to carry on the war in Brabant: they judged, and very justly, that the ruin of their

* See Voltaire's History of the War 1741, p. 245.

Barrier was more owing to the divisions among themselves than to the power of the enemy. Hitherto the magistrates, the burghers, and the populace seemed to be of different interests; but now, from a sense of danger, all united in the choice of the Prince of Orange for Stadt-holder and Captain-general. And the King of / Great Britain was determined to make his enemy feel the effects of his power in the different quarters of the globe. The superiority at sea was visibly on his side; and, to obtain the same by land, he once more sent his own Son to take upon him the command of the army. For this purpose he set out in the month of January, and arriving at the Hague, entered immediately into a conference with Prince Waldec upon the plan of operation; and though nothing could divert him from his main business, yet he received not only the compliments of the States from their Deputies, but likewise those of the Emperor and Empress, and of all the foreign ambassadors, with as much ease and complacency, as if he had only come upon a visit of congratulation and ceremony. The States of Holland went so far as to offer him the command of their troops; the Emperor soon followed their example. Never was Prince more honoured and respected. The States seemed to be unusually gay, and felicitated him upon his glorious success, and the honour he had gained. Poems were addressed to his sister, the Princess of Orange, on the battle of Culloden, in Dutch, French, Latin, and English. However, his Highness did not come over in quest of applause or empty commendation: his design was to lay open the source of the distasters in the Netherlands, and to awaken the States-general into a sense of the danger they were in: that in consequence of this they might send forth their full complement of troops, pay the subsidies punctually to the allies, as the Crown of Britain had set them the example: and in a conference with the Grand Pensionary, at which M. de Van Haaren was present, he told them, That he believed the people of Holland would not suffer more without fortified towns, than as they were. I, continued he, never looked / upon a fortified place to be a real fence to any state, unless it commands the only entrance to that state to which it is the barrier: a well-disciplined and numerous army, under the direction of an able commander, who has orders to fight, is their best security. There are many ways by which an enemy can come into the United Provinces: which they would not be so ready to enter, if there was a body of good troops to give them a warm reception. The observation of his Highness was extremely just; for the States of Holland can never be safe by any barrier but the good œconomy of their finances, the regularity of their government, the respectable situation of their troops, and the proper condition of their marine. The Prince of Orange saw thoroughly into the extent of the argument, and became convinced of its force. Experience has shewn, that by means of these forts almost thirty thousand prisoners had fallen into the hands of the common enemy; who, elated with success, threatened at times to penetrate into the very heart and bowels of the state; and yet he could not think of a proper remedy. For, walking one day with his Royal Highness nigh the House in the Wood, he observed, that the troops which were hired from the petty princes of the Empire proved of very little use against the French, except in the defence of fortresses. These princes, said he, live almost in the neighbourhood of France, their connections with the subjects of that crown are strict, and in some cases natural: some time or other they have been in the pay of that crown; nor is there a prince this day in the Empire whose troops have not, at least some of them, served in the armies either of France or of Spain. However, we must endeavour to make them as useful to the state as possible; and, depend upon it, nothing shall be wanting on my part to have a / proper army on foot, and to bring them early into the field, for the good of the common cause. This being over he set out from Loo, on his return to England; where he laid down the subject of the several conferences which he had with the Generals of the army, with the Deputies of the States, and with the Prince of Orange.

'Tis the character of the people of England to improve a hint to more advantage, and even to a further extent, than had entered the heart of him who first proposed it. The British ministry began to see clearly what so often had been complained of in former wars, that the want of success in the Netherlands was greatly owing to the backwardness of the Court of Vienna to send out her full complement of troops conformable to treaties, and as their own interest required. It was a common thing for a regiment of foot to be stated at 1200 in the bill, when payment was required, and yet in reality not to consist of more than half the number. The same thing might be said of their horse, their dragoons, their artillery, their carriages, nay and their incidental charges. The Court of Britain was convinced of this treatment from that of Vienna, and from the inferior princes: and now was the question, What to do? The Danes being in the neighbourhood of Sweden, and over-awed by Russia, could not spare any quota. Sweden was in the same situation: and so the matter seemed to be carried to its utmost, when his Royal Highness said, And where is the impropriety of taking a body of Russians into pay, more than a body of Swedes or Danes? The first may be easily transported, though not perhaps with the same facility as the others: yet wherever there is a true zeal, wherever there is a real desire of entering into action, a few days march will be in a manner nothing. My / advice is, that we should negotiate with the Empress of Russia for a body of 50,000 men; which may be landed near Hamburgh or Bremen, and may soon be up with the grand army, without being intercepted. If these once join the British and Hanoverian troops, my life for giving a good account of the enemy. The Russians will be subject to orders, and will fight as veterans, especially when at a distance from their own country. He observed, that the forces of all nations fought best when in another country, or immediately upon the frontiers of their own; and that the Russians had very lately given a shining proof of the first in their war with the Turks, and more lately had shewn to the world an evidence of the latter in their war with the Swedes. The King and his chief ministers agreed to the project; and directly wrote to the Earl of Hyndford, the British ambassador at Petersburgh, to enter into a negotiation for 50,000 effective men.

That nobleman, so famous for having negotiated a peace between the King of Prussia and the Empress Queen, was already in high favour in the Russian empire, and soon brought about the bargain for the body of troops proposed; for which the Empress was to receive the annual sum of 100,000 *l.* Their rendezvous was to be at Dunebere in Livonia; and they were to consist of those who had so lately signalized themselves at the taking of Oczakow and the battle of Czaslaw against the Turks, or in the fierce and terrible encounter with the Swedes at Wilmanstradt.

Since the beginning of the war there was not so much business in the different theatres of action as in the year 1747; for in that period the marine of France was reduced to one single man of war. She had in the preceeding year lost an immensity of / treasure both in Asia and America: several French and Spanish ships, with very rich cargoes (to the amount of 8,500,000 *l.*) suddenly arrived at Louisburgh, some from the East Indies, others from Peru and Mexico, and cast anchor in the harbour, without knowing that the same had changed masters. Every capture was an addition to the strength of Great Britain, and a diminution of the power of her enemines. The British fleet rode triumphant in every quarter. On the 16th of May six large French men of war and seven East India ships were taken by Lord Anson (who had sailed round the world) and Admiral Warren: the Centurion, which had traversed the globe, came up the Thames with the news. Two-and-twenty waggons loaded with the gold and silver taken on board the French fleet yielded a more general satisfaction to the merchants and trading people of the great metropolis, than the account of a complete victory over the armies of France either in Germany or Flanders. And no wonder; for by this capture the enemy lost to the amount of 1,609,000 *l.* Nay, the victors might have taken the whole Martinico fleet, which was under the convoy of these ships, had not the Marquis de la Jonquiere, the French commodore, by standing between them and the British squadron, given them an opportunity to escape.

The French had no more than seven men of war to escort their merchant ships to the American colonies: these were met in the Bay of Biscay by Admiral Hawke's fleet, which was double the number of theirs: the two squadrons engage, and out of the seven, six were taken; so that now the marine of France was reduced to one ship only and that of Spain was every day mouldering away: her seamen had in a manner lost all sort of courage; whereas the British sailors were so heartened, that / the Dartmouth, a small ship of 40 guns commanded by the gallant Captain James Hamilton, encountered the Gloriosa of 74: they were off the rock of Lisbon, where the latter had landed the money which she had brought from Porto Bello but the day before. The engagement continued for six glasses almost within pistol shot of each other, when a cannon placed upon the poop burst, by means of an immoderate quantity of powder brought by an unskilful hand, the Dartmouth blew up, and with her the captain and the whole ship's crew, except twenty-six, who (all but Capt. Obrien) were wounded; some lost their arms, some had their thighs broke, and others were disjointed. The gentleman, Thomas Scott, a relation of mine, from whom I had the story, declared that he was splicing the shrouds, when all of a sudden a mist came over his eyes, and deprived him of his senses; that when the boat of one of the three privateers, which some time raked the Gloriosa afore and aft, during the engagement, came to take him up, he found himself upon an oar, bending cross his breast, and his left leg broke in two places. Mr. Obrien was more fortunate, and his case was still more astonishing; for he had been drinking a can of flip with Lieutenant

Mackenzie, and while holding the same out to the other gentleman, the explosion happened. He was no less stunned than my friend, and all at once found himself sitting in the carriage of the gun in the middle of the water, which was smooth, and as much at ease as if placed in an easy chair in his own room. Short-lived was the triumph of the Gloriosa, for she was taken next day by the Russel of 70 guns, though those on board her were mostly invalids, wounded and maimed.

The taking of Madrass, and relieving Pondicherry in the East Indies, was of no substantial detriment to the affairs of Great Britain, while the / very victories which France gained tended no less to impoverish her, than the Allies which hitherto she had supported. The Genoese were become burthensome, and the more so, as the Austrians had drained from them above 5,000,000 *l.* the Infant Don Philip, with the King of Naples, drew daily upon the French treasury for immense sums; her scheme of setting the Pretender on the throne of Britain had proved abortive, notwithstanding the same had been supported at the expence of several ships, about 3000 men, and 200,000 *l.* France and Spain had lost very fine armies in Italy, notwithstanding the address of the Prince of Conti; while the King of Sardinia and the Austrians extended their conquests as far as the Var, and even crossed into Provence.

To vindicate the credit and reputation of the French arms, there was nothing to be done, except on the borders of Holland. All the force of France was in a manner collected here, and to give the further eclat to her enterprizes, the grand monarch again set out from Paris for the army in Brabant. He reached the quarters of M. de Saxe at Liege on the 27th of April, and having given all possible encouragement to his troops, who were more numerous than ever, he sent Count Lowendahl to reduce the towns and fortresses, while he and his General Count Saxe marched to seek out the army of the Allies in the field, or to hem them in on every quarter.

At this time the Confederate army was more numerous than in either of the preceding campaigns: the Dutch, by means of the Prince of Orange's party, had come more heartily into the quarrel, and the Empress Queen saw the absolute necessity of acting up to her dignity: she had no less than 20,000 foot, and 10,000 horse under the / command of Field Marshal Bathiani, a nobleman of Bohemia, an officer of years and experience, one who had served at the battle of Peterwaradin under the famous Prince Eugene, and had fought both in Flanders and Germany against the armies of France. The Dutch troops consisted of 20,000 men; the national troops of Great Britain amounted to fifteen regiments, those raised for quelling the rebellion having been continued, and the Duke of Kingston's horse being declared to be the Duke of Cumberland's regiment of dragoons. Besides these were 10,000 Hanoverians and 5000 Hessians.

To forward the operations of the troops, the Duke of Cumberland set out from St. James's about four in the morning of the 1st of February, attended by Lord Bury, Lord Cathcart, and Colonel Fitzwilliams, and by the way of Harwich and Helvoetsluys arrived next day at the Hague, where he found things more to his satisfaction than hitherto; he was every day in conference with the Deputies, the Pensionary or with the Prince of Orange, of whom it will not be improper to draw a character.

William Henry Friso was the posthumous son of that Prince of Orange, who fought with an astonishing intrepidity at the battle of Malplaquet: he was an orphan before he saw the light of the world; like William III. Prince of Orange and King of England, he no sooner came to years of maturity, than he met with very hard usage from the same quarter as our great Deliverer; the States of Holland slighted him, and neglected to confer upon him the high office of his ancestors; but he bore all with true magnanimity, a greatness of mind superior to fortune, and a resignation to the Divine Providence, which never abandons those who confide in it; like his illustrious predecessor, / he was possessed of a wonderful sagacity, a quick discernment, and a solid judgment; he was munificent, serene, and temperate, and so moderate in respect to titles and honours, as to neglect those he had the justest right to. It was no wonder if two such great souls as the Duke of Cumberland, and the Prince of Orange, should unite together in all the bonds of mutual affection, being connected together not so much by the tie of affinity, as of a similarity of manners, and a likeness of disposition and genius. The reason of his Highness continuing here so long was to wait for the troops from England and Scotland, which accordingly arrived on the 11th of March at Williamstadt, where by order of the Prince of Orange they were very hospitably received. Next morning the Duke went from the Hague to review them, and on the 16th returned, in order to settle the further operations, which being adjusted, he set out on the 27th to take upon him the command of the Confederate army, which then began to assemble about Tilbourg: he came to them in an open chaise, to which there was free access; above two hundred petitions were presented to him from different persons: he received and read them all as much as possible, and finding their purport to be, that the men might be eased of the burden of giving four pence *per* week out of their pay, for receiving their money in the coin of the country, and of four pence more for camp equipage; he directly called the general officers together, and after remonstrating upon the impropriety of putting any hardship upon private men, matters were so settled, that they were paid ever after in the currency of the country to the utmost extent. And here he could not help expressing a peculiar satisfaction at seeing the regiments, who had gone with him through the winter / campaign of 1745, and who had fought at Culloden battle.

The French Generals had not been idle: Marshal Saxe had arrived at Brussels on the 19th, when the troops under his command filed off by different routs, and immediate preparations were made for opening the campaign. Count Lowendahl entered the Dutch territories at the head of 25,000 men, and soon reduced Sluys, Sas Van Ghent, and Fort Philippines, Axel, and Hulst; and to hurt the States General still more, the Marshal de Contades entered by the Scheld a little below Antwerp, and soon mastered Doel, Perli, Liehenshack, and Lillo, no walls being able to resist the shock of their enormous artillery. The States remonstrated upon this irruption into their territory, and the French endeavoured to pacify them by an assurance, that the places garrisoned by the troops of the Republic, but the property of the Austrians, should be restored so soon as ever the States of Holland should give convincing proofs of their furnishing no succours to the power with whom the French were at war.

So striking a declaration awakened the people out of their lethargy. A resolution was taken of making an augmentation of 30,000 men to their troops. Mynheer Van Hoey was recalled from Paris, the Importation of French goods was prohibited, and every other precaution was taken, except the actual declaration of war.

While the detachments under Count Lowendahl and Marshal Contades were effecting the total reduction of Dutch Flanders, and while the French and the States politicians were carrying on a paper war, the grand armies of France and of the Confederates were preparing for a decisive action; which might influence the conference for a general / peace which M. de Thiel, the French plenipotentiary, and M. de Macanas, the Spanish minister, had proposed to be held at Aix la Chappelle, Worms, or any other place which the Count de Wassenaer should fix on. The French troops were cantoned between Mechlin and Louvain, and those of the Allies lay encamped near Antwerp, till the 15th of May, when they made a motion, by the direction of the Duke of Cumberland, in order to encamp between the Great and Little Nethe with the right at Lieres and the left at Cinq Fontaines. This alteration was of the utmost advantage, as it secured a safer and more easy communication with the Schelde, and by encamping upon a fresh ground it tended much to the health and ease of the soldiers; hospitals were erected in the most commodious situation and at proper distances, every inconvenience was avoided, and the troops in general were more hearty and well. This motion of his Royal Highness obliged M. Saxe to quit his cantonments on the 21st, when the infantry marched to the camp marked out for them behind the Dyle: so that the two armies were now within ten miles of each other. Here they might have continued for some time, had not the French King arrived there on the 31st, and given immediate orders for calling in all the detachments, while a battery was erected upon the Schelde, to hinder all communication by water betwixt the Confederate army and Holland.

After several marches and counter marches, which sufficiently demonstrated the skill and address of the two great commanders the Duke of Cumberland and M. de Saxe, the armies came in sight of each other on the 18th of June, the Allies being about Lonakin, and the French at Tongres. The former consisted of very fine troops, and such as had been acquainted with battles: they were commanded / by generals of experience and conduct, among whom were the Prince of Wolffenbuttle, and Count Daun, the same who beat the King of Prussia at Czaslaw and at Hochkirchen. The French generals had been inured to fields of danger; and to prompt them to exert themselves, they were favoured with the presence of their King, under whose eye they had already proved victorious: they had besides the superiority of numbers, and a large train of artillery.

But though they were near each other, yet they did not come so near as to engage until the 1st of July, when the Duke of Cumberland, who had been indefatigable, always on horseback by daybreak, and ever busy in procuring the best intelligence, purposed to Prince Waldec to march up to the enemy. A salutary proposal indeed, as their artillery had not arrived; but in this he was opposed both by the Marshal and the Prince, between the latter of whom and him there was a visible reserve ever after.

On the 2d in the morning the army of the Allies was drawn up in order of battle; the Austrians on the right, the Dutch in the center, and the British troops upon the left, having the village of Val in their front; and this was taken possession of by six battalions of foot, and defended by a battery of six pieces of cannon. In the mean time the enemy advanced, when a champion came out from their lines, and called out for a man to fight him. The Earl of Hume being at the head of the guards, answered in French, *I m'avancerai immediatement,* and accordingly rode forward. These two charged each other with their swords, and so closely that the victory continued in suspense for twenty minutes, when his Lordship cleft the Frenchman from the crown of this head to the collar bone, and laid / a side of his head upon each of his shoulders. In the mean time the enemy was advancing, in the form of a wedge, toward the village of Val, where the British guards, with the divisions of Howard, Wolf, and Mordaunt were placed. The enemy had twelve battalions in front, and were twelve deep; but the second line more extended than the third, and this more than the second, and so on successively to the last: and to the right of the first line was Count Tallard's regiment of horse, with that of the French cuirassiers. Three squadrons of the regiment of Greys moved forward to attack them, engaged them, and cut them in pieces: no less than six-and thirty squadrons came up to succour the corps that was broke; and these engaged the victors. The fight was bloody and obstinate: however numbers carried it, so that the Greys were obliged to retire, but not in disorder; neither indeed were they pursued; though as they were returning they received a full discharge from a body of foot that had been lodged behind some hedges to intercept them. The column advanced toward Val, where his Royal Highness had posted himself in the front line, to animate them by his presence. The artillery there was served with great order, and fired the whole time the enemy was advancing, as well upon their front as upon the squadrons of horse that supported the right and left flanks.

At ten o'clock the cannonading began on the enemy's side against the village, with the field pieces which their infantry had brought with them. By the second shot from which the Baron de Zigifaer, a German, aid de camp to his Highness, was killed: this was soon followed with an attack from the brigades of Dillon, Vaiffeaux, Navarre, La Marque, Monaco, and their Gens d'armes: but these were soon dispersed, with prodigious loss, as / were their second, third, and fourth divisions: however, fresh troops always came up, so that the regiments in Val were obliged to give way. They fell back a little, when the Earl of Hume rallied them, and again brought them back to the charge, recovered their post, and joined the regiments of Wolf, Charles Howard, Conway and Hants, who had now supplied their places and were closely engaged with the enemy. The carnage was great; and yet the French still appeared more numerous: they kept pouring in fresh lines of foot, so that the village was lost and regained five different times; or in other words, the British and Hanoverian battalions were four times driven from it, but as oft regained their former station: till wearied out by fatigue they quitted at the fifth time, and neither returned nor yet were pursued.

The instant that the enemy made the first general discharge of small arms at the village, his Highness sent an aid de camp express to M. Bathiani, to inform him that the left was attacked; that the enemy seemed determined to make their whole effort upon Val, and therefore desired he would be attentive to support him speedily and effectually. The Marshal returned for answer, that he had dispatched Count Daun with fourteen battalions for that very purpose, and would likewise support him further as much as possible; and besides this infantry, part of the squadrons of Count Daun's corps was ordered to Val likewise; nine of these battalions arrived time enough to do great execution, but the other five, being ordered from the corps de reserve, did not arrive till after, having a larger extent of ground to march through.

About twelve o'clock affairs went on so well, that his Royal Highness ordered the whole left wing to advance upon the enemy, whose infantry / gave way on every quarter, but were still supported by fresh troops, and by great bodies of cavalry, who constantly appeared upon their flanks; but, above all, by a monstrous train of artillery, which directed all their force against the left wing. M. Bathiani could give but a faint assistance; for the troops and batteries on the hill of Herdeeren, which guarded the left of the enemy, kept him in awe; and the Prince of Waldeck, fearing they might fetch a compass round another village called Bilsen, and attack the right in flank, which in time might put him between two fires, he continued almost without any movement. It is true Bathiani's wing advanced a little toward Herdeeren, and drove a detached party from the village of Elohl, that lay in the front thereof; and here they stopt; which Count Saxe observing, he ordered the batteries to be fully prepared in case they proceeded further; and at the same time commanded the infantry of the reserve to reinforce the troops that were engaged with the left wing. The French right wing, and the left of the Allies, were now more closely engaged than ever; there was nothing but thunder and smoke. Unfortunately for the latter, some squadrons in the center of the line wheeled toward the right, in order to attack the French cavalry on the left flank of their right wing; and riding inadvertently among the five battalions of the corps de reserve, which were marching toward Val, these were entirely overthrown before the mistake was discovered; a mistake which tended more to deciding the action, than either the inactivity of the Dutch, or the lukewarmness of the Austrians. His Royal Highness rode immediately between the lines, and in the midst of the firing to the head of the cavalry, and with the assistance of the Dutch Major-General Cannenburgh endeavoured to rally / them, but in vain; the enemy pressed into the opening, and like a strong wedge split the Confederate army in two. The Duke saw it with concern, but without either anger or inquietude; he rode toward the left wing on a full stretch without being stopt, as the enemy in the midst of the smoke took him for one of their own general officers. And here the battle was kindled into the fiercest rage, the right flank of the left wing being charged by the squadrons that had broke in, and the front exposed to all the fire of the numerous infantry that every moment multiplied against them.

Things being in this situation, the cavalry of the left, with some squadrons of the Imperialists, under the command of Major-General Bournonville, were led on by Sir John Ligonier, charged the French cavalry, and once more overthrew all before them on that quarter; but too eager in the pursuit, they received a sharp fire from a body of foot, which were posted in a hollow way, and among some hedges, to favour the flight of their own horse, by which they suffered greatly: however, they dispersed that body of foot, as also some fresh squadrons that were sent to sustain them; but all was in vain while the army was cut in two. At this very time Sir John Ligonier advised his Royal Highness to retire to a place of safety, and in the mean time he would throw himself in the enemy's way to be taken prisoner. The advice was too salutary to be neglected, and there being even an honour to be obtained in getting through the French ranks, he directly clapt spurs to his horse, and never halted till he had joined the wing that was so hard pressed; and yet not until he had sent an aid de camp to the Marshal, and another to Prince Waldeck, to inform them of the resolution he had taken to retreat to Maestricht, whither he / desired they would follow in the best manner they could. Accordingly he called off the left wing, with which he retired orderly and slowly, and with them the heavy artillery, though these has been planted before the village of Val. The enemy cannonaded a little, but attempted nothing further, seeing the good order they were in, and knowing how greatly they themselves had already suffered. About five o'clock the Duke arrived at Maestricht, and at seven the Austrians and Dutch. The enemy seemed to have a mind to attack the Prince of Wolfenbuttle, who made the rear-guard; but after exchanging some small shot, found it too difficult, and retired.

Such was the battle of Val, in which the British troops, with the Hanoverians and Hessians, procured the greatest honour and applause, having sustained for almost five hours the repeated attacks of a superior army, and retired unbroken at last. On their side were killed about 4930 men, among whom were 2110 of the British, with 382 horse; 2435 of the Hanoverians, with 525 horses; and of the Hessians 385, with 176 horses: there were also taken one thousand prisoners; among whom were Sir John Ligonier, and count Yssemberg of the Hessians, which last was wounded, as was Major-General Bland, and Lieutenant-General Drachtleben of the Hanoverians, with above 1000 subaltern officers of the different corps. The loss of the French was much greater; the brigades of Navarre, La Marque, the Irish, Monaco, the Royal des Vaisseaux, and several others, were totally ruined, four lieutenant-generals were killed, with 1200 other officers, and 8000 men; 700 of the French were taken prisoners, with about 60 officers, among whom were the Brigadier Marquis de Blondel, and Colonel Dillon of the regiment of that name: they / likewise took five standards, and seven pair of colours. Without dwelling any further upon particulars, his Royal Highness next day crossed the Maese, in order to cover Maestricht, and the enemy without loss of time proceeded to the siege of Bergenopzoom, a town advantageously situated upon the confines of Brabant, Flanders, Holland and Zealand, strong by nature as well as art, on account of the morasses that surround it, and already famous for baffling the efforts of the Prince of Parma in 1588, and of the Marquis de Spinola, who lost 10,000 men before it in 1622; nor would Louis XIV. risk his glory in attacking it, anno 1672.

While the French army lay encamped at Tongres, the Count de Lowendahl, after several feints, appeared on the glacis of the place on the 12th of July, and began to draw a line of circumvallation round it; but notwithstanding all his attention, the Prince of Saxe Hilburghausen entered the lines with twenty battalions and fourteen squadrons, tho' to no purpose: the French were determined to have it, and nothing could resist their destroying batteries: the poor peasants were forced to work in their ditches, and driven by the enemy toward the ramparts of the town. Sometimes the firing was terrible, and many of the best buildings, with the steeples of the churches, were beat down. Baron Cronstrom the governor, depending too much on the strength of the place, was not at due pains to keep the outworks properly manned, except at the time when they were attacked. M. Lowendahl was convinced of the oversight, and therefore contrived to surprize the garrison on the 11th of September: for this purpose he made great preparations all that day, as if he intended to begin the attack on the west quarter, while his real design was upon the south east. He had made some prisoners / from among the parties that had sallied out of the town, and from these he had information of the real force of the garrison: he knew the situation and strength of their galleries, the number of their mines, and the casemates to which the workmen resorted. All at once about four in the morning a mine was sprung before the ravelin of Dedem, while an immense quantity of bombs were thrown from all the batteries. In the mean time fifty companies of grenadiers, supported by sixteen battalions, threw themselves into the fosse, and having cut off the communication between the outworks and the town, some attacked the ravelin of Dedem by the breach, whilst others got into it from behind: there were but thirty men upon the gorge, and some of these retired without firing; others were taken prisoners, and were forced with ropes about their necks to conduct the assailants through the galleries, in one of which they surprized the workmen, killed some, and made others prisoners. At this very instant another party forced their way through the sallee ports, scaled the walls of the town with their ladders, mounted the narrow breaches of the lunettes of Cucelle and Pohorn, and spread along the inner talus of the curtains as they arrived, while the first who entered proceeded to the market-place, where they were met by such as edged through the galleries; the French colours were fixed in a moment; the Prince of Hesse Philipstal appeared with Collier's Scots regiment, and the Swiss regiment of Deutz, in order to stop their progress. These kept the assailants in play till the other corps belonging to the garrison should assemble; but they were overpowered, about 400 of Collier's were killed, with as many of Deutz, and the Prince himself was wounded in the leg; the garrison was driven out of the town, and pursued / to the gate of Steenbergen, which was immediately closed upon them; the troops in the lines followed, so that by six in the morning Bergenopzoom was wholly in the hands of the besiegers; they seized upon the governor's papers, the military chest, all the cannon in the arsenal, and every thing that was valuable, and among others seventeen small ships that had been sent with provision for the garrison. When the Grand Monarch heard of this important conquest, he came out of his closet next day, and being surrounded by a great number of general officers, he said, 'Bergenopzoom is taken, Count Lowendahl is a Marshal of France, and M. Saxe is governor-general of the conquered Netherlands.'

But what was gained in the Netherlands was lost in Italy and Provence; for it is observable, that every advantage in the Low Countries was balanced by some loss in these parts. Genoa, which had been possessed and impoverished by the Austrians, had from a love of liberty risen up against their oppressors, and expelled them from the city, and almost from the other territories of the state. The Court of France, from a motive of private interest, sent the Duke de Boufflers with 8000 men to support them: however, their wounds were too deep to be soon healed, and the succours sent them by sea were frequently picked up by the English fleet which lay there to intercept them; the beautiful county of Provence was desolated by Marshal Brown's army, and on the 19th of July, just seventeen days after the battle of Lafelt, a brother of the Marshal Belleisle, one of the best engineers in Europe, lost a great part of his army, and his own life also in attacking the Piedmontese, who were intrenched at the Collo di Tende in Piedmont near to Exilles: her colonies were exposed, / her commerce was at a stand, and her navy destroyed. In short, the very name and reputation of France would have been sunk, had it not been for her efforts in the Netherlands, or rather the disagreement among those, who led the troops in that quarter against her.

All the different powers at war were losers thereby: France was impoverished, and had lost above 300,000 effective men in the course thereof: Great Britain has been drained of immense treasures by supporting a land war; but these had been supplied from the vast captures that were made: the States General were in the most dismal situation, being open to the inroads of an enemy, whose losses had rendered them still more rapacious: one half of Germany, Italy, and the Netherlands was ravaged promiscuously by friends and by enemies, when all of a sudden a new turn was given to affairs by the ministry of France and of Great Britain, who at this time breathed the same sentiments of humanity: the Earl of Chesterfield and the Marquis de Puysieux were both convinced, that a kingdom is more happy in time of peace than of war, be it ever so fortunate. How happy for a nation to have a man of consideration and temper as a minister of state!

The French Monarch always affecting a kind of moderation in the midst of his success, had signified already his inclination for peace to Sir John Ligonier, and declared his personal regard for his Brother Monarch. The Court of Great Britain, notwithstanding her signal advantages, was not averse to what might be of such public utility; for at the meeting of the new Parliament, his Majesty, in his speech from the throne, after informing them, that the want of success in the Netherlands was not owing to the British troops, he / told them, that propositions of peace were made him on the part of France, which he was not averse to; the addresses from both Houses were full of loyalty and affection, and expressed a pleasure at hearing of the step made toward a general pacification; and his Royal Highness arriving the day after the Parliament sat, gave still the more satisfaction; plenipotentiaries were appointed to meet at Aix la Chapelle as soon as conveniently they could.

This complacency on the part of France was not so much on account of a desire of putting an end to the war, notwithstanding the ruinous state of her affairs, as from an apprehension that the new Parliament would act more vigorously than ever, and that the Russians, when once joined with the British troops, would be more than a match for any armies which she could send into the field: she knew that nothing but a disagreement among the Confederate generals had been the occasion of her success, and well foresaw that the Russians would be as much at the beck of his Royal Highness, as either the Royal or Electoral troops of his father. Prince Repnin was ready to set out on the 1st of January 1748, and actually began his march on the 6th with 30,000 men, besides 7000 recruits to fill up the vacancies. They had a numerous artillery, with plenty of ammunition and military stores: they would have come by sea to Lubeck, but the ice in those parts hindered them; so that they took the rout of Lithuania and Poland, and would have soon been up with the grand army, had not the cessation of arms prevented it.

As the approach of the Russians might influence the congress at Aix la Chapelle, and that his Royal Highness the Duke of Cumberland had crossed over to Flanders in March 1748, so Marshal Saxe endeavoured / to ballance this weight by a coup d'eclat, in reducing the town of Maestricht, the capital of Brabant, notwithstanding it was defended by strong forts, a numerous garrison, a large and well-served train of artillery, and had the allied army in its neighbourhood: to draw off which he sent bodies of troops three different ways; one filed off toward Luxemburgh, another to Breda, a third toward Tongres, and a fourth toward Tirlemont; and, while every one was in suspense where these were to meet, he sat down before Maestricht with an army of 110,000 men, an irresistible train of artillery and mortars, under the direction of the most experienced engineers. The States General remonstrated against this as the conferences were soon to begin: and, after some arguments on both sides, it was agreed, that the Russians should halt, that the French should send back a number equal to that of the Russians, and in the mean time to be put in possession of Maestricht; which on the conclusion of the peace was to be restored, with all its artillery and magazines, on the faith of a Prince and the honour of a Christian. This settled, the summer was spent in a state of inactivity, and in August the conferences began, which terminated in a general peace, concluded and signed on the 7th of October, at Aix la Chapelle. By this treaty Lewis XV. secured the kingdom of the Two Sicilies to Don Carlos, grandson of Lewis XIV. He settled his son-in-law Don Philip in Parma, Placentia, and Guastalla: and his ally the Duke of Modena, son-in-law to the Regent Duke of Orleans, was restored to his dominions. Genoa recovered all her rights; but it was a work of time before she could recover the credit of her Bank, and the 5,000,000 *l.* sterling, of which she had been fleeced. /

The Court of Great Britain neither lost nor gained any territory, as Cape Breton was delivered back to France; and the Dutch had all their towns restored to them. In short every thing was put in the same situation as at the beginning: only the King of Prussia preserved the conquest of Silesia, and the Queen of Hungary yielded to his Sardinian Majesty a part of the Milanese: and, as in other cases, the prisoners on both sides were restored.

There was nothing in the peace dishonourable to Britain but the circumstance of sending two hostages to the Court of France, until Cape Breton should be restored; which was done in about eight weeks: and so soon as this news arrived of the delivering it up, the two hostages set out from Paris, notwithstanding the declaration of the French King, that he would look upon it as a mark of his Britannic Majesty's confidence, if they might be permitted to stay somewhat longer, as he expressed for them the highest personal honour and regard. The greatest rejoicings were made at Paris and at London by fireworks, illuminations, and every other emblem of satisfaction; and on the day when the peace was proclaimed through the metropolis, his Majesty appeared at the window, attended by his two Sons and a brilliant company of Nobles, lifted up the sash, and was accosted with loud and incessant acclamations. The Courts sent ambassadors immediately to each other: the Earl of Albemarle was dispatched from Great Britain to Paris, and the Marquis, afterwards Duke, de Mirepoix was sent hither on the part of France.

The End of the NINTH BOOK. /

THE LIFE OF WILLIAM DUKE OF CUMBERLAND.

BOOK X.

CONTENTS.

The Consequences of the Peace, – the Character of the Prince of Wales, *and of the Earl of* Crauford, *– the Hospitality of the Duke of* Cumberland, *– Account of the* Shetland *Fishery, – the Review of the* Hanoverians *on* Coxheath, *– and the Regulation with respect to* Chelsea Hospital.

AFTER the peace, his Royal Highness applied himself wholly to promote the welfare and happiness of those who had served in the war. His Majesty gave 50,000 *l.* out of his privy-purse, toward supporting such as should be discharged, and recommended to his parliament to make provision for such as had deserved so well of their country. An act soon passed both for the benefit of soldiers and sailors, by which they had liberty to settle and / follow business in any City, Town, or Corporation through England, except in the two universities of Oxford and Cambridge: and to enlarge the provision still more, the vast tract of ground known by the name of Acadia, or Nova Scotia, began to be peopled, by a colony sent out on the Government's expence: a project which, however uninviting at first, on account of the piercing cold in that quarter, has, by the prudence and conduct of General Cornwallis and after governors, turned out to the great advantage and support of many poor people who were starving in their mother-country. The town of Hallifax, which but twenty years before was covered with wood to the very beach, is now a place of taste, elegance, and commerce, and contains ten thousand houses, besides arsenals and magazines: it is a staple of trade for the fisheries in North America; the country on each side of it is productive of wheat, rye, and every other grain; and, by the unanimous consent of travellers, very rich mines of iron, of lead, and of coal, have been discovered there: so that in a few years that place, which was looked upon with indifference both by the Courts of France and Great Britain, will become as flourishing and wealthy as any other part on the northern district of the British empire. Many of those who served so well under his Royal Highness now live in easy and opulent circumstances; and in an after war it has been seen, that a due attention paid to the right forming of an army in that particular part, has been the ground-work of those laurels which adorned the British arms in that part of the world.

From this time the King gave his Royal Highness the sole power of granting commissions, and doing every thing relative to the army in all the different departments of the British empire. It is / observable, that he was always happy in the choice of his officers: and was particularly attentive to their reception in the regiment where they were appointed.

He had bestowed a commission upon a man's son who had done something very agreeable to his Highness in the course of the rebellion: but the other officers not looking upon him as a gentleman, he was so far despised, that none of these would keep him company: his Highness was of a nobler way of thinking; he went one day to review them, and observing the slighted officer, he called him out, walked with him in the most familiar manner along the lines, ordering him to put on his hat, 'as all soldiers served the same Master, and all officers bore the King's commission equally.' The other officers observing what was done, they from that time forward kept up the same correspondence with the gentleman as with any other.

He took a delight in the company of old commanders, and such as had seen foreign armies; and in a particular manner of the Earl of Crauford, who had made the art of war his study from his infancy. He had served in the armies of Sweden, of Sardinia, of Germany, and England: he was full of courage and humanity, the most agile man in Europe before he received his wounds; the best swordsman, and never at a loss for resources in the midst of the greatest dangers. His Highness and he would be shut up together for hours in close and serious conversation.

Of the different improvements in possession of his lordship, nothing exceeded an invention, which though easy in itself now that it is found out, yet was never thought of till the beginning of this century, when Charles XII. of Sweden discovered it in Saxony, and shewed it to Marshal Renchild, / one of the ablest of his generals. It was deduced from the same principles with the diversion known by the name of the game at draughts in England. He had ordered twenty thousand statues of men in armour, each about six inches high, and formed in battalions or squadrons upon a board, to be cast by a founder. He would set them upon a table opposite to each other, sometimes ten against ten, five against fifteen, seven against thirteen, in all the different positions; and range them in the same manner in order of battle: and, as in the game at draughts, he would draw out a party from the wings or center, and shew the advantage or disadvantage resulting therefrom; would erect a hill, a village, a farm-house, or some such incumbrance. The attention of his Highness was fixed the more closely, as he never had fought but against more numerous forces and a superior artillery. From a greatness of soul, derived from the greatest of fathers, did his Highness communicate the scheme to the King, who daily became more and more enamoured with Lord Crauford: so that on hearing that his death, which happened in November 1751, was occasioned more from the narrowness of his circumstances (the consequence of the expensive equipage which he kept when abroad) than from the breaking out of his wounds, he lamented the same with a becoming sympathy, and said, 'Would to God I had known the situation of his affairs, for no money should have been wanting toward relieving so worthy and so great a man.'

Never was a son more endearing to a father than the Duke of Cumberland; for being daily with him, he was in his anxieties a comfort, in his troubles an assistance, in his prosperity an honour and delight; in every thing was he aided by his happy genius, which was ever elevated, and swelling / with the greatest designs: the circumstance of being a son was not the greatest of his recommendation; his virtues, which would have added lustre to any character more than the ties of blood, prevailed on the heart of the King; who in March 1751 found a singular comfort in the time of a distress which every parent looks upon as of the most trying and serious kind.

At that time Frederic Prince of Wales, father to our present Sovereign, died suddenly at Leicesterhouse, in the forty-sixth year of his age; leaving behind him five sons and three daughters, a disconsolate consort and a child unborn. He was certainly a prince of a most amiable character; free, generous, open, gracious, and humane. The deaths of the Prince and Princess of Orange soon followed, and the Queen of Denmark did not long survive, for she died in childbed in the December following. His Majesty was comforted in the midst of these afflictions by a Son who had fought his battles and supported his crown, so far as to look upon the deaths of these only as the forerunner of his own, and to be intirely resigned to Him who gives and who takes away!

It is observable that men born with a military genius do, upon a recess from war, apply themselves to agriculture and improving the ground: to do which to the greatest advantage his Highness retired to Windsor, the antient Residence of former Kings, and there he employed about five hundred different people, who otherwise must have been greatly distressed. He enlarged and cleansed the canals, and added a new one, more grand and convenient than any of the former. He caused menageries to be built for animals which were sent him from different nations, from the lion to the lowest quadruped, and from the eagle to the meanest / reptile: feeders were appointed, and these had suitable salaries. He delighted much in horse courses, so as never to fail being at Newmarket, where his Highness kept open house during the time of the races: and in a few years had so fine a breed of horses that the like were never seen in any one part of England before. The collection of shells, of metals, and of ores was no less valuable: and the encouragement which he gave to gardening rendered Windsor a nursery for all kind of trees as good as any in the known world. His collection of curiosities was inestimable; the largest telescopes, microscopes, and every other kind of optical glasses. His memory was so retentive that if he ever had seen a man he would have known him again: nay, I have heard it declared by the workmen about Windsor, that if he once had seen a horse ploughing, though among many others, yet if he had come a second time, though never so long after, he would have missed any of them, and would ask the owner about it, even though supplied by one in its place.

But his application to things of curiosity did not take off his attention from what was moral and becoming; if ever he knew that a workman had used his wife ill, that man was sure to be discharged; whatever children they brought with them were sure of employment; if ever a soldier came to the lodge, he was sure of entertainment, and of a present besides. He delighted much in shewing hospitality to such of the army as had fought under him; for when Barrel's regiment marched for Portsmouth, and through Windsor in their way to Gibraltar, he gave a general invitation to all the officers, whom he entertained in a splendid and magnificent manner in the great hall, while the private men had a substantial dinner prepared for them; beer, / rum, and brandy were set upon the green for regaling them; and after all was over, each company was ordered ten guineas, he himself walking along their lines with the utmost complacency, and reminding them of their bravery upon Culloden field. And yet this assiduity in domestic affairs did not hinder his attention to public business; such as being present at the proofs of new pieces at Woolwich, reviewing the troops, introducing among them an easier exercise, and sometimes attending the meetings of the Antiquarian and Royal Societies; and notwithstanding his good nature, yet he could not help reflecting on the impropriety of admitting people of no genius or application as members thereof: he laid himself out to promote the manufactories and fisheries in the King's dominions; among which the white and herring fishery on the coast of Shetland; his brother the Prince of Wales became the first president of the society for encouraging of it. An alarming scheme indeed to the States General, who gain about one million sterling to their revenue yearly, and employ in networking, shipping, cooperage, and other branches necessary toward carrying it on, no less than 40,000 different persons; so that supposing each to have a family of four persons to maintain, then by this fishery no less are supported than 160,000 individuals.

The isles of Shetland, the ancient patrimony of Denmark, was in 1469 looked upon with so little regard, as to be mortgaged for a small sum, payable as the portion of a Princess of Denmark married to King James III. of Scotland, and afterward to King James I. of England. In 1596 their poor were the most abject of mortals, the rich mines that surround them not being properly known; nor indeed was the intrinsic value discovered till about / the beginning of this century, when it was found that these northern seas contained as full and teaming a vintage as the verdant banks of the Thames.

To Arthur Nicholson of Lochend, and Magnus Henderson of Gairdie, was owing the wonderful discovery; the former had as extensive a genius for trade as any merchant in Europe, and the latter, not to mention a dignified and majestic aspect, which even distinguished him among the great, and by which he was admired at the Courts of Copenhagen, Stockholm, and Petersburgh, did not so much enoble him as this great and important event: his skill in the Dutch and Swedish languages, his alertness in the French, the German, and Italian tongues, with the more refined accomplishments of the understanding, did not so much enoble him, as a goodness of heart, which never looked upon the poor without feeling for them: the relief of those who were starving amidst the most exuberant plenty, more than any personal interest, prompted him to enquire into all the articles that might promote the herring, the cod, the ling, and the tusk fisheries.

These amiable gentlemen began with sending out a few lasts of fish to Hamburgh, and in time shipped off several vessels with fish and oil to Genoa, Leghorn, and other ports of Italy, and all the Hanse towns: a politeness and generosity to strangers drew many to settle in these remote places: their punctual payments rendered their bills incontestible on every Exchange, while their kindness, which was always sincere, procured them an universal applause. Many houses have been erected through the island in the most elegant taste, adorned with the richest furniture, and the poor have had bread; but all these have shared the calamities of war for want of the countenance of government. Here / the French land with impunity, and strip men, women, and children; their privateers ride in safety to wait the arrival of our ships from the East Indies, and from Greenland.

What pity that this fishery was not properly encouraged, since the cod and ling in these seas are preferable to what is caught upon the banks of Newfoundland, and can much sooner be carried to the markets of Italy.

Whatever was of public utility engrossed the care of his Highness; and observing the impropriety of reckoning time by the old stile, he promoted the bill for altering it to the new, in conformity with other nations; and accordingly it commenced in England on the 3d of September 1752, which was called the 14th.

In 1753 he discovered some uneasiness at naturalizing the Jews; for looking upon them as a strolling people, without King, without Priest, and without Prophet, he judged any encouragement of them to be hurtful to a commercial state, and in time to bid fair for jostling out the Christian religion.

It was not till the year 1754, when Mr. Pelham, the grand promoter of the naturalization bill, died. In consequence of the death of this prime minister, there arose a number of candidates, who wanted to supply his room; the most conspicuous of whom was Henry Fox, Esq; and Mr. Pitt, formerly named. The encroachments of the French upon the back settlements in North America were then at first talked of, and individuals began to complain: a rupture with France was easily foreseen, and the question was, what way to prepare best against any event, as the militia was not properly armed. Some were for bringing over a body of regular troops as the best security, while others laughed at the / proposal as inconsistent with the dignity of the crown, and an useless expence to the subject. Mr. Fox had espoused the first opinion, and Mr. Pitt had adopted the latter. The winter of the year 1754 was spent in arguments and consultations; however the party of Mr. Fox prevailed. About 10,000 Hanoverians and 6000 Hessians came over in the next summer, the first being stationed at Coxheath in Kent, and the other at Chatham and other places: they looked extremely well, and were obliged to observe the strictest discipline. The Generals Kilmansegg and Sporcken took care that every thing should be agreeable to the people, and these in return took a pride in doing offices of generosity and kindness to the troops. His Royal Highness went down to the camp, where he reviewed them with the utmost seriousness and attention upon the 28th of September 1755. Though Coxheath be one of the most wholsome places in England, and is no less spacious and convenient than Wyehill, or any other place of appointment for farmers and planters, yet it never appeared with such lustre as on that day. The country people shew with a kind of pleasure, bordering upon admiration, the very place where his Highness stood during the time of the review. The troops went through all the evolutions of the military exercise before him with surprizing alacrity; so that the most strenuous in the opposition to calling in foreign troops could not help acknowledging the order, regularity and decorum which the whole corps of Hanoverians and Hessians observed. The disputes about them soon subsided, as they were soon called over to the continent, where France brought on a war, in which his Royal Highness expected to have an opportunity of engaging the enemy upon more equal terms than hitherto, both / as the troops under his command would be more numerous, and as by his many generous and princely actions he had procured their entire and universal good-will, having interested himself in rectifying the abuses that had crept into the public charities, and set the most brilliant and laudable example of humanity and goodness toward the private men, as will best appear from the following example.

Among many useful and distinguishing foundations in Great Britain, there is none which deserves more to be admired than that of Greenwich for decayed seamen, and that of Chelsea for such as have served their country by land. It was first begun by King Charles II. who was the man to lay the first stone thereof. King James II. prosecuted the work, and succeeding Sovereigns have gloried in enlarging the charity. Lord Ranelagh and other nobles have imitated the example of their Kings, and it has been generally among the first articles of the Parliament's business to make provision for the same.

Such as lived in the house, and were under the immediate inspection of a governor and proper officers, were abundantly happy; but indeed the out-pensioners were most cruelly and miserably abused by a number of usurers, some of them publicans, whose frauds and impositions were even shocking to humanity.

By the statutes of the legislature every out-pensioner was to receive *7l.* 12*s.* 2*d. per annum*, a noble help indeed toward the support of a poor man, when grown old in the service of the government; but which was mostly engrossed by a false and odious set of men.

The poor creatures were generally imposed upon when in liquor, notes of hand were solicited from / them, and these shewn when they came to ask for what was their own; if they offered to complain they were browbeat by a volley of oaths, curses, and imprecations, and threatened to be turned altogether off the list: sometimes the name of a justice of peace would be forged to a certificate, attesting a pensioner to be alive, when he was really dead; and by this method his money might be taken up for seven or eight years: the miserable creatures were by their dismal appearance, owing to the cruel rod of their oppressors, a disgrace to the public, many of them being obliged to beg, while their usurers were feasting upon what should have sustained them; and in these and such like ways did these unworthy men proceed in their wickedness, till by the superintendency of an all-powerful and watchful Providence the matter came to an end.

One day the Earl of Rothes met a pensioner, who asked charity of him; which his Lordship, however willing to succour the needy upon every occassion, hesitated at that time to bestow; and finding by the man that his usurer was the cause of this misfortune, his Lordship sent for the dealer, and confronted him with the pensioner. The evasions of the one could not stand against the innocent and positive assertions of the other; and so his Lordship withdrew, and that very afternoon waited on his Royal Highness the Duke of Cumberland with an account of what had passed upon the occassion. He was heard with complacency; a scheme was immediately formed for putting a stop to the iniquitous practice; he even spoke to several members to second the motion for bringing in the bill whenever the same should be made; Mr. Pitt introduced it into the House of Commons; the officers of the army, who were members, seconded it with a becoming eloquence; arguments / flowed in its favour from every mouth, and the daily objects of misery rendered these irresistible: so that it soon passed into a law, the poor men were delivered from their oppressors, who had carried matters to such a degree of insolence, that the very people who lived upon the spot were refused payment of their pension, and with an authoritative contempt were ordered to apply to their usurer, who at most paid only six guineas for the 7 *l.* 12 *s.* 2*d.* while others gave only 5 *l.* or by their dilatoriness obliged the poor wretches to squander the better part of it in liquor, and in their own houses.

The practice of usury being put down gave such satisfaction, that in the war which was now breaking out the people wanted only an opportunity to serve under his Highness's command.

The boundaries of the French and British empires not having been properly settled, gave rise to mutual claims, complaints, and blows; which last began with the defeat of M. Washington. A piece of ground, which a Quaker of the name of Jeffreys wanted to improve, as lying contiguous to him, was the source of a bloody and terrible war. Matters might soon have been compromised, had it not been for the ambition of the Court of France, which from the conclusion of the last peace had been preparing for another rupture.

Scarce was the treaty of Aix la Chapelle signed, when she purchased from the Court of Sweden a squadron of twenty men of war, with vast quantities of materials, such as iron, plank, deal, cordage, and tar, with other articles necessary for ship-building; many merchant ships were fitted out at Gottenburgh and Carelscrona; and to reinstate her marine still more, vast quantities of wood were cut in the Pyrenean forest, in which the different / parts of a ship's fabric were prepared, and afterward conducted to Marseilles, Rochfort, and Brest, nay even to St. Maloes itself, where the carpenters had only to join them. As after the peace of Utrecht she recovered herself, and soon became more flourishing; the States of Italy being divided among the branches of her House, were more ready to take the furs and fish caught upon the banks of Newfoundland from the French than from British merchants.

In consequence of the melancholy advices daily received of the situation of our back settlements in North America, the King sent a message to his Parliament by Sir Thomas Robinson, one of his Secretaries of State, intimating the necessity of augmenting their forces, and preparing their marine. Braddock was sent to Virginia with a body of troops, consisting of 1500 men; he marched with these to Fort Du Quesne, where he fell into an ambush, and on the 9th of July was defeated and killed. A very unlucky circumstance for Admiral Boscawen, who, notwithstanding he and Admiral Mostyn had been sent out with twenty-four men of war, and had taken two French ships of the line, yet they could not entirely remedy that disaster: that affair was not properly rectified till September, when General Johnson gave a total defeat to the French, and took General Dieskau prisoner. As the blows were mutual, the French ambassador withdrew from the Court of London without taking leave, and the Earl of Albemarle dying at Paris of a surfeit, which he had contracted at a supper in company with the Duke de Montmorenci a short time before; the two Courts were liable to be imposed upon by misrepresentation and falshood. By the advice of the Duke of Newcastle the French merchantmen continued to be / seized both in Europe and in America, while the Court of France, affecting a kind of moderation for eight months, suffered the British vessels to trade unmolested in their ports; but in the mean time they marched their troops to the Mediterranean, to the channel, and to the ocean, and in March 1756 the Duke de Choiseul, then Prime Minister of France, wrote a letter to Mr. Fox, one of the Principal Secretaries of State, requiring the restitution of the ships that had been taken by Admiral Boscawen, whom he charged with piracy, and used such other expression, as plainly shewed that the Court of France was intent upon a rupture.

Neither France nor Spain can be at war with Great Britain, but the shock, in whatever part it is given, must be felt even at the remotest place of the globe; if the industry and boldness of our modern nations have in any respect the advantage over the rest of the world, and over all antiquity, it is certainly in defensive and offensive fortification, and in our naval expeditions. The Manillas beyond China, and the Gulph of Mexico, have at one and the same time been visited; the most powerful empires have been spectators of a skilful fury, which they have not attained; in Africa is the dispute about slaves, and in Europe the sword is sometimes drawn for promoting luxury and extravagance.

Scarce was the coal of dissention kindled in North America, till the blaze extended to Europe, and in a short time set all her States in a flame. France begun with sending the Duke de Richlieu with an army of 20,000 regular troops to take Minorca, and to reduce the strong fortress of St. Philip. General Blakeney, whose good fortune had triumphed over the Pretender in Scotland, / sunk under that of the Duke de Richlieu; the strong reinforcement destined to succour Blakeney had been prevented by the fleet under Admiral Galissoniere from entering the island; Admiral Byng had fought, conquered, and retreated on the 20th of May; and General Blakeney suffered the fort to be taken by surprize on the night of the 29th of June thereafter. The Admiral and the General in their turn had both fought, but were not equally rewarded; for Byng was shot to death*, and Blakeney was created an Irish Peer for his bravery. And now France had recourse to the stratagem of involving Great Britain in a land war upon the continent; and accordingly war was declared by Great Britain on the 18th of May, and by France on the 16th of June thereafter; and in the mean time the States General embraced a neutrality.

For this purpose a league offensive and defensive was concluded at Paris, on the 14th of May 1756, between the Courts of Versailles and of Vienna; between which last and Courts of Petersburgh and Dresden there was a treaty, brought about by the policy and address of France, for stripping the King of Prussia of such parts of his dominions as lay contiguous to these respective powers. / The North of Germany was soon in a flame. The King of Prussia marched into Saxony, August the 28th, and reduced the strong camp at Pirna, and the Austrian and Prussian armies, October 1st, cut each other in pieces at Lowitschutz; the beautiful city of Prague was once more besieged by a numerous army and a terrible artillery; at

* His charge was for not having, according to the 12th article of war, done his utmost to destroy the enemy's ships on the day of the engagement. After a trial, which lasted fourteen days, he was found guilty; but some circumstances appearing favourable to the court-martial, they earnestly recommended him to mercy: a sentence which the King referred to the consideration of his Parliament, which, after very long debates, at which the Duke of Cumberland was sometimes present, but never offered to speak, was confirmed; and accordingly the Admiral was shot at Portsmouth on board the Magnanime, March 14, 1757.

Kollin the Prussian monarch was obliged to yield to the superior skill and conduct of Count Daun: and, to spread the flames of war still further, a French army, of 110,000 men, marched toward Hanover, under the command of the Marshal Count'd Etrees, one of the best officers in France. He had been formed under the old Duke de Villars; was acquainted with all the feints and stratagems of war, had fought at Fontenoy, Rocoux, and Lafelt: he was an officer of consummate prudence and discretion, endowed with all the qualifications of a great general; sedate in his temper, strict in his behaviour, cool in his proceedings, wise in his conduct, and stated in his schemes: more dangerous after a defeat than an ordinary general after a victory; fit indeed to conduct an army; capable of repairing by his wisdom what seemed irreparable, and endowed with so large a share of virtue as to procure the esteem and veneration of the troops under his command, which at this time were the very flower of the French army; there scarcely being a single man among them who was not an hardy veteran. Nor is it the least of the Duke of Cumberland's praise that the Court of France should send out so well appointed a body of troops against a much less numerous corps under the command of his Highness.

As the French army advanced toward Westphalia, so the Duke of Cumberland, who had crossed the sea to head the Hanoverian army, thought proper / to march to the east side of the Weser, in order to incommode them in their rout, and actually would have made a stand and given them battle, had the forces under him bore any proper proportion to those of the enemy. He had no more than 36,000 men, and many of these had never seen an engagement. He had indeed endeavoured to get a body of 10,000 of the national British troops; but the British ministry would not consent to the demand: he even asked but three regiments, and at last came so low as to desire no more than his own dragoons, which were absolutely refused.

To deal with so superior an army was a task of no little importance, and which none but a commander of penetration and sagacity was equal to. The French forces were even assisted by the subjects of the States General in their march to the Weser, by bringing them provision and other necessaries. It was not till the middle of June 1757 that they reached the banks of the Weser, which separates Westphalia from Hanover. The Duke of Cumberland retreated over the river, as the other advanced.

To cross a river in the face of an enemy, or to prevent a passage over it, has been looked upon as one of the most arduous tasks of a general: the French frequently endeavoured it by a bridge of boats; but the Duke's batteries were so placed as to command the fords, and to flank each other; and iron spikes were driven into the bed of the stream. The Count d'Etrees, the Duke of Orleans, and the Duke de Grisors went up to an high mountain, whence they surveyed the Hanoverian camp and the adjacent country. The intelligence which his Highness received was so good, that wherever the enemy intended to cross there was a strong party, with a large battery of cannon and mortars, / to oppose them. At last, on the night of the 20th of July, the Marquis d'Armentieres effected a landing twenty miles from their grand army, with fourteen thousand men and ten pieces of cannon, in order to draw the army from the river and to raise contributions: the cavalry soon followed, and the infantry hastened as fast as possible, crossing as they arrived. His Highness endeavoured to get betwixt them and the capital, and to prevent their seizing upon the copper mines, which are very considerable in these parts: for this he took up his quarters at a village called Hastenbeck, where the French army came in view of him on the 25th, about six in the evening: and towards eight the two armies fronted each other, a morass being only between them: that night they cannonaded each other very smartly, and next day the action began. The Duke's army was supported by batteries on each of the wings and in the center, and besides all this there was a battery of seven pieces of cannon placed upon the left wing, a little inclining toward the enemy, forming a right-angle with the extremity of the line: it was supported by ten battalions, under the command of General Sporcken, and greatly annoyed the enemy: whose dispositions were easy and free, having the infantry in the center and the cavalry in the wings. For two hours the cannonading continued with great fury: the two armies still drawing nearer to each other, when the firing from the small arms began from right to left, and became general. The victory hung in suspence for two hours; the Duke of Cumberland being in the hottest places of the action, animating the troops with his voice, his hand, and his example; and the Generals Kilmanseg, Zastrow, and Dulemback were at the head of the lines, and inspired the different bodies under their respective commands. / The Count d'Etrees, the Duke de Orleans, and the Count de Broglio did the same on the side of the French; and all at once the Duke de Grisors, son to the Marshal de Belleisle, fetched an half compass round the eminence whereon the battery under General Sporcken was placed: he brought up a superior artillery against it, and twice the number of troops that supported it. The crisis of the battle turned upon what could be done here: the Duke of Cumberland sent three battalions from the reserve to support those under General Sporcken; but too late, for the battery was taken, and the guns were turned against the Hanoverians. In this situation his Highness judged proper to sound a retreat, which was effected with as much order and regularity as if no disaster had befallen them: and, what is pretty singular, they were not pursued.

Such was the battle of Hastenbeck, which determined the fate of Hanover, and in which there were five thousand killed on the side of the Allies, and seven thousand on that of the French, who likewise took about a thousand prisoners, and the seven pieces of cannon formerly named. His Highness did not retire with precipitation; but in so cool and sedate a manner as to order out parties for carrying off the best and most valuable effects both of the King his father and of the principal Inhabitants of the Electorate, to the most commodious place of safety. Stadt was the place fixed on, and thither the archives, the plate, the mint, nay and the fine set of horses belonging to the stables of Herenhausen, were soon conveyed, as to a place of the greater safety; and, to be still more secure, an English ship of twenty guns was sent to bring over the plate, the money, and the jewels of the Electoral palace into England. /

By the way of Bremen, Verden, and Carlstat did the Hanoverian and Hessian army retire, and were followed at a slow pace by the numerous forces of France; sometimes they were pretty near each other; but the superiority of numbers, and the vast disproportion between the artillery of either, still hindered an engagement: nor was the French general desirous of wasting his troops by a battle against forces who were every day more and more enraged, and under the direction of so great and so illustrious a commander, whose ears were every day wounded by the cries of women and orphans, earnestly beseeching that an end might be put to the war.

After a continued march of one month, his Royal Highness arrived at Stadt, a strong fortification near the Elbe, and subject to the Electorate of Hanover. Frederic V. King of Denmark, did not chuse such powerful armies to be in his neighbourhood, and the Republic of Hamburgh applied for the protection of the Court of Vienna in the midst of the dangers that threatened. The former sent word to his ambassador both at Paris and at London, offering his mediation, that things might not come to extremities, and in the mean time advertised the Duke of Cumberland and the Duke de Richlieu (which last had come to supersede the Count d'Etrees) of the steps he had taken. All at once the hands of these great commanders were tied, a cessation of arms for twelve days took place, at the end whereof a courier arrived from France, accepting the mediation of Denmark, and soon after a Letter from the King of Great Britain, desiring that his Highness would enter into a convention, for the preservation of Hanover and the states depending thereon. After several days conferences between the deputies on the part of France, Denmark, / and Hanover, an agreement was drawn up, in order to be signed by his Royal Highness on the one hand, and by the Marshal de Richlieu on the other. Accordingly these two great commanders met in an antichamber at a gentleman's seat called Closter Severn. Richlieu paid the same compliments to him as if he had been at London or at Kensington: he began with these words; 'Your Highness and I are not enemies: I always entertained the highest sense of your merit and great abilities, and now that I have the honour of being in your presence, nothing could give me more pleasure than an opportunity of doing what might be agreeable to you.' The Duke heard him with a seeming complacency, and on the 28th of September the convention was signed, first by his Highness and then by the M. de Richlieu: who no sooner heard that the Hanoverians had disbanded than he made a demand upon Hamburgh for 100,000 *l.* The principal article of the agreement was, That the Hanoverians and Hessians, composing the army under the command of his Royal Highness, should retire to their own houses, with their arms; that they were to be safe in their persons, properties, and estates, and not to serve against France during the course of the war: and that the French were immediately to quit the Electorate:

Things being thus settled, the Hanoverians and Hessians were disbanded, and the Duke of Cumberland, after paying a visit to the Court of Prussia, (in which he laid open the letter and spirit of the late convention) returned to England, where the King his father, however fond at other times, discovered a kind of reserve toward him: however, fidelity and a good conscience supported his Highness: he convinced the King of the uprightness of / his conduct; but declined ever after to take upon him any principal command. He told his Majesty, that though there was a difference betwixt the Sovereign and his General, which might be owing to a misapprehension on the side of the one, and to too hearty an inclination to obey on the side of the other, yet that was no reason why any difference should exist between a father and a son. His Highness indeed had much to say, and yet he contented himself with saying very little: he accused no body, he complained of no body, notwithstanding he had all the reason in the world to complain; for had his plan been pursued, Hanover would have been sooner rid of her enemies than she actually was. His Highness had fought an army three times as numerous as his own, and at last retreated unbroken. Perhaps since the retreat of Marshal Turenne at Mariendal, or of Count Schulemberg, who eluded the fortune of Charles XII. and King Stanislaus, there has not been a more honourable retreat than that performed by the Duke of Cumberland from the plains of Hastenbeck: and now he wanted an opportunity of engaging them at a more convenient season. From his usual sagacity he foresaw, that as winter was approaching, the national troops of France must moulder away: he had sent express after express to the King of Prussia for a single body of ten thousand men; but that Monarch, if willing, had his hands so full that he could not answer the demand: however, this did not dishearten him; his intention was to march by the way of Harburg and Lunenburgh to the Weser, in order to cut off any supplies that might come to M. de Richlieu; who in that event might be exposed to the fire of an ally and of the Hanoverians at a convenient season: but of all this the convention deprived him.

The End of the TENTH BOOK. /

THE LIFE OF WILLIAM DUKE OF CUMBERLAND.

BOOK XI.

CONTENTS.

The Hanoverians *take up Arms, – Battles in* Saxony, Silesia, *and* Westphalia, – *Mons.* Bussy*'s Negotiation, – the Operations of the* British *Fleet in* Europe *and* Asia, – *Death of King* George II. – *the Accession, Marriage, and Coronation of King* George III. – *Origin of the Paper called* The North Briton. – *The Character of* J. Wilkes – *The Death of the Duke of* Cumberland. – *His Elogium.*

AFTER the convention he never appeared on the theatre of action: but yet assisted in contriving all the plans of operation that were laid down for bringing the war to a speedy conclusion: for by his advice five regiments were raised from among the Scots Highlanders, one of which was committed to Simon Frazer, eldest son of Lord / Lovat, whose whole life was one continued scene of contradiction and impropriety. There was one from Ross, two from Argyleshire, and one from Caithness and Sutherland. The two first were mostly made up of those people who had been in the rebellion 1745, and were animated by the late act of parliament dissolving the vassalage and servitude, of which the Clergy took care to inform them: enraged at the perfidy of the French in leading them into such sloughs of difficulty and hardship, they heartily engaged in the cause of their country; and, without any murmuring, appeared ready to bear arms where their service might be most desired.

These adventurers wanted an opportunity of atoning for the guilt which unluckily they had contracted, and the rather as they were told, that they had been raised by the advice of the Duke of Cumberland. In this disposition of mind they were conducted to Nova Scotia in the latter end of the year 1757; and from the moment of their landing at Hallifax became the instruments of procuring the most substantial advantages, and contributed as much as any one corps of the King's army toward obtaining the laurels which adorned the British standards in the years 1758 and 1759. In the reduction of Louisburgh they behaved with uncommon alertness and intrepidity; they braved the seasons and the sword at Martinico and Guadaloupe in April 1758. On the 25th of July 1759 they assaulted camps and stormed armies at Ticonderoga, where our troops were repulsed, and the gallant Colonel Townshend was killed. They climbed up rocks and precipices at Quebec when it fell by the British arms on the 18th of September thereafter*. The repulse which the army met with on the 13th, when the French lines were attacked, only tended / to inflame their courage, On the 28th of April 1760, when the French endeavoured to retake Quebec, they performed prodigies of valour; they dyed their swords in the blood of our enemies, and were only fought down by the superiority of numbers, assisted by the regiment of Rousillon. They beat their assailants in a second encounter; and following them to Montreal, the place of their rendezvous, they by the reduction thereof finished the conquest of North America: and when the war broke out with Spain, they not only behaved with their usual fortitude and intrepidity at the Havannah in August 1762, but likewise upon the confines of Portugal. So hearty was the Scots nation in the service of their country, that the antiquated distinction of Lowlanders and Highlanders was laid aside: the antipathy between these gave place to the common zeal for promoting the glory of the kingdom. Near one-half of these Highland regiments consisted of men from the Lowlands of Scotland; and from these parts were about seventy thousand men in the service of the Government.

But North America was not more the scene of action than Senegal and Goree on the coast of Africa, both of which were taken in the course of this commercial war, which all this time was raging in the North of Germany with uncommon fierceness and devastation, not only between the

* Here fell the brave General Wolf, greatly lamented.

armies of France, and those of his Britannic Majesty, but likewise between the Allies of both.

The empire of Germany, from the time of the King of Prussia's irruption into Saxony, which had been twice conquered, and twice regained in the course of three years, was in the most dismal situation. In the year 1758 it was for several months ravaged by no less than eight armies, one of these commanded by the Marshal Duke de Richlieu, / another under the command of the Prince Saxehilburghausen and the Prince of Soubise, a third under Prince Charles of Lorrain and Count Daun, a fourth under the Duke of Bevern, a fifth army of Russians under M. Apraxin, a sixth of Swedes, commanded by Field Marshal Ungern Sternberg, a seventh of Prussians, and the eighth was composed of the troops of Hanover and Hesse-Cassel, to whom, in a short time after, a body of 20,000 of the national British troops were afterward joined. All these, except the last two, were at war with the King of Prussia, who had battles with each of them, and in which there was spilt abundance of blood.

Hanover and Hesse-Cassel, with the countries of Westphalia and Paderborn, had already found to their smart that an enemy was in their bosom. From the time the French army crossed the Rhine, and had access to East Frizeland, and the other territories of the King of Prussia, their support and maintenance became exceeding easy to them; the adjacent countries, except such as belonged to the States of Holland, were on some pretext or other laid under contribution. No sooner was the conquest of Hanover effected, than provisions and forage of all kinds abounded in the French camp; horses were taken up for remounting their cavalry, whole regiments of dragoons were supplied with them, their German regiments were recruited, excesses of the worst kind were committed upon the estates of the burghers and landed gentlemen, and the country was so harrassed, that the peasants chose rather to die with their swords in their hands, than to be exposed to all the hardships of a rapacious enemy; they only wanted an opportunity of taking up arms to free them from their oppressors, / which soon was given them, and this by an instrument, from whom it was least expected.

The Electorate of Saxony, so famous for the industry and trade of her inhabitants, now bled under the sword of a neighbouring potentate: the peasants and burghers were harrassed every where, and treated with all the rigour of a conqueror: the Saxon army, which had rendezvoused at

Pirna, in order to wait for the succours from Count Brown's army, had been compelled to surrender themselves prisoners of war before the arrival of the reinforcement; and the King of Poland, on the 12th of October, retired with his favourite Count Bruhl to Warsaw, leaving his Electorate to the mercy of an enraged enemy, who triumphed every where, except in Dresden, where the Queen of Poland still resided with her family.

To recover Saxony was no less a pretext to France for marching her armies into Germany, than the treaty of Westphalia, of which she represented herself to be the guarantee. The Duke de Richlieu sent the Prince de Soubise with an army of 36,000 men to join the army of execution* under the Duke de Saxehilburghausen, in order to dislodge the Prussians. By the nearest rout they approached toward Leipsic, of which M. Keith was governor, and on the 1st of November summoned him to surrender the town, which being refused, they broke ground before it within two hundred yards of the glacis, and in the mean time sent parties about the country to raise contributions, especially from among those who were in the Prussian interest.

His Prussian Majesty, being advertised of the danger of Leipsic, hastened to its relief, and on / the 5th of November, when at a village called Rosbach, he gave the enemy a total defeat, taking all their baggage and artillery, killing 4000 men, and taking 6000 prisoners, among whom were eight generals, and 250 subaltern officers, and this only with the loss of 300 men killed, and as many wounded, among whom were Prince Henry, the King's brother, with the Generals Pelitz and Muneike.

Never did an army appear in a more shattered and miserable condition than that of the Allies, particularly the French after the battle of Rosbach. Few of them retained their swords, many of them wanted hats and shoes, their clothes were ragged, and, to complete their disaster, the country people either knocked them on the head, or refused them the common acts of humanity, while the inclemency of the weather made havock of the remainder.

From this time the troops, which composed the army of the empire, listed in the Prussian regiments, while the service of the French soldiers was absolutely and scornfully refused; their only safety was to fly toward the reinforcements that were sent by Marshal Richlieu to relieve them. The battle of Rosbach was just a month before that of Lissa in Silesia,

* An army consisting of the troops of different German princes for securing their territories.

whither the King of Prussia repaired with nineteen battalions, and thirty-three squadrons, in order to retake Breslau, and to relieve the Prince of Bevern, who, on the 23d of November, was defeated and taken prisoner. About one o'clock on the 5th of December, the Austrian and Prussian armies had a view of each other, and soon came to a general action, in which the former had 12,000 men killed, 14,000 wounded, and 21,000 taken prisoners, most of whom listed in the King of Prussia's service; they lost about 240 pieces of cannon, all their tents, ammunition, and military stores, and, / what was still more, Breslau and the other towns in Silesia, except Schweidnitz, surrendered to the conqueror, who from this time, poured in his forces upon Bohemia, the half of which was soon reduced to his obedience.

Thus in the space of thirty days the force of the Houses of Austria and Bourbon was broken; the Russians had already retired from the frontiers of Brandenburgh for want of provision; the Swedes, who fought against their will, had retreated from before a superior army to Straelsund; a military spirit daily diffused itself through the subjects of Prussia, and, to crown all, a change in the British ministry had taken place; Mr. Pitt and his party had got the better of Mr. Fox and the Duke of Newcastle; the old Lord Chancellor Hardwicke had resigned, the consequence of which was, that the Prussian monarch had an annual subsidy granted him of 670,000 *l.* to be paid at two terms without discount.

So large a subsidy, and his late successes, impowered him to send Prince Ferdinand of Brunswick with a detachment of 20,000 men into Hanover to cover Saxony on that side, and to watch the motions of the French, whom he now considered as his enemy.

Prince Ferdinand was perhaps one of the most cool and deliberate commanders that had appeared in Germany for many years; he was a lieutenant - general in the Prussian service, and nephew to the Prussian Monarch. He published a manifesto as he approached the confines of Hanover, inviting all who had any regard for their country, or for the Protestant religion, to join him in taking up arms against the enemies of both. The people, considering the flagrant breach of the convention on the part of Marshal Richlieu's army, and the / cruel oppressions daily exercised upon the inhabitants without regard to age, sex, dignity, or character, did take up these arms, which a false policy, and the apprehensions of a neighbour, had caused them to lay down. Prince Ferdinand soon saw himself at the head of 40,000 men; he was declared generalissimo and commander in chief of the army of the Allies that was to be mustered against France; the troops of Brunswick and Zell were taken into British pay, and joined him; and soon after his Britannic Majesty had so far interested himself in the prosecution of this war, that, in opposition to Mr. Pitt's superior eloquence, a body of 20,000 of the national British troops under Lord George Sackville, second son to the Duke of Dorset, were sent over to join; they were transported to Embden, and landed, some at Bremen, and others at Verden, as more commodious than to march through the territories belonging to the States General.

The French army, and that of the Allies, did not differ more in their religious principles, the one being Roman Catholics, and the other Protestants, than in their situation and circumstances; for while the latter were hearty and vigorous, the former was in such a deplorable condition, that when the Prince de Clermont came to take upon him the command in the room of M. Richlieu, who was recalled, he wrote to his Court, 'that one third of the army was below ground, another above ground, and a third in the hospitals.' They quitted Hanover almost without stroke of sword, and his Highness found himself obliged to seek them out in another country.

There was nothing more in this German war than what might be expected; the armies marched after each other from place to place, and embraced / the opportunity of fighting when the generals saw it for their advantage. Westphalia and the Country of Paderborn were the theatres thereof: these countries were sometimes mastered by one army, sometimes by the other; and the whole Langraviate of Hesse Cassel was twice lost and twice gained in the course thereof. There were four pitched battles and above twenty different encounters between detached parties: the plains of Fraudlingen, of Crevelt, and of Rheda were dyed by the blood of the French, and their troops were beat out of the field: however, of all these engagements that at Minden, on the 1st of August 1759, was the most general and important. The French army, amounting to 80,000 men, was commanded by the Marshal de Contades and by the Duke de Broglio, and the Confederates, who were 70,000 strong, was headed by Prince Ferdinand, who obtained a signal victory, owing to a division that subsisted between Broglio and Contades, but more to the superior bravery of the troops under his Highness's command; and particularly the British corps under the command of the Generals Waldegrave and Kingsley. The French cavalry was routed, and the English cavalry did not engage: an event owing to a misapprehension of the orders delivered to Lord George Sackville; between whom and Prince Ferdinand there never existed that zeal, confidence, and personal regard as are requisite to finish a campaign with glory. Perhaps his Highness thought, that another might be more generous and profuse: and therefore in the orders issued out next day, thanking the different generals for their valour and conduct, there was an implied censure upon his*. Lord George applied for his Majesty's permission to return / to England, in order to answer such accusations as might be brought against him; which having obtained he arrived at his house in Pallmall on the 8th of September; at which time the whole kingdom seemed to have imbibed an unfavourable opinion of his behaviour, to remove which he issued out a short address to the public, representing how much he thought himself injured abroad by an implied censure upon his conduct, and still more unfortunate at home, by being publicly represented as having neglected his duty and disobeying the positive orders of his Serene Highness Prince Ferdinand. 'As I am,' continued he, 'conscious of neither neglect nor disobedince to orders; as I am certain I did my duty to the utmost of my abilities; as I am persuaded, that the Prince himself would have found that he had no just cause of complaint against me, had he condescended to have enquired into my conduct, before he had expressed his disapprobation of it, from the partial representation of others; so I have applied for his Majesty's permission to return to England, in order to answer any accusations that should be brought against me:' and so concluded with claiming that justice which is due to every Englishman, 'of being heard before he is condemned.'

In consequence of his Lordship's desire, a courtmartial was appointed, and composed of such officers as his Royal Highness the Duke of Cumberland recommended. They sat at the Horse-guards in March 1760; where, after fourteen days sitting, Lord George was, by a plurality of voices, declared unworthy of serving his Majesty in any station ever after. So that his place of commander in chief of the British forces in Germany, with that of master-general of the ordnance, was conferred / upon the Marquis of Granby, a nobleman who, ever since the winter of the rebel-

* Had the Marquis of Granby been at the head of the cavalry, the victory had been more complete and brilliant.

lion 1745, had by his liberality and generous behaviour to the soldiers, procured their universal esteem and regard.

The summer of 1760 was, like others, spent in skirmishing, retreats, encounters, and encampments: and it is somewhat remarkable through the course of the war, that if the King of Prussia prevailed, the Allied army met with a disaster, and if the last obtained an advantage, the Prussians sustained a loss. About twelve days after the battle of Minden, the Prussians, commanded by the King in person, were defeated by the Muscovites, at Custrin, under Count Soltikoff: and though I would shun as much as possible to enter into the minute circumstances of battles, especially in a narrative where is such a variety, yet we cannot pass over an entertaining circumstance here.

Whoever examines the conduct of the King of Prussia at different engagements, and he has fought twenty battles, he will find, that his Majesty's uniform practice was to direct more than ordinary force either against the center or one of the wings of the enemy. Count Soltikoff was apprized of his method, and prepared accordingly. The King encountered the center with uncommon fierceness, after a feint attack upon the right wing; but the other sustained his efforts, which were redoubled seven different times, and as often proved abortive: at the eighth the Muscovites right seemed to retire, and the Prussians began to pursue: thus were they decoyed to an eminence fortified with eighty pieces of cannon, which pouring in upon them, they were soon between two fires, and cut down in their ranks with a terrible slaughter. The same thing might be observed of the battle of Hochkirken, October 14th 1758; for when his army was routed by / Count Daun, and when M. Keith (his master in the art of war) was killed, about that time Westphalia and Hanover were freed; so the successes and losses seemed reciprocal. When Saxony fell to the King of Prussia, Hanover was possessed by the French; and if these lost the country of Paderborn, the Prussians recovered Silesia: and in this manner the war continued in that quarter. It really seemed as the French generals were not bent upon conquest. M. de Broglio appeared gay, even after a disaster: and, as Alsace and Lorrain were open behind him, his troops could be reinforced at pleasure. This observation is not meant to diminish the fame of those who fix the chief place of glory in war and in conquest. The bravery of a general may appear as great in a defeat as in a victory: the repulse of the Hereditary Prince of Brunswick does not less enoble him, than the advantages which he gained: and the victory obtained by the Marquis of Granby at Harbourgh, over M. de Huy (the gentleman in whose arms the Dauphin of France died Dec. 20th 1765) does not add more lustre to his military character, than the address with which the French general brought off the shattered remains, does honour and dignity to his. If there had been no war in any other part of the world with France, she could have continued her armies in Germany for ten years, tho' she had lost a battle every year.

In Asia her affairs were as unsuccessful as in America. Sir George Pocock defeated her fleet on the 3d of August 1758, near Fort St. David. Her army, under M. de Lally, met every-where with disasters: her troops were shamefully repulsed before Madrass, and Pondicherry was taken. Nor were her misfortunes small even upon her own / coasts, which were four times attempted in the course of four months.

In June 1758 Charles Duke of Marlborough landed at Cancalle Bay with an army of 20,000 men, and, marching to St. Maloes, burnt an hundred sail of ships, raised contributions, triumphed with all the badges of a conqueror, and in nothing more than in his moderation and goodness; for he would not suffer those under his command to do any hurt to the innocent inhabitants: yet the damage sustained by France on that occasion was computed at two millions sterling. At Cherburgh the harbour, one of the brightest monuments of Cardinal Fleury's ministry, was demolished in the August thereafter. And though the attacks at Lunaire under General Bligh*, September the 11th, and on the coast of Gascony by Sir John Mordaunt, were not so hurtful to the French as the other two, yet even these shewed to the world that Great Britain was capable of acting vigorously against her enemies, and that her councils were inspired and directed by courage and sagacity. The destroying of M. de Clue's squadron upon the coast of Portugal, and the repeated blows given to her marine in the Mediterranean, and indeed in every other part, but particularly off the coast of Belleisle Nov. 20th 1759, when Admiral Hawke totally routed the Brest fleet, under M. de Conflans, exposed the weakness of France in the most evident manner.

The engagements between the fleets of France and of Great Britain have ever had something uncommonly terrible in them, and few more

* His Royal Highness the Duke of York was on board the same ship as Commodore Howe, and gave such signal instances of a truly great soul and real goodness of heart as procured esteem and veneration from all who saw him.

that the encounter we have mentioned. The infatuation of / the French was singular, for when the signal was given that the English fleet was approaching, instead of drawing up in order of battle, they steered different ways, and yet determined to stand an engagement. The Magnanime, commanded by Lord Howe, was the first to begin the fight with the sternmost ship of the enemy, a vessel of 80 guns, commanded by M. de St. Andre. The firing on both sides was brisk, when Sir Edward Hawke in the Royal George came up, and the French ship struck. M. de Conflans in the Soleil Royal endeavoured to decoy the British admiral among some shallows, where he must inevitably be stranded, yet not before the two had exchanged seven broadsides against each other. A view of the two ships with the ensigns of the Lion flying at the top mast head of the one, and that of the Flower de Lys at the top of the other, yielded a glorious appearance at first; but when these ships poured out fire and smoke at each other, the scene was greatly altered, and became terrible and moving; and still more shocking, as two ships sunk without any possibility of saving them. It seems the French had opened their lower guns, and the sea being tempestuous, the water poured in at the port-holes and overset the vessels in a moment. Some that were on board Admiral Hawke's ships have told me, that the poor men got from the decks upon the sides of the ship, and as she was sinking, raised the most pitiful cries significant of their miserable distress. Some boats were hoisted out to take them in, but very few were saved, as the swell was so large. In a word, the French fleet, which had been blocked up for four months, was totally ruined; two of their capital ships were burnt, two were sunk, and the rest were either taken or so miserably shattered as to be unfit for use during the course of the war; and all / with the loss of one ship, the Resolution, which had run aground through the eagerness of the pilot to pursue.

When the news of the engagement reached Britain, there was the greatest joy and satisfaction; and his Royal Highness taking part therein, notwithstanding he did not attend the court-days so frequently as before, yet on this occasion he waited on the King at St. James's to pay his compliments, and was received with all the fondness of a father. The Court resounded with the praise of Admiral Hawke, and the British Parliament returned their thanks to him; which concluded in these very words: 'The defeat of the French fleet has been the safety of England in this age of glory, as the destruction of the Spanish Armada had been in another.'

Though this coup d'eclat might have completed the distresses of the enemy, yet they had others still more terrible. Their vintage that year was blasted, their crops were withered, their harvest had been as bad as that in Britain was plentiful; their cattle were slaughter'd, and after being packed up on board their vessels had been picked up by privateers or by the British men of war. Being in continual alarms of an invasion from England, the ties of humanity were broken, connections were loosed, fears within and terrors without prey'd upon her vitals: jealousy, like a moth, insinuated into the inmost recesses of her councils; her Monarch spent his time among his women, the Dauphin among the priests and clergy of the different orders; the kingdom was so drained of specie, that the King's plate with that of some of the greatest peers was sent to the mint to be coined: nay, to such distress was the French Court driven, that she could not support the poor prisoners, twenty thousand of / whom were now in England confined, at Sigenhurst, Hawkhurst, Winchester, &c.

Among the many transcendent virtues which adorned the Duke of Cumberland, that of real goodness of heart shone brilliant and glorious. No difference of nation, religion, interest, or any other external circumstance could in the least efface the noble and elevated principles of generous, diffusive, and disinterested benevolence and charity, so deeply rooted in him. He never looked on the poor without feeling for them, nor could any of his favourites lay a greater obligation upon him than to point out a way by which he might be more extensively useful. Many of the letters in the public papers from the gaols of Newgate, the Compters, the Marshalsea, and Whitechapel, thanking unknown benefactors, might with great propriety have been directed to him: and at this time his royal heart bled for those who became prisoners through the doubtful fortune of war. He sent a thousand pounds to Sigenhurst by a sure hand; but at the same time laid the strongest injunctions upon him, not to mention from whom the present came, and with it he sent a letter, signed *Britannicus,* desiring that a note might be taken of the number of those who were of the same trade, and an estimate be made of what they were able to do for their living: accordingly some were found to be shoemakers, some taylors, some clothworkers in all its branches. Suitable materials were bought for working upon; some dressed leather, some made clothes and shoes for the country people, others spun and knit stockings, some of which I have seen; and in this manner did many of these unfortunate strangers gain their living. The example of his Highness was followed by many of the nobility of both sexes, to the immortal honour of him who was the instrument / of giving alms in secret, and yet was content to be unknown; and the Parliament soon took their case into consideration, and gave them relief.

The affairs of France in the year 1759 were not in a worse condition, than those of Great Britain were prosperous and fortunate. The fame of Mr. Pitt was greater than that of any other minister; the fondest hope or the most ardent wishes could not have dared to entertain the most distant thoughts of what had been brought about through his means: he restored his country to that dignity of which she seemed to be deprived at the beginning of the war: he healed her divisions, cancelled the distinction of party, and united his fellow subjects in one common cause: he inspired our councils with resolution and wisdom, and piloted our natural strength through the proper channel to glory and success, under the influence of his ministry, hitherto unparalleled for concord and unanimity. Britannia's sons by sea and land were habituated to conquest, and victory seemed to sit brooding between the knees of our aged Sovereign, at a time when the brilliance of his diadem received a lustre from the silver colour of his grey hairs. The same spirit of concord and harmony diffused itself through the fleets and army, to such a degree that every one seemed to fight the cause of his neighbour no less than his own.

That year the Parliament voted the continuation of the war, and made provision for it: and accordingly it continued to rage with its usual fierceness in Germany, where the French, by the superiority of numbers, and from a motive to wipe off their disgrace, had exerted themselves so far as to get possession of Paderborn, and several estates belonging to the Electorate of Hanover. Incidents which could not but affect the heart of our King: he died / suddenly at Kensington, about half an hour after seven in the morning of the 25th of October 1760, wanting only sixteen days of seventy-seven years, after having reigned thirty three years four months and fourteen days: and here it will not be improper to give a character of him.

He was certainly a Prince of excellent endowments, of spirit, and of vivacity. By the innate strength of his own genius he at once commenced a general and a hero: never discouraged by difficulties, he sometimes executed what others judged impossible: active and indefatigable, he discerned as by intuition. By his evenness of temper, hitherto proof against misfortunes, he baffled the efforts of conspiracy and distress; and if at any time his calamities multiplied, his virtues shone with the brighter lustre. As a Sovereign he was a man, a citizen, a legislator, and a patriot. His ambition was to see things with his own eyes, and to make justice and humanity his ministers of state: for, entertaining an unconfined good will to mankind, he gave an universal toleration, the decisive characteristic of true religion: he equally abhorred the guilt of making martyrs and the folly of making proselytes. His Majesty encouraged the industrious, and honoured the learned: was of such uncommon sympathy that he always felt for the unfortunate; never signing a dead warrant without a visible concern: and such was the feeling of his Royal heart, that once in Hyde-park, at an experiment for firing a cannon three times in a minute, when one of the matrosses had his hand and arm torn by the explosion, he refused to look at any more trials that day, notwithstanding he was entreated by all who were round him.

Next day his grandson, our present Sovereign, was proclaimed through London and Westminster, / by the name of George III. whom may God Almighty long preserve.

It is one of the maxims of this constitution, that a King of Great Britain never dies; and in this event the maxim was verified; for the new Sovereign in his very first speech to his Parliament declared his unalterable resolution to support the government in church and state, and to preserve the toleration inviolable. The officers of state were retained; a resolution was taken of continuing the war; and, for the better distribution of justice, the salaries of the puisne judges were augmented from 1500 *l.* to 2000 *l. per ann.* That Session of Parliament, tho' the last in the course of things, was no less forward than any of the preceding; and, having finished their business, they were dissolved, and a new one was called.

As things were in this situation a conference was proposed on the side of France; and the Court of Britain was not averse to it. Accordingly Sir Hans Stanley was sent from London to Paris, to confer with the French ministry, in June 1760, and M. de Buffy came over to London, to negotiate with ours. He was well acquainted with the British nation, and with the public funds: he had formerly been an ambassador at the British Court, and in the year 1743 followed the King to Hanover, where he negotiated with the Earl of Harrington. M. Buffy, knowing that his Court only wanted to gain time, and that a compact had been entered into with that of Madrid for curbing the growing power of the British nation, came over partly with a view of diverting the British ministry from prying into the secret articles of the treaty. The Spanish flota had left Carthagena in New Spain in the month of February, so that, had the Family Compact been known, the same might have been intercepted. /

Before leaving Paris he artfully caused some emissaries to publish through Britain and Holland, that the war would become every day more serious and terrible; and, the French army having got possession of Hesse Cassel and defeated two or three detached parties of the Confederates strengthening the conjecture, his design was answered: the stocks fell considerably, and he, by his agents at Amsterdam and at the Hague, bought shares to the amount of 400,000 *l.*

By his coming to England, where after once and again conferring with the Duke of Newcastle and with Mr. Pitt, the hopes of peace began to revive, and the stocks rose considerably. At this very time he sold out the shares he had bought, and by his bargain gained 70,000 *l.* This being done, he embarrassed the negotiation, by intermixing the claims of the Court of Madrid, which, he said, his Master ardently desired might be adjusted. Mr. Pitt soon detected the latent fire that lay concealed under these plausible terms, and Buffy soon broke off the conferences; which he attributed only to Mr. Pitt's obstinacy: 'For (said he) the Duke of Newcastle is a reasonable downright honest man; but I know not what to make of Mr. Pitt: he is tenacious, and no way disposed to reconcile.'

It was somewhat surprizing, that the Court of France should be so refractory after so many losses and disappointments: for that very summer she lost the beautiful island of Belleisle, by the surrender of the garrison of Palais, on the 5th of June, to Commodore Keppel and General Hopson. By this conquest the British nation was put in possession of almost the whole trade in the bay of Biscay: and indeed the best use was made of it during the remaining part of the war, as a squadron was constantly kept there, so that no ship could either go / in or come out of Brest, Rochfort, &c. without imminent danger of being taken.

The hurry of war did not divert consulting a method for perpetuating the blessings which this constitution in church and in state daily brought about: for his Majesty declared in council, that he had fixed upon Charlotta Sophia, the younger sister of the reigning Duke of Mecklenburgh

Strelitz, as partner of his bed and of his throne. That Princess had once danced at a ball where some of the British officers were present, and these had made so handsome a report of her person and virtues, as to captivate the heart of the King. The rank of her family, though the same had given a King to Norway and had been connected with the best in the Empire, was the least of her recommendation; the brilliance of her character, the goodness of her heart, and the fullness of her reputation were decisive circumstances in her favour. The Earl of Harcourt, with a grand retinue, went over, while the Dutchess of Hamilton (lady to the Marquis of Lorn) and the Dutchess of Ancaster were sent to accompany her to the dominions over which she was to govern. She travelled by land to Stadt, escorted by a body of her brother's guards, where she embarked for England: and, arriving upon the 8th of September, was received at the garden-gate by his Royal Highness the Duke of York, who handed her out of the coach, and conducted her through the entrance, where she was received by his Majesty, who, before she could fully kneel, took her up in his arms, embraced her, and conducted her up stairs to his mother and sisters, who received her with all the tenderness of a friend: his Highness the Duke of Cumberland with the King's four brothers were also present, and all of them paid their compliments, welcoming her to / the country. The Chancellor and other Officers of State were immediately sent for; and, all agreeing that the nuptials should be solemnized immediately, they were married that very night. The Duke of Cumberland acted the part of father and gave her away; about ten they joined hands, which was intimated to the people by the great guns drawn out in the park for that purpose. It seems that foreigners when married to a native of England must repeat the words of the ceremony in the English tongue, some of whom make a poor figure in the uttering of them: however it was not so with the Royal Bride; for people who were present declared, that she pronounced the different sentences as properly as a native; and about the time of the death of the Duke of Cumberland she spoke the English tongue incomparably well.

Fourteen days after this marriage was the coronation, perhaps the most brilliant and splendid that ever had been in England; at least the Royal Family were more numerous than on any other occasion, there being no less than eleven immediate descendants of the last King, besides the Princess Dowager of Wales and the Queen.

George the Third, King of Great Britain, is a prince endowed with such external qualities of person, as speak the more refined and admirable accomplishments of the understanding. Under the eye of the best of fathers he learned to read and pronounce with singular elegance and propriety; formed to virtue by his precepts and excited by his example, he began to have an early love for his country, and in a manner to court the favour of those over whom he was once to govern. His genius for letters was spirited and free. In love with liberty from his infancy he could act the part of Cato in the tragedy of that name, in a manner that would / have done honour to the best performers: he delighted much in architecture, botany, and the fine arts; and looked upon his father's friends as his own.

The childish amusements and trifling employments too frequent about courts, had never got any ascendant over him: and though these might for a while obscure a little of that precious seed which had been sown in his heart, yet no sooner did he take into his hands the reins of government, than the great and noble principles he had imbibed, and which had taken deep root during the course of his education, had entirely got the upper hand: the death of his royal father had made the first impression; that of his grandfather had made it more sensible; the marriage bed (which is but a forerunner of the death bed) tended to mollify him the more, and his coronation still improved what was begun: for, receiving a surfeit at worldly greatness, and observing the vanity of earthly splendor, he set his mind upon the King of kings. It was delightful to see a young man passing in all the pomp of majesty and all the splendor of greatness, beyond whatever Greece or Rome beheld at their most exalted triumphs, beckoning to crowded multitudes, with his hands, his head, and the whole of his deportment. How elevated the expression, 'I do not chuse to take the sacrament with the crown upon my head, for I am in the presence of the King of kings!' And again, 'Pray read over the oath distinctly, for I am in the presence of God, and am resolved to observe it.'

The crown was set upon his head by Dr. Secker, Archbishop of Canterbury, the same who had baptized him, married him, and afterward baptized three of his sons. The sermon was preached by Dr. Hay Drummond, Archbishop of York, / from the words of the Queen Sheba to King Solomon*. It was a rhetorical discourse upon the duty of a chief magistrate in a limited constitution like that of this country.

* 1 Kings, chap. x. vers. 9.

Scarce was the coronation over, when an event happened which not a little startled the people of all ranks, as Mr. Pitt resigned the seals on Monday October the 5th. He and his lady's brother, Lord Temple, had insisted in a debate that happened in the Privy-council, on declaring war immediately against Spain. These two courtiers 'submitted in writing and signed by them, their sentiments for taking that step;' which being over-ruled by the unanimous opinion of his Majesty's other servants, Mr. Pitt resigned the seals, in order that he might not remain responsible for measures which he was no longer allowed to *guide*. However, on his resignation the King bestowed upon him a pension of 3000 *l. per annum,* the title of Baroness on Esther Mr. Pitt's lady, and the name and dignity of Baron of Chatham on her male issue.

This resignation only raised the love and esteem of the nation: for on the lord mayor's day following the infatuated populace huzzaed Mr. Pitt more than the King himself, and crowded about his coach in such multitudes, that they were like to raise the wheels thereof from the ground. And here his Highness attended the King, and, without being moved, beheld the shiftings of popular applause.

The time was approaching when the war was to be brought to a period: the British nation exerting herself with a becoming vigour, a revenue was raised of no less than 196, 161, 19 *l.* 19 *s.* 9 *d.* for the service of the ensuing year. The Courts of Madrid and London emitted reciprocal declarations of war; and, to involve Great Britain still more, / the Kings of France and Spain both declared war against Portugal.

In the midst of these gathering storms, the Duke of Cumberland, who never was absent from the Privy-council, when affairs of importance came upon the carpet, advised to send a body of 14,000 men to Portugal; and likewise a number of land forces and a strong squadron of ships to besiege the Havannah in the Isle of Cuba in the West Indies, while a ship should be dispatched to Admiral Cornish and Colonel Draper in the East Indies, requiring them to sail directly to the Isle of Manilla, in the extremity of Asia, to distress Spain in these two opposite quarters. He named the officers and regiments to be employed in Portugal and in the West India expedition. The Earl of Loudon, whose name was already sufficiently known, acted with all the spirit and vigour of a brave officer on the Portuguese frontiers, while Sir George Pococke and the Earl of Albemarle reduced the Havannah, after having stormed El Moro castle, which lies at the mouth of the harbour, and hitherto was accounted impregnable: and, to render the conquest still more glorious and important, no less than twelve ships of the line, with twenty-seven merchant-men and 5,000,000 *l.* fell into the hands of the victor; with territory capable of the utmost improvement, and so situated as to be in a manner the key to Mexico and Peru. The French made a diversion by landing upon Newfoundland; but were soon beat off with loss, and had it not been for the fogs, which are immoderately thick in that quarter, the whole would have been taken.

The Spaniards sustained another great loss at the commencement of this war, in a large ship, named the Hermione, which had sailed from the western shore of Panama, laden with silver, with gold and / with jewels, to the amount of 1,500,000 *l.* fell providentially into our hands: the money taken out of which was conducted to London, and just came in sight of St. James's as the King had the first account of the birth of his son*. That year there was an installment of the Knights of the most noble Order of the Garter at Windsor, when his Majesty, attended by the Queen, visited his Royal Uncle, and witnessed the grand solemnity; after which they were most magnificently and royally entertained.

The elegance of the entertainment was but the least article of their amusement: their Majesties walked thro' his gardens, where they were struck with an amazing variety; and being attended by a prodigious and splendid retinue, they all admired the grandeur of his apartments, the choice of his curiosities, the variety of his pictures, his animals and shells, the order and regularity of his houshold, the fineness of his horses, and the harmonious distribution and laying out of the different grounds. After being delighted with the whole of his Highness's improvements the Duke, their Majesties, and the illustrious company visited Eaton School; where they conversed freely with the different masters, and received in the most gracious manner, such noblemen and gentlemen students as were introduced to them.

The glory of the British arms was brilliant both in the West and in the East Indies. Manilla fell before its Governor so much as heard that there was a rupture between the two Crowns. The conduct of Colonel Draper and the bravery of Admiral Cornish were every way noble, and at the sametime temper'd with an humanity which great souls generally regard more than any resolution or intrepidity. They entered into an agreement

* August 12th, 1762.

for ransoming / the Manillas for four million of dollars: but, under the pretences that some of our private men had misbehaved (an event which discipline itself cannot totally prevent) and that the La Santissima Trinidada and Philippina, two rich Acapulco ships, which had been taken by the British fleet, were included, the Spanish Court have hesitated in fulfilling the engagements for the ransom; which, however, by means of warm and serious remonstrances, are at the time of writing this like to be complied with.

The loss of the Havannah in the West and the disaster at the Manilla (where never enemy had before penetrated in an hostile manner) would not have disposed France to an accommodation: her ministry were infatuated and obstinate, and therefore endeavorued to make a figure on the Weser. However, the olive branch seemed to have come from the quarter where it was discovered at the period of the former war: for the Empress of Russia (the only surviving child of Peter the Great) dying January 1762, she was succeeded by her nephew Peter III. who, embracing a different system from his predecessor, ordered the Russian army to quit Colberg and the other states of Prussia; while the Swedes clapt up a peace, and returned to their own country: nay, the system of Russia was so much changed in a few months, that Peter III. who was murdered July 9th, by a conspiracy among his clergy and officers of state, would have sent an army to join the Prussians, and to act as their Monarch should direct them. But, as the powers on the continent seemed all glutted with blood and with rapine, an accommodation was proposed: and indeed it was time it should take place, for Paderbon, Westphalia, Hanover, and Hesse Cassel were exhausted; the sword and / famine had with united force visited the inhabitants. Bohemia, Saxony, Silesia, and Moravia had been ruined by the armies of contending Potentates: Prussia, Pomerania (both Swedish and Prussian) together with Brandenburgh, had been filled with horror and calamity. The Queens of Poland and Prussia died of grief; the one for the miseries of her husband, the other for the misfortunes of her son. The temples had been violated, the altars had been profaned, and, what is shocking to humanity, the bodies of the dead had been taken out of their coffins, and stripped of their grave clothes. It was hard to say, whether the Muscovite Cossacks or the Austrian Croats exceeded in brutality.

To bring this accommodation to a period, the Duke of Bedford repaired to Paris, in September 1762, on the side of Great Britain, and the Duke de Nivernois came over to London on the part of France.

The Duke de Nivernois was a nobleman of as bright parts, deep penetration and sagacity, as any about the Court of Versailles. With all the advantages of birth and education, he early took the tour of Europe: the clearness of his understanding increased with his years: well acquainted with the interest of Princes, he investigated the several springs that move the Courts of Vienna and Berlin: well knowing the strength and weakness of Great Britain, he saw where she was sound, and where she was diseased: he had thoroughly digested the interests of the Courts of Madrid and Lisbon; was possessed of a readiness of thought, and nervousness of expression, that rendered him entirely fit for holding an argument: to him was owing the alliance formed between the Courts of Vienna and Versailles, as it was foreseen that, in consequence of this step, the King of Prussia would / become an expensive ally of Great Britain; sensible of our connections with Portugal, he knew how to adapt his speech toward raising compassion in the breasts of her friends. And indeed at this time their case was wretched; their very existence was threatened by two powerful neighbours; the people were discontented with their King, their Sovereign was distrustful of his subjects, two armies within her bowels, the one wanting to rob her of her being, and the other composed of Protestants and Roman Catholics*, only united in place, but disjointed in religion, sentiments, and discipline: add to this, that the French negotiator was so cool, as never to alter his countenance, even when informed of the most disastrous events. He was dining with the Earl of Bute, one of his Majesty's Principal Secretaries of State, when the news came of taking the Havannah; he read the contents of the letters without any alteration of countenance, and continued to spend his time with the same gaiety and chearfulness as before. The Duke of Bedford was no less regaled in Paris, than the Duke de Nivernois was at London; and on the 3d of November the preliminaries for a general peace were signed. The news of this event was transmitted to the several places where the war was raging, and at once put an end to hostilities in Germany, where the armies were in motion, as if in the hottest time of the war. The French had got possession of the beautiful city of Cassel, which the Allies were no less desirous to recover, than they were earnest to retain:

* The Portuguese army and the British auxiliaries.

the party to succour the garrison under M. de Stainville, and the body of forces intended to prevent them under the Marquis of Granby, had a most sharp and terrible encounter, in which both of them performed the / part of the greatest and most experienced in the art of war: however, the latter prevailed, and got betwixt the other and the town; so that when the news of the cessation of arms came, and was intimated by the French generals, both Prince Ferdinand and the Marquis declared, that they rejoiced in every opportunity of preventing the effusion of human blood, and even agreed to let provisions go into the garrison.

When the preliminaries of peace were sent to St. James's, his Majesty ordered the same to be laid before his Parliament, who, on the 9th of December following, took them seriously into consideration: both Houses were extremely full; and Mr. Pitt, notwithstanding an excruciating pain, attended, though his feet and legs were wrapt up in flannel; and that he was obliged to be carried between two men from his chair to his seat in the House of Commons, and when there to be three times recruited with drops prescribed for his disorder, yet he spoke for three hours and an half on the important subject, till his malady increasing, he was obliged to withdraw two hours before the final resolve on an address to his Majesty, approving what had been done: the numbers for the address were 319 to 65, or five to one nearly. Many speeches for and against them were that day uttered, which might have adorned any assembly that ever Greece or Rome beheld; Mr. Pitt, Mr. Fox, Mr. Charles Townshend, and Mr. Dempster, spoke with distinguished eloquence; and the healths of the Minority were drank at several magnificent and grand entertainments.

In the other House the debates likewise ran high; the Dukes of Newcastle and Grafton spoke upon the subject, as did the Earls Temple, Hardwicke, and Halifax, the Lord Chancellor Henley, Earl / of Northington, and the Lord Mansfield. In the course of the debate it was shewn, that the King of Prussia was not a natural, but an accidental ally; that the subsidy paid to him was more than was given to any other potentate; and that though the treaty between the Courts of London and Berlin had expired before the last negotiation was begun, yet the Prussian interest had been taken as much care of, as if the treaty had subsisted in all its force. In a word, the address was agreed on; and the Earl of B – very candidly owned, 'that was he to die next day, he would desire no more honourable inscription on his tomb, than that he was the man to advise his Majesty to agree to the preliminary articles, which now lay before them;' and were afterward signed, Feb. 10, 1763.

By this treaty the French were driven from the East Indies, Great Britain had the whole of North America, from the bottom of the Gulph of Florida to Quebec inclusive; as also Cape Breton and Senegal: Cuba was restored to Spain, Martinico and Guadaloupe, with the other isles, to France, &c. and in other respects things were mostly settled as before.

Though this treaty of peace, so glorious for the armies and navies of Great Britain, of whom the King, in his answer to the address of the City of London on the conquest of the Havannah, said, 'Too much cannot be said in their praise;' yet loud and bitter complaints were made against it without doors, and the Earl of Bute being a favourite was blamed; however, it had the approbation of both Houses of Parliament, the trading part of the City of London, the merchants and corporations of the other great cities and towns in the united kingdom, of the universities, the convocation in England, and the assembly of the / church of Scotland. Though Lord Bute was nephew to John and Archibald, Dukes of Argyle, and by the mother was descended from the famous Lieutenant-General Talmash, he was yet treated in the most contemptible manner on account of his being from the north side of the Tweed. A paper called the North Briton appeared weekly, containing aspersions upon him, and the most false and glaring misrepresentations of the country, which evidently proved, that the author was grossly ignorant of Lord Bute's character, and that he was an utter stranger to the geography and inhabitants of Scotland. Every person of discretion and prudence laughed at reflections upon people for the place of their birth; but others carried the matter so far, that the bowels of compassion, so warmly recommended by the Christian religion, were shut against the cries of the poor. It was no new thing to hear a well-dressed gentleman say to a sailor, who had lost a limb in the cause of his country, 'Go to Lord Bute, ask charity of him, don't ask it of me.' The lower class of the natives of Scotland about London were great losers at that period; for if a Scotsman kept a shop or a stall, he was sure to be singled out by such tools as were employed to inflame. And here it is observable, that wretches of a mongrel descent were readier than those who were of an English family, that had existed before the conquest: the immediate descendants of Dutch Jews, Italian rope-dancers, or French cooks by Irish strollers, or prostitutes from the Isle of Man; nay, some of those Englishmen were the sons of African or Jamaica blacks by Asiatic negroes from Canton, or from Bengal. Among the number of these enemies to the people of North Britain was J. Wilkes, though descended from those of that country, a man of life and wit, / but neither correct nor equal in them: being a man of spirit and vivacity, he had, like others, spent a large fortune which he had by his lady: he was frequently obliged to do things, which otherwise he would not have done: he wrote periodic papers himself, and encouraged others to employ their pen against Lord Bute's administration; and carried his rashness to such a height, as to give a low and invidious turn to the several parts of his Majesty's speech from the throne: for in the North Briton, No. 45, he told the people, that the speech delivered April 19, 1763, was not the speech of the King, but of the Minister; that the advantages received by the last peace were not to be regarded; and that the tract of ground interjacent between the eastern shore of the Missisippi, and the ocean, were nothing, while those on the opposite side of that river were not in our power. On this he was dismissed from being Colonel of the Buckinghamshire militia, and by a general warrant from Lord Halifax, then one of the Principal Secretaries of State, his papers were seized, as in cases of high treason; he himself was apprehended and confined to the Tower, from whence he was brought up, May 5th, before the Common Pleas, in consequence of a complaint entered against his hardships.

That day the Court-house was crowded with persons of the first distinction, and he had counsel to assist him: however, so spirited was he, that far from committing his cause to the worthy gentlemen, he stood up, and after having told, how the constables entered his house, he with great warmth said, 'I have been worse used and treated than if I had been a Scots rebel.' On this the Court found that he had been illegally taken up, as his name was not specified in the warrant, which was / only general. This application to the Court of Common Pleas proceeded from the spirit of party, which at that time ran exceeding high: some looked upon it as an indignity done to the Court of King's Bench, before whom indeed, in the nature of things, matters of sedition are brought more properly; the reason of this contempt was, that Lord Mansfield, the Chief Justice, was born in Scotland. Wilkes, in an after trial before Lord Camden, obtained 1000 *l.* damages of the messengers, others had decisions in their favour;

and Lord Camden received the thanks of some corporation town for what he had done.

In all points that are dubious there is a diversity of sentiment: the question of searching houses by virtue of a general warrant was debated in both Houses of Parliament without being determined: the House of Commons ordered that Wilkes should attend to answer to the charge against him for writing the seditious paper, intituled, North Briton, No. 45. He answered the first summons by an excuse, proceeding from a wound he had received in a duel with one Mr. Martin; a second and third were given him, but in the time of the Christmas holidays he thought proper to retire beyond sea, and at last settled in Paris, where his circumstances were not only bad, but he had the mortification to hear first of his being expelled the House of Commons, and afterwards in March 1764 of being found guilty by two different juries of writing blasphemy against his God*, and sedition against his King.

As Lord Bute observed so strong and impetuous a stream against him, he resigned his office of First / Lord Commissioner of the Treasury, and retired wholly to his farm; yet after this resignation the peace of the kingdom was not settled: for whatever minister was preferred, there were still complaints against him; events which tended not a little toward rendering the Sovereign uneasy, notwithstanding he had extended his sway beyond any other potentate†; that there was a reciprocal confidence between him and his Parliament; that his domestic happiness was secured by the increase of his family, with the conduct and behaviour of the Queen.

Some of Lord Bute's friends could not help admiring the penetration of the former ministry, for resigning at a time when a general peace was expected; they knew that no peace ever pleased all the people; they observed the press teeming with productions dictating the terms to be insisted on by the Ministers of State; and that the vast acquisitions in the East and West Indies, with those on the shore of Africa, were more extensive and more important ones than had ever come before the senate of ancient Greece or Rome; they knew Lord Bute to have been a

* In a pamphlet called, 'Essay on Woman,' a most impious and detestable contrivance, burlesquing the most sacred expressions, using the must odious representations, and the most immodest terms.

† Super et Garamantas et Indos
Protulit imperium –
Afric and Indus did his power obey.

favourite with the King's father, and no less with the King himself. The circumstance to endear that nobleman to his Majesty was, according to my information, owing to an accident, which does honour both to the Sovereign and to him.

One day his Lordship came into the room, where the Prince's tutor was demonstrating the 47th proposition of the first book of Euclid's Elements, which is, that in a right-angled triangle the square of the hypothenuse is equal to the squares of the / two containing sides; a discovery* more glorious for Pythagoras, than the overthrow of the Persian empire was to Alexander the Great. As the preceptor's demonstration was somewhat perplexed, perhaps owing to a want of presence of mind, or to confusion, which might arise from being in the room with strangers, his Highness could not understand it. Lord Bute observed the situation of the pupil, and of the master, and being an adept in these things, he begun the illustration of the figure with such perspicuity and conciseness, that his Royal Highness instantly comprehended the same, and from that time commenced the high and personal regard, which the King entertained for him ever after; nor would any thing, but the express commands of his Sovereign, have prevailed upon his Lordship to accept of the place of First Lord of the Treasury, and office which involved him in a certain expence, and diverted his attention from the affairs of his own immense and opulent fortune. The old Duke of Argyle foresaw the storm, and advised him, as he was but little known, not to accept of any station at so critical a period: a caution worthy of his Grace to give, and of his Lordship to have taken. And here it will not be improper to draw a character of the first-named nobleman, as he had been a Lord of Parliament for the space of fifty-four years.

The high office of Lord Justice General of Scotland, and Keeper of the Great Seal there, with a numerous train of titles and dignities, did not so much honour to him, as they derived lustre from him; and though he was adorned with all the / crowns that glory itself could fix upon the head of a subject, yet these, and the confidence of four succeeding Sovereigns, did not so much ennoble him, as his own merit and personal accomplishments, which rendered him a competent judge both of men and of things.

* Upon this proposition the trigonometrical tables are constructed, and by it several of the most intricate problems both in algebra and fluxions are solved: in short, its use is universal.

He could write a letter in eight different languages: he understood botany, chemistry, and all the practice of physic; the ingenious and noble construction of watches and clocks, and of all the machines depending upon mechanism, with all the branches of the mathematics, of natural and moral philosophy: he had digested the laws of his country, so as to speak upon them with a majestic and distinguishing sedateness, a charming and irresistible eloquence: he was a true friend, no cruel enemy; and besides the Scheme of raising the Independent Highland companies, and promoting the manufactories and fisheries through the King's dominions, by which multitudes have had bread, and millions unborn may find entertainment, he at a moderate computation settled fifty-four thousand individuals in civil and military employments: a man like Cæsar, chief in peace and war. While at the school of Inverary, and college of Glasgow, he was no less remarkable for a prodigious strength of body and surprizing agility, than admired afterward in the Senate and in the Privy Council, where

Actions his words, and words his actions grac'd!
He tho' from heaven remote to heaven did move,
With strength of mind, and trod th' abyss above;
Well pleas'd was he to walk along the sphere
Of shining stars, and travel with the year;
With more than human skill he scal'd the height
Of Atlas, who sustain'd the heavenly weight: /
And now his condescending eyes survey
Mistaken mortals wandring from the way.

I should not have dwelt so long upon the character of this great man, to whom I had the honour of being known, had it not been that in the circle of his Majesty's dominions, there was not a single person who had an higher opinion of his Royal Highness the Duke of Cumberland; for when the foundation of his palace was laid at Inverary in September 1746, the first stone, which was fixed by this present Duke of Argyle, had this inscription cut out upon it:

Gulielmus Cumbriæ Dux – nobis hæc otia fecit.

The Duke of Argyle was not single to admire his Royal Highness: every one, in proportion to their being known to him, reverenced him for his every virtue, and for none more than for an incorruptible candour, and such integrity of heart, that he was looked upon as one of the honestest men that ever lived; his abilities in peace being no less conspicuous than his talents in war: he had been already declared Chancellor of the universities of Dublin and of St. Andrews: his picture was in every house, and the Lords of the Admiralty had added a ship to the navy, to whom they had given the name of the CULLODEN, in commemoration of the Good he had done to his country.

However, his character in public was not more meritorious than in private life, being a promoter of every charity that was of general utility; and in his private benefactions, his only care was to fix upon proper objects, and to keep the name of the donor concealed. When the poor Palatines came over to England in quest of a settlement in / one of the new acquisitions, he sent them a purse of one thousand guineas; and I have heard it affirmed by people who knew things well, that he bestowed no less than 6000 *l.* yearly in private charities.

He had endeavoured to be free from the noise and tumult of a court, and to be rid of the turmoils of party and faction, which ever since the peace had raged in a strange manner. He never came to court, except to pay his compliments on the increase of the Royal Family, or to set off its lustre, as at the marriage of the hereditary Prince of Brunswick with his niece the Princess Augusta, January 16th 1764: and whenever he appeared, he was wearied out with compliments and congratulations; for, convinced that the convulsions in the ministry did not flow from public spirit, from a design to lessen the price of provisions, or to do what might be for the benefit of the poor, he heard of their animosities with dissatisfaction and concern. And yet toward the latter end of his days, he was obliged, out of love to his nephew the King, to appear at court oftner than he had for some time before.

About the latter end of the year 1764 and the spring 1765, the King had been so indisposed as not to appear upon the stated court-days till toward the middle of April; and on the 24th he delivered a speech from the throne; the import of which was, that the Parliament would deliberate whether a regency should be immediately settled, or if the nomination should be committed to him, in case of an accident: the first of which measures was agreed to be pursued; and in the act of regency the Duke and all the Royal Family were named.

He beheld with regret the growing price of provisions, without a proportioned augmentation of / the price of labour and industry: nor was he less affected with the bitter complaints that were daily thrown out by the lower set of people, for the hardships put upon them by their superiors. The poor seamen proceeded with displayed banners to St. James's, complaining of their being imposed on in the distribution of prize-money, and other hardships: the silk-weavers in and about Spitalfields proceeded three days successively to Westminster, craving that no French silks might be imported. The behaviour of the justices of the peace, but partiularly of Sir John F – g*, was greatly disapproved by the House of Lords, as some noblemen were insulted: however, no bad consequence followed.

Under the pressure of these alarming tumults, the King sent for his Royal Uncle to Richmond, and unbosomed himself to him, as to his best and his kindest friend. His Highness told him, 'that little danger might be apprehended from the late turmoils: that popular clamours would soon subside, and that his Majesty needed not make himself uneasy.' Though these softening expressions not a little satisfied that heart which so graciously felt for his people, yet it could not restrain from desiring, that his Highness would endeavour to remove the prevailing discontents, and settle the ministry in such a manner as might be most agreeable: and, accordingly, at his Majesty's request, he set about these important matters. /

He visited Mr. Pitt at Hayes, where he dined and conversed with him upon the present posture of affairs: but that gentleman chose not to throw up a certain income of 3000 *l. per ann.* to please the discontented, notwithstanding he was highly in their favour. This circumstance determined his Highness to look out for such noblemen and gentlemen as had been most popular.

Of the number of these was General Henry Seymour Conway, esq; brother to the Earl of Hertford; an officer of great abilities, prudence, and foresight; great by his family, more important by his connections, and still more considerable for his merit and fagacity: he had been dismissed from his Majesty's service by a court artifice, and without any visible reason; and the populace seemed to be offended at what was done. This gentleman was made principal secretary of state: lord chief justice Pratt (whose

* This magistrate, (the greatest terror of rogues since J. Wylde's exit) told their Lordships, that this was not such a mob as authorized him to read the proclamation, though he well knew that the Duke of Bedford, a truly sweet tempered nobleman, had been assaulted and wounded in his way from the House, while the most outrageous and treasonable expressions were used by some people, tending to excite the mob to open rebellion against the person of his most sacred Majesty King George.

decisions in the cases of Wilkes, Beardmore, &c. had been mightily cried up) was created Lord Camden: the Marquis of Rockingham was made first lord of the treasury. 'Tis needless to enumerate a catalogue of names, as the public neither lost nor gained by the change; which whether it be for the welfare or detriment of the community his Highness did not live to see: for, on the 31st of October 1765, he came from Windsor to wait on their Majesties, who received him very affectionately; and, going to his house in Upper Grosvenor street, he ordered some coffee and chocolate to be got ready about eight o'clock, as he expected company. About that time the Duke of Newcastle came to wait on his Highness; but, on the valet de chambre's going with the message, behold! his head lay backward upon the great chair whereon he sat: he was quite dead; and, from the coldness of his skin (notwithstanding a large fire / near him) it seemed that he had expired several minutes before it was known; an event not unlikely, he being exceeding corpulent, and addicted to sleep, notwithstanding the great exercise he had taken to keep his body low.

Thus lived and died William Augustus Duke of Cumberland, one of the most illustrious princes that ever lived. Any person to look at him would readily expect from him any thing that could be imagined or executed by the wit or force of man. He was of that stature which makes a man become all parts of exercise; his height was graceful on occasion of state and ceremony; and, though always inclined to corpulency, he was no less adapted for aglity and dispatch. His aspect was erect and composed; his eyes lively and thoughtful, and yet rather vigilant than sparkling: his actions and address so easy, that he appeared to be more afraid of putting a person out of countenance than they of offending against his dignity. His behaviour in an assembly was peculiarly graceful, in a certain art of mixing insensibly with the rest, and becoming one of the company, instead of receiving the courtship of it. There was in his look something sublime, which did not seem to arise from his dignity and character, but the innate disposition of his mind. He suffered the presence of much company, instead of taking delight in it; and he appeared in public rather to return good-will or to satisfy curiosity, than to gratify any taste he himself had of being popular. As his thoughts were never tumultuous in danger, so they were as little discomposed on occassions of pomp and magnificence: enterprizing like Alexander, couragious as Charles the XIIth; and possessed of the justice and humanity of Cæsar himself. His mind was capable of contemplation as well as enterprize; / ever ready for great exploits, but never impatient for occasions to perform them. He had wisdom and valour in as high perfection as man could enjoy them: free from ostentation, vain-glory, ambition, and all other vices which might intrude upon his mind, and shake the evenness of his temper: in short, among the most couragious and intrepid the most charitable and humane; one of the most candid, upright, and honest men of those, who lived in his days.

The city of London sent a deputation to his Majesty, to know in what manner the Lord Mayor's day should be observed; but though it was left intirely to themselves, as he was to be buried that very evening in King Henry the VIIth's Chapel, all the usual ceremonies, that distinguish this great metropolis above any other city in Europe, were dispensed with. The Lord Mayor Elect and the Court of Aldermen walked through Westminster-hall, in a manner expressive of their grief, for the Defender of their religion and liberties: the two Houses of Parliament in their Addresses, of the 18th of December, took notice of the loss his Majesty had sustained by the death of his Royal Uncle: such officers and soldiers as had been with him in the day of battle lamented him with their tears: his servants wept for him as for their father: the whole Royal Family were bitterly afflicted; and most of the Courts in Europe put on mourning when they heard of the change.

His death raised the more concern as it was unexpected: and his nephew Prince Frederic William, a youth of real goodness of heart and humanity, was so grieved at it, that it was thought to hasten his death, which happened on the 29th of December following.

THE END. /

Gulielmi Cumbriæ Ducis Encomiasticon.
Conditur hoc tumulo decus et tutela Britanni
Nominis, et puræ religionis amor!
At vivit totum quæ gloria compleat orbem
Hæc mensura bono vix fuit æqua duci.
Gallorum timor ille fuit, quo præside rerum,
Angligeno generi fat tribuere Dii:
Præterit ille dies qui nil nisi corporis hujus
Jus habet: impavidus jam fine fine viget.
Parte sui meliore viget, super alta perennis
Astra quidem fertur, nomen ubique sonat;
Nam si pro meritis tumuli mensura fuisset

Arcta foret tumulo terra Britanna viri.

AND. HENDERSON.

A LETTER TO Dr. SAMUEL JOHNSON, ON His JOURNEY to the WESTERN ISLES.

By ANDREW HENDERSON,

AUTHOR of the LIFE, of the Late
DUKE of CUMBERLAND.

Procul o procul este profani. VIRG.

Printed for the Author, and Sold by J. HENDERSON, *Westminster Hall;* J. MILLAN, *Charing Cross;* J. WILLIAMS, *Fleet Street;* W. NICOL, St. *Paul's Church Yard.* /

A LETTER TO DR. SAMUEL JOHNSON.

SIR,

As your journey to the Western Isles has occasioned a variety of publications, it may not be improper to send some thoughts upon the subject, as my knowledge of Scotland, and of the Isles has been somewhat considerable.

A production from a writer who passes a dictatorial sentence upon men of the most distinguished abilities, might have raised the curiosity of the public, which indeed has been much disappointed, as little or nothing / has been found in your performance, except some few common observations, and an ill natured assertion that the poem of Fingal was a modern production in the last century: Beda, an antient author, who died in the year 735, began his ecclesiastical history of the Angles with a curious description of the situation of Britain, its antient inhabitants, and the produce of her Isles: he takes notice of the cattle and corn of Scotland, and the Orcades, the nature of her fowls, ærial, aqueous & domestic, her rivers abounding with fish, and her medicinal waters; the beauty and variety of her shells, on which he makes judicious and manly observations with her mines of brass, iron, lead, silver, and precious ores; all which you have in a manner totally neglected.

Had you given yourself the trouble to pry into the natural or artificial productions of North Briton, you might have deserved well of your country, but in this you have been greatly wanting, your time being spent rather in idle and trifling amusements, than in solid investigation and search. The city of St. Andrew's itself might have furnished matter for many manly and judicious remarks, it having been a seminary / of learning for more than a thousand years, and rendered a royal foundation in 1412, during the captivity of K. James I. then in England, but who had improved in the several branches of literature then in use, so well, and had conceived such an opinion of the English colleges of Oxford and Cambridge, that the University of St. Andrew's was modelled thereby: Here have been educated men of the highest literary merit: George Buchanan, whom you yourself affect to commend, was an alumnus there, so was Lord Napier the wonderful inventor of Logarithms, as also David Gregory, whose book of optics is a work coeval with the sun.

The reign of James II. was no less auspicious to the sciences than that of his father: He founded the college of Glasgow, anno 1453, and endowed it with every privilege in the power of a sovereign to grant, the diploma erecting it into an university being wrote in such ample terms, and in such elegant Latin, that I doubt if you Dr. Samuel Johnson could go beyond it; here men of real learning have frequently resided, among whom Mr. Robert Simpson, whose conic sections and other works are sufficient to enoble him to the latest posterity. / What need I mention the two universities of Aberdeen and Edinburgh, the one founded by King James IV. the same who married lady Margaret Tudor, and the latter by King James VI. great grandson to the former prince, and who afterwards ascended the throne of England; both these universities have produced men of the most extensive knowledge and abilities.

The counties of Berwick and East Lothian so beautifully diversified with trees, and with corn, so well peopled, so full of villages and gentlemens seats, so remarkable for the fine situations of three royal boroughs, might claim the attention of a stranger come to observe; I am sure no country abounds in better wheat and is crowned with more exuberant harvests: Here are many mines of coal, works of salt, and the coast is one continued fishery, neither is Fife inferior to the Lothians; it consists of 200,000 inhabitants, one city, thirteen royal boroughs and was frequently the residence of kings, its coals and salt are inexhaustible: Here are beautiful gardens, some of them laid out in the nicest taste and nutrive of any species of trees; the gardens of Sir Robert Henderson, both at Fordel and Otterstoun, may vie with any I have / seen; strange you should so much dwell upon the want of trees in a country where garden ground does so much abound.

Your crossing over to Dundee, has indeed taken up some writing, while the meandrings of the Tay the finest river in Scotland is almost neglected, and indeed so has the town, tho' but few excell it in pleasantness of situation, neatness of streets, stateliness of buildings, extent of prospect, convenience of living, and adapted to every public utility; it stands in the neighbourhood of a district as remarkable for fine wheat as any in the British empire. Upon the Tay stands the castle of Broughtie, first built by Agricola, the same who on the moor of Munrouman not far from Dundee routed with a terrible slaughter anno 85, the united army of the Britons, then commanded by the Galdach, i.e. the Caledonian King.

It seems you have been in great haste when at Aberbrothic, a very beautiful town, and once so remarkable for a large and voluminous abbey, where not only parliaments were held, but the ashes of kings and princes were deposited; the letter wrote from the nobility of Scotland to the Pope, on the 13th of April 1320, and dated at Aberbrothick / is in such pure Latin, that I doubt much if yourself could exceed it; you might indeed pretend in an assuming tone to condemn, but sure I am, your censures like some of your observations would be ill founded. At this very time is to be seen the burial place of William the Lyon, whose ashes were interred there.

'Tis needless to follow you thro' your dry and tedious perambulation till your arrival in Coll, where it seems you spent more time than in places of greater consequence, for I truly believe, that among the Western Isles there is not one more barren in its soil, or of fewer natural advantages; the island is about 12 miles long, and 4 broad at a medium, but so poor that there are not in it above sixty families, or in other words, not above six hundred inhabitants: it has neither church, chapel or any place of worship. Tyriff, and it form but one parish; and the former is by far the most populous, as it contains about 2 thousand inhabitants, though but eight miles long and four broad; the name of the Isle itself is from the galick Tyriff, the country of the racers; there being a plain about a mile over, as fine as any in the universe, and having in the middle a rising every way / delightful; it has the finest hard sands to be met with; its horses are small, like those of Shetland, but more spirited, lively, and better shaped; the name of the harbour Scaranish is half Danish, half Irish, but many of the Hamlets are entirely from the Danes, Kirkipol, Heylepol, Hulapul, and Crossapul, it's soil is capable of any improvement, and at this very time the proprietor the Duke of Argyle has a thousand pound sterling per annum of rent from it. Here are some beautiful caves, and at the southern part a considerable high mountain, from whence on the 13th of December 1737, I had perhaps as full a view of the Hebrides as perhaps ever any person had before or since.

It was about eight in the morning when by means of a strong and lively refraction, I beheld this wonderful sight, the morning was adorned with the refulgent beams of the east, and appeared in her saffron dress ushering in the sun as he advanced. From the time of my being on the summit, till the upper limb of the sun appeared was half an hour, during which the Isles became gradually more visible; when half up, the view was most distinct, but when wholly up it was fainter. From this place I beheld / the several isles with wonder and astonishment, and only lament that I did not adore the God of nature sufficiently for the sight that I saw. The isles except such as were hid by the higher, or lay too near to be discerned then, appeared to advantage: The Isle of Skie which is near forty two miles long and eight broad at a medium, and whose hamlets and harbours are generally from the Danish language, was abundantly discernible, the southern parts of the long isle were no less so, Barra an island five miles over, and at the foot of south Uist appeared like a sugar loaf: The Isle of Mull about 24 miles long and generally broad, was very visible, as was Jona 2 miles long, that once famous seminary of learning, and burial place of the Scottish Kings: Cairnburgh, a small island, about half a mile long, and naturally so strong by means of an impetuous current that no ship could lye against it, was apparent, notwithstanding it is so contiguous to Mull, as to be separated by a channel only 500 yards over; here are the remains of a fort built by the Danes, who also gave it the name; Gometra and Ulva, being small, seemed by reason of their nighness to form but one continent with Mull; but to the W. b S. of these, the Island of Jura about 24 miles long and 16 / broad, appeared whole and entire; its paps vitz two high mountains rose gradually by means of the sun's refraction in the form of a sugar loaf, and making nine tenths of a regular cone, the diameter of whose base is each about 130 yards, and the height about 500; to the south of this, lyes the island of Isla, only separated by a sound, and in extent 24 miles long and equally broad; it was the residence of the lord of the isles, and is now worth an hundred thousand pound sterling: It is separated by a channel about 21 miles over from Ireland, of which I had as clear a view as if seen by the naked eye in a clear day at the distance of 20 miles, for in September 1766, the coast of France did not appear more visible about ten in the morning from the gate of Dover Castle, than did the coast of Ireland from the mountain of Tyriff: However, this extensive view was lost in the horizon; in this manner I continued two hours, when the whole were absorbed in the brightness of the sun. How did it become me to say with extasy? how wonderful are thy works O God? every one of which is an earth full of thy wisdom? Never man had an ampler view of them at one time, a view ten thousand times nobler than what could be conveyed by a map, or any other representation. /

But, Sir, as you dwell so long on Coll, 'tis astonishing you saw nothing of M'Lean the poet, a man so universally known there and in Tyriff, and this leads to consider your assertion that the poem of Fingal was modern, and composed in the last century.

On entering into this debate, I would beg to inform you, that I am no way connected with James M'Pherson, nor yet Mr. Becket the publisher of Fingal, these gentlemen are abler than I to refute your argument; the former being a native Highlander, the Irish language was natural to him, whereas by me, it was but partly acquired, besides as the M'Pherson's are the most ancient branch of the Clancattan, and so numerous as to possess the whole district of Badenoch, and to consist of 500 heads of families, and so high minded as every one to be called by the name of the farm they live in; 'tis strange you did not mention any of the battles between them and the clan Cameron, which were frequently exceeding fierce; for I remember in April 1741 – M'Pherson of Innernachaun, shewed me the spot where the Camerons and M'Phersons fought a pitched battle, whereon according to him the latter were victorious, / but when talking to the Camerons on the subject, I was told a quite contrary tale?

I do not remember to have heard much of heroic poetry in Earse, while in the north Highlands, but indeed in the west where the Earse is more pure and incorrupted, I heard of some sublime productions in that language.

Mr. M'Lean of Leadh, brother to Hector M'Lean, of Coll, told me at Breakachie, that M'Lean the poet had by him compositions as elevated and sublime as any to be met with in Homer or Virgil: I saw the manuscript in Colls hand, and heard him read several passages every way heroic: I own that the district of Morvern, which is but barren and does not exceed 50£ per annum, does not seem to me to have been the scene of action; it certainly was another Morvern, from whence the present has derived its name.

If the scene of action happened in Morvern, there occurs a pretty strong argument that the poem of Fingal was either of a much older date than you would admit, or else that the composer had purposely passed over an incident which might have been / wrought up to a perfect embellishment of any Epic Poem.

The harbour of Tobermorrie in the Isle of Mull is almost opposite to the western part of Morven, and separated from it by a sound about a mile over, nor ever did I read the striking account of the sea fight between the Phenician and Egyptian fleets so nobly described in the second book of Telemachus, without Tobermorie (i.e. the king's Great Well) occurring to my mind; it lies within six miles of the ocean, and forms a beautiful deep bay in the form of a Demi Ellipse, bounded by the transverse axis, the length of which from the rock of Muisnish to the upper end of the little island Calva, is three miles nearly, and its Demi lonjugate running into the shore is about a mile, it is on every point sheltered from the winds, and the short sound between Calva and Mull might be a place of safety for numbers of small craft, as the same is about half a mile long, and two hundred yards broad at a medium.

Sure I am the harbour of Tobermorrie deserved a place in Fingal, fully as well as Tenedos in the Æneid or Lemnos itself in the Iliad. /

Besides had Fingal been modern, it certainly would have made mention of the Gallicia, the Spanish admiral's ship, which in the year 1588, after traversing the eastern coast of Scotland, and doubling Strathnavern, retired in a leaky condition into the sound of Mull for shelter; but here she was sunk within about thirty yards of the shore, some of the crew who landed, were hospitably entertained by the natives, but the greater part travelled in a dismal situation; however, they fished for their bread, and so introduced the method of profiting by this necessary article of subsistence, in this setting an example to the natives which I am sorry to say, they till very lately almost totally neglected: Trials have been made for fishing up the wreck, and so late as August 1737; Captain Roe, a man who had fished up several wrecks upon the coast of Shetland, and understood the properties of the diving bell to perfection, for near two months rode at anchor almost above the very spot where the wreck itself lay conceal'd: Several times the divers went down, found her of a vast size, equal to one of our ninety gun ships, upon her right side, her decks which were entire facing the westward and her head in toward shore; the windlass whole, the gangway sound, her mizen and / foremast still standing, and her stern but little festered or corrupted: However, the hatchways were so strongly barricaded, that it was impossible to get into the cabin or hull, where 'tis thought the money was deposited, which in the opinion of every person was very considerable, as the military chest for paying the troops was there.

Had any person intended to pass a compliment on James M'Pherson, he could not have thought of a nobler than that of stiling him the author of Fingal.

The several epic poems that have appeared in the world, do in most things resemble each other, whereas Fingal is almost an original; many things in the Iliad and Æneid are alike, whole lines, nay periods have been translated, though it is not in the nature of a genius to be a copiest, and when he does copy he falls short of the original, a just punishment for having clogged his own invention with the fetters of imitation; when he appears an original then he excells; the affront given by Æneas to Queen Dido, being the assigned cause for a stated enmity between Rome and Carthage, and the calling out of the womb of time, a series of heroes from Æneas to Augustus Cæzar, are / perhaps nobler Episodes than ever entered into the heart of any other poet. Lucan undertook a poem, the subject of which was a recent history: the nighness of the times and notoriety of the event were a clogg to his poetical invention.

The greater the subject the greater the difficulty: Cæsar and Pompey were certainly men of more consequence than Agamemnon or Æneas, and the war waged before the walls of Troy, were but frays of children when compared with the civil wars of Rome, in which her most warlike sons fought for the empire of the world.

No characters were better drawn than those of Cato, of Cæsar and of Pompey; the gods are laid aside, as fables more adapted to the age of Priam and Latimus, than to the wars of Rome, wherein Cæsar gave a deadly wound to the superstition of the druids, by commanding to cut trees in the forest of Marseilles, in order to be made into warlike instruments, notwithstanding the frightful stories, that the wood was haunted by Furies, and that immediate death would be the fate of him who should strike the blow: If the author of Fingal / was indebted to any poet it was to Lucan, since each of them sung real not imaginary heroes, and yet the presumption is that the Fingal was prior to the Pharsalia.

Where is the improbability of a poem being wrote in the Earse language, more than in the Latin or Greek? the rage and passion of superiors, the valour and ferocity of inferiors being no less among the speakers of Earse, than those of Greek and of Latin: many words of the latter are derived from the former, as Arduus from the celtic ard high, solstice from sol, and that from seul the eye, amunition from munio to fortify and that from mun the back, animated from the Greek and Latin animus, and that from the celtic anam the soul; the Earse language is full, strong, manly and significant; it can be turned into every species of verification, and originally had an alphabet of its own.

You certainly have heard of the book of Psalms, or collection of Poems made by Ezra the Priest, and as much preferable to those of Greece or Rome, as the meridian light of the sun is to the morning or evening twilight; the subject of the first is the great God, his works of creation, providence / and redemption, whereas that of the latter is various, sometimes of fictitious deities, sometimes of kings who had deluged the earth with blood; at another time of wrestlers, racers, coursers and sorcerers; or if you will of Cæsar and the sun: Had you read the Psalms with that attention, which you would fain have people think you had given to the plays of Shakespear, you would have spoken less illiberally of Mr. Knox and the other reformers of North Britain, 'Tumults and violence, nay ruffians of reformation' are phrases which an Englishman should never drop from his pen: And what is more you have attributed to the 'waste of reformation' the ruins of the cathedral of Elgin; whereas that stately structure was destroyed almost 200 years before the reformation, and that by the Earl of Buchan, from a pique at the bishop of Murray, anno 1347, after it had stood 127 years. Other noble edifices fell a victim to rage and not to the reformation: The famous abbey of Melrose was destroyed by the English in 1544, that of Dryburgh by the same, Aberbrothwick was burnt by accident, and the cathedral of Aberdeen which had been ninety years in building was after standing twenty years ruined by the barons of the Mearns, who demolished the / monasteries of the black and grey Friars, robb'd the cathedral, spoiled it of its costly jewels and ornaments, destroyed the chancel, and shipped the lead, bells and other utensils for Holland, with an intent to dispose of them there, but in this they were disappointed, for the whole was sunk not far from the Girdleness, almost in sight of the town. Was one to form a judgment of you from your words in p. 48 about this matter, I should be apt to conclude you was a Roman Catholic: 'I hope every reader will rejoice that this cargo of sacrilege was lost at sea.' I presume that the order of council for taking away the lead that covered the cathedral of Elgin was long after, I am apt to believe it was in the time of Montrose, anno 1645, he had a numerous band of Roman Catholics, viz. 1800 M'Donalds from the north of Ireland, and nearly the same number from the Hebrides, who were of the same principles.

As you are ignorant of the Earse, I must beg leave to inform you, that the version of the Psalms in that tongue is as noble, elevated and melodious as that in the English by Tate and Brady. /

Your inference from Mr. Hector M'Leans saying that he did not use the Earse translation of the new testament because he could make the text more intelligible to his auditors, by an extemporary version, is far from being just; for the language of the translation is no less the language of the isle of Coll, than the language of the English translation is that of Sheepy, Thanett or the Isle of Wight.

You was much mistaken, in thinking 'that you lost some of his good will by treating an heretical writer with more regard than in his opinion an heretic could deserve.' As I knew the gentleman, so I can with freedom and pleasure remove any sinistrous sneer at his 'orthodoxy which you honoured not much censuring his asperity.' Of which last word if I can have any idea, it was very improperly applied to Mr. M'Lean: Heretic is in no use with the Scots clergy, and more frequent in Italy than in North Briton. I wish the ill natur'd epithets, sectary and hereitic were never to be heard: Your acquaintance with the Rev. Mr. M'Queen in Skye, and the other Mr. M'Lean in Mull, was a sufficient recompence for your tour to the Isles, they being ministers of great learning, politeness / and generosity; I was intimate with them, and heartily join in whatever can be said either to their praise, or to that of Mr. M'Leod of Raasa, and Sir Allan M'Lean: I wish they had seen your manuscript before it went to the press; many errors, natural, historical, and geographical would have been corrected, and a parcel of idle tales more fit for children than men of understanding would have continued in darkness or oblivian; your forced conclusions so unbecoming a man the least acquainted with syllogism would have been suppressed.

These gentlemen would have told you that the Earse language is adapted to poetry, and that the meridian brightness thereof, was in the time of Columbus and his followers, it being not only the vernaculum of the isles, but of Scotland in general, as the names of rivers, and their districts with other local disignations abundantly show; according to Beda, there were no less than five different tongues spoken in Britain at one period, viz, that of the Angles who came from Jutland, that of the Britons, that of the Picts, and that of the Scots, besides the Latin language, which from the perusal of the scriptures became common to the whole; The Earse was then in the highest / esteem; the English nobility were sent to Scotland to be educated; nay Oswin, King of Mercia, and of the southern provinces, was baptized and brought-up in the Scots seminaries, and instructed in their language, so as to speak it fluently: Cedda whom we formerly named, is called interpres vigilantissimus, and Eatta Abbott of Melrose is termed vir reverendissimus ac mansuetissimus from the celtic manis (pity) I fear your warm and adventitious expressions about the reformers, will preclude you from this last appellation, no less than your sneering expression, P. 276. 'A Scotchman must be a very sturdy moralist who does not love Scotland better than truth, he will always love it better than enquiry, and if falshood flatters his vanity, will not be very diligent to detect it, neither ought the English to be much influenced by Scotch authority.' Strange that a man pensioned by the Government should write so unlike a gentleman, revive the national distinction abolished by the Union, the very first article of which ought to make you ashamed.

If you love truth better than England, pray think charitably of your fellow subjects? For the North Britons whom you mention, deserve / your good opinion, difference of countrys is nothing at all, 'tis what every good man looks on with detestation according to the words of Mr. Hill, in the Poem called the North Star.

> Perish the peevish thought, to custom grown,
> That makes Men blind to merits, but their own;
> Britons and Russians differ but in name,
> In natures sense, all nations are the same;
> One Universe, claims one Creators care,
> And man is reasons subject every where.

This quotation is from a real gentleman who without doubt had a chearfulness in his own breast, known only to those who feel it, when speaking or writing in terms expressive of universal good-will, poor man I wish I could say the same thing of you? 'Tis hoped that neither Englishmen nor Scotchmen will be influenced by your authority, for I assure you it is not good.

Had you perused that glorious composition the first psalm, you wou'd have nipped your pevishness in the bud, but now you sit in the seat of the scorner: Had you read Beda who I believe loved truth and peace, you would have found that in the time of Columbus and his followers, people could / read, write and investigate things with propriety: he was present at the contest between the delegates about keeping Easter, which happened in 664 and when he himself was 19 years old, universally respected and regaled: Charity which thinketh no evil inclines me to believe that the image of God is every where, that there are men of real integrity in all countries, and to my certain knowledge those whom you mention are every way so.

The corruption of the Celtic flowed from the invasion of the Danes, no less than the corruption of the Latin, from the irruption of the Goths and Vandals into Italy: While these possessed the Hebrides, they built forts, in the most considerable isles, and introduced their language with their arms: The conquest of small islands, separated by dangerous sounds, became easy to people who had large vessels, and provided they had not invaded the main land, they might have retained the isles for many centuries, as the fleet of Scotland was not able to cope with that of Denmark.

The destruction of the Danes upon the continent was the cause of abandoning the isles, yet not without leaving behind them / every vestige of cruelty: They pulled down forts and castles, destroyed churches, violated the monuments of the dead, burnt the beautiful monastery of Icolmkill, that repository of manuscripts and records, that seat of the Muses and nursery of the learned: It is now no more than a pendicle of a farm possessed by a tenant of the Duke of Argyle; the noblest stones, carv'd in the most curious manner, are now to be found among the dykes and enclosures: It constitutes a part of the parish of Ross, at the southern end of Mull, of which last place you have given an erroneous account, when you say Page 320. 'The isle of Mull is perhaps in extent, the third of the Hebrides, it is not broken by waters or shot into promontories, but is a solid and compact mass, of breadth nearly equal to its length. – I am willing to estimate it at about 300 square miles.' So that according to you, the length of the isle of Mull may be 15 miles, and one third i.e 586 yards nearly.

That it is longer I am positive, for from the Ferry, that separates it from Lorn, to the Western Point, is 24 computed Miles, which I have passed over oftner than once, when Tutor to Collonel Dugald Campbell, whose / father was sheriff in those parts, and extremely kind to me: About half way stands the ruinous castle of Aros, at which is a water, a bay, and a promontory; three miles to the south of which water stands Killicronan and Teloan, at the head of a very large bay, whose two shores, the one stretching twelve miles westward, and the other twenty miles southwards, form almost a right angle, or at least an angle of eighty degrees, besides almost opposite to the inch the residence of Sir Allan M'Lean, the shore stretching southerly, bends somewhat eastwardly so as to form an inward angle of about 150 degrees, nor do I believe that between the shore stretching westward from Killicronan to Treisnish opposite to Cairnburgh, and that from Aros to the west point of Muishnish, over against Coll, there is any one part broader than eight miles: There are other inlets which might further expose your strange and glaring assertions.

I should not have dwelt so long on this, if it was not to show what little credit is to be given to a man who can represent things with impunity, and in the second place to draw an argument in favour of the antiquity of Fingal, which if composed since the Danish invasion, it is somewhat singular, that / such desolating scenes should not so much as be touched at.

Can any person believe that the invaders got possession of these without bloodshead? though many carns and obelisks erected in different parts show the contrary: It is likewise reasonable to suppose that the conflagration was general, that the burning of Icolmkill would afford as tremendous a blaze by means of the Firth between it and Mull, as did that of the temple of Æsculapius at Carthage, I had almost said that of Troy by the image formed in the sea of Dardanelles.

You should have had more sense than to be prejudiced against a country which in most places you depreciate; you say that 'the students for the most part go boys to the Scots universities, and depart before they are men, they carry with them little fundamental knowledge, and therefore the superstructure cannot be lofty.' By fundamental knowledge I presume you mean Shakespear's plays, in which they are certainly not conversant, but then they are at the age of fourteen or fifteen, adepts in the whole variety of grammar, can turn a piece of English into good Latin and vice versa, / well acquainted with prosody, and all the kinds of versification; the grammar schools are generally well supplied with men extremely well skilled in classical learning, and in their business they are diligent and laborious.

You say 'Men bred in the universities of Scotland, cannot be expected to be often decorated with the splendours of ornamental erudition, but they obtain a mediocrity of knowledge, between learning and ignorance, not inadequate to the purposes of common life; which is I believe very widely diffused among them, and which countenanced in general by a national combination so inviduous that their friends cannot defend it, and actuated in particulars, by a spirit of enterprize so vigorous, that their enemies are constrained to praise it, enables them to make their way to employment, riches, and distinction.'

Here, Sir, might be room for a lecture to explain your meaning, and sufficient subject to employ two cavillers for hours; was I to interpret it, perhaps I should pay but a sorry compliment either to the depth of / your judgment, or to the goodness of your heart.

But what do you mean by the splendours of ornamental erudition: If you mean a man of learning, then there are many in Scotland, who understand one thing well, and has such a general knowledge of other things as to yield satisfaction to himself, and be agreeable to those with whom he converses: The institution of universities favours this definition, which if not a just one, I am afraid you will be obliged to renounce the name of learned.

But what is your mighty learning; perhaps an acquaintance with Shakespear's plays, and a study of the English language, so as to compile a dictionary under the patronage of a stage player, a task to which many were more adequate as more fully masters of the different tongues whereof the English is composed.

The body of the English language is German: The generality of words in one syllable are from thence, as are some of two, but very few of three, less of four, and not one of five; almost all the words ending in ion as action, creation, division, are from the / Latin; words ending in ty are under the same predicament, as cavity, gravity, divisibility: The most part of the words in or are also from the Latin or French: A proper knowledge of these and the Greek would enable a man to do fully as much as you have done, while an acquaintance with the Hebrew, the Spanish, Portugueze and Celtic or Earse would assist him to do much more, and after all what is the knowledge of the English language, to that of the Sciences, or if you will to that of classical learning: I have been acquainted with people who knew the English poets well, and yet were not masters of 100 Greek or Latin lines: If a deep search into mathematical learning constitutes a real scholar, then Scotland has produced a Napier the inventor of logarathims, a Keil and a M'Laurin, which last understood the French and Latin so well as to corespond in those with Doctor Celsius, professor of mathematics at Upsal, and with M. de Clairault and M de Maupertuis, who communicated to him their progress in measuring, anno 1736, a degree of the Meridian so near the pole as Torneo in Sweden: To him nothing was difficult if within the reach of the human understanding, and in consequence of this correspondence, and the Data sent him from these great men, he about three days / before his death, though in a languishing condition, computed the axis of the equator to be to that of the poles as 122 to 121 nearly: How much he was master of the Latin may be seen in his Geometria Organica, which he dedicated to Sir Isaac Newton, whose knowledge of men and of things, and unconfined goodness of heart would not suffer him to speak in the peevish manner you have done; if a profound knowledge of the sacred scriptures proclaim a man learned, there are many such at this day in Scotland, as Dr. Patrick Cumming, Dr. Henry, Dr. Wiseheart, Dr. Plenderleith, and Mr. James Nasmith; in experimental and moral philosophy, and all the branches of physic, the universities of Scotland are universally admired; if translation be an accomplishment, then Scotland can boast of two translators, viz George Buchanan and Dr. Arthur Johnston, who wrote the Latin tongue in all the elegance of the Augustan age, and in the several kinds of verse used by the Greek and Latin poets: I have known men in Scotland who could explain a classic author with any in the world, and if the justness of translation is more to be considered than the style, then the version of Virgil by Dr. Gavin Douglass, Bishop of Dunkeld, anno 1520 is preferable / to that of Trapp, of Pitt, or of Wharton.

I am sorry to find you advancing that the cathedral of Glasgow was the only one left standing 'in the rage of reformation' since the cathedral of St. Giles at Edinburgh is still whole and entire; it will readily be allowed that the seizing on church lands was the occasion of letting cathedrals go to decay, but that the reformers pulled them down is in great part erroneous; many of these were very antient, that of Glasgow was built in 1135, and that of Dumferling in 1057 by Malcolm Kenmore, i.e. Malcolm the Great, in whose time, and not before, the English language and titles of dignity were introduced into Scotland: He had been an exile from his native country, even when a child at the breast, but being nephew to the Earl of Northumberland, he had a liberal education and was trained up at the court of Edward the confessor, where he had occasion to be acquainted with the Duke of Normandy, afterward known by the name of William the Conqueror. While at Westminster School he was frequently with the royal family, and being restored to the throne by the assistance of the English, he in gratitude married Margaret the / sister of Edgar Atheling, a woman every way brilliant in her character, and glorious in the goodness of her heart*, she was a blessing to the Scots and English in her life time, and was in a manner adored by them both: She saved many of the latter from horror and all the devastations of conquest, and as to the former, she erected manufactures and schools; her memory is still in the highest veneration, Margaret (a pearl) is the most frequent name in North Britain, and the passage over an arm of the sea called the Queen's Ferry, has its appellation from her.

It is evident thro' your book, that you are neither a friend to North Britain nor her sons; tho' no man ought to be an enemy to a country, least he should become an enemy to truth, the ready way of becoming a stranger to the pleasing entertainment arising from a good conscience: how ungrateful the task to heighten the defects of a country, depreciate their seminaries of learning, and deprive them of the honour of an epic poem, little inferior to that of Dante the Italian, or Camouens the Portugueze. How unfortunate for your character, not to pry into the advantages the isles might be of to / the main land, or not to account for the frequent impression made by these islanders upon the state: In this I beg leave to point out some of your defects, which are but too numerous and glaring not to be adverted to.

In your perambulation along the east coast of Scotland, you have taken notice of trifles, and passed over things of moment; the ecchoing grove in the neighbourhood of Aberbrothwick has eluded you, as have the fine salmon rivers and stately bridges built over them: Gardens, plantations of timber, nay woods have escaped you, and as for Murray a most plentiful

* See my Life of William the Conqueror, p. 157.

country, abounding with wheat and blessed with an inexhaustible fishery, you have said but little, tho' three stately structures, viz. Elgin, Kinloss, and Pluscardy can be traced out, and a very high obelisk in commemoration of the defeat of the Danes be still standing, yet all these gave place to the incident of being on the road where Macbeth met the witches, who predicted his advancement to the throne? this last is a discovery which I really believe no mortal found out but yourself: It seems witchcraft is the same in all ages, since the sorcerers who met Macbeth used the same articles of enchantment as did Medea about / 2000 years before Macbeth was born. In Murray are more gentlemens seats built of free stone and of considerable antiquity, than in any other county of the same extent, and at Nairn where is a good harbour, a fine salmon river and the remains of a castle, there are vast mountains of sand, which were covered much about the time when those of Goodwin began. Could you have vouchsafed to give an account of the rise of fort George at Arderseir, it would not have been ill-timed, as it is built after the model of Bergenopzoom.

From the earliest period, a castle was thought to be absolutely necessary at Inverness, and accordingly it continued on one spot, till Oliver Cromwell blew it up, and erected another near the harbour; at the restoration this was pulled down and the old one being rebuilt, continued to be augmented with many out-works at a vast expence, particularly in 1732, till the 18th of March 1746, when major George Grant surrendered it into the hands of the young chevalier, who ordered the works to be blown up.

After the battle of Culloden, the Duke of Cumberland saw the impropriety of / re-building a fort at Inverness, though he approved the erecting of one at Arderseir, opposite to Rossmarkney in Rosssire, between which places is a gutt two miles over, beginning at the great sea that spreads between Norway and Scotland.

In your way to fort Augustus, you passed over or at least nigh to the spot, where the clans of M'Donald and Frazer fought almost to their mutual extinction; tho' this battle be taken notice of in our annals, yet the cause of the broil is not hinted at, and yet the same is acknowledged by the descendants of both familes.

The younger Clanranald was married to a daughter of Lord Lovat, whom maternal fondness kept in Morwich in the Aird, till she should be delivered of her first child. She brought forth a son, and in the mean time her husband died; some years after Lord Lovat demanded the estate for his grandson; the M'Donald's refused to admit the claim, alledging that the child of the marriage had died, and that they did not chuse a Chieftain, a Frazer, and an impostor. As Clanranald was possessed of lands, viz. Knoidart and Moidart upon the continent, so it was judged, these could / be easily seized: Each clan armed in support of the right contended for, and the M'Donalds of Glengary and Keppoch joined those of Clanranald, who are certainly the last branch from the Lord of the Isles: All these marched to the district of Stratherrick in order to save their own lands from becoming the scene of action: On the 15 of July, 1544 during the minority of an infant Queen, and the distracted condition of the Kingdom, governed by a stranger, a Regent, a Princess, unacquainted with our language, our customs, and our laws, they came in sight of each other at a common 12 miles from Inverness: A champion of the Frazers, marched out to challenge the Host of the M'Donalds to single Combat: A champion of these walked out to meet him: They accordingly met half way between the Lines, saluted each other with their bonnets and a flourish of their swords, which being over they entered upon action, now out, now in, now here, now there, shifting in their turn, while the respective Clans stood almost motionless, and anxious for the event: After an hour's contest, M'Donald prevailed, and taking out the dead man's heart, fixed it upon a pole, and moved forward, while it was bleeding and the Clans began to follow: The Frazers no way intimated, stood their / Ground, and sustained as terrible an onsett as is to be found in the Iliad; they fought almost to the extirpation of each other, and the shattered remains retired each to their respective homes: Among the killed on the side of the Frazers were eighty new married men, each of whose widows in a few months after, brought forth a son.

'Tis surprising you did not endeavour to account for the frequent disturbances given by the Islanders to the Kings of Scotland, as the same is but gently touched at, notwithstanding the cause be every way obvious.

The Lord (i.e. Thearn) of every Island, was in a manner King thereof, and the people seeing none greater, were insensibly led to reverence him the more: The descendants from his family were daily about him, honoured him as their head and support: Their vicinity to the main land, gave them an opportunity to cross over unexpectedly, and even to advance far into the country, before a proper force could be raised to make head against them. One of these incursions gave rise to the family of Douglass, anno 767, when Donald Bane, i.e. White came with numerous forces from the western isles, / and was encountered by Soluathius then King of Scotland, whom he almost routed: A man of uncommon prowess rallied some of the fugitives at a distance, returned with these to the charge, and wrested the victory out of the hands of the conqueror when all was over, and the particulars of the action were laid before the King, he desired to see the man who had been the deliverer of his country: On this one pointed at him saying Sholto Douglass, (see that black grey man) from thence replied the King, that shall be his name.

From their nighness to each other, the inhabitants are jealous, and severally trained up to arms; it being a maxim with them, that to secure peace, one ought to be always prepared for war: The tract of land from the north point of Lewis to the southern extremity of south Uist is about 120 computed miles, forming in a manner one island, tho' in three different places there is a channel, in which the sea ebbs and flows twice in 24 hours; the whole is about twelve miles over at a medium and possessed by distinct families, Lewis by the M'Kenzies and M'Leods which last possess Harris 12 miles long, part of north Uist 24 miles long, the other part is the property of the M'Donalds, as is south Uist, an isle equally long: The Militia of / which is among the best in the British empire: Before the Union they received Wines from France in exchange for their black cattle, and at the easiest rate: But you have been in few isles and some of these inconsiderable, manifesting your credulity in every page. You say the isle of Mull is filled with M'Leans, whereas three fourths of it belongs to the Duke of Argyl, the name of the steward and principal taxmen is Campbell, contains three parishes, whereof Ulva, Scaffa, Gometra, Inch, Calva, Carnburgh and Jona, are constituent parts, and the inhabitants may be 5000.

Alas, you have not been desirous to detect the falshoods that flattered your vanity, your account of the Scots Earse being grossly sophistical; you say it never was a written language or a cultivated tongue as the Welsh and Irish are; poor man, the Earse and Irish were originally the same, and now differ only in dialect, there are Irish or Earse manuscripts to be had both in Paris and in Rome, where the deficiencies of our own annals occasioned by the invasion of Foreigners, and intestine broils, are amply supplied, from Tacitus 'tis evident that the Galdeach or speakers of the Earse, were a nation which knew the use of writing, the deeds of their / ancestors, the actions of their neighbours, of the Irish, the Germans and other upon the continent; the feint glimmerings of a battle, fought on the declivity of Mount Grampus, arising from the name Munrouman Moor, and the tradition of a terrible slaughter being once upon it, are amply cleared up by the Roman historian: The heroic expression of Galgacus is generously recorded, 'As you advance into the field think on your ancestors, look forward on your posterity?' the genius of the times is set forth in all their ghastly attire: Sint omnes jugulati being the sentence of the conqueror upon the captives whenever any new prisoners were brought in.

Every nation has signs for preserving the memory of past transactions; the Egyptians had their hieroglyphics, the Chinese and Tartars their characters, which made up an alphabet at last, for writing and the matter on which it was impressed, had its formation, its birth, its infancy, nonage and maturity; the Indians themselves have their symbols to perpetuate. Was any person to enter a Huskanawed Penn, the chief would shew ranged pieces of wood, describing the deeds of his ancestors, perhaps for 500 years back: If any of them killed a / wild beast, the same would be cut out so as to be distinguished, and the age of the warrior marked by notches. Suppose one of their Priest's should come to England and learn to write, would he not be able to convey his meaning in English characters. Every mortal knows the Hebrew may be wrote in these, as Samuel and other names. I own that the English alphabet, first used by the Romans after the destruction of Troy is a noble improvement, since every one of its letters is expressed either in one breath, or at most in one short syllable, whereas those of the Hebrew and Greek are mostly sounded in two syllables, and sometimes in three: Strange that you will not allow as much sagacity to the speakers of Earse as to the Indians, especially as there was a Christian seminary among them; as also men of learning and probity: Can a man be interpres vigilantissimus, and yet unable to write or preach in his mother tongue? Every language is noble if rightly understood.

If the Earse was the language of the Scots in time of Columbus anno 565, and the Latin language was taught at that time, it follows that the Earse was written, since no dead language can be acquired but by comparing it with the living: This method was prescribed / by Cicero to his son Marc, and is every where adopted; nay the readiest way to learn a living language is by reciprocal translation: For my part I cannot look upon the fifth and sixth century as ages of total darkness, for there were good poets, pious divines, and men of curiosity: On the 14th of March 528 an eclipse of the sun was observed carefully from 1 o'clock till 3. On the 12th of July 540 was another, which began about 15 minutes after 2, and at 3 when nine digets were covered, some stars became visible and so continued almost half an hour, when the moon had advanced three digits beyond the eastern limb of the sun, they faded gradually, till absorbed in the broad day light of the luminary.

Your assertion that Scotchmen loved Scotland better than truth is peevish and false; In Scotland the sacraments are solemnly administered, and church discipline exercised, the happy effects of which appear in this, that fewer people come to an untimely end through Scotland in 30 years, than at Tyburn in one; nor can any Scotchman be branded with not being desirous to detect falshood, when it flatter'd his vanity except the Earl of Bute, and that in a matter you will not condemn. /

Vain to find the colossus of learning, a man like himself of a good heart, and the parent of a numerous offspring, he procured you a pension of 300l. a year, but in every thing he was mistaken; you being but a novice in ancient and modern learning, a weak reasoner while your conjectures prove your malignity, and want of natural affection to your fellow subjects, whom policy and the sacred scriptures denominate the children of our King the common father of us all; and as you are without natural affection, a crime 'worthy of death,' I leave you with the second sight, the very notion of which during my abode for 15 months in the Isles, every person of common sense treated as a relick of Paganism introduced by the Danes who possessed the Hebrides for 160 years, a treasure indeed, being surrounded with an inexhaustible fishery, which might turn out to more advantage, and be more durable, than the pearls of India, or the golden mines of Peru.

I cannot conclude without observing that your ill natured phraze. 'The Scots first took up arms against the royal family of Hanover,' is a downright assertion that the whole part of the united kingdom called / Scotland was in actual rebellion, whereas there were but few, not above the hundred part of the inhabitants being Jacobite, even in the year 1715, when the friends of the government mustered up in its defence, the Dukes of Roxburgh and Douglass, with the Earls of Haddington, Rothes, Leven, and Loudon engaged as volunteers at the action of Sheriffmuir, where the Earl of Islay, who died Duke of Argyl received two wounds, and Archibald Douglass Earl of Farfar twenty two. John the second Duke of Argyle commanded the King's forces, and the late Duke of Argyle whose virtues I admired, having had the honour of being personally known to him, was chief Aid de camp on that ever memorable day.

I have only to add that I am perhaps your master in the knowledge of these things and of the Isles, which I wish some man of temper, and acquainted with the Earse would traverse and survey; though not decorated with the splendours of ornamental erudition, I yet either in Greek, Latin, or in English can keep up a logomachy at this diversion, for half an hour with you.

Incipe tu doctor, vis tu contendere mecum
Maxime si tu vis cupio contendere tecum.

FINISH.

A SECOND LETTER TO Dr. SAMUEL JOHNSON.

In which his wicked and opprobious Invectives are shewn; the Conspiracy against Mr. MACKLIN clear'd up; an Anecdote submitted to DAVID GARRICK Esq;

WITH

An impartial Character of Doctor SMOLLET; and a Method laid down for adding to the BRITISH Revenue 1,000,000 Sterling.

By ANDREW HENDERSON,

AUTHOR of the former LETTER.

LONDON:

Printed for J. Henderson, and J. Fox, Westminster Hall; J. Millan, Charing Cross; J. Williams, Fleet Street; W. Nicoll, St. Paul's Church Yard; W. Goldsmith, Pater-noster Row.

(Price Six-PENCE.) /

LETTER II.

TO
Dr. SAMUEL JOHNSON.

HAVING in my former letter hinted at some of your scurrilities thrown out against the Scots nation, her seminaries of learning, and antiquity of the Earse language, I come now to a matter, which once employed your own pen, and has much distorted the learned.

In your Journey to the Æbuda, you speak of the place where Macbeth met the witches, a whim which Shakespear would have laughed at, since the several articles of enchantment mentioned in his Macbeth, are contained in the 7th book of Ovid's Metamorphoses, a work / That will defy the rage Of sword, of fire, and time's rolling age.

It seems that Shakespear was not only acquainted with Ovid, consequently more with the Latin language than you have allowed, but that he believed less in the doctrine of witches, and the second sight than you do? nay the noble inscription upon his tomb, and taken from himself, is but a parody of that glorious expression in Metam. lib 1, fab. 6.

Quo mare, quotellus, correptaque regia cœli
Ardeat, et mundi moles operosa laboret:

There was no translation of Ovid in Shakespear's time. The right understanding the story of Macbeth might have prevented a scene that lately engrossed the public attention.

Several criticks have remarked the impropriety of a man but twenty or thirty years old, acting the part of Macbeth, and arrayed rather like a Marquis in 1775 than a Scots chief, in the dress of 1057, Mr. Garrick himself with all his ability, was in a manner a contrast to that formidable warriour, being low in stature, and naturally diminutive: / whereas Macbeth was strong, [illeg.] nervous, fierce, and gigantic: he had managed the war against the Danes for several years, destroyed their troops, attained the crown at a time when he must have been upwards of forty years, and reigned above seventeen more; this mistake of Macbeth's age occasioned the conspiracy against Mr. Macklin, Nov. 24th 1773, exposed the inattention of some lawyers; February 24th 1775, when Mr. Miles, Aldus, Leigh, James, and Clarke were convicted of the plot against him; a plot whose atrociousness was fully explained May 12th by him, whose words and actions generally surpass those of other men: and when the fine compliment paid to master Macklin did no greater honour to his merit, than to Lord Mansfield's goodness of heart. Mr. Macklin never acted better 'than to day, by moderating matters beyond what could be expected.' Macbeth when killed was 60 years old.

Your nonsense about Macbeth and the second Fight might conclude you rather to be a wizard, than a philosopher: you too much show your weakness in every particular? If you describe a country as Mull, one would think you had been drunk while on the island, in which you say there is no / water, nor road, whereas in your way from Tobermorrie to Ulva, you, yourself crossed the water and road of Aros; your impudence in representing the isle as a solid square without promontories and waters, was condemned by several shipmasters, since to follow your direction might be attended with the loss of many lives. Mull has actually several bays, promontories, two Istmus's several patent roads, and three large waters, abounding with variety of fishes. Poor man, you went to the country from a malignant motive; if the names of martyrs for the truth, drop from your pen, you revile their actions; your sneers are dealt promiscuously among individuals, seminaries of learning, nay and a whole nation! in short you show such baseness, as would have subjected a school-boy to as severe a flagellation, as ever Dr. Busby himself was known to use in the course of 46 years.

For a man to go to the Æbudæ, and depreciate them because they are not capable of producing corn like Staffordshire; is equally absurd as to ridicule you for not being capable of dancing: the character of Cato so directly contrary to yours was

Naturamque sequi, patriaeque impendere vitam! / judge of a country from that where with nature has endowed it, which leads me to point at something on which people of more ability may improve.

The Æbudæ in number 310 are among the brightest gems in the British crown, and some of these are very extensive (see letter 1. p. 287) all productive of peas, oats, barley, flax, lint and the most substantial vegetables: nor is there an isle except Coll, the fifth part of whose ground is not arable; and yet by not duly attending to their natural advantages, they only contain 25 parishes, and about 48000 inhabitants, including women and children; tho' the soil be more generous than that upon the same parallels of latitude, they neither have towns nor villages; in this the Shetland and Orkney isles excell them, there being in the former two large towns, and in the latter, a royal borough & a stately cathedral; they have the best water, the finest harbours, and all of them surrounded by an inexhaustible fishery; the air is in most parts pure, the climates wholesome, the natives hospitable and brave, and so terrible in an attack, that it is almost impossible to resist the fury of their first charge; many families both in north and south Britain are descended from / the M'Donalds, your own name (M'Ean) is from them.

The western seas are covered with fish, the cod, the ling, the tusk, the herring, with myriads of others, equally differing in species, as land animals; every creature whether of the land or sea, has its peculiar relish, form, taste, colour, instinct; and each feed upon some resembling themselves, and next to them in magnitude; those of the lesser size being to them, what venison, wild or domestic fowls are to quadrupeds that feed upon animals. The whale delights in the herring, a fish about a foot long, with a beautiful head ⅛ of its length, six inches round at the breast, and tapering gradually to the tail which is long, fibrous and muscular, adorned throughout with a refulgence that is inexpressible; they engender between lat. 74 and 83 where after a night of 11 weeks, viz. from the 14 of November to January 27th, when the benumbed whale, half famished with hunger, quits the caverns of the deep, and begins a dreadful havock, sucking in perhaps an hogshead of water at a glut and five hundred herrings between his jaws; then the herrings finding their own Climate untenable, set out and being continually joined by new shoals, / they by the time of their arrival at lat. 73, become innumerable: here they separate, one large flota extending along the shore of Nova Zembla, and Great Tartary; another that of Greenland, and Iceland, and a third run down the coast of Norway, whence they again divide, one part steering westward towards Bressa, Faro, and the Orkneys, or to the eastern coast of Scotland; when near Shetland, viz. lat. 61 they again subdivide, one branch flows toward the Orkneys and Pentland Firth; thro' which they are whirled with rapidity, and the other toward the western isles; they have their king, fight battles, engage, fly and retire: On the coast of Norway their food is not so generous as on that of Skye and of Lewis; besides on this last they are better secured from the ravages of the whale, than in higher latitudes.

What pity that a fishing company was not set up in these isles, and a borough erected in five of the largest, where those of every nation might be invited, whether Dutch, Danes, Russians or Swedes: a law ought certainly to be made that no vessel was to fish in these seas, whose master did not with his family settle upon the coast, notwithstanding / he might dispose of his cargo where he pleased.

Let the city of London give the first encouragement for bringing cargoes of fish to her markets, this would lower the price of butchers meat, and give bread to the labouring poor. If once the canal from the Clyde to the Forth was finished, a ship with herrings or cod, &c. might be brought from Isla to Blackwall, as soon as from Shetland to Hamburgh or Amsterdam, which last are enriched by that article of commerce. Above 3000 busses are employed yearly, to the great encouragement of ship builders, net knitters, coopers, and every manufacturer; many of these make three voyages in a season; not only supplying Holland, but Flanders and the Hanse towns? by this trade a million of people have bread, and about a million sterling is gained to their revenue. Our advantages are beyond theirs? every thing is to be brought by them from afar; whereas we have every thing within ourselves, and when the canal is finished, salt may be had from Sir Robert Henderson's pans, opposite the Queens Ferry, no way inferior to that of France or of Poland. I wish twenty shipmasters were appointed, each with the yearly salary of 50 l. to begin / the fishery, the town would soon be stocked with inhabitants, and 'tis a doubt if any temporary grant to the Dutch could over set that great law of nature, that whatever potentate is possessed of a country, he certainly has an unalienable power to so much of the sea as runs along the coast, and is bounded in the ordinary way; at least he has a power to enact laws, regulating the police and fishing upon it; nay, when two continents, such as Sweden and Denmark line the same strait or sound, the same is equally divided between them.

'Tis surprizing you should say so little of the palace of Inverara, built after the model of that of the Doge at Genoa, nor yet of Lochow, a lake of 24 miles in length, and abounding with isles. Lochfine was overlooked by Sam. Johnson, though it communicates with the sea, and contains an inexhaustable fishery. You might have seen the place where were fought two battles at Falkirk, the first on the 22d of July 1296, between the victorious King Edward I. and the guardian of Scotland; and the second on the 18th of January 1746, between the king's troops and the Pretender to the crown. You might have observed the spot where was the decisive engagement / 24th June 1314, between the renowned Robert Bruce, and the unfortunate Edward II. As also another in 1483, between King James III. and his son; the wall of Severus was passed over, as also the spot where stood the temple of Terminus, of whose stones the dykes and mills now are composed; here is an exuberant district, (the carse of Falkirk) whose wheat is little inferior to any in Europe; the manufactures, fine rivers, populous villages of the shire of Air where you was most politely entertained by Lord Loudon, with the stateliest monuments so descriptive of former times, gave place to the monument of Dr. Smollet, of whom, it will not be improper to draw a short but impartial character.

Tobias Smollet, son to the (goodman) i.e. farmer of Unghern, in the shire of Dumbarton, was a man of very little learning, and always remarkable for perverseness, obstinacy, and revenge. Being an apprentice to a Surgeon at Glasgow, he eloped from his master, went abroad as third mate to a Surgeon in 1739, but soon took to another trade; for returning with a creole to Britain, he commenced Doctor, Manmidwife, / Historian, and Romancer at Chealsea, where every Sunday, his assistants criticized the monthly sixpenny pamphlets, heard the decisions of their host, and then retired with horror and ridicule.

In 1753 he was found guilty of a cowardly assault upon an innocent man, Mr. Patrick Gordon, the real compiler of Rhoderic Random, and striking the man after he was down; he was afterwards found guilty of writing a libel against Admiral Knowles, fined and confined three months to the prison of the King's Bench for his pains; he was fluctuating in his friendship, and if an enemy his tender mercies were cruel; a sanguine temper appears in all he has done; his characters as of William I. are contrasts to themselves; that of King John the granter of magna charta, contains thirteen epithets, each blacker than another, while that of Mary Queen of Scots is a profusion of encomium. His account of the Duke of Cumberland's conduct in Scotland is shocking; 'for fifty miles round all was silence, horror and desolation'? whereas there was scarce a hut pulled down, a stone displaced, or a person killed who was not actually in arms, even on the day of the battle of Culloden, much less afterwards, / nor have I the least reason to alter the account contained in my history of the rebellion, a book which underwent five editions, and was first published by Mr. Griffiths Anno 1748, when he invited me to write the history of Scotland.

Smollets disposition was roving and unsettled; nor had he judgment to investigate a matter with sagacity: however, he had some humour, but then it was of a kind ludicrously cruel, and if once prejudiced he would propogate with his utmost dexterity of insinuation, a report hurtful to the innocent, would first condemn anonymous productions, and then ascribe them possitively to people who did not know what size they were of: However it is a kind of honour to his tomb, that it was taken notice of by Doctor Samuel Johnson, the man who could represent an island as an entire square, which in many places is actually indented with Bays.

I dare say your execrable treatise went to press without consulting Mr. Boswell, whose politeness and generosity of sentiment could not suffer him to harbour the remotest suspicion that he was carrying a viper in his bosom: a man freight with venom / and malignity; and however his natural goodness may confine him to a silent contempt, certain it is that you would have been recokned a Scelestus by the Pagans of antient Rome who would not have entered the same boat, nor lodged under the same roof with a betrayer of the secrets of Ceres, or a violator of the ties of hospitality.

But passing your baseness, I heartly wish that the litigation about your assertions, may open the eyes of the state and make them give that due attention to the improvement of our fisheries, which nature has furnished us with: Sometimes no less than 400 vessels are employed at the Lewis at one time: the fish are like the sand upon the sea shore about the vessels, and 'tis observable that those caught next the shore are sweeter than those at a further distance, a proof that the fish love rest, and that nigh these shores, they find a food that agrees with them: By a proper attention to these, the revenue of Great Britain might annually gain above a million sterling. Cargoes from any part of the long isle, or from Skye might be carried to the Bay of Biscay, the coasts of Spain, Portugal, and the Mediterranean, much sooner than from Orkney, or Shetland, and / far sooner than from Nefoundland, or any other part upon the Continent of America.

I have long considered the isles as a mine hitherto neglected by those who ought to have taken care thereof, during the unatural wars between

South and North Britain, the inhabitants were generally in an interest opposite to that of their sovereign? the Edwards during their wars were assisted so far by the Islanders, that they gave no assistance to their natural sovereigns, nay, sometimes made a diversion in favour of those with whom they were fighting hence number of other clans came in among them: that Coll whom you saw was the thirteenth laird of Coll, and the first of these was son to the third laird of Mac Lean. Since the union with England, their cheiftains were generally in the interest of France, the captain of Clanranald, almost the cheiftain of the Mac Donalds, and from whom the family of Antrim in Ireland is descended, was an officer in the French and Spanish service almost 27 years.

I have here to add that a desire of promoting the fisheries is more my aim, than any view towards raising my own fame, by making observations upon your productions / so full of impudence, so replete with faults, nonsense and ridicule: 'tis truth I seek, but neither praise nor victory: the pension you receive from the Government, may according to you palliate your execrable treatise taxation, no tyranny, so justly condemned, as contrary to the principles of magna charta the very spirit of the institution of parliaments, and so diametrically opposite to the very first principle, that 'Taxation without representation, is slavery' in the sense of the word; as may be seen in the letter to Lord North, in favour of the Colonies: but indeed what excuse you can have for condemning things of which you was ignorant, surpasses my comprehension: the conclusion of my former letter proceeds from no vanity in me, nor should I think it a great thing to be thought preferable to you, as many worthy gentlemen both of Great Britain and Ireland are every way superior: but I have not so much to do with your defects in the literary way, as with your neglect and extravagance; for in a country abounding with natural and artificial curiosities, a prodigious variety of fish, of shells, and of land animals, in a vast diversity of ores, minerals, and fossils, adorned with the remains of the most stately fabricks, cloud capt towers, gorgeous palaces, high / obelisks; and solemn temples, you have entertained yourself and the public with a parcel of idle, hyperbolical, false and execrable tales, that if a common footman was to utter them he would be debarred the society of his fellow servants, and be consequently turned from his place.

Every person possessed of an estate ought narrowly to pry into whatever might be of public utility. The british parliament have for many years given the utmost countenance to such enquiries, many large heaths, boundless commons and extensive waste grounds have been improved since the begining of the century; 'tis a question if nine tenths of the kingdom of England, be not taken in and improved since the conquest: with these improvements came population, and the number of inhabitants grew exceedingly: Trade followed of course, notwithstanding it frequently shifted her residence, yet commerce still continued to flourish, and 'tis hoped it always will, a becoming emulation is far from being blameable, every proprietor is to seek for his own advantage, and when this is found out the same will naturally be turned to the public utility not only of those in the neighbourhood but extend in a manner toward all. /

To pry into the conveniences of what is within a man's cognizance, and is included within his own property, is a duty incumbent upon every person of fortune, it is what he owes to himself, to his family, to his King, to his country, and to his God? every generous breast has considered such investigation as acts of the noblest kind, the effect of an high and elevated Genius: Fellow-Citizens have honoured them with wreaths of encomium, and adorned them with the civic crowns of applause; Cicero the greatest orator that adorned the bar of antient Rome, and whose goodness of heart, took in the whole of mankind, preferred the founders of Citys to the most extensive and amazing conquerors: the construction of Forts, founding of Towns, erecting Harbours at places which had not so much as a name, adorning Cities, embellishing them with squares, laying out Streets and Lanes to the greatest advantage, in short every thing, the effect of mens hands, owed its rise first to mens ingenuity and goodness.

Here it is observable that tho' the royal Boroughs in Scotland in number sixty-three among which four cities, viz. Edinburgh, Aberdeen, St. Andrews, and Glasgow, are but few in comparison of those in England, / yet many of them are more antient than those of the latter, many of them are greatly decayed: while others are vastly augmented: thus the city of Glasgow is twice larger than at the beginning of the century; lying in the midst of an excellent country, they have a vast consumption for goods imported from America as well as for the produce within themselves: her seminary of learning so famous over the world, draws Students, and consequently wealth from the several Provinces and Colonies of either Indies, and from the Carribee Isles: the mode of education in Scotland is certainly of the best kind, and in my humble opinion, 'tis better for a young man to study for half a year without a vacation, that to intermitt thro' the intervention of terms; such eminent masters as have flourished either in England, or upon the continent, are well known there by their works and by their names; 'tis pity that any man should endeavour to interupt the harmony that now subsists among the learned: Sir Isaac Newtouns principia with that divine work upon the understanding are honoured and taught at Edinburgh, and the other Universities, while Mr. Maclaurins Fluxions, and Mr. Simpsons conic sections are received at Cambrige and quoted by those that are connoisseurs, / many of the other towns in the west are enriched by the flourishing condition to which Glasgow by the industry of its inhabitants now is arrived; in a word the west of Scotland might be singularly benefited, if their inhabitants had the countenance of government, and knew the rich and over growing mines of which they are possessed.

If we take a view of the northern district, we will find many of her towns more flourishing than in antient times, and only the inland places going to decay: Aberdeen is now twice more populous than formerly, her trade to the Baltic and to London is enlarged, and might be still more so, if the fisheries were properly encouraged: her seminary of learning is in high repute, she only prostituted her dignity, by conferring favours upon you.

There is not a place in the kingdom, which might not be greatly assisted, was this fishery to take place; the cities of St. Andrews and Edinburgh are famous for learning, but might be still more enobled, provided the scheme which you should have proposed, had been steadily and properly pursued. /

Several people have gone to these isles, with as few connections as you had, and all unanimously speak well of their natives, as a brave, spirited and martial people, and possessed of advantages which nothing but the want of encouragement could keep from being of the most singular utility to England, nay might adorn and embellish her throne. The peevish thought that England and Scotland are in a manner distinct, and at variance, has but too much prevailed upon you: Blind to your own peace you have cultivated every kind of perverseness, and like a person void of sense and humanity, have acted things more deserving correction, than either a pickpocket or an highwayman.

The southern and eastern parts of Scotland, being every way so like those of England which lye so contiguous, that a person may go from the one to the other without boat or vessel, nay without bridge, waggon, horse, or any kind of vehicle, 'tis needless to trouble you or myself with much about them; further than that they contain many mines of coal, nay lead mines of inestimable value, by which many thousands have bread and more still may have entertainment. /

The inexhaustible lead mines belonging to the duke of Queensbury and to the earl of Hopton are a treasure indeed, and were found out by an application and industry that deserve for ever to be admired.

A Gentleman of curiosity having one day observed the lead dust from the side of an eminence, concluded that a lead mine was there. Many people were set to search for it, but their labours were abortive for ten full years, when the vein was discovered in this accidental manner.

A man having a long pole in his hand, with which he was probing the mountain in quest of the vein, had despaired of finding it out, when a rat sprung suddenly out of an hole that had escaped him; he run against it with fury and resentment; the reptile leaped into the hole, the man darted at it, and missed it, however with the force of the blow, the pole struck the very body of the vein, and could not be got out till the earth covering it was removed, and then the whole was detected: 'tis a question with me, whether or not there be many mines of metals more precious than lead, in some of these subterraneous caverns of North Britain. People of your stamp and / disposition would discourage every investigation, but men of real sense and goodness will highly approve, nay, they will rejoice in the event.

I have only to say that if those in the administration countenanced your malignant scheme, they were traitors to their country, or else they wanted you should expose your perverseness and obstinacy, which have now been made manifest and beyond the possibility of being doubted; as for myself, I assure you that I am sorry for your ignorance, but more concerned that such baseness should enter into the heart of a man, who could go to a kingdom, where he met with the kindest usage, and the most cordial hospitality, and on his return, entertain the public with a parcel of stupid tales about witches and the second sight; with execrable raillerys against her reformers, detractions from her seminarys of learning, the grossest falshoods about her produce, the state of the country, and with little or nothing about that inexhaustible treasure her fisheries.

FINIS.